C. G. JUNG
AND ANALYTICAL
PSYCHOLOGY

GARLAND REFERENCE LIBRARY
OF SOCIAL SCIENCE
(VOL. 38)

C. G. JUNG
AND ANALYTICAL
PSYCHOLOGY
A Comprehensive Bibliography

Joseph F. Vincie
Margreta Rathbauer-Vincie

GARLAND PUBLISHING, INC. • NEW YORK & LONDON
1977

Library of Congress Cataloging in Publication Data

Vincie, Joseph F
   C. G. Jung and analytical psychology.

   (Garland reference library of social science ; v. 38)
   Includes indexes.
   1. Jung, Carl Gustav, 1875-1961--Bibliography.
2. Psychoanalysis--Bibliography. I. Rathbauer-Vincie,
Margreta, joint author. II. Title.
Z8458.75.V55   [BF173.J85]   150'.19'54   76-52695
ISBN 0-8240-9874-9

PRINTED IN THE UNITED STATES OF AMERICA

CONTENTS

v

INTRODUCTION

We were led to begin the compilation of titles that was to evolve into this bibliography when we encountered difficulties in doing research for our own work. The extraordinary growth of interest in Jung's work which began in the 1960's made a bibliography mandatory, while the lack of any comprehensive set of references made serious research all but impossible. Standard psychological indices and abstracts are unreliable and neglect large portions of Jungian material. Even articles in the major journals, *The Journal of Analytical Psychology* and the *Zeitschrift für Analytische Psychologie*, are not abstracted with any regularity. Thus, the present work offers the first complete international bibliography of material related to both C. G. Jung and the Jungian school of thought. Entries in all major European languages cover subjects ranging from psychology to philosophy, religion to myth, literary criticism to aesthetics.

We have not included works by Jung himself since a complete bibliography of his writings will form Vol. 19 of the *Complete Works* published by Princeton University Press; all other Jungian material is listed. A work was defined as Jungian if the author concerned himself with Jung, his work, or Analytical Psychology, if his article was published in a journal sponsored by a Jungian organization, or if he claimed to have been working within the Analytical Psychological tradition. We have not evaluated any of these claims but have taken the authors at their word. It was our decision not to determine orthodoxy, but merely to organize and present the broad range of material offered under the aegis of C. G. Jung. Finally, keeping in mind Jung's close connection with Olga Froebe-Kapteyn, the founder and director of Eranos, his continued participation in the Eranos Conferences, as well as the spiritual affinity of his concerns with the subjects of the yearly meetings at Ascona, we have included all the papers appearing in the *Eranos Jahrbücher.*

The body of the work consists of three major sections: a list of works about Jung and Analytical Psychology; a list of book reviews of Jung's works; and author and subject indices.

The works are arranged chronologically and alphabetically within each year. In cases where there is insufficient published material, several years have been grouped together. Anonymous works appear alphabetically by title at the end of each year's entry. Undated works and those for which we were unable to determine a date appear at the end of the list. Every published appearance of a work has been separately indicated and all multiple listings and translations have been fully cross-referenced so that the researcher can easily find the most accessible and useful edition of the work. Books are noted by an asterisk placed before the reference number. Whenever possible we have listed separately all the individual selections contained in edited collections of articles and papers.

The bibliography contains all works published through the end of 1975. It is as comprehensive as possible, but given the nature and extent of the task, we have undoubtedly overlooked a number of articles. There has been one deliberate omission: short reviews or abstracts of public lectures which have appeared in Swiss newspapers. The Kristine Mann Library of the C. G. Jung Foundation in New York and the library of the C. G. Jung-Institute in Zurich possess complete files of these lecture reviews. We have chosen not to include them for several reasons: they are very short, generally only a single paragraph; there are a great number of them; and there are tentative plans to publish the catalogue in the near future.

Reviews of works contained in the bibliography are included with the particular work in question. Thus, even if the review appeared several years after the publication of the book, it is listed with it. Reviews of Jung's works, however, are presented in the second part. These are also arranged chronologically and alphabetically within each year. Reviews were more difficult to uncover than were articles and books, and although the list remains incomplete, the approximately 800 reviews that are included provide an adequate cross section of the response that Jung and his followers evoked from their contemporaries.

The final section of the work consists of the indices. The author index lists the author of every book, article, and review contained in the bibliography while the subject index, extensively cross-referenced for maximum convenience and use, catalogues all key words and important terms. Reviews of works appearing in the bibliography are identified in the author index by an R and reviews of Jung's works by an RJ before the reference number.

J.F.V.
M.R.V.

ABBREVIATIONS

Amer	American	Proc	Proceedings
An	Annals	Q	Quarterly
Assoc	Association	Rev	Review
Bull	Bulletin	Soc	Society
J	Journal	Supp	Supplement
Jahr	Jahrbuch	Zeit	Zeitschrift

Periodicals

AP	*Analytische Psychologie* (see ZAP)
APCLA	Analytical Psychology Club of Los Angeles
APCNY	Analytical Psychology Club of New York
BJMP	*British Journal of Medical Psychology*
CGJISF	C. G. Jung Institute of San Francisco
CGJIZ	C. G. Jung-Institute, Zurich
Du	*Du: Schweizerische Monatschrift*
DV	*Le Disque Vert*
EJ	*Eranos Jahrbuch*
GofPP	Guild of Pastoral Psychology
Harv	*Harvest*
JAP	*Journal of Analytical Psychology*
JPP	*Jahrbuch für Psychologie, Psychotherapie und Medizinische Anthropologie*
JppF	*Jahrbuch für Psychoanalytische und Psychotherapeutische Forschungen*
NSR	*Neue Schweizer Rundschau*
NTPsy	*Nederlandische Tijdschrift voor Psychologie*
NTTid	*Nederlandische Theologische Tijdschrift*
NZZ	*Neue Zürcher Zeitung*
Paps APCNY	*Papers of the Analytical Psychology Club of New York*
PEY	*Papers from the Eranos Yearbooks*
PMLA	*Publications of the Modern Language Association*

Quad	*Quadrant*
Schweiz ANP	*Schweizer Archiv für Neurologie und Psychiatrie*
SMW	*Schweizer Medizinische Wochenschrift*
SR	*Schweizer Rundschau*
SZP	*Schweizerische Zeitschrift für Psychologie und ihre Anwendung*
TLS	*Times Literary Supplement*
ZAP	*Zeitschrift für Analytische Psychologie* (became AP with Vol. 5)
Zentral	*Zentralblatt für Psychotherapie und ihre Grenzgebiete*
ZPGP	*Zeitschrift für Parapsychologie und Grenzgebiete der Psychologie*

The Works of Jung

CW1	*Psychiatric Studies*
CW2	*Experimental Researches*
CW3	*The Psychogenesis of Mental Disease*
CW4	*Freud and Psychoanalysis*
CW5	*Symbols of Transformation*
CW6	*Psychological Types*
CW7	*Two Essays on Analytical Psychology*
CW8	*The Structure and Dynamics of the Psyche*
CW9-I	*The Archetypes and the Collective Unconscious*
CW9-II	*Aion: Researches into the Phenomenology of the Self*
CW10	*Civilization in Transition*
CW11	*Psychology and Religion: West and East*
CW12	*Psychology and Alchemy*
CW13	*Alchemical Studies*
CW14	*Mysterium Coniunctionis*
CW15	*The Spirit in Man, Art, and Literature*
CW16	*The Practice of Psychotherapy*
CW17	*The Development of Personality*
Alch	*Psychologie und Alchemie*
Allg	*Allgemeines zur Komplextheorie*

Aspec	*Aspects du Drame Contemporain*
Assoz	*Assoziations-experiment*
Aufs	*Aufsätze zur Zeitgeschichte*
Br	*Briefe*
Contem	*Essays on Contemporary Events*
Darstellung	*Versuch einer Darstellung der psychoanalytischen Theorie*
Dyn	*Die Dynamik des Unbewußten*
Ener	*Über psychische Energetik*
Erz	*Psychologie und Erziehung*
Essays	*Two Essays on Analytical Psychology*
ETG	*Erinnerungen, Träume, Gedanken*
F-J Let	*Freud-Jung Letters*
Freud	*Freud und die Psychoanalyse*
Gegen	*Seelenprobleme der Gegenwart*
Geistes	*Symbolik des Geistes*
Gest	*Gestaltungen des Unbewußten*
Gött	*Das göttliche Kind*
Hiob	*Antwort auf Hiob*
Integ	*Integration of the personality*
Job	*Answer to Job*
Kind	*Über Konflikte der Kindlichen Seele*
Let-I	*Letters-I*
Let-II	*Letters-II*
Man	*Man and his Symbols*
MDR	*Memories, Dreams, Reflections*
Mod	*Modern Man in Search of a Soul*
Mod Myth	*Ein Moderner Mythus*
Myth	*Essays on a Science of Mythology*
Natur	*Naturerklärung und Psyche*
Nature	*The Interpretation of Nature and the Psyche*
Paps	*Collected Papers on Analytical Psychology*
Port	*The Portable Jung*
Prac	*Analytical Psychology: Its Theory and Practice*
Praecox	*Psychology of Dementia Praecox*
PuPP	*Zur Psychologie und Pathologie sogenannter occulter Phänomene*

Reflec	*Psychological Reflections*
Rel	*Psychology and Religion*
Relig	*Zur Psychologie westlicher und östlicher Religion*
Sauc	*Flying Saucers: a Modern Myth*
Schelm	*Der göttliche Schelm*
Seele	*Über die Energetik der Seele*
Self	*The Undiscovered Self*
Symboles	*Metamorphoses et Symboles de la Libido*
Typen	*Psychologische Typen*
Types	*Psychological Types*
Über	*Die Psychologie der Übertragung*
Unbew	*Die Psychologie der unbewußten Prozesse*
Unc	*Psychology of the Unconscious*
Wandl	*Wandlungen und Symbole der Libido*
Welt	*Psychoanalyse und Weltanschauung*
Winz	*Von den Winzeln des Bewußtseins*

WORKS ON JUNG
AND ANALYTICAL PSYCHOLOGY

Before 1916

1. Assatiani, M. M. "The present state of the question of the theory and practice of psychoanalysis according to the opinions of Jung." (in Russian) Psychotherapie, 1 (1910), pp. 117 ff.

2. Bleuler, Eugen. "Antwort auf die Bemerkungen Jungs zur Theorie und Negativismus." JppF, 3:1 (1911), pp. 475-79.

3. Eitington, Max. "Über das Unbewußte bei Jung seiner Wendung ins Ethische." Int Zeit für ärztliche Psychoanalyse, 2 (1914), pp. 99-104.

4. Goodhart, S. P. "Jung's modification of the Freudian theory of neuroses." Medical Record, 83 (1913), pp. 374 ff.

5. Hoch, August. "Jung's recent experimental studies of mental associations." J of Abnormal Psychology, 1:2 (1906), pp. 95-100.

6. Lang, Joseph B. "Über Assoziationsversuche bei Schizophrenen und den Mitgliedern ihrer Familien." JppF, 5:2 (1913), pp. 705-55.

*7. Loy, R., ed. Psychoanalytische Zeitfragen. Ein Briefwechsel mit C. G. Jung. Leipzig: 1914.

8. Maeder, Alphonse. Über die Funktion des Traumes." JppF, 4:2 (1912), pp. 692-707.

9. _____. "Über das Traumproblem." JppF, 5:2 (1913), pp. 647-86. (see *19 below for English edition)

10. _____. "Zur Frage der teleologischen Traumfunktion." JppF, 5:1 (1913), pp. 453-54.

11. Martins, G. "Über synthetische und analytische Psychologie." Bericht über der Kongress für experimentale Psychotherapie (Leipzig), 5 (1912), pp. 261-81.

12. Wolff, Toni. "Oberst Chabert." Wissen und Leben, 9 (1912-13), np.

13. "Jung's Resignation." Int Zeit für Psychoanalyse, 2 (1914), pp. 405-06.

14. "Portrait of Jung." Everybody's, 32 (June 1915), p. 742.

15. Bertine, Eleanor. "Health and morality in the light of the new psychology." Proc of the Int Conference of Women Physicians. Vol 4. Moral Codes and Personality. New York: The Woman's Press, 1920, pp. 5-14.

16. Burrow, Trigant. "Noted with reference to Freud, Jung and Adler." J of Abnormal Psychology, 12:3 (1917), pp. 161-67.

17. Hinkle, Beatrice M. "Jung's libido theory and the Bergsonian philosophy." New York Medical J, 22 (1919), pp. 99 ff.

18. _____. "Moral conflict and the relation of the psychological types to the functional neurosis." J of Abnormal Psychology, 14:3 (1919), pp. 173-89.

*19. Maeder, Alphonse. The Dream Problem. New York: Nervous and Mental Disease Pub. Co., 1916. (see 9 above for German edition)

20. Meyer, Adolf F. "Dr. C. G. Jungs Psychologie des unbewußten Prozesse. Int Zeit für ärztliche Psychoanalyse, 4 (1916), pp. 302-14.

21. Oppenheim, James. "What Jung has done." New Republic, 7 (May 20, 1916), pp. 67-68.

22. Putnam, Marion C., Burrow, T., and White, W. A. "The theories of Freud, Jung, and Adler." J of Abnormal Psychology, 12 (1917), pp. 145-73.

1921-25

23. Barnes, Hazel E. "Some reflections on the possible service of analytical psychology to history." Psychoanalytic Rev, 8 (1921), pp. 22-37.

24. Crichton-Miller, Hugh. "The outlook for analytical psychology in medicine." Medical Press, 113 (1922), pp. 499-501.

25. Corrie, Joan. "Personal experience of the night journey under the sea." British J of Psychology, Medical Section, 2:4 (1922), pp. 303-12.

26. Downey, J. E. "Jung's psychological types and will-temperament

patterns." J of Abnormal Psychology, 18:4 (1924), pp. 345-49.

27. Harding, M. Esther. "The development of love." The New Era, 4:
14 (1923), pp. 175-81.

28. Hinkle, Beatrice M. "An introduction to analytical psychology."
In An Outline of Psychoanalysis. J. S. von Teslaar, ed. New
York: Boni and Liveright, 1923, pp. 218-54.

29. _____. "The spiritual significance of psychoanalysis." British J of Psychology, Medical Section, 2:2 (1922), pp. 209-29.

30. _____. "A study of psychological types." Psychoanalytic Rev.
9:2 (1922), pp. 107-97.
        Rev. by C. E. Long. Brit J of Psychology, 2:4 (1922),
        pp. 229-33.

*31. Hoop, J. H. van der. Character and the unconscious; a critical
exposition of the psychology of Freud and Jung. New York:
Harcourt, Brace & Co., 1923.

32. Kantor, J. B. "Jung's psychological types and Levine's The Unconscious." J of Philosophy, 20:23 (1923), pp. 636-40.

*33. Oppenheim, James. The psychology of Jung. Girard, Kansas: Hal-
deman Julius Co., 1925.

34. Reik, T. "The science of religion." Int J of Psychoanalysis, 2:
1 (1921), pp. 80-93.

35. Reich, Wilhelm. "Trieb und Libidobegriffe von Forel bis Jung."
Zeit für Sexualwissenschaft, 9 (1922), pp. 17-19, 44-50, and
75-85.

1926-1928

36. Baynes, Helton Goodwin. "Freud versus Jung." BJMP, 8 (1928),
pp. 14-23. (see 351 and 602 below for other editions in English)

*37. Corrie, Joan. A B C of Jung's psychology. London: Kegan Paul;
New York: Frank-Maurice, 1927.

38. Gernat, A. "Die psychoanalytischen Richtungen Freud, Adler,
Jung; Typen in der Handschrift." Charakter, 2 (1926), pp.
37-43.

39. Giese, Fritz. "Analytische Psychologie als verstehendes erzien-

3

endes Verfahren." Zeit für psychoanalytische Pädagogik, 28 (1927), pp. 433-46.

40. Heyer, Gustav Richard. "Psychologische Lehren von C. G. Jung." Der Nervenarzt, 1 (1928), p. 743.

41. Kemlers, H. "Tiefen- und Typenpsychologische Probleme bei C. G. Jung." Die neue deutsche Schule, 2 (1928), pp. 759-73.

42. Rickman, J. "On some of the standpoints of Freud and Jung." BJ MP, 8 (1928), pp. 44-48.

43. Prinz Rohan, Karl Anton. "Der Kampf gegen die Neurose und die Erneuerung Europas." Neue Freie Presse, (2 Feb. 1928), np.

44. Schmitz, Oscar A. H. "Psychologie." Zeit für Menschenkunde, 3 (1927), pp. 245-55.

45. Seillière, Ernest. "M. Ernest Seillière expose les théories psychanalystes du Professeur Jung." Comedie Paris, (27 May 1928), np.

46. Stockmayer, W. "Analytische Psychologie und Erziehung." Ärztliche Rundschau, 37 (1927), pp. 115-18.

47. _____. "Das Unbewußten im Seelenleben." Ibid., pp. 1-9.

*48. Wickes, Frances G. The inner world of childhood: a study in analytical psychology. Intro. by C. G. Jung. New York: Appleton Century Crofts, 1927/1940. (see *76 below for German, *2413 for English, and *3687 for Dutch editions)

49. "Psychologie der Persönlichkeit. Wells über Jung. Jungs Psychologie und die Praxis des Arztes." Neue Zürcher Zeitung, (11 Nov. 1928), np.

1929

50. Garthe, O. W. "Zur Eigenart seines Werkes. C. G. Jung." Stuttgarter Neues Tagblatt, (21 Feb. 1929), np.

51. Götz-Heinrich, Hertha. "Das Ich und das Unbewußte bei C. G. Jung." Zeit für Sexualwissenschaft, 15 (1929), pp. 476-78.

52. Graber, Gustav Hans. "Zur Psychoanalyse der Individuation," Zeit für psychoanalytische Pädagogik, 3 (1928-29), pp. 462-67.

53. Hattingberg, Hans von. "Psychological types." Allg ärztliche

Zeit für Psychotherapie und psychische Hygiene, 2 (1929), pp. 129-56.

54. Korner, __. "The clinical significance of the collective unconscious." Loc. cit.

55. Künkel, F. "Individual Psychology's note on C. G. Jung's report on 'Goals of Psychotherapy'." Loc. cit.

56. Paneth, Ludwig. "Über das Problem der Psychosynthese bei Jung." Deutsches medizinisches Wochenscrift, 55 (1929), pp. 736-39.

57. Schmitz, Oscar A. H. "Die Psychologie von C. G. Jung." Der Lesezirkel (Zurich), 16 (1929), p. 21.

58. _____. "Carl Gustav Jung, der Topograph des Unbewußten," Psychologische Rundschau, 1 (1929), p. 8.

59. Sigg-Boeddinghaus, M. "C. G. Jung über die Ziele der Psychotherapie." Ibid., pp. 153-57.

60. Stockmayer, W. "The development of the inferior function in psychotherapy." (see 53 above)

61. Wittels, Fritz "C. G. Jung." In his Sigmund Freud. Vienna: E. P. Tal & Co., 1929, pp. 159-78.

1930

62. Kirsch, James. "Das Problem des modernen Juden." Zurich: Psychologischer Club, Zürich, 1930.

*63. Kranefeldt, Wolfgang M. Die Psychoanalyse, Psychoanalytische Psychologie. Leipzig and Berlin: de Gruyter, 1930. (see *80 below for English, and *641 and *1253 for German editions)

64. Lubbeke, H. "Seelenkunde und Seelenführung (Adlers Psychologie von Jung as betrachtet)." Preussische Kirschenzeitung, 21 (1930), pp. 316-21.

65. Rittmeister, J. "C. G. Jungs Energetik der Seele." Ärztliche Rundschau, 10 (1930), pp. 17-20.

66. Steinitz, Hans. "Die Lehre der Libido bei Freud und bei Jung." Der Nervenarzt, 3 (1930), pp. 150-52.

67. Stockmayer, W. "Figuren des kollektiven Unbewußten." Zentral,

5

10 (1930), pp. 587-98.

1931

68. Heyer, Gustav Richard. "Die Bedeutung C. G. Jungs." Die Medizinische Welt (Berlin), 5 (1931), pp. 47-52.

69. _____. "Bericht über C. G. Jungs analytisches Seminar." Zentral, 4 (1931), pp. 2-6.

*70. _____. Seelenräume. Stuttgart: Kohlhammer, 1931.

71. Kirsch, James. "Darstellung somatischer Phänomene im Traum." 6. Allgemeiner ärztlicher Kongress für Psychotherapie, Dresden: 1931.

72. Kranefeldt, Wolfgang M. "Bericht über das Zweite Deutsche Seminar von C. G. Jung in Küsnacht-Zürich von 8-10 Oktober, 1931." Zentralblatt für Psychotherapie, 3 (1931), pp. 129-31.

73. Sergeant, E. S. "Doctor Jung: a portrait." Harper's, 162 (May 1931), pp. 740-47.

74. Sigg-Boeddinghaus, M. "C. G. Jung über Seelsorge und Psychotherapie." Psychologische Rundschau, 3 (1931), pp. 1-4.

75. _____. "Die praktische Verwendbarkeit der Traumanalyse von C. G. Jung." Ibid. pp. 141-46, 207-10.

*76. Wickes, Frances G. Analyse der Kinderseele. Stuttgart: Julius Hoffman Verlag, 1931/1951. (see *48 above and *2413 below for English editions, and *3687 below for Dutch edition)

1932

77. Hauer, Jakob Wilhelm. "Seminar notes on the Kundalini Yoga." Zurich: 1932 (multigraphed).

78. Heun, Eugen. "Individualität und Kollektivität in der analytischen Psychologie C. G. Jung." Archiv für angewandte Soziologie, 4 (1932), pp. 238-52. (see 93 below)

79. Kirsch, James. "Die Anima in Goethe's Faust." 1932.

*80. Kranefeldt, Wolfgang M. <u>Secret ways of the mind</u>. H. Holt, trans.
    New York: Holt, 1932; London: Kegan Paul, 1934. (see *63
    above, *641 and *1253 below for German editions)

81. Scharf, C. "Grundzüge der Psychologie C. G. Jung." <u>Psychologi-
    sche Rundschau</u>, 4 (1932), pp. 100-106.

82. Schmid, G. "C. G. Jungs Lehre von dem Unbewußten." <u>Schulwarte</u>,
    8 (1932), pp. 498-511.

83. Schnackenberg, __. "Aus ein Handschriftenmappe." <u>Zeitschrift
    für Kirchenmusiker</u>, 13 (1932), p. 138.

84. Vetter, August. "Denker der Zeit / C. G. Jung." <u>Vossische
    Zeitung</u> (Berlin), (6 March 1932), np.

                              1933

85. Baudouin, Charles. "La psychologie de C. G. Jung." <u>Rev de psy-
    chologie appliquée de l'est</u>, 3 (1933), pp. 58-72.

86. _____. "La Pensée de C. G. Jung." <u>Présence</u> (Geneva), 1933,
    np.

87. _____. "La psychologie de C. G. Jung." <u>Action et Pensée</u>,
    (June-July, Aug.-Sept., 1933).

88. Buonaiuti, Ernesto. "Meditation und Kontemplation in der römisch-
    catholischen Kirche." <u>EJ</u>, 1 (1933), pp. 327-48.

89. Davie, T. M. "Jung's theory of psychological types: a critical
    estimate." <u>J of Mental Science</u>, 79 (1933), pp. 247-85.

*90. Harding, M. Esther. <u>The way of all women; a psychological</u> inter-
    pretation. New York: Longman's Green & Co., 1933. (see below,
    *147 German, *207 Dutch, *407 French, *448 Italian, and *2802
    English editions)

*91. Heidbreder, Edna. <u>Seven Psychologies</u>. New York: Appleton-Cen-
    tury-Crofts, 1933.

92. Heiler, Friedrich. "Die Kontemplation in der Christlichen Mystik."
    <u>EJ</u>, 1 (1933), pp. 245-326. (see 1678 below)

93. Heun, Eugen. "Individualität und Kollektivität in der analyti-
    schen Psychologie C. G. Jungs." <u>Fortschritte der Medizin</u>,

                              7

51 (1933), pp. 689-94. (see 78 above)

94. Heyer, Gustav Richard. "Sinn und Bedeutung östlicher Weisheit
für die abendländische Seelenführung." EJ, 1 (1933), pp. 215-
44.

95. Hoop, J. H. van der. "Verschiedene Wege der Psychotherapie."
Zentralblatt für Psychotherapie, 6:1-3 (1933), 145-61.

*96. Ramos, Arthur. Freud, Adler, Jung. Rio de Janeiro: 1933.

97. Rhys Davids, Mrs. C. A. F. "Religiöse Übungen in Indien und der
religiöse Mensch." EJ, 1 (1933), pp. 95-134.

98. Rouselle, Erwin. "Seelische Führung im lebenden Taoismus." Ibid.,
pp. 135-200. (see 1721 below for English edition)

99. Tuinstra, Coenrad Liebrecht. Het symbool in de psychanalyse.
Beschrijving en teologische Critiek. (Doctoral dissertation).
Amsterdam, 1933.

100. Wandeler, J. "Freud, Adler, und Jung. Bemerkungen zu den neueren Richtungen in der Psychologie." Schweizer Rundschau, 33
(1933), pp. 48-55.

101. Wolff, Toni. "C. G. Jung: L'homme, le charactère." Rev d'Al-
lemagne, 7:70 (15 Aug. 1933), np.

102. Zimmer, Heinrich. "Zur Bedeutung des indischen Tantra-Yoga."
EJ, 1 (1933), pp. 9-95. (see 1743 below)

103. "Jung in Frankreich." Neue Schweizer Rundschau, NF1 (1933), pp.
379.

1934

*104. Adler, Gerhard. Entdeckung der Seele; von Sigmund Freud und Al-
fred Adler zu C. G. Jung. Zurich: Rascher, 1934.

105. _____. "Ist Jung Antisemit?" Judischer Rundschau, 62 (1934),
p. 2.

106. Bally, Gustav. "Deutschstämmige Psychotherapie." Neue Zürcher
Zeitung (Morgenausgabe), 343 (27 Feb. 1934), p. 1.

107. Bernoulli, Rudolf. "Zur Symbolik geometrischer Figuren und Zah-
len." EJ, 2 (1934), pp. 369-416.

8

*108. Bodkin, Maud. Archetypal patterns in poetry; psychological studies in imagination. London: Oxford University Press, 1934.

109. Buber, Martin. "Sinnbildliche und sakramentale Existenz im Judentum." EJ, 2 (1934), pp. 339-68. (see 1648 below for English edition)

110. Buonaiuti, Ernesto. "Symbole und Ritus im religiöse Leben einiger Orden." Ibid., pp. 305-38. (see 2537 below for English edition)

111. Cammerloher, M. C. "Die Stellung der Kunst im psychologischen Weltbild unserer Zeit. (Ein Beitrag zur Funktionenlehrer). Ibid., pp. 449-86. (see 1652 below for English edition)

112. Froboese-Thiele, Felicia. "C. G. Jung." Veirteljahrschrift, 10 (1934), p. 115.

113. Hauer, J. W. "Symbole und Erfahrung des Selbstes in der indo-arabischen Mystik." EJ, 2 (1934), pp. 35-96.

114. Heiler, Friedrich. "Die Madonna als religiöses Symbol." Ibid., pp. 263-304.

115. Heun, Eugen. "Grundunterschiede in der modernen Tiefenpsychologie (Freud, Adler, Jung)." Münchener medizinische Wochenschrift, 81 (1934), 52-57.

116. _____. "Über das kollective Unbewußte." Zeit von Menschenkunde, 9 (1934), pp. 237-43.

117. Heyer, Gustav Richard. "Dürers Melancolia und ihre Symbolik." EJ, 2 (1934), pp. 231-62.

*118. _____. Organiser of the mind; an introduction to analytic psychology. E. & C. Paul, trans. New York: Harcourt Brace, 1934.

119. Jung, Emma. "Ein Beitrag zum Problem des Animus." In C. G. Jung, Wirklichkeit der Seele. Zurich: Rascher, 1934/1939. (see 275 and 1369 below for English editions)

120. Kranefeldt, W. M. "C. G. Jungs Typenlehre." Süddeutsche Monatshefte (Stuttgart), 1 (1934), np.

121. _____. "Freud und Jung." Zentralblatt für Psychotherapie, 7 (1934), pp. 24-38.

122. Rhys-Davids, Mrs. C. A. F. "Zur Geschichte des Rad-Symbols." EJ, 2 (1934), pp. 153-78.

123. Rouselle, Erwin. "Drache und Stute, Gestalten der mythischen Welt chinesischer Urzeit." EJ, 2 (1934), pp. 11-34. (see 2635 below for English edition)

9

124. Schatten, E. C. G. Jungs Stellung zum Judentum." <u>Judischer</u>
     <u>Rundschau</u>, 62 (1934), p. 2.

125. Speer, Ernst. "Ergebnisse aus der Psychotherapeutischen Praxis
     zum Typenproblem." <u>Zentralblatt für Psychotherapie</u>, 7:1-6
     (1934), pp. 240-54.

126. Strauss-Kloebe, Sigrid. Über die psychologische Bedeutung des
     astrologischen Symbols." <u>EJ</u>, 2 (1934), 417-48.

127. Swami Yatiswarananda. "Flüchtiger Blick auf religiöser Hindu-
     Symbolik in ihrer Beziehung zu geistigen Übungen und zur Höh-
     erentwicklung." <u>Ibid.</u>, pp. 487-528.

128. Zimmer, Heinrich. "Indische Mythen als Symbole." <u>Ibid.</u>, pp.
     97-152.

129. "Zur Psychologie Sigmund Freuds und C. G. Jungs." <u>Der Landbote</u>
     (Winterthur), (15 Sept. 1934), np.

                              1935

130. Alm, Ivar. "Die analytische Psychologie als Weg zum Verständnis
     der Mystik." In <u>Die Kulturelle Bedeutung</u> (see *161 below), pp.
     298-313.

131. Bacon, Leonard. "Analytical psychology and poetry." <u>Ibid.</u>, pp.
     365-69.

132. Baudouin, Charles. "Le point de vue de C. G. Jung et la réalité
     de l'âme." <u>Présence</u> (Geneva), (June 1935), np.

133. Baumann, Hans H. "Betrachtungen über die Symbolik der Pyrami-
     den." In <u>Die Kulturelle Bedeutung</u> (see *161 below), pp. 327-48.

134. Baynes, Helton Goodwin. "Analytical psychology and the English
     mind." <u>Ibid.</u>, pp. 377-97. (see 600 below)

135. _____. "The provisional life." <u>Zentralblatt für Psychother-</u>
     <u>apie</u>, 8:2 (1935), pp. 83-94. (see 476 and 607 below)

136. Bernoulli, Rudolf. "Seelische Entwicklung im Spiegel der Alche-
     mie und verwandter Diziplinen." <u>EJ</u>, 3 (1935), pp. 231-88.
     (see 1643 below for English edition)

137. Bianchi, Ida. "Vom Werdegang des inneren Menschen." In <u>Die</u>
     <u>Kulturelle Bedeutung</u> (see *161 below), pp. 493-508.

138. Breuss, E. "Die Psychologie von C. G. Jung." Erziehungs Rundschau, 8 (1935), p. 153.

139. Buonaiuti, Ernesto. "I. Die gnostische Initiation und die christliche Antike. II. Die Exerzitien des hl. Ignatius von Loyola." EJ, 3 (1935), pp. 289-322.

140. Curtius, O. "Das kollective Unbewußte C. G. Jungs, seine Beziehung zur Persönlichkeit und Gruppenseele." Zentralblatt für Psychotherapie, 8 (1935), pp. 265-79.

141. Durham, Willard H. "Analytical psychology and the art of teaching." In Die Kulturelle Bedeutung (see *161 below), pp. 370-76.

142. Eisler, Robert. "Das Rätsel des Johannesevangeliums." EJ, 3 (1935), pp. 323-512.

143. Fierz, H. E. "Über die psychologischen Grenzen der dramatischen Gestaltung." In Die Kulturelle Bedeutung (see *161 below), pp. 434-61.

144. Fierz-David, Linda. "Frauen als Weckerinnen seelischen Lebens." Ibid., pp. 462-92.

145. Gilli, Gertrude. "C. G. Jung in seiner Handschrift." Ibid., pp. 509-15.

146. Harding, M. Esther. "The mother archetype and its functioning in life." Zentralblatt für Psychotherapie, 8:2 (1935), pp. 95-108. (see 227 below)

*147. _____. Der Weg der Frau. Eine psychologische Deutung. Intro. by C. G. Jung. L. Heyer, trans. Zurich: Rhein-Verlag, 1935/1943. (see *90 above and *2082 below for English, *207 below for Dutch, *407 for French, *448 for Italian editions.)

*148. _____. Woman's mysteries; ancient and modern. London: Longman's Green, 1935. (see below, *547 for German, *833 for French, *1058 for English, and *3234 for Italian editions.)

149. Hauer, Jakob Wilhelm. "Die indo-arische Lehre vom Selbst im Vergleich mit Kants Lehre vom intelligiblen Subjekt." In Die Kulturelle Bedeutung (see *161 below), pp. 220-36.

150. Heyer, Gustav Richard. "Die Institution als ordnendes Prinzip." Ibid., pp. 416-33.

151. _____. "Von Umgang mit sich selbst." EJ, 3 (1935), pp. 135-78.

152. Hoop, J. H. van der. "Persönliches, unpersönliches und überpersönliches in der Psychotherapie." Zentralblatt für Psychotherapie, 8:1-6 (1935), pp. 162-74.

11

153. Keller, Adolf. "Analytische Psychologie und Religionsforschung." In Die Kulturelle Bedeutung (see *161 below), pp. 271-97.

154. Lang, J. B. "Paulinische und analytische Seelenführung." EJ, 3 (1935), pp. 513-43.

155. Laszlo, Violet de. "Versuch einer Traumdeutung auf Grundlage der Analytischen Psychologie." Zentralblatt für Psychotherapie, 8:2 (1935), pp. 119-32.

156. Le Lay, Y. "La psychologie de l'inconscient et l'esprit français." In Die Kulturelle Bedeutung (see *161 below), pp. 396-415.

157. Lévy-Bruhl, Lucien. "Remarques sur l'initiation des medicine men." Ibid., pp. 214-20.

158. Medtner, Emil. "Bildnis der Persönlichkeit in Rahmen des Gegenseitigen Sich Kennenlernens." Ibid., pp. 556-616.

159. Meier, Carl Alfred. "Moderne Physik - Moderne Psychologie." Ibid., pp. 349-64.

160. Oeri, Albert. "Ein paar Jugenderinnerungen." Ibid., pp. 524-28.

*161. Psychologischen Club Zürich. Die Kulturelle Bedeutung der Komplexen Psychologie. Festschrift zum 60. Geburtstag von C. G. Jung. Berlin: Springer, 1935.

162. Rhys-Davids, Mrs. C. A. F. "Der Mensch, die Suche und Nirvana." EJ, 3 (1935), pp. 207-30.

163. Rouselle, Erwin. "Chinesische Kontemplationen." In Die Kulturelle Bedeutung (see *161 above), pp. 195-213.

164. _____. "Lau-Dsis Gan durch Seele, Geschichte und Welt. Versuch einer Deutung." EJ, 3 (1935), pp. 179-206.

165. Seifert, Friedrich. "C. G. Jung und die moderne Psychologie." Adelsblatt, (1935), pp. 1878-80.

166. _____. "Ideendialektik und Lebensdialektik. Das Gegensatzproblem bei Hegel und bei Jung. In Die Kulturelle Bedeutung (see *161 above), pp. 237-71.

167. _____. "Die Komplexe Psychologie von C. G. Jung." Neue Schweizer Rundschau, NF 3 (1935), pp. 236-44.

168. Trüb, Hans. "Individuation, Schuld und Entscheidung. Über die Grenzen der Psychologie." In Die Kulturelle Bedeutung (see *161 above), pp. 529-55.

169. Werner, H. "Zur modernen Psychologie. Die Tiefenpsychologie C. G. Jungs." Kölner Zeitung, (28 July 1935), np.

170. Wolff, Toni. "Einführung in die Grundlagen der Komplexen Psychologie." In Die Kulturelle Bedeutung (see *161 above), pp. 1-170. (see 1629 below)

171. Wyscheslavzeff, B. "Selbstbesinnung. Eine philosophische Meditation." Ibid., pp. 314-26.

172. Zimmer, Heinrich. "Die Geschichte vom indischen König mit dem Leichnam." Ibid., pp. 171 - 94.

173. "Prof. Dr. C. G. Jung zum 60. Geburtstag." Zentralblatt für Psychotherapie, 8 (1935), pp. 145-46.

1936

174. Alm, Ivar. Den Religiösa Funktionen I Människosjälen. Studien Till Fragan om Religionens Innebörd och Människans väsen I Modern Psychologi Särskilt Hos Freud och Jung. (Doctoral dissertation). Stockholm: Svenska Kyrkans Diakonistyrelses Bokförlag, 1936.

175. Baumann, Hans H. "Jungs Psychologie im Ausland." Neue Schweizer Rundschau, NF 4 (1936), np.

176. Buonaiuti, Ernesto. "Die Erlösung in den orphischen Mysterien." EJ, 4 (1936), pp. 165-82.

177. Ikin, Alice Graham. "New concepts in healing: medical, psychological, and religious." Rev American Education. New York: Association Press, 1936.

178. Kranefeldt, Wilhelm M. "Über zwei Arten archetypischen Zuordnung." Zentralblatt für Psychotherapie, 9:1-6 (1936), pp. 321-34.

179. Laiblin, Wilhelm. "Das Urbild der Mutter." Ibid., pp. 66-96.

180. Masson-Oursel, Paul. "Die indischen Erlösungstheorien im Rahmen der Heilsreligionen," EJ, 4 (1936), pp. 113-34. (see 1119 below for English edition)

181. Meier, Carl Alfred. "Die Grundlinien der analytischen Psychologie (C. G. Jung)." Schweizer ANP, 38 (1936), 329-38.

182. Oppenheim, E. A. "C. G. Jung im Spiegel seiner Schule." Basler Nachrichten, (29 March 1936), np.

183. Puech, Henri-Charles. "Der Begriff der Erlösung im Manichäis-

13

mus." <u>EJ</u>, 4 (1936), pp. 183-286. (see 2628 below for English edition)

184. Rhys-Davids, Mrs. C. A. F. "Erlösung in Indiens Vergangenheit und in unserer Gegenwart." <u>Ibid.</u>, pp. 135-64.

185. Vetter, August. "Die Bedeutung der unbewußten Seele bei C. G. Jung." <u>Zeitwende</u>, 12 (1936), pp. 213-34.

186. Wysheslavzeff, B. "Zwei Wege der Erlösung." <u>EJ</u>, 4 (1936), pp. 287-329.

1937

/

187. Baynes, Charlotte A. "Der Erlösungsgedanke in der christlichen Gnosis (Originaltexte und Kommentare)." <u>EJ</u>, 5 (1937), pp. 155-210.

188. Buonaiuti, Ernesto. "Die Ecclesia Spiritualis." <u>Ibid.</u>, pp. 293-353. (see 885 below for English edition)

189. Danzel, Theodor Wilhelm. "Zur Psychologie der altmexidanischen Symbolik." <u>Ibid.</u>, pp. 211-40. (see 1659 below for English edition)

190. Karpf, F. B. "Dynamic relationship therapy: II. The Jungian and Adlerian backgrounds." <u>Social Work Technique</u>, 2 (1937), pp. 107-17.

*191. Kellner, K. <u>C. G. Jungs Philosophie auf der Grundlage seiner Tiefenpsychologie.</u> Düren: Spezial-Diss Buchdruckerei, 1937.

192. Layard, John. "Der Mythos der Totenfahrt auf Malekula." <u>EJ</u>, 5 (1937), pp. 241-92. (see 1702 below for English edition)

193. Massignon, Louis. "Die Ursprünge und die Bedeutung des Gnostizismus im Islam." <u>Ibid.</u>, pp. 55-78.

194. Masson-Oursel, Paul. "Die indische Auffassung der psychologischen Gegebenheiten." <u>Ibid.</u>, pp. 79-92.

195. Przyluski, Jean. "Die Erlösung nach dem Tode in den Upanishaden und im ursprünglischen Buddhismus." <u>Ibid.</u>, pp. 93-136.

196. Speiser, Andreas. "Der Erlösungsbegriff bei Plotin." <u>Ibid.</u>, pp. 137-54.

197. "Jung's lectures at Yale entitled 'Applied Psychology and

Religion'." <u>Commonweal</u>, 27 (5 Nov. 1937), p. 32.

198. "Portrait of Jung." <u>Time</u>, 30 (8 Nov. 1937), p. 30.

1938

199. Adler, Gerhard. <u>Consciousness and Cure</u>. London: GofPP Lecture # 5, May 1938. (see 396 below)

200. Barrett, Clifford. "Jung on Religion." <u>New York Times Book Rev</u>, (20 March 1938), p. 14.

201. Baudouin, Charles. "Les dernières découvertes sur la réalité intérieure." <u>La Grande Rev</u> (Paris), 154 (1938), pp. 248-56.

202. Bertine, Eleanor. "The individual and the group." <u>Paps APCNY</u>, <u>Vol 1</u>. 1938.

*203. Bumke, Oswald. <u>Die Psychoanalyse und ihre Kinder</u>. Berlin: Springer, 1938.

204. Buonaiuti, Ernesto. "Maria und die jungfräulische Geburt Jesu." <u>EJ</u>, 6 (1938), pp. 325-402.

205. Collum, V. C. C. "Die schöpferische Mutter-Göttin der Völker keltischer Sprache, ihr Werkzeug, das mystische 'Wort', ihr Kult und ihre Kult-Symbole." <u>Ibid</u>., pp. 221-324.

206. Eranos Archive. "Image of the Great Mother throughout the ages." <u>Paps APCNY</u>, <u>Vol 2</u>. 1938.

*207. Harding, M Esther. <u>Der Vrouwen Levensweg</u>. A. W. E. D. Sterck, trans. Leiden: E. J. Brill, 1938. (see *90 above for English edition, *147 for German, and see below, *407 for French, *448 for Italian, and *2802 for English editions)

208. Heyer, Gustav Richard. "Die Große Mutter im Seelenleben des heutigen Menschen." <u>EJ</u>, 6 (1938), pp. 445-91.

209. Laws, Frederick. "The mystic in the laboratory. <u>New Statesman and Nation</u>, 15 (1938), pp. 660, 662.

210. Massignon, Louis. "Der gnostische Kult der Fatima im schiitischen Islam." <u>EJ</u>, 6 (1938), pp. 161-74.

211. Meier, Carl Alfred. "Über die Bedeutung den Jungschen Assoziationsexperimente für die Psychotherapie." <u>Zeit für Neurologie und Psychiatrie</u>, 161 (1938), pp. 483-86.

212. Picard, Charles. "I. Die Ephesia von Anatolien. II. Die Große Mutter von Kreta bis Eleusis." _EJ_, 6 (1938), pp. 59-120.

213. Przyluski, Jean. "Ursprünge und Entwicklung des Kultes der Mutter-Göttin." _Ibid._, pp. 11-58.

214. Rosenfeld, Paul. "Psychoanalysis and God." _Nation_, 146 (1938), pp. 510-11.

215. Virolleaud, Charles. "Ischtar, Isis, Astarte." _EJ_, 6 (1938), pp. 121-60.

216. Waals, H. G. van der. "Über die Beziehungen zwischen dem Associationsexperiment nach Jung und der Psychodeagnostik nach Rorschach." _Schweizer ANP_, 42:2 (1938), pp. 377-403.

*217. Wickes, Frances G. _The inner world of man_. New York: Farrar & Rinehart, 1938. (see *519 below for English and *874 for German editions)

218. Wolff, Toni. "Betrachtung und Besprechung von 'Reich der Seele'." _Zentralblatt für Psychotherapie_, 10:4-5 (1938), pp. 239-78.

219. Zimmer, Heinrich. "Die indische Weltmutter." _EJ_, 6 (1938), pp. 175-221. (see 219 below for English edition)

220. "Symbols and religion." _Time_, 31 (7 March 1938), pp. 28 ff.

1939

221. Allberry, Charles R. C. "Symbole von Tod und Wiedergeburt im Manichäismus." _EJ_, 7 (1939), pp. 113-50.

222. Alveredes, F. "Die Wirksamkeit von Archetypen in den Instinkthandlungen der Tiere." _Zoologischer Anzeiger_ (Leipzig), 109 (1939), np.

223. Buonaiuti, Ernesto. "Wiedergeburt, Unsterblichkeit und Auferstehung im Urchristentum." _EJ_, 7 (1939), pp. 291-320.

*224. Eggman, O. _Die Begriffe Anima und Animus und ihre Bedeutung für die Tiefenpsychologie_. Bern: 1939.

225. Feuerborn, H. L. "Der Instinktbegriff und die Archetypen C. G. Jungs." _Biologie Generale_, 14 (1939), pp. 456-506.

226. Fordham, Michael. _The Analysis of Children_. London: GofPP Lecture # 4, June 1939.

227. Harding, M. Esther. "The Mother archetype and its functioning in life." Paps APCNY, Vol 2. 1938-39. (see 146 above)

228. Henderson, Joseph L. "Initiation rites." Paps APCNY, Vol 3. 1939.

229. Kirsch, James. The religious aspect of the unconscious. London: GofPP Lecture # 1, March 1939.

230. Knickerbocker, H. R. "Psychologie des dictateurs: le cas Hitler; interview." Europa Nouvelle, 22 (9 Sept. 1939), pp. 984-86.

231. Leisegang, Hans. "Das Mysterium der Schlange." EJ, 7 (1939), pp. 151-250. (see 1109 below for English edition)

232. Massignon, Louis. "Die Auferstehung in der mohammedanischen Welt." Ibid., pp. 11-20.

233. Meier, Carl Alfred. "Spontanmanifestationen des kollektiven Un-bewußten." Zentralblatt für Psychotherapie, 11 (1939), pp. 284 -303.

234. Moritz, Eva. "Materialismus gegen Logik und Komplexe Psychologie." Ibid., pp. 303-317.

235. Nagel, Hildegard. "Eranos conference, 1938." Paps APCNY, Vol 2. 1938-39.

236. Otto, Walter F. "Der Sinn der eleusinischen Mysterien." EJ, 7 (1939), pp. 83-112.

237. Pelliot, Paul. "Die Jenseitsvorstellungen der Chinesen." Ibid., pp. 61-82.

238. Pratt, Jane Abbott. "Early concepts of Jahweh." Paps APCNY, Vol 3. 1939.

239. Stephenson, W. "Methodological consideration of Jung's typology." J of Mental Science, 85 (1939), pp. 185-205.

240. Thurnwald, Richard. "Primitive Initiations- und Wiedergeburtsri-ten." EJ, 7 (1939), pp. 321-98.

241. Virolleaud, Charles. "Die Idee der Wiedergeburt bei den Phöni-zien," Ibid., pp. 21-60.

242. Watts, Alan W. "Psychology of acceptance; the reconciliation of the opposites in eastern thought and in analytical psychology." Paps APCNY, Vol 3. 1939.

243. Westman, H. The Old Testament and analytical psychology. London: GofPP Lecture # 3, May 1939.

244. Zimmer, Heinrich. "Tod und Wiedergeburt im indischen Licht."

<u>EJ</u>, 7 (1939), pp. 251-90. (see 2236 below for English edition)

245. "Portrait of Jung." <u>Time</u>, 33 (8 May 1939), p. 22.

1940

*246. Baynes, Helton Goodwin. <u>Mythology of the Soul</u>. London and Baltimore, Md.: Tindall, 1940. (see *993 and *2663 below)
   Rev. M. Esther Harding. <u>J of Abnormal Psych</u>, Aug 1940, p. 939.
   Violet de Laszlo. <u>Bull. APCNY</u>, 3 (May 1941), p. 5.

247. Bertine, Eleanor. "Concerning Nazi Dynamism." <u>Paps APCNY, Vol 4</u>. 1940, pp. 1-7.

*248. Frayn, R. Scott. <u>Revelation and the unconscious</u>. London: Epworth Press, 1940.

249. Frei, Gebhard. "C. G. Jung: Psychologie und Religion." <u>Schweizerische Rundschau</u>, 40 (1940), pp. 329-31.

250. Goldbrunner, Josef. <u>Die Tiefenpsychologie von Carl Gustav Jung und Christliche Lebensgestaltung</u>. (Doctoral dissertation). Freiburg im Breisgau, 1940.
   Rev. Pedro Meseguer. <u>Razón y fe</u>, (May 1943), pp.465-68.

251. Harding, M. Esther. "Totalitarianism at home." <u>Paps APCNY, Vol 4</u>. 1940, pp. 21-29.

252. Henderson, Joseph L. "Historical factor of the European War." <u>Ibid</u>., pp. 8-9.

253. Henley, Helen G. "What will become of our values." <u>Ibid</u>., pp. 10-15.

254. Hinkle, Beatrice M. The Evolution of woman and her responsibility to the world of today." <u>Ibid</u>., np.

*255. Jacobi, Jolande. <u>Die Psychologie von C. G. Jung; eine Einfuhrung</u>. Zurich: Rascher, 1940. (see below, *292 for English, *451 for Spanish, *557 for Dutch, *634 for French, *556 for Italian, *717 for English, *1585 for German, *2034 for Dutch, *2180 for French, and *2595 for English editions)

*256. Macintosh, Douglas Clyde. <u>The problem of religious knowledge</u>. London: Harper and Brothers, 1940.

257. Mann, Kristine. "The present war from the religious standpoint."
Paps APCNY, Vol 4. 1940, np.

258. _____. "In the shadow of death." Ibid., np. (see 1922 below)

259. Nagel, Hildegard. "The other side of darkness." Ibid., pp. 16-
20.

260. Oertly, Walter. "Neutrality." Ibid., pp. 30-35.

1941

261. Adler, Gerhard. "The study of a dream. A contribution to the
concept of the collective unconscious and to the technique of
analytical psychology." BJMP, 19 (1941), pp. 56-72.

262. Baker, Lillian E. "One aspect of the movement within Germany."
Spring 1941, pp. 122-26.

*263. Baynes, Helton Goodwin. Germany Possessed. London: 1941.

264. _____. "Jung's conception of the structure of personality in
relation to psychical research." Proc of the Society for Psychical Research, London, 46 (1941), pp. 377-88. (see 605)

265. Bertine, Eleanor. "Some positive aspects of the times in which
we live." Spring 1941, p. 109.

266. Buonaiuti, Ernesto. "Gnostische Erfahrung und gnostisches Leben
im fruhen Christentum. EJ, 8 (1940-41), pp. 231-56.

267. _____. "Christologie und Ecclesiologie bei Sankt Paulus."
Ibid., pp. 295-335.

268. Eckstein, Alice Raphael. "The Third Reich and Goethe." Spring
1941, pp. 52-61.

269. Estes, Lula. "Hero and shadow." Ibid., pp. 114-15.

*270. Haendler, Otto. Die Predigt. Tiefenpsychologische Grundlagen
und Grundfragen. Berlin: Alfred Topelmann, 1941/1949.

271. Harding, M. Esther. "The dragon and the hero." Spring 1941, pp.
11-26.

272. Henley, Helen G. "Our American Eros." Ibid., 1941, pp. 119-21.

273. Holmes, S. W. "Browning's Sordello in the light of Jung's theory of types." PMLA, 56 (Sept. 1941), pp. 758-96.

274. Hoppin, Hector (Courtland). "Analytical Psychology Clubs today." Spring 1941, pp. 106-07.

275. Jung, Emma. "On the nature of the animus." C. F. Baynes, trans. Spring 1941, pp. 27-51. (see 119 above for German edition, and 1369 below)

276. Kerényi, Carl. "Mythologie und Gnosis." EJ, 8 (1940-41), pp. 157-230.

277. Laszlo, Violet de. "Some dreams connected with the present war." Spring 1941, pp. 62-80.

278. Little, Dorothy. "Trends in American education." Ibid., pp. 115-17.

279. Pulver, Max. "Christus und Paulus." EJ, 8 (1940-41), pp. 257-94.

280. Speiser, Andreas. "Die platonische Lehre vom unbekannten Gott und die christliche Trinität." Ibid., pp. 11-30.

281. Stone, M. Eleanor. "Democracy and the Incarnation." Spring 1941, pp. 112-14.

282. Thayer, Ellen. "Unconscious attitudes toward the group." Ibid., pp. 117-19.

283. Westman, H. The Golden Calf. London: GofPP Lecture # 10, 1941.

284. Wickes, Frances G. "A question." Spring 1941, pp. 107-09.

285. Wolff, Toni. "A few thoughts on the process of individuation in women." Ibid., pp. 81-103. (see 1630 below for German edition)

286. Zimmer, Heinrich. "The involuntary creation: a Hindu myth." Ibid., pp. 1-10.

1942

287. Briner, Mary (comp.). "Index to: Psychological analysis of Nietzsche's Zarathustra." Zurich: 1942 (typescript).

288. Dawson, Eugene E. "The religious implications of Jung's psychol-

ogy." <u>Trans of the Kansas Academy of Science</u>, 52 (1942), pp. 88-91.

289. Harding, M. Esther. "Individuation and the nation at war." <u>Spring</u> 1942, pp. 93-99.

290. _____. <u>Psychic energy: its source and goal</u>. London: Vision, 1942, (see below, *488 for German, *489 for English, *777 for French, and *2022 for English editions)

291. Henley, Helen. "Child of Pan." <u>Spring</u> 1942, pp. 59-70.

292. Jacobi, J. <u>The psychology of C. G. Jung: an introduction</u>. K. W. Bash, trans. London: Kegan Paul, 1942; New Haven Conn.: Yale University Press, 1943. (see 255 above for German edition and complete list of other editions)
  Rev. Leonard Bacon. <u>Saturday Rev of Literature</u>, 26 (25 Dec. 1943), p. 9.
  M. Brierly. <u>Inter J of Psychology</u>, 35 (1943), pp. 81-84.
  Julian Hammersley. <u>Spectator</u>, 168 (15 May 1942), p. 468.
  Violet de Laszlo. <u>Bull APCNY</u>, 5 (April 1943), pp. 5-7.
  Unsigned. <u>Christian Century</u>, 60 (22 Dec. 1943), p. 1507.
  Unsigned. <u>Scientific Book Club Rev</u>, 14 (Dec. 1943), p. 2.

293. Kerényi, Carl. "Hermes der Selenführer (Das Mythologem vom männlichen Lebensursprung.)." <u>EJ</u>, 9 (1942), pp. 9-108.

294. Lang, J. B. "Der Demiurg des Priesterkodex (Gen. I bis II, 4a) und seine Bedeutung für den Gnostizismus." <u>Ibid.</u>, pp. 237-88.

295. MacMonnies-Hagard, Berthe. "The Tarot and the accomplishment of the great work." <u>Spring</u> 1942, pp. 31-42.

296. Mann, Kristine. "Individuation and the family problem." <u>Ibid.</u>, pp. 80-93.

297. Nagel, Georges. "Le dieu Thoth d'après les textes égyptiens." <u>EJ</u>, 9 (1942), pp. 109-40.

298. Oertly, Alda. "Kundry." <u>Spring</u> 1942, pp. 71-79.

299. Pulver, Max. "Jesu Reigen und Kreuzigung nach den Johannes-Akten." <u>EJ</u>, 9 (1942), pp. 141 - 78. (see 1151 below for English edition)

300. Whitney, Elizabeth. "Tarok, Tarot, or Taroc." <u>Spring</u> 1942, pp. 13-30.

301. Zimmer, Heinrich. "The Hindu view of world history according to

the Puranic myths." <u>Rev</u> <u>of</u> <u>Religion</u>, (Feb. 1942), pp. 249-69. (see 2237 below)

302. _____. "The guidance of the soul in Hinduism." <u>Spring</u> 1942, pp. 43-58.

1943

303. Chein, I. "Personality and typology." <u>J</u> <u>of</u> <u>Social</u> <u>Psychology</u>, 28 (1943), pp. 89-109.

304. Jacobi, Jolande. "Ein Gespräch mit C. G. Jung über Tiefenpsychologie und Selbsterkenntnis." <u>Du</u> (Zurich), 3:9 (1943), pp. 15-18.

305. _____. "Interview with C. G. Jung." <u>Horizon</u> (London), 8:48 (1943), pp. 372-81.

306. Kerényi, Carl. "Vater Helios." <u>EJ</u>, 10 (1943), pp. 81-124.

307. Lander, K. Forsaith. <u>Map</u> <u>of</u> <u>the</u> <u>psyche</u>. London: GofPP Lecture # 24, Sept. 1943.

308. Massignon, Louis. "Les infiltration astrologiques dans la pensée religieuse islamique." <u>EJ</u>, 10 (1943), pp. 297-304.

309. Nagel, Georges. "Le culte du Soleil dans l'ancienne Egypt." <u>Ibid</u>., pp. 9-56.

310. Pulver, Max. "Die Lichterfahrung im Johannes-Evangelium, im Corpus Hermeticum, in der Gnosis und in der Ostkirche." <u>Ibid</u>., pp. 253-96. (see 1713 below for English edition)

311. Rahner, Hugo. "Das christliche Mysterium von Sonne und Mond." <u>Ibid</u>., pp. 305-404.

312. Schär, Hans. "Die Bedeutung der Religionspsychologie." <u>SZP</u>, 2 (1943), pp. 175-85, 255-65.

313. Schmitt, Paul. "<u>Sol</u> <u>invictus</u>. Betrachtungen zu spätrömischer Religion und Politik." <u>EJ</u>, 10 (1943), pp. 169-252.

314. Sen, Indra. "The integration of the personality." <u>Indian</u> <u>J</u> <u>of</u> <u>Psychology</u>, 18 (1943), pp. 31-34.

315. Valangin, Aline. "C. G. Jung." <u>Annabelle</u>, Sondernummer 6:60 (Feb. 1943), pp. 10-12, 59.

22

316. Virolleaud, Charles. "Le dieu Shamash dans l'ancienne Mésopotamie." EJ, 10 (1943), pp. 57-80.

317. Wili, Walter. "Die römischen Sonnengottheiten und Mithras." Ibid., pp. 125-68.

*318. Witcutt, W. F. Catholic thought and modern psychology. London: Burns, Oates and Washbourne, 1943.

319. Zimmer, Heinrich. "Integrating the Evil: a Celtic myth and a Christian legend." Spring 1943, pp. 32-66.

320. "Biography of Jung." Current Biography, 1943.

1944

321. Abegg, Emil. "Worte des Nachrufes." In H. R. Zimmer, Das Weg Zum Selbst. Zurich: Rascher, 1944, pp. 7-10.

322. Baum, Julius. "Die symbolischen Darstellungen der Eucharistic." EJ, 11 (1944), pp. 327-46. (see 991 below for English edition)

323. Berlucchi, C. "La caratterologia di Jung." Cont Lab Psicol, Milano, 12 (1944), pp. 525-26.

324. Bertine, Eleanor. "The great flood." Spring 1944, pp. 33-53.

*325. Fordham, Michael. The life of childhood. London: Kegan Paul, 1944. (see 2786 below)

326. Gray, Horace. "Jung's psychological types and marriage." Stanford Medical Bull, 2 (1944), pp. 37-39.

327. Henderson, Joseph L. "The drama of love and death." Spring 1944, pp. 62-74.

328. Kerényi, Carl. "Mysterien der Kabiren." EJ, 11 (1944), pp. 11-60. (see 1092 below for English edition)

329. Koppers, Wilhelm. "Zum Ursprung des Mysterienwesens im Lichte von Völkerkunde und Indiologie." Ibid., pp. 215-76. (see 2610 below for English edition)

330. Lander, K. Forsaith. Anima. London: GofPP Lecture # 32, Nov. 1944.

*331. Layard, John. Lady of the hare; being a study in the healing power of dreams. London: Faber & Faber, 1944.

332. _____. "Primitive kinship as mirrored in the psychological structure of modern man." BJMP, 20:2 (1944), pp. 118-34.

333. Lockwood, Marian. "The Christmas stars." Spring 1944, pp. 26-32.

334. Meier, Fritz. "Das Mysterium der Ka'ba." EJ, 11 (1944), pp. 187-214. (see 1125 below for English edition)

335. Menasce, Jean de. "Les mystères et la religion de l'Iran." Ibid., pp. 167-86. (see 1126 below for English edition)

336. Nagel, Georges. "Les 'mystères' d'Oseris dans l'ancienne E-gypte." Ibid., pp. 145-66. (see 1134 below for English edition)

337. Pratt, Jane Abbott. "Theories of mythology." Spring 1944, pp. 54-61.

338. Pulver, Max. "Vom Spielraum gnostischer Mysterienpraxis." EJ, 11 (1944), pp. 277-326.

339. Rahner, Hugo. "Das christliche Mysterium und die heidnischen Mysterien." Ibid., pp. 347-49. (see 1153 below for English edition)

340. Rodewald, Alice. "The venerable sign." Spring 1944, pp. 75-90.

341. Röösli, Josef. "Der Gottes- und Religionsbegriff bei C. G. Jung." Schweizerische Kirchenzeitung, 26 (1944), pp. 302-04.

342. Schmitt, Paul. "Antike Mysterien in der Gesellschaft ihrer Zeit, ihre Umformung und späteste Nachwirkung." EJ, 11 (1944), pp. 107-44. (see 1170 below for English edition)

343. Sergeant, Elizabeth Shipley. "Redskin Nephew." Spring 1944, pp. 91-110.

*344. Teillard, Ania. Traumsymbolik. Ein Traumbuch auf tiefenpsychologischer Grundlage. Zurich: Rascher, 1944.

345. White, Victor. "St. Thomas and Jung's psychology." Blackfriars, 25 (1944), pp. 209-19.

346. Wili, Walter. "Die orphischen Mysterien und der griechische Geist." EJ, 11 (1944), pp. 61-106. (see 1193 below for English edition)

347. Abenheimer, Karl M. "On narcissism—including an analysis of
Shakespeare's King Lear." BJMP, 20:3 (1945), pp. 322-29.

348. Adler, Gerhard. "C. G. Jung's contributions to modern consciousness." Ibid., pp. 207-20.

349. Barnes, Hazel E. "Neo-Platonism and analytical psychology."
Philosophical Rev, 54 (1945), pp. 558-77.

350. Baudouin, Charles. "Position de C. G. Jung." SZP, 4 (1945), pp.
263-75.

351. Baynes, Helton Goodwin. "Freud vs. Jung." Spring 1945, pp. 49-
75. (see 36 above and 602 below)

352. Bonaventura, Enzo. La Psicoanalisi. Verona: Arnoldo Mondadori
Editore, 1945.

353. Desoille, Robert. La rêve eveillé en psychothérapie; essai sur
la fonction de régulation de l'inconscient collectif. Paris:
PUF, 1945.

354. Feldman, S. S. "Dr. Jung and National Socialism." Amer J
of Psychiatry, 102:2 (1945), pp. 262 ff.

355. Fordham, Michael. "The analytical approach to mysticism." SZP,
4:3-4 (1945), pp. 188-204. (see 1460 below)

356. _____. "Professor C. G. Jung." BJMP, 20:3 (1945), pp. 221-
35.

357. Forel, O. L. and Morgenthaler, W. "Carl Gustav Jung." SZP, 4:
3-4 (1945), pp. 171-72.

358. Foster, Genevieve. "Archetypal imagery of T. S. Eliot." PMLA,
60:2 (1945), pp. 567-85.

359. Frei, Gebhard. "C. G. Jung zum 70. Geburtstag." Schweizerische
Rundschau, 45 (1945), pp. 312-19.

360. Frischknecht, Max. Die Religion in der Psychologie C. G. Jungs.
Bern: Paul Haupt, 1945.

361. Gray, Horace and Wheelwright, Joseph B. "Jung's psychological
types including the four functions." J of General Psychology,
33 (1945), p. 265.

362. Harding, M. Esther. "The shadow." Spring 1945, pp. 10-27.

363. Hediger, Hans. "Von Traum der Tiere." Ciba Zeit, 9:99 (1945), pp. 3558-65.

364. Hendrickson, Marion Vaux. "A paper on Dante Alighieri." Spring 1945, pp. 28-48. (see 2578 below)

365. Holmes, S. W. "Browning: semantic stutterer." PMLA, 60 (March 1945), pp. 231-55.

366. Jacobi, Jolande. "Komplex, Archetypus, Symbol. Versuch einer Begriffsabklärung vom Standpunkt der Jungschen Psychologie." SZP, 4:3-4 (1945), pp. 276-313.

367. _____. "Traumbücher." Ciba Zeit, 9:99 (1945), pp. 3567-80. (see 1690 below for English edition)

368. Kerényi, Carl. "Apollon-Epiphanien." EJ, 13 (1945), pp. 11-48. (see 924 below for English edition)

369. _____. "Heros Iatros: Über Wandlungen und Symbole des ärzlichen Genius in Griechenland." Ibid., 12 (1945), pp. 33-54.

370. Kirsch, James. "Psychology and the New World." Presidential Address, Analytical Psychology Club, Los Angeles, 1945.

371. Layard, John. "The incest taboo and the virgin archetype." EJ, 12 (1945), pp. 253-307.

372. Massignon, Louis. "L'ideée de l'esprit dans l'Islam." Ibid., 13 (1945), pp. 277-82.

373. _____. "Thèmes archétypiques en onirocritique musulmane." Ibid., 12 (1945), pp. 241-52.

374. Meier, Fritz. "Der Geistmensche bei der persischen Dichter 'Attaar." Ibid., 13 (1945), pp. 283-354. (see 1705 below for English edition)

375. Menasce, Jean de. "L'espérience de l'esprit dans la mystique chrétienne." Ibid., pp. 355-84. (see 2620 below for English edition)

376. Piaget, Jean. "Hommage à C. G. Jung." SZP, 4:3-4 (1945), pp. 169-71.

377. Pulver, Max. "Das Erlebnis des Pneuma bei Philon." EJ, 13 (1945), pp. 111-32. (see 953 below for English edition)

378. Rahner, Hugo. "Erdgeist und Himmelsgeist in der patristischen Theologie." Ibid., pp. 237-76. (see 954 below for English edition)

379. _____. "Die seelenheilenden Blume." Ibid., 12 (1945), pp. 117-240.

380. Schär, Hans. "Voraussetzung der Seelsorge beim Pfarrer und beim Arzt." SZP, 4:3-4 (1945), pp. 238-62.

381. Schmidt, Karl-Ludwig. "Das Pneuma Hagion als Person und als Charisma." EJ, 13 (1945), pp. 187-236.

382. Schmitt, Paul. "Archetypisches bei Augustin und Goethe." Ibid., 12 (1945), pp. 95-116.

383. _____. "Geist und Seele." Ibid., 13 (1945), pp. 133-87.

384. Schoch-Bodmer, Helen. "Die Spiral als Symbol und als Strukturelement des Lebendigen." SZP, 4:3-4 (1945), pp. 324-32.

385. Speiser, Andreas. "Geist und Mathematik." EJ, 13 (1945), pp. 95-110.

386. _____. "Platos Ideenlehre." Ibid., 12 (1945), pp. 23-32.

387. Spinks, Alfred G. S. Archetypes and Apocalypse. (Doctoral dissertation). University of London, 1945.

388. White, Victor. "Psychotherapy and ethics." Blackfriars, 26 (1945), pp. 287-300.

389. _____. "Psychotherapy and ethics: a postscript." Ibid., pp. 381-87.

390. Wili, Walter. "Die Geschichte des Geistes in der Antike." EJ, 13 (1945), pp. 49-94. (see 970 below for English edition)

391. _____. "Probleme der Aristotelischen Seelenlehre." Ibid., 12 (1945), pp. 55-94.

392. Wilwoll, Alexander. "Vom Unbewußten im Aufbau religiösen Erlebens." Annalen der philosophischen Gesellschaft Innerschweiz, 2 (1945), pp. 25-55.

393. Wolff, Toni. "Zum 70. Geburtstag von C. G. Jung." Basler Nachrichtung, (21 July 1945), np.

394. "The Jung Method." Life and Letters Today, 45 (June 1945), pp. 129-36.

395. Abenheimer, Karl M. "Shakespeare's Tempest, a psychological analysis." Psychoanalytic Rev, 33:4 (1946), pp. 399-415.

396. Adler, Gerhard. "Consciousness and cure." Spring 1946, pp. 33-46. (see 199 above)

397. _____. Psychology and the atom bomb. London: GofPP Lecture # 43, April 1946.

398. Bash, Karl W. "Gestalt, Symbol und Archetypus; über einige Beziehungen zwischen Gestalt- und Tiefenpsychologie." SZP, 5:2 (1946), pp. 127-38.

399. Bertine, Eleanor. "Men and bombs." Spring 1946, pp. 47-63.

400. Carp, Eugène A. D. E. "Der Mensch-beschouwing bij Jung, Freud, en Adler." Nederlandische Tijschrift von der Psychologie, 1 (1946), pp. 213-49.

401. Dessauer, Friedrich. "Galilei, Newton und die Wandlung des abendländischen Denkens." EJ, 14 (1946), pp. 282-331.

402. Elkisch, F. B. "Some practical points of Jung's analytical psychology." Blackfriars, 27 (Dec. 1946), pp. 461-66.

403. Fordham, Michael. "Analytical psychology applied to children." The Nervous Child, 5:2 (1946), pp. 134 ff.

404. Gray, Horace. "Brother Klaus; with a translation of Jung's commentary." Journal of Nervous and Mental Diseases, 103:4 (1946), pp. 359-77.

405. _____. "Jung's psychological types in relation to occupation, race, body build." Stanford Medical Bull, 4 (Aug.-Nov. 1946), pp. 100-103.

406. _____, and Wheelwright, Joseph B. "Jung's psychological types their frequency of occurrence." J of General Psychology, 34 (1946), pp. 3-17.

*407. Harding, M. Esther. Femmes de demain. Adapted and trans by E. Hugenin. Neuschatelle: Editions de la Baconniere, 1946. (see *90 above for English edition and a complete list of other editions.)

408. _____. "The unconscious as fate: a psychological study of l' Avocat by Brieux." Spring 1946, pp. 64-79.

409. Harms, Ernest. "Carl Gustav Jung - defended of Freud and the

Jews. A chapter of European psychiatric history under the Nazi yoke." Psychiatric Q, 20 (April 1946), pp. 199-230.

410. _____. "A fundamental concept for analytical psychology of childhood: paternus and materna. The Nervous Child, 5 (1946), pp. 146-63.

411. _____. "Jung." Psychiatric Q, 20 (April 1946), pp. 199-230.

412. Kaegi, Werner. "Wandlung des Geistes in der Renaissance." EJ, 14 (1946), pp. 228-81. (see 923 below for English edition)

413. Kerényi, Carl. "Die Göttin Natur." Ibid., pp. 39-86.

*414. _____. Prometheus; die menschliche Existenz in griechischen Deutung. Zurich: Rhein, 1946.

415. Linera, A. A. de. "Un nuevo type de psychanályse." Rev Filos, 5 (April-June 1946), pp. 280-89.

416. _____. "'El psicoanálisis y sus satélites.' del Dr. Oswald Bumke." Ibid., pp. 323-25.

417. Mann, Kristine. "The self-analysis of Emanuel Swedenborg." Rev of Religion, 10:3 (1946), pp. 266-93.

418. Massignon, Louis. "La nature dans la pensée islamique." EJ, 14 (1946), pp. 144-48. (see 2616 below for English edition)

419. Meier, Carl Alfred. "Considerations on medical and non-medical therapy." (in German) SZP, 5:4 (1946), np.

420. Meier, Fritz. "Der Problem der Natur in esoterischen Monismus des Islams." EJ, 14 (1946), pp. 149-227. (see 935 below for English edition)

421. Nagel, Hildegard. "The challenge of fire." Spring 1946, pp, 24-32.

422. Portmann, Adolf. "Die Biologie und das Phänomen des Geistigen." EJ, 14 (1946), pp. 521-67. (see 950 below)

*423. Schär, Hans. Religion und Seele in der Psychologie C. G. Jungs. Zurich: Rascher, 1946. (see *670 and *2401 below for English editions)
          Rev. Max Frischknecht. Theologische Zeit, 2 (1946), pp 388-93.

424. Schmidt, Karl-Ludwig. "Die Natur- und Geisteskräfte im Paulischen Erkennen und Glauben." EJ, 14 (1946), pp. 87-143.

425. Schmitt, Paul. "Natur und Geist in Goethes Verhältnis zu den Naturwissenschaften." Ibid., pp. 332-84.

426. Schrödinger, Erwin. "Der Geist der Naturwissenschaft." Ibid.,
pp. 491-520. (see 958 below for English edition)

427. Speiser, Andreas. "Die Grundlagen der Mathematik von Plato bis
Fichte." Ibid., pp. 11-38.

*428. Witcutt, W. F. Blake, a psychological study. London: Hollis
& Carter, 1946.

429. Wolff, Toni. Christianity Within. London: GofPP Lecture # 42,
May 1946. (see 1627 below for German edition)

1947

430. Baeck, Leo. "Individuum ineffabile." EJ, 15 (1947), pp. 385-
436.

431. Bänziger, Hans. "Persönliches und Archetypisches im Individua-
tionsprozess." SZP, 6 (1947), pp. 272-82.

432. Barker, Culver. Some positive values of neurosis. London: Gof
PP Lecture # 50, Feb. 1947.

433. Bertine, Eleanor. "Jung's greatest contribution to his time."
Spring 1947, pp. 11-29. (see 998 below for French edition)

434. Binder, Hans. "The concept of neurosis." Schweiz medizinische
Wochenschrift, 77 (1947), pp. 157-63.

435. Childs, Grace H. "The black ball." Spring 1947, pp. 94-102.

436. Christoffel, Hans. "Über-Ich und Individuation. Ein kritischer
und entwicklungspsychologischer Versuch." SZP, 6 (1947), pp.
283-89.

437. Creegan, Robert F. "Carl G. Jung." In P. L. Harriman, Encyclopaedia of Psychology, 1947, pp. 313-18.

438. Dessaure, Friedrich. "Mensch und Kosmos." EJ, 15 (1947), pp.
75-148.

*439. Fierz-David, Linda. Der Liebestraum des Poliphilo; ein Beitrag
zur Psychologie der Renaissance und der Moderne. Zurich:
Rhein, 1947.

440. Fordham, Michael. Analytical psychology and religious experience.
London: GofPP Lecture # 46, March 1947. (see 1458 below)

30

441. _____. "Integration and disintegration and early ego develop-
      ment." The Nervous Child, 6:3 (1947), pp. 266-77.

442. _____. "Psychological methods of treatment." The Medical
      Press, 217 (30 April 1947), p. 5634.

*443. Gebsattel, Viktor Emil von. Christentum und Humanismus. Wege
      des menschlichen Selbstverständnis. Stuttgart: Ernst Klett,
      1947.

444. Graber, Gustav Hans. "Probleme der Übertragung bei Freud und bei
      Jung." SZP, 6 (1947), pp. 131-36.

445. Gray, Horace. "Jung's psychological types: meaning and consis-
      tency of the questionnaire." J of General Psychology, 37
      (1947), p. 177.

446. _____. "Psychological types and changes with age." J of Cli-
      nical Psychology, 3:3 (1947), pp. 273-77.

447. Harding, M. Esther. "She: a portrait of the anima." Spring
      1947, pp. 59-93.

*448. _____. La strada della donna. A. & T. Carini, trans. Rome:
      Astrolabio, 1947. (see *90 above for English edition and a
      complete list of other editions)

449. Hawkey, M. Lawry. "The witch and the bogey: archetypes in the
      case study of a child." BJMP, 21 (1947), pp. 12-29.

450. Hoppin, Hector (Courtland). "The psychology of the artist."
      Spring 1947, pp. 30-39.

*451. Jacobi, Jolande. La psicología de C. G. Jung. Madrid: Espasa-
      Calpe, 1947/1963. (see *255 above for German edition and a
      complete list of other editions)

452. Kerényi, Carl. "Urmensch und Mysterium." EJ, 15 (1947), pp. 41-
      74.

453. Kesser, Armin. "Die Übertragung und das Kulturproblem. Zur Psy-
      chologie von C. G. Jung." Weltkultur (Tubingen), 15:687 (1947),
      p. 5.

454. Linera, A. A. de. "La psicología de C. G. Jung." Rev Filos, 6
      (Oct.-Dec. 1947), pp. 784-88.

455. Massignon, Louis. "L'homme parfait en Islam, et son originalité
      eschatologique." EJ, 15 (1947), pp. 287-314.

456. Metman, Eva. C. G. Jung's essay on 'The Psychology of the Spi-
      rit.' London: GofPP Lecture # 49, June 1947.

457. Muralt, A von. "Jungs Stellung zum Nationalsozialismus." Schwei-

zer _Annalen_, 2 (1946-47), pp. 692-702.

458. Parelhoff, Albert D. "Dr. Carl G. Jung." The Protestant, (June 1946-Feb. 1947), np.

459. Pearson, M. H. "Some ideas on science and religion." Spring 1947, pp. 40-58.

460. Portmann, Adolf. "Das Ursprungsproblem." EJ, 15 (1947), pp. 11-40.

461. Postle, Beatrice. "Religion in the psychologies of Jung and Freud." Ohio State Medical J, 43 (1947), pp. 947-50.

462. Pratt, Jane Abbott. "The inner mountain." Spring 1947, pp. 103-18.

463. Quispel, Gilles. "La conception de l'homme dans la gnose Valentinienne." EJ, 15 (1947), pp. 249-86.

464. Rahner, Hugo. "Das Menschenbild des Origens." Ibid., pp. 197-248.

*465. Röpke, Wilhelm. The solution of the German problem. E. W. Dickes, trans. New York: G. P. Putnam's Sons, 1947.

466. Schärf, Rivkah. King Saul and the spirit of God. London: Gof PP Lecture # 47, April 1947. (see 511 below for English and 1167 for German editions)

467. Schmidt, Karl-Ludwig. "Homo imago Dei im Alten und Neuen Testament." EJ, 15 (1947), pp. 149-96.

468. Strauss, E. B. "Quo Vadimus?" BJMP, 21 (1947), pp. 1-11.

469. Sumner, Oswald and Elkish, F. B. "Modern psychology and introspection." Downside Rev, 65 (1947), pp. 33-44. (see 583 below for French edition)

*470. Trüb, Hans. Vom Selbst zur Welt. Der zweifache Auftrag des Psychotherapeuten. Zurich: Speer, 1947.

471. White, Victor. "Anthropologia rationalis (The Aristotelian-Thomist conception of man)." EJ, 15 (1947), pp. 315-84.

472. Wickes, Frances G. "A disciple of Jung on dream symbols." In The World of Dreams, Ralph L. Woods, ed. New York: Random House, 1947, pp. 674-83.

473. "La psicología de C. G. Jung." Arbor, 8 (Sept.-Oct. 1947), pp. 284-85.

474. Abenheimer, Karl M. Problem of individuation in Friedrich Nietzsche's writings. London: GofPP Lecture # 54, May 1948.

*475. Adler, Gerhard. Studies in Analytical Psychology. London: Rout-
ledge & Kegan Paul; New York: Norton, 1948. (see *1306 and
*1307 below for English and French editions)
    Rev. F. Moellenhoff. Psychological Q, 18 (1949), pp.
    388-89.

476. Baynes, Helton Goodwin. "The provisional life." Spring 1948,
pp. 13-25. (see 135 above and 607 below)

477. Bertine, Eleanor. "Fromm looks at Jung." Bull APCNY, 10 (Feb.
1948), pp. 9-10.

478. _____. "Men and women." Spring 1948, pp. 70-92. (see 528 below)

*479. Bitter, Wilhelm. Die Angstneurose. Entstehung und Heilung. Mit
2 Analysen nach Freud und Jung. Bern: Huber, 1948/1972.
    Rev. Eberhard Jung. ZAP, 4:4 (1973), p. 295.

*480. Carp, Eugene A. D. E. De analytisch-psychologische behandelings-
methode volgens Jung. Een Critische Uiteenzetting. Amsterdam:
H. Meulenhoff, 1948.

481. Dracoulides, Nicholas N. "The individual and collective guilt in
post-war societies." Proc First Int Congress on Mental Health.
London: H. K. Lewis, 1948.

482. Fierz, Markus. "Zur physikalischen Erkenntnis." EJ, 16 (1948),
pp. 434-60.

483. Fordham, Michael. "Reflections on individual and collective psychology." BJMP, 21:2 (1948), pp. 90-103. (see 1467 below)

484. _____. Repression in Christian practices. GofPP Lecture #
57, Dec. 1948. (see 1468 below)

485. Frei, Gebhard. "Zur Psychologie des Unbewußten." Gloria Dei,
2:3 (1948), np.

486. Glover, Edward. "Freud or Jung: applied Jungian psychology."
Horizon, 15 (Oct. 1948), pp. 227-58; 16 (Nov. 1948), pp. 303-
18; 19 (March 1949), pp. 209-28.

487. Gray, Horace. "Jung's psychological types in men and women."
Stanford Medical Bull, 6 (1948), pp. 29-36.

*488. Harding, M. Esther. Das Geheimnis der Seele. Ursprung und Ziel der psychischen Energie. E. von Pelet, trans. Zurich: Rhein, 1948. (see *290 above for English and complete list of other editions)

*489. _____. Psychic energy: its source and goal. New York: Pantheon Press (Bollingen Series X), 1948. (see *290 above for complete list of other editions)
      Rev. Eugene H. Henley. Bull APCNY, 10:2 (1948), pp. 10-15.
      Helen H. Henley. Bull APCNY, 10:3 (1948), pp. 8-14.

490. Harms, Ernst. "Awakening into consciousness of subconscious collective symbolism as a therapeutic procedure." J of Child Psychiatry, 1:3 (1948), pp. 208-38. (see *549 below)

*491. Hondius, J. M. Religie en werkelijkheid in het licht der psychologie van C. G. Jung. Deventer: A. E. E. Kluwer, 1948.

492. _____. "Religie en werkelijkheid in het licht der psychologie van C. G. Jung." Arch Philos, 1:2 (1948), pp. 67-95.

493. Hoppin, Hector (Courtland). The psychology of the artist. London: GofPP Lecture # 55, June 1948. (see 450 above)

494. Jacobi, Jolande. "C. G. Jung." Hamburger Akademische Rundschau, 2:1-2 (1947-48), pp. 20-23.

*495. Kerényi, Carl. Der Göttliche Arzt; Studien über Asklepios und seine Kultstätten. Basel: Ciba, 1948. (see below *496 for French, *1251 for German, and *1588 for English editions)

*496. _____. Le medicin divin; promenades mythologiques aux sanctuaires d'Asclépios. V. Baillods, trans. Basel: Ciba, 1948. (see *495 above for German and complete list of other editions)

497. _____. "Mensch und Maske." EJ, 16 (1948), pp. 183-208. (see 1694 below for English edition)

498. Laterno, E. H. "Agape and Jung's Eros." J of Religious Thought, 5 (1948), pp. 186-95; 6 (1949), pp. 49-66.

499. Layard, John. "The making of man in Malekula." EJ, 16 (1948), pp. 209-84.

500. Leeuw, Gerardus van der. "L'homme et la civilisation; ce que peut comprendre le term: évolution de l'homme." Ibid., pp. 141-82.

*501. Maeder, Alphonse. Selbsterhaltung und Selbstheilung. Zurich: Rascher, 1948.

502. Neumann, Erich. "Der mystische Mensch." EJ, 16 (1948), pp. 317-74. (see 1829 and 2624 below for English editions)

*503. _____. Tiefenpsychologie und neue Ethik. Zurich: Rascher, 1948. (see below *940 for Dutch and *2726 for English editions)

504. Pagel, Walter. "Jung's views on alchemy." Isis, 39:1-2 (1948), pp. 44-48.

505. Parellhoff, A. D. "Jung and the Nazis." Saturday Rev of Literature, 30 (6 Sept. 1947), p. 21. Discussion, 30 (6 Sept. 1947), p. 21; (20 Dec. 1947), p. 20; 31 (21 Feb. 1948), p.17.

506. Portmann, Adolf. "Der naturforschende Mensch." EJ, 16 (1948), pp. 461-88.

507. Pugliesi, A. "C. G. Jung: Tipi psicologia." Ric Filos, 3:2 (1948), pp. 77-78.

508. Quispel, Gilles. "L'homme gnostique (La doctrine de Basilide)." EJ, 16 (1948), pp. 89-140. (see 2630 below for English edition)

509. Rahner, Hugo. "Der spielende Mensch." Ibid., pp. 11-88.

510. Sborowitz, Arië. "Beziehung und Bestimmung. Die Lehren von Martin Buber und C. G. Jung in ihrem Verhältnis zueinander." Psyche, 2 (1948), pp. 9-56.

511. Schärf, Rivkah. "King Saul and the spirit of God." Trans. by the author with B. Hannah. Spring 1948, pp. 47-69. (see 466 above for English, and 1167 below for German editions)

512. Schöneck, Gebhard Frei. "Die Grundgedanken der Psychologie von C. G. Jung." Annalen der Philosophischen Gesellschaften Innerschweiz und Ostschweiz, 4:3 (1948), pp. 73-103.

513. Staub, Josef. "Die Auffassung von Gott und Religion bei C. G. Jung." Ibid., pp. 1-37.

514. Sumner, Oswald. St. John of the Cross and Modern Psychology. London: GofPP Lecture # 57, Aug. 1948.

515. Teillard-Mendelssohn, Ania. "Anima-animus (l'amour selon Carl Jung)." Psyché (Paris), 3 (1948), pp. 191-202.

516. _____. "Introduction à Jung." Ibid., pp. 582-83.

517. Weyl, Hermann. "Wissenschaft als symbolische Konstruktion des Menschen." EJ, 16 (1948), pp, 375-433.

518. Wickes, Frances G. "The creative process." Spring 1948, pp. 26-46.

*519. _____. The inner world of man. New York: Henry Holt, 1948; London: Methuen & Co., 1950. (see *217 above for English, and

*874 below for German editions)

*520. Zimmer, Heinrich. De weg tot het zelf. Leer en leven van de In-
dische heilige, Shri Ramana Maharishi. Forw. by C. G. Jung.
's Graveland: De Driehoek, 1948.

1949

521. Adler, Gerhard. "A discussion on archetypes and internal objects.
III. A contribution of clinical material." BJMP, 22 (1949),
pp. 16-22.

522. _____. "Reply to Glover." Horizon, 19 (June 1949), p. 454.

*523. Bash, Karl W. Consciousness and the unconscious in depth and
gestalt psychology. Amsterdam: North Holland Pub. Co., 1949.

524. Baum, Julius. "Darstellungen aus der germanischen Götter und
Heldensage in der nordischen Kunst." EJ, 17 (1949), pp. 335-
58.

525. Baumann, Carol. "Interview with C. G. Jung." Bull APCNY, 11:8
(1949), pp. 1-9.

526. Baynes, C. F. "What about Dr. Jung?" Saturday Rev of Literature,
32 (15 Oct. 1949), pp. 23-25.

527. Beirnaert, Louis. "La dimension mythique dans le sacramentalism
chrétien." EJ, 17 (1949), pp. 255-86. (see 611 below for
English edition)

528. Bertine, Eleanor. Men and women. London: GofPP Lecture # 60,
Aug. 1949. (see 478 above)

529. Cambon, G. G. "C. G. Jung: 'L'io e l'inconscio'. Prolegomeni
allo studio scientifico della mitologia." Riv St Filos, 4:1
(1949), pp. 78-80.

*530. Campbell, Joseph. Hero with a thousand faces. New York: Pan-
theon (Bollingen Series XVII), 1949.
          Rev. Margaret Flenniken. Bull APCNY, 11:5 (1949), pp.
          5-7.

531. Corbin, Henry. "Le récit d'initiation et l'hermetism en Iran."
EJ, 17 (1949), pp. 121-88.

532. Dawson, Eugene E. Religious implications of Jung's psychology.
(Doctoral dissertation). Boston University, 1949. (see 1559

36

below)

533. Ewald, P. "Vegetatives System, emotionelles Erleben und Psychotherapie." Allg Z Psychiatrie, 124:1-4 (1949), pp. 235-43.

534. Ewer, James. "C. G. Jung." Forward, 15:1 (1949), pp. 15-23.

535. Fordham, Michael. "The contribution of analytical psychology to
psychotherapy." Brit Medical Bull, 6:1-2 (1949), pp. 24-27.
(see 1457 below)

536. _____. "A discussion of archetypes and internal objects. I.
On the reality of the archetypes." BJMP, 22:1-2 (1949), pp.
3-7.

537. Franz, Marie-Louise von. "The 'Passio Perpetuae'." E. Welsh,
trans. Spring 1949, pp. 85-127.

538. Frei, Gebhard. "Magie und Psychologie." Schweizer Rundschau,
48:8-9 (1948-49), pp. 680-88.

539. _____. "Schriften um C. G. Jung." Ibid., pp. 806-07.

*540. Glover, Edward. Freud or Jung. Oxford & London: Blackwell,
1949; London: Allan & Unwinn, 1950; New York: W. W. Norton,
1950. (see below, *709 for Spanish, and *909 for French editions)
        Rev. T. A. C. Rennie. New York Times, (6 May 1951), p.
        7.
        Erich Fromm. New York Herald Tribune Book Rev,
        (11 March 1951), p. 12.
        A. D. Harris. New Statesman and Nation, 40 (12 Aug.
        1950), p. 177.
        Robert Orton. Manchester Guardian, (6 June 1950),
        p. 4.
        Unsigned. San Francisco Chronicle, (1 April 1951),
        p. 25.

*541. Goldbrunner, Josef. Heiligkeit und Gesundheit. Freiburg: Her-
der, 1949. (see below, *1047 for English, and *2164 for German editions)

*542. _____. Individuation. Die Tiefenpsychologie von Carl Gustav
Jung. Krailing vor München: Wewel, 1949. (see below, *1048
for English, *1787 for Portugese, *1896 for Spanish, *2165 for
English, and *2363 for German editions)

543. Granjel, Luís S. "La psicología de C. G. Jung en la historía de
las relaciones entre medicina y religión." Archivos ibero-ame-
ricanos de historía de la medicina, 1 (1949), pp. 189-297.

544. Gray, Horace. "Freud and Jung: their contrasting psychological
types." Psychoanalytic Rev, 36 (1949), pp. 22-24.

37

545. _____. "Jung's psychological types: ambiguous scores and
     their interpretation." J of General Psychology, 40 (1949),
     pp. 63-88.

546. Hafner, Theodor. "Die Typenlehre von C. G. Jung und ihre päda-
     gogische Verwertung." Schweizer Schule, (15 Nov. 1949).

547. Harding, M. Esther. Frauen-Mysterien: Einst und Jetzt. F. du
     Bois-Reynard, trans. Zurich: Rascher, 1949. (see *148 above
     for English and complete list of other editions)

548. _____. "An old tale retold: the Babylonian creation." Spring
     1949, pp. 57-84.

*549. Harms, Ernst. Awakening into consciousness of subconscious col-
     lective symbolism as a therapeutic procedure. New York: Child
     Care Pubs., 1949. (see 490 above)

550. Heimann, Paula. "A discussion on archetypes and internal objects.
     II. Some notes on the psychoanalytic concept of introjected ob-
     jects." BJMP, 22 (1949), pp. 8-13.

551. Hinkle, Beatrice M. "The re-creating of the individual. A Study
     of psychological types and their relation to psychoanalysis."
     New Education. New York: Dodd Mead, 1949.

552. Hübscher, Arthur. "C. G. Jung." In Philosophen der Gegenwart.
     Munich: 1949, pp. 90-92, 159-60.

553. Jacobi, Jolande. "Aspects psychologiques de l'homme religieux."
     Etudes Carmélitaines, (1949), pp. 115-35.

554. _____. "Frau und Seele." Schweizer Rundschau, 48:8-9 (1949),
     pp. 633-808.

555. _____. "Gedanken über den Standort der Jungschen Psychologie."
     Hamburger Akademische Rundschau, 3:4-5 (1949), pp. 382-90.

*556. _____. La psicologia de C. G. Jung. A. Vita, trans. Torino:
     Einaudi, 1949. (see *255 above for German and complete list of
     other editions)

*557. _____. De Psychologie van C. G. Jung. M. Drukker, trans.
     Amsterdam: Contact, 1949. (see *255 above)

558. James, E. O. "Myth and Ritual." EJ, 17 (1949), pp. 79-121.

559. Jensen, Adolf E. "Die mythische Weltbetrachtung der alten
     Pflanzer-Völker." Ibid., pp. 421-74.

560. Jones, C. "Jung: anti-totalitarian." Sat Rev Lit, 32 (10 Sept.
     1949), p. 27.

561. Kerényi, Carl. "Mythologisches Mädchenbildnis." Du, 5 (1949),

pp. 11 ff. (see 2719 below for English edition)

*562. _____. Niobe, neue Studien über antike Religion und Humanität. Zurich: Rhein, 1949.

563. _____. "Die Orphische Kosmogonie und der Ursprung der Orphik." EJ, 17 (1949), pp. 53-78.

564. Kirsch, James. "The role of instinct in psychosomatic medicine." American J of Psychotherapy, 3 (1949), pp. 253-60.

565. _____. "The story of the seven beggars, a contribution to the understanding of Jewish psychology." Los Angeles: Analytical Psychology Club, Oct. 1949.

566. Lambert, Kenneth. Psychology and personal relationships. London: GofPP Lecture # 58, Feb. 1949.

567. Leeuw, Gerardus van der. "Urzeit und Endzeit." EJ, 17 (1949), pp. 11-52. (see 1380 below for English edition)

568. Marmy, Emile. "C. G. Jung et le problème de l'éducation." Nouv Rev Pédagogique, 5 (1949), pp. 450-65.

*569. Meier, Carl Alfred. Antike Inkubation und moderne Psychotherapie. St ad CGJIZ, I. Zurich: Rascher, 1949. (see *2491 below for English edition)

570. Muralt, Alex von. "C. G. Jungs Stellung zum Nationalsozialismus." Hamb Akad Rundschau, 3:7 (1949), pp. 547-57.

571. Nagel, Hildegard. "Goethe's Mephistopheles." Spring 1949, pp. 21-39. (see 2623 below)

572. Neumann, Erich. "Die mythische Welt und der Einzelne." EJ, 17 (1949), pp. 189-254.

*573. _____. Ursprungsgeschichte des Bewußtseins. Zurich: Rascher, 1949/1968. (see *943 below for English edition)

574. Nott, K. "Topographical illusion (reply to Glover)." Horizon, 19 (May 1949), pp. 367-71.

575. Parelhoff, A. D. "Letter to the Editor." (see 560 above) Sat Rev Lit, 32 (16 July 1949), pp. 21.

576. Parin, Paul. "Zur Kritik der geisteswissenschftlichen Richtungen in der Tiefenpsychologie." SZP, 8 (1949), pp. 67-84.

577. Portmann, Adolf. "Mythisches in der Naturforschung." EJ, 17 (1949), pp. 475-514.

578. Radin, Paul. "The basic myth of the North American Indians." Ibid., pp. 359-420.

579. Scholem, Gershom G. "Kabbalah und Mythus." <u>Ibid.</u>, pp. 287-334.

580. Scott, W. Clifford M. "A discussion on archetypes and internal objects. IV. The psycho-analytic views of mandala symbols." <u>BJMP</u>, 22 (1949), pp. 23-25.

581. Sigaux, G. "Aspects du drame contemporain d'après Jung." <u>Table Ronde</u>, 13 (Jan. 1949), pp. 121-23.

*582. Stocker, Arnold. <u>Psychologie du sens moral</u>. Geneva: Suzerenne, 1949.

583. Sumner, Oswald, and Elkisch, F. B. "Psychologie moderne et introspection." <u>Psyche</u>, 4 (1949), pp. 637-50. (see 469 above)

584. Sutermeister, H. von. "Zum heutigen Stand der Traumforschung." <u>Grenzgebiete Medizin</u>, 2:11 (1949), pp. 485-92.

585. Waldighofer, Josef. "Was ist Tiefenpsychologie?" <u>SR</u>, 48:8-9 (1948-49), pp. 674-79.

586. White, Victor. "Some notes on Gnosticism." <u>Spring</u> 1949, pp, 40-56.

587. Wylie, P. and Wertham, F. "What about Dr. Jung?" <u>Sat Rev Lit</u>, 32 (30 July 1949), pp. 6-8 ff.

588. "Doctor Jung: reply." <u>Commonweal</u>, 48 (24 Sept. 1949), pp. 568-69.

589. "In defense of Jung." <u>Sat Rev Lit</u>, 32 (9 July 1949), p.25; (16 July 1949), p. 23.

1950

590. Adler, Gerhard. "Zur Dynamik des Selbst." <u>Der Psychologe</u>, 2:7-8 (1950), pp, 314-23. (see below, 687-88 for English, 977 for French, and 1206 for English editions)

591. Aeppli, Ernest. "Zum 75. Geburtstag C. G. Jung." <u>Ibid.</u>, pp. 246-49.

592. Allenby, Amy I. <u>Relationship as the basis of the religious attitude</u>. London: GofPP Lecture # 66, Dec. 1950.

593. Aramus, Rudolf. "Autorität à tout prix. Ein Blick in die Problematik von C. G. Jung." <u>Die Kommenden</u>, 4:8 (1950), p. 5.

594. Aumüller, Anneliese. "Jungian psychology in wartime Germany." _Spring_ 1950, pp. 12-22.

595. Bänziger, Hans. "Der Glaube als archetypische Haltung." _EJ_, 18 (1950), pp. 377-412.

596. Bash, Karl W. "Begriff und Bedeutung des Archetypus in der Psychologie C. G. Jungs." _Der Psychologe_, 2:7-8 (1950), pp. 302-10. (see 879 below)

*597. Baudouin, Charles. _De l'instinct à l'esprit; precis de psychologie analytique_. Bruges and Paris: 1950.

598. _____. "La psychologie analytique." In R. Bayer, _Philosophie_. Paris: 1950, pp. 3-38.

*599. Baynes, Helton Goodwin. _Analytical psychology and the English Mind_. London: 1950.

600. _____. "Analytical psychology and the English mind." In _AP&EM_ (see *599 above), pp. 34-60. (see 134 above)

601. _____. "Demonstration of analytical practice." _Ibid._, pp. 19-33.

602. _____. "Freud vs. Jung." _Ibid._, pp. 97-129. (see 36 and 351 above)

603. _____. "Ghost as a psychic phenomena." _Ibid._, pp. 154-67.

604. _____. "The importance of dream-analysis for psychological development." _Ibid._, pp. 130-53.

605. _____. "Jung's conception of the structure of personality in relation to psychical research." _Ibid._, pp. 168-79. (see 264 above)

606. _____. "On the psychological origins of divine kingship." _Ibid._, pp. 180-203.

607. _____. "The provisional life." _Ibid._, pp. 61-75. (see 135 and 476 above)

608. _____. "Psychological background of the parent-child relation." _Ibid._, pp. 76-96.

609. _____. "The unconscious as the real objective of psychology." _Ibid._, pp. 1-18.

610. _____. "What is it all about?" _Ibid._, pp. 204-38.

611. Beirnaert, Louis. "The mythic dimensions in christian sarcamentalism." _Cross Currents_, 1 (1950), pp. 68-86. (see 527 above for French edition)

612. _____. "Le symbolism ascensionnel dans la liturgie et la mystique chrétiennes." EJ, 19 (1950), pp. 41-64.

613. Brinkmann, Donald. "Romantik und Tiefen-psychologie." Der Psychologe, 2:7-8 (1950), pp. 250-56.

614. Brunner, Cornelia. "Betty, a way of individuation." Inward Light, 37 (Fall 1950), pp. 10-29.

615. Buytendijk, F. J. J. "Zur Phänomenologie der Begegnung." EJ, 19 (1950), pp. 431-86.

616. Cahen-Salabelle, Roland. "La psychothérapie de la deuxième moitié de la vie d'aprè C. G. Jung." Semaine des Hôpitaux de Paris, 26 (1950), pp. 2291-93.

617. Choisy, Maryse, "Freud, Jung et Adler." Psyché, 5 (1950), pp. 450-63.

*618. _____. Psychoanalyse et catholicisme. Paris: L'Arche, 1950.

619. Clark, Tom C. "Jung's psychology as a background for studying the Cayce material." The Searchlight, 3:3-4 (1950), pp. 17-26.

620. Corbin, Henry. "Le Livre de Glorieux de Jâbir ibn Hayyân." EJ, 18 (1950), pp. 47-114.

621. _____. "Rituel Sabéen et exégèse Ismaélienne du rituel." Ibid., 19 (1950), pp. 181-246.

622. Cunardi, G. "Un contributo alla conoscenza dell'opera de Jung." Riv di psicologia (Florence), 46:1 (1950), pp. 48-50.

623. Cutner, M. "Analysis in later life." BJMP, 23:1-2 (1950), pp. 75-86.

624. Debrunner, Hugo. "Ein Handdruck von C. G. Jung." Der Psychologe, 2:7-8 (1950), pp. 256-63.

625. Eliade, Mircea. "Psychologie et histoire des religions--à propos du symbolisme du 'Centre'." EJ, 19 (1950), pp. 247-82.

*626. Fierz-David, Linda. Dream of Poliphilo; related and interpreted. M. Hottinger, trans. New York: Pantheon (Bollingen Series XXV), 1950.
    Rev. M. Esther Harding. Bull APCNY, 13:1 (1951), pp. 1-5.

627. Froböse-Thiele, Felicia. "Die religiöse Funktion des Unbewußten." Der Psychologe, 2 (1950), pp. 343-51.

628. Fromm, Erich. "Freud and Jung." Pastoral Psychology, 1 (1950), pp. 11-15.

629. Frye, Northrop. "Archetypes of literature." The Kenyon Rev, (Winter 1950), pp. 92-110.

630. Hannah, Barbara. Victims of the creative spirit: a contribution to the psychology of the Brontës from the Jungian point of view. London: GofPP Lecture # 68, July 1950.

631. Henley, Helen G. "What can we ask of marriage?" Spring 1950, pp. 23-39.

632. Hoppin, Hector. "An introduction to astrology." Ibid., pp. 40-55.

633. Jacobi, Jolande. "Der Beitrag Jungs zur Psychologie des Kindes." Der Psychologe, 2:7-8 (1950), pp. 286-94.

*634. _____. La Psychologie de C. G. Jung. V. Baillods, trans. Neuchatel: Delachaux & Niestlé, 1950. (see *255 above for German and complete list of other editions)

635. _____. "Zur Symbolik des Feuers." Du, 10:10 (1950). pp. 10-13.

636. Jaffé, Aniela. "Bilder und Symbole aus E. T. A. Hoffmans Märchen 'Der Goldene Topf.'" In C. G. Jung, Gestaltungen des Unbewußten. Zurich: Rascher, 1950, pp. 239-593.

637. Kemp, R. "La psychologie de Jung." Nouv Lit Art Sci, 29:1207 (1950), p. 2.

638. Kerényi, Carl. "Dramatische Gottesgegenwart in der griechischen Religion." EJ, 19 (1950), pp. 13-40.

*639. _____. Labyrinth-Studien; Labyrinthos als Linienreflex einer mythologischen Idee. Zurich: Rhein, 1950.

640. Kirsch, James. "Dreams of a movie-maker." Spring 1950, pp. 56-70.

*641. Kranefeldt, Wolfgang M. Therapeutische Psychologie: Ihr Weg durch die Psychoanalyse. Berlin: de Gruyter, 1950. (rev. ed. of *63 above, see *80 above for English and 1253 below for German editions)

642. Kraus, Fritz. "Aus der Welt der Urbilder." Deutsche Beiträge, 4 (1950), pp. 467-73.

643. Laiblin, Wilhelm. "Erneurung aus der Ursprung; Zur Symbolik des Wiedergeburts-Motivs." Der Psychologe, 2:7-8 (1950), pp. 276-85.

644. Lauffenburger, __. "La musique et l'inconscient collectif." Polyphonie, 7-8 (1950), pp. 10-23.

645. Layard, John. "Initial stages in analysis: leading to the problem of opposites." London: APC of London, 1950.

646. Leeuw, Gerardus van der. "Unsterblichkeit." EJ, 18 (1950), pp. 183-206. (see 2193 below for English edition)

647. Leisegang, Hans. "Der Gottmensch als Archetypus." Ibid., pp. 9-46.

*648. Linssen, Râm. Etudes psychologiques de C. G. Jung à J. Krishnamurti. Brussels: "Etre Libre", n.d. (ca.1950).

649. Massignon, Louis. "Le rite vivant." EJ, 19 (1950), pp. 351-56.

650. Matthews, Richard C. "Analytical psychology." Encyclopedia Americana, 1950.

*651. Meier, C. A. Zeitgemässe Probleme der Traumforschung. Zurich: Eidgenössische Technische Hochschule, 1950.

652. Meier, Fritz. "Die Welt der Urbilder bei Ali Hamadani." EJ, 18 (1950), pp. 115-72.

653. Metman, Philip. "C. G. Jung's psychology and the problem of values." (Burning Glass Paper # 21) Shorne, Kent, Great Britain: Ridgeway House, 1950.

654. Neumann, Erich. "Betrachtung über den Schatten." Der Psychologe, 2:7-8 (1950), pp. 295-302.

655. _____. "Über den Mond und das matriarchale Bewußtsein." EJ, 18 (1950), pp. 323-76. (see below, 852 for German, and 942, 1263, and 3285 for English editions)

656. _____. "Zur psychologischen Bedeutung des Ritus." Ibid., 19 (1950), pp. 65-120.

657. Nitsche, Roland. "Weltdeutung aus der Seele." Die Zeit (Hamburg), 5:30 (1950), p. 5.

658. Ostrowski-Sachs, Margaret. "Die Wandlungen des Prometheus-Mythus." Der Psychologe, 2:7-8 (1950). pp. 334-43.

659. Petro, Carlo. "Su l'introversione et l'estroversione." Cervello, 26:3 (1950), pp. 137-48.

660. Pettazzoni, Raffaele. "Der babylonische Ritus des Akiitu und das Gedicht der Weltschöpfung." EJ, 19 (1950), pp. 403-30.

661. Pimenta de Souza Monteiro, José Alfredo. "A psicología analítica de Jung." Riv Port de Filosofía, 16 (1950), pp. 48-72.

662. Poli, C. "Sull'inconsciente psicanalitico." G Psichiat Neuropat,

73:4 (1950), pp. 413-37.

663. Portmann, Adolf. "Das Problem der Urbilder in biologischer Sicht." EJ, 18 (1950), pp. 413-32.

664. _____. "Riten der Tiere." Ibid., 19 (1950), pp. 357-402.

665. Quispel, Gilles. "Anima naturaliter christiana." Ibid., 18 (1950), pp. 173-82.

666, Radin, Paul. "The esoteric rituals of the North American Indians." Ibid., 19 (1950), pp. 283-350.

667. _____. "The religious experience of an American Indian." Ibid., 18 (1950), pp. 249-90.

668. Sanford, John A. St. John Climacus: the psychology of the Desert Fathers. London: GofPP Lecture # 63, Feb. 1950.

*669. Schär, Hans. Erlösungsvorstellungen und ihre psychologische Aspekte. St ad CGJIZ, II. Zurich: Rascher, 1950.

*670. _____. Religion and the cure of souls in Jung's psychology. R. F. C. Hull, trans. New York: Pantheon (Bollingen Series, XXI), 1950; London: Routledge & Kegan Paul, 1951. (see *423 above for German, and *2401 below for English editions)
     Rev. Erdman Smith. Christian Century, 67 (2 Aug. 1950), p. 923.
     School and Society, 71 (13 May 1950), p. 302.

671. Schärf, Rivkah. "The image of the marriage between God and Israel as it occurs in the Prophets of the Old Testament, especially Ezekiel xvi." Spring 1950, pp. 70-89.

672. Schmidt, Karl-Ludwig. "Jerusalem als Urbild und Abbild." EJ, 18 (1950), pp. 207-48.

673. Schmitt, Paul. "Das Urbild in der Philosophie des Nicolaus de Cusa." Ibid., pp. 291-322.

674. Seifert, Friedrich. "Das Unbewußte bei C. G. Jung." Der Psychologe, 2:7-8 (1950), pp. 263-75.

*675. Sierksma, Fokke. Phaenomenologie der religie in complexe psychologie: een methodologische bijdrage. Assen: Van Gorcum, 1950.

676. Simon, W. "Schizophrenia: fundamental concepts of eight noted psychiatrists." Military Surgeon, 105:5 (1950), pp. 375-81.

677. Smith, J. W. D. "A study of sin and salvation in terms of C. G. Jung's psychology." Scottish J of Theology, 3 (1950), pp. 397-408.

*678. Suares, Carlo. Le mythe Judéo-chrétien d'après la Genèse et les Evangiles selon Matthieu et Jean. Paris: Cercle du Livre, 1950.

679. Tedeschi, G. "Dall'inconscio personale di Freud all'inconscio collettivo di Jung." Rassegna de Neuropsichiatria, 4:2 (1950), pp. 103-11.

680. Teirich, H. R. "Die Psychologie C. G. Jungs in der Alltagsprax-is." Der Psychologe, 2:7-8 (1950), pp. 330-33.

*681. Thurneysen, Eduard. Seelsorge und Psychotherapie. Munich: Kaiser, 1950.

682. Valangin, Aline. "Das musikalische Mandala." Der Psychologe, 2:7-8 (1950), pp. 310-14.

683. Wellisch, E. "The psychological conception of personality." J Trans Victoria Inst, 82 (1950), pp. 113-30.

684. Zeller, Max. "Unconscious material in a conflict situation." (paper # 3) Los Angeles: APCLA, 1950.

685. "Das Jung-Institut in Zürich." Weltkultur, 18:876 (1950). p. 7.

1951

686. Abel, Assia. "Some aspects of the cultural significance of depth psychology." Spring 1951, pp. 78-97.

687. Adler, Gerhard. "The dynamics of the Self." Spring 1951, pp. 98-111. (see 590 above for German and complete list of other editions)

688. _____. "Notes regarding the dynamics of the Self." BJMP, 24: 2 (1951), pp. 97-106. (see 687 above)

689. Bach, Hans I. "Freud and Jung." N. Gateman, trans. Bull APCNY, (Supplement, Nov. 1951), 13:7.

690. _____. "Freud und Jung." NSR, NS 18:11 (1951), pp. 679-88.

691. Bänziger, Hans. "Sinnbild und Urbild in der Psychoanalyse." Du, 7 (Oct. 1951), pp. 41-46.

692. Baudouin, Charles. "L'échelonnement des instances morales selon la psychologie analytique." Vie Spirituelle, 17 (1951), pp. 212-25.

693. Baumann, Carol. "Time and Tao." <u>Spring</u> 1951, pp. 21-46. (see 2119 below)

694. Bertine, Eleanor. "The psychological meaning of initiation." <u>Ibid</u>., pp. 46-60.

695. Bitter, Wilhelm. <u>Freud</u>--<u>Adler</u>--<u>Jung</u>. Stuttgart: Ernst Klett, 1951.

696. Bodkin, Maud. <u>Studies of type-images in poetry, religion and philosophy</u>. London: Oxford University Press, 1951.

697. Campbell, Robert. "Le psychologisme de Jung." <u>Rev de Paris</u>, 58 (March 1951), pp. 123-25.

698. Choisy, Maryse. "Freud and religion: another view." <u>Commonweal</u>, 54 (20 July 1951), p. 362.

699. Corbin, Henry. "Le temps cyclique dans le Mazdéism et dans l'Ismaélisme." <u>EJ</u>, 20 (1951), pp. 149-218. (see 699 below for English edition)

700. Curtis, Monica Mary. <u>Jung's essay on the transformation symbol in the Mass</u>. London: GofPP Lecture # 69, May 1951. (see 766 below)

701. Daim, Wilfred. <u>Umwertung der Psychoanalyse</u>. Vienna: Herold, 1951.

702. De Falco, Carmella. "L'inconscio ed il mito nella psicologia di K. G. Jung." <u>An Fac de Lettere e Filosofia</u> (Naples), 1 (1951), pp. 191-212.

703. Eliade, Mircea. "Le temps et l'éternité dans la pensée Indienne." <u>EJ</u>, 20 (1951), pp. 219-52. (see 1328 below for English edition)

704. Fierz-Monnier, Antoinette. <u>Initiation und Wandlung; zur Geschichte des altfranzösischen Romans im zwölften Jahrhundert von Chrétien de Troyes zu Renault de Beaujeu</u>. Berlin: A. Francke, 1951.

705. Fordham, Michael. "The concept of the objective psyche." <u>BJMP</u>, 24:4 (1951), pp. 221-31. (see 1459 below)

706. _____. "Some observations on the self in childhood." <u>BJMP</u>, 24:2 (1951), pp. 83-96. (see 1341 below)

707. Franz, Marie-Louise von. <u>Archetypal patterns in fairy tales</u>. Zurich: (privately printed), 1951.

708. _____. "Die passio perpetuae." In C. G. Jung, <u>Aion: Untersuchungen zur Symbolgeschichte</u>. Zurich: Rascher, 1951.

*709. Glover, Edward. _Freud_ o _Jung_. Buenes Aires: Nova, 1951. (see
       *540 above for English, and *909 below for French editions)

710.   Goodenough, Erwin R. "The evolution of symbols recurrent in time
       as illustrated in Judaism." EJ, 20 (1951), pp. 285-320.

711.   Hannah, Barbara. The _problem_ of _contact_ with the _animus_. Lon-
       don: GofPP Lecture # 70, Aug. 1951.

712.   Hawkey, Lawry. "The use of puppets in child psychotherapy." BJ
       MP, 24:3 (1951), pp. 206-14.

713.   Henley, Eugene H. "A man's world." Spring 1951, pp. 61-77.

714.   Hindel, Robert. "Der archetypische Gott C. G. Jungs und die Re-
       ligion." Wort und Wahrheit, 7 (1951), pp. 565-71.

715.   Hoop, J. H. van der. "Het typologische en het phenomenologische
       gezichtspunkt." Algem Neder Tijds Wijabeg Psychol, 43:5
       (1951), pp. 239-55.

716.   Hupfer, Joseph. "Der Begriff des Geistes bei C. G. Jung und bei
       R. Steiner." Abhandlungen zur Philosophie und Psychologie, 1
       (1951), pp. 57-79.

*717. Jacobi, Jolande. The _psychology_ of C. G. _Jung_: an introduction.
       Rev. ed., K. W. Bash, trans. New Haven, Conn.: Yale Univer-
       sity Press, 1951. (see *255 above for German and complete list
       of other editions)

718.   Keyserling, Graf Herman. "Meine Begegnung mit C. G. Jung."
       Weltkultur, 19:899 (1951), p. 5.

719.   Knoll, Max. "Wandlungen der Wissenschaft in unserer Zeit." EJ,
       20 (1951), pp. 387-436. (see 1376 below for English edition)

720.   Laroque, P. "A propos de 'De l'instinct à l'esprit' de Charles
       Baudouin." Evolution Psychiatrique, 3 (1951), pp. 497-516.

721.   Leibbrand, Werner. "C. G. Jungs Versuch einer psychologischen
       Deutung des Trinitätsdogmas." Zeit für Religions- und Geistes-
       geschichte, 3 (1951), pp. 122-34.

722.   Leonard, A. "La psychologie religieuse de Jung." Supplément de
       la Vie Spirituelle, 5 (1951), pp. 325-34.

723.   Mahr, Werner. "Arbeitstagung der deutschen Gesellschaft für Psy-
       chotherapie und Tiefenpsychologie." Psyche (Heid.), 5:1 (1951),
       pp. 70-79.

724.   Massignon, Louis. "Le temps dans la pensée Islamique." EJ, 20
       (1951), pp. 141-48.

725.   Meseguer, Pedro. "La educación como problema de energetica psi-

quica." <u>Razón</u> y <u>Fe</u>, 143:639 (1951), pp. 375-83.

726. Metman, Eva. <u>Woman</u> and <u>the</u> <u>animus</u>. London: GofPP Lecture # 71, Nov. 1951.

727. Metman, Philip. "Notes on the post-insulin analysis of a schizo-phrenic man." <u>BJMP</u>, 24:1 (1951), pp. 55-63.

728. Neumann, Erich. "Kunst und Zeit." <u>EJ</u>, 20 (1951), pp. 11-56. (see below, 1134 for French and 1392 for English editions)

729. Orelli, Aloys von. "Persönlichkeit, Selbst und Person." In Ernst Speer, <u>Die</u> <u>Vorträge</u> <u>der</u> <u>2</u>. <u>Lindauer</u> <u>Psychotherapiewoche</u>. 1951, pp. 158-66.

730. Plessner, Helmuth. "Über die Beziehung der Zeit zum Tode." <u>EJ</u>, 20 (1951), pp. 349-86. (see 1396 below for English edition)

731. Pötzl, Otto. "Über einige Grenzfragen der Tiefenpsychologie. I. Auslösermechanismus (K. Lorenz) und Archetypen (C. G. Jung). <u>Wien</u> <u>Arch</u> <u>Psychol</u> <u>Psychiat</u> <u>Neurol</u>, 1 (1951), pp. 135-49.

732. Portmann, Adolf. "Die Zeit im Leben der Organismen." <u>EJ</u>, 20 (1951), pp. 437-58. (see 1398 below for English edition)

733. Puech, Henri-Charles. "La Gnose et le temps." <u>Ibid</u>., pp. 57-114. (see 1400 below for English edition)

734. Quispel, Gilles. "Zeit und Geschichte im antiken Christentum." <u>Ibid</u>., pp. 115-40. (see 1402 below for English edition)

735. Read, Herbert. "Jung at mid-century." <u>Hudson</u> <u>Review</u>, 4:2 (1951), pp. 259-68.

736. Richer, J. "Nerval et ses fantômes (la psychologie de Jung dans l'oeuvre de Nerval). <u>Mercure</u> <u>Fr</u>, 312 (June 1951), pp. 282-301.

737. Sborowitz, Arië. "Nachwort." <u>Heilung</u> <u>aus</u> <u>der</u> <u>Begegnung</u>, (1951), pp. 117-24.

738. _____. "Das religiöse Moment in der Tiefenpsychologie." <u>Psyche</u>, 5 (1951), pp. 278-89.

739. Schirren, J. "Beitrag der analytischen Psychologie C. G. Jungs zu den Grundlagen der Psychotherapie." <u>Kongressbericht</u>. <u>Ana-lytische</u> <u>Psychotherapie</u> <u>und</u> <u>Erzieungshilfe</u>. Berlin: 1951, pp. 16-26.

*740. Sierksma, Fokke. <u>Freud</u>, <u>Jung</u> <u>en</u> <u>de</u> <u>religie</u>. Assen: Van Gorcum & Co., 1951.

741. Thum, Beda. "Theologie und Psychologie." <u>Gloria</u> <u>Dei</u>, 5 (1950-51), pp. 81-91.

742. Tramontin, J. A. "Jung y el inconsciente colective." Día Médico (Buenes Aires), 42 (1951), pp. 1754-60.

*743. Walder, Peter. Mensch und Welt bei C. G. Jung. Die anthropologischen Grundlagen der komplexen Psychologie. Zurich: Origo Verlag, 1951.

744. Wap-Van Pesch, __. "Jung en Krishnamurti." Perspektiven, 8:9 (1951), pp. 21-27.

745. Whyte, Lancelot Law. "Time and the mind-body problem. A changed scientific conception of process." EJ, 20 (1951), pp. 253-70.

746. Wilhelm, Helmut. "Der Zeitbegriff im Buch der Wandlungen." Ibid., pp. 321-48. (see 1422 below for English edition)

747. Wolff, Toni. "Strukturformen der weiblichen Psyche. Eine Skizze." Der Psychologe, Sonderheft 3:7-8 (1951). (see 1302 and 1633 below for English editions)

*748. Woltereck, Heinz. Das Tor zur Seele. Seebruck am Chiemsee: Heering Verlag, 1951.

749. Wormer, E. "Enkele begrippen mit de psychologie van Jung." Psychologische Achtergronden, 14 (1951), pp. 181-91.

1952

750. Abenheimer, Karl M. Reassessment of the theoretical and therapeutic meaning of anal symbolism. London: GofPP Lecture # 72, Feb. 1952.

*751. Adler, Gerhard. Zur analytischen Psychologie. Zurich: Rascher, 1952.

752. d'Arcy, Martin. "The power of Charitas and the Holy Spirit." EJ, 21 (1952), pp. 285-324.

*753. Axele, __. Freud -- Adler-- Jung. I Psychoanalysis. II Individual psychology. III Complex psychology. (in Greek). Athens: Biblioteque encyclopédique, 1952.

754. Bach, Hans I. C. G. Jung's Aion. London: GofPP Lecture # 74, Dec. 1952. (see 812 below)

755. Bash, Karl W. "Die Übertragung in der Praxis der Jungschen analytischen Psychologie." Psyche, 6:5 (1952), pp. 276-92.

756. _____. "Zur experimentallen Grundlegung der Jungschen Traum-
      analyse." SZP, 11 (1952), pp. 282-95.

757. Bertine, Eleanor. "Speaking of good and evil." Spring 1952,
      pp. 76-91.

758. Beveridge, W. E. The Jungian psychology and the origin of reli-
      gion. (B. Litt. dissertation). Trinity College, Dublin, 1952.

759. Bixler, Ray H. A comparison of the incidence of complex signs
      in association of normal subjects to the Jung word-list and to
      self-selected words. (Doctoral dissertation). Ohio State Uni-
      versity, 1952.

760. Boss, Medard. "Über Herkunft und Wesen des tiefenpsychologischen
      Archetypus-Begriffes." Psyche, 6 (1952), pp. 584-97.

761. Buber, Martin. "Antwort nach C. G. Jung." Merkur, 6 (1952), pp.
      474-76. (see 817 below for English edition)

762. _____. "Religion und modernes Denken (drei Auseinandersetz-
      ungen mit Sartre, Heidegger und Jung). Merkur, 6:2 (1952), pp.
      101-20.

763. Bügler, Käthe. "The turning point: a case of climacteric psycho-
      sis." H. Nagel, trans. Spring 1952, pp. 44-58.

*764. C. G. Jung-Institute, Zurich. Zeitlose Dokumente der Seele. St
      ad CGJIZ, III. Zurich: Rascher, 1952.

*765. Caruso, Igor. Psychoanalyse und Synthese der Existenz. Vienna:
      1952. (see *2131 below for English edition)

766. Curtis, Monica M. "Jung's essay on the transformation symbol in
      the Mass." Spring 1952, pp. 1-24. (see 700 above)

767. Dessauer, Philip. "Bemerkungen zum Verhältnis von Psychotherapie
      und Seelsorge." Anima, 7 (1952), pp. 112-20.

768. Diel, P. "La theorie des archeytypes chez C. G. Jung." J de Psy-
      chologie Normale et Pathologique, 43 (1952), pp. 97-109.

769. Eichinger, F. "Die Stellung von Jungs Typen der Intro- und Extra-
      version im System der Typenlehren." SZP, 11:2 (1952), pp. 146-
      56.

770. Eliade, Mircea. "Puissance et Sacralité dans l'histoire des re-
      ligions." EJ, 21 (1952), pp. 11-44.

771. Evans, Erastus. Soul and Death. London: GofPP Lecture # 73,
      Aug. 1952.

772. Fierz, Heinrich Karl. "Die Bedeutung des Kontaktes in der klini-
      sch-psychiatrischen Therapie." SMW, 82:29 (1952), pp. 687-92.

773. Fordham, Michael. "Psychotherapy in schizophrenia." The Medi-
      cal Press, (24 Dec. 1952), pp. 601-05.

774. Franz, Marie-Louise von. "Der Traum des Descartes." In Zeitlose
      (see *764 above), pp. 49-120. (see 2557 below for English
      edition)

775. Gutscher, Klaus. "Brücke zu Jung." Kirchenblatt für die reform-
      ierte Schweiz, 108, (1952), pp. 226-28.

776. Harding, M. Esther. "The anima and the animus: a Curtain Lec-
      ture." Spring 1952, pp. 25-43.

*777. _____. Réalité de l'ame; l'energie psychique, son origine et
       son but. Pref. by C. G. Jung, E. Huguenin, trans. Neuchatel
       and Paris: Baconnière, 1952. (see 290 above for English edi-
       tion and complete list of other editions)

778. Hauser, Irene. "Tiefenpsychologie in der heilpädagogischen Prax-
      is." Heilpädag Werkbl, 21 (1952), pp. 141-43.

779. Hochheimer, Wolfgang. "Abriss der Jungschen Lehre als Beitrag
      zur Synthese und Amalgamdiskussion in der Psychotherapie."
      Psyche, 6 (1952), pp. 508-35.

780. Hurwitz, S. "Archetypische Motive in der Chassidischen Mystik."
      In Zeitlose (see *764 above), pp. 121-212. (see 2592 below
      for English edition)

781. Jacobsohn, H. "Das Gespräch eines Lebensmüden mit seinem Ba."
      Ibid., pp. 1-48. (see 2598 below for English edition)

782. Kirsch, James. "A contribution to the psychology of the North
      American Indians." Los Angeles: APCLA, 1952.

783. Knoll, Max. Quantenhafte Energiebegriffe in Physik und Psycholo-
      gie." EJ, 21 (1952), pp. 359-414.

784. Koepgen, Georg. "Hiob, das große Lehrgedicht des Alten Testa-
      ments. Zu den Deutungen C. G. Jungs und Martin Bubers." Glo-
      ria Dei, 7 (1952), pp. 228-37.

785. Lang, R. "Die Frage der Urreligion in der Tiefenpsychologie."
      Wissenschaft und Weltbild, 5 (1952), pp. 46-53.

786. Langer, James. "Psychology and Religion." Today, 15 (1952), pp.
      54-56.

787. Laszlo, Violet de. "The goal in Jungian psychotherapy." Spring
      1952, pp. 59-75. (see 844 below)

788. Löwith, Karl. "Die Dynamik der Geschichte und der Historismus."
      EJ, 21 (1952), pp. 217-54.

789. Meseguer, Pedro. "La aceptacion de la 'sombra', según C. G. Jung, y su paralelo cristiano. _Razón y fe_, 145 (1952), pp. 166-78, 393-402.

790. Neumann, Erich. _Amor und Psyche. Mit einem Kommentar von Erich Neumann. Ein Beitrag zur seelischen Entwicklung der Weiblichen_. Zurich: Rascher, 1952. (see *1261 below for English edition)

791. _____. "Die Psyche und die Wandlung der Wirklichkeitsebenen." _EJ_, 21 (1952), pp. 169-216. (see 1267 below for English edition)

792. Orelli, A. von. "Der anthropologische Ort der Psychologie C. G. Jungs." _Zeit für Psychotherapie und medizinische Psychologie_, 2 (1952), pp. 20-21.

793. Pauli, Wolfgang. "Der Einfluss archetypischer Vorstellungen auf die Bildung naturwissenschaftlicher Theories bei Keppler." In Jung and Pauli, _Naturerklärung und Psyche_. _St ad CGJIZ, IV_. Zurich: Rascher, 1952, pp. 109-194. (see 1142 below for English edition)

794. Portmann, Adolf. "Die Bedeutung der Bilder in der lebendigen Energiewandlung." _EJ_, 21 (1952), pp. 325-58.

795. Progoff, Ira. _C. G. Jung's psychology in its significance for the Social Sciences_. (Doctoral dissertation). New School for Social Research, 1952.

796. Quispel, Gilles. "Mensch und Energie in antiken Christentum." _EJ_, 21 (1952), pp. 109-68.

797. Read, Herbert. "The Dynamics of Art." _Ibid._, pp. 255-84.

798. Schär, Hans. "C. G. Jung und die Deutung der Geschichte." _Schweizerische Theologische Umschau_, 22 (1952), pp. 91-96.

799. Schneider, Ernst. "Zur Psychologie des Unbewußten." _SZP_, 11 (1952), pp. 99-120.

800. Scholem, Gershom G. "Zur Entwicklungsgeschichte der Kabbalistischen Konzeption der Schechinah." _EJ_, 21 (1952), pp. 45-108.

*801. Speer, Ernst, ed. _Die Vorträge der 2. Lindauer Psychotherapiewoche_, 1951. Stuttgart: Georg Thieme, 1952.

*802. Uhsadel, Walter. _Der Mensch und die Mächte des Unbewußten. Begegnung von Psychotherapie und Seelsorge_. Kassel: Johannes Stauda, 1952.

803. White, Victor. "Challenges to Religion." _Commonweal_, 55 (14 March 1952), pp. 561-62.

804. _____. "Four challenges to religion: II. Jung." Blackfriars, 33 (1952), pp. 203-07.

805. Whyte, Lancelot Law. "A scientific view of the 'creative energy'
of man." EJ, 21 (1952), pp. 415-46.

*806. Xerotyris, I. I. The psychology of Freud, Adler, and Jung as
it pertains to the task of education. (in Greek) Heraclion:
By the author, 1952.

807. "Antwort auf Jungs Antwort auf Hiob." Für ein jüdisches Lehrhaus
Zürich, 2 (Sept. 1952), pp. 22-24.

808. "Personality." Time, 60 (7 July 1952), p. 37.

809. "Religion und Psychology. Dr. C. G. Jung." Merkur, 6:5 (1952),
pp. 467-73.

1953

810. Allers, Rudolf. "Mental trouble and moral life." Books on Trial,
(June 1953), pp. 342-43.

811. Bach, Hans I. C. G. Jung on synchronicity. London: GofPP Lecture # 77, Oct. 1953.

812. _____. "C. G. Jung's Aion; a synopsis." Spring 1953, pp. 11-
21. (see 754 above)

813. Benz, Ernst. "Die heilige Höhle in der alten Christenheit und
in der östlichorthodoxen Kirsche." EJ, 22 (1953), pp. 365-
432.

814. Boss, Medard; Fierz-Monnier, H. K., and Maeder, Alphonse. "Her-
künft und Wesen des Archetypus-Begriffes: eine Diskussion."
Psyche, 7 (1953), pp. 217-40.

815. Brunner, A. "Theologie oder Tiefenpsychologie." Stimmen der
Zeit, 152 (Sept. 1953), pp. 401-15.

816. Buber, Martin. "Religion and modern thinking." In his The E-
clipse of God. Studies in the relation between religion and
philosophy. London: Victor Gollancz, 1953, pp. 87-122, 179-
84. (see 762 above for German edition)

817. _____. "Reply to C. G. Jung." Ibid., pp. 171-76. (see 761
above for German edition.)

818. Ciarlo, Héctor Oscar. "Nota sobre la teoría de los complejos de Alfredo Adler y los tipos psicológicos de C. G. Jung." <u>Filos e Perón</u>, 6 (1953), pp. 55-60.

*819. Clark, Robert Alfred. <u>Six talks on Jung's psychology</u>. Pittsburg: Boxwood Press, 1953.

820. Corbin, Henry. "La Sophia éternelle." <u>Rev de culture européenne</u>, 3 (1953), pp. 11-44.

821. _____. "Terre Céleste et corps de résurrection d'après traditions Iraniennes." <u>EJ</u>, 22 (1953), pp. 97-194.

822. Daim, Wilfred. "Der Grundfehler C. G. Jungs. Zu einer gnostischen Entgleisung." <u>Wissenschaft und Weltbild</u>, 6 (1953), pp. 58-67.

823. Daniélou, Jean. "Terre et Paradis chez les Pères de l'Eglise." <u>EJ</u>, 22 (1953), pp. 433-72.

824. Dannwitz, Rudolf. "C. G. Jungs Wissenschaft von der Seele." <u>Merkur</u>, 7 (1953), pp. 418-38.

825. Eliade, Mircea. "La Terre-Mère et les hiérogamies cosmiques." <u>EJ</u>, 22 (1953), pp. 57-96. (see 1034 below for English edition)

826. Flew, Anthony. "Coincidence and synchronicity." <u>J of the Society of Oriental Research</u>, 37 (1953), pp. 198-201.

*827. Fordham, Frieda. <u>An introduction to Jung's psychology</u>. Harmondsworth: Penguin, 1953/1966/1968. (see below, 1666 for German, 2149 for Dutch, 2553 for Italian, and 2785 for Spanish editions)

828. Fordham, Michael. "A child guidance approach to marriage." <u>BJM P</u>, 26:3-4 (1953), pp. 197-203. (see 1333 below)

829. Gebsattel, V. E. von. "Psychoanalyse und Tiefenpsychologie, ihre psychotherapeutische Grenzen." <u>Jahr für Psychologie und Psychotherapie</u>, 1 (1953), pp. 409-420.

830. Haendler, Otto. "Komplexe Psychologie und theologische Realismus." <u>Theologische Literaturzeitung</u>, 78 (1953), pp. 199-218.

831. Hannah, Barbara. "Some remarks on active imagination." <u>Spring</u> 1953, pp. 38-58.

832. Harding, M. Esther. "Our search for mental health, Dr. Jung's contribution." <u>Ibid.</u>, pp. 22-37.

*833. _____. <u>Les mystères de la femme dans les temps ancien et modernes</u>. Intro. by C. G. Jung, E. Mahyère, trans. Paris: Payot, 1953. (see *148 above for English and complete list of other editions)

834. Henderson, James L. "Jung and education." _J of Educational Psychology_, 11 (1953), pp. 149-155.

835. Heun, Eugene. "Psychotherapie und Seelsorge." _Zeit für Psychotherapie und medizinische Psychologie_, 3 (1953), pp. 76-81.

836. Hoek, Kees van. "Carl Gustav Jung. Eine Porträtskizze." _Europa_, 4:47 (1953), pp. 15-16.

837. Hübscher, Arthur. "C. G. Jung über das Mariendogma." _Glaube und Erkenntnis_, 3 (1953), p. 13.

838. Jacobi, Jolande. "Ich und Selbst in der Kinder zeichnung." _SZP_, 7:1 (1953), 51-62.

839. Johnson, Hiram K. "Carl Jung, a contemporary appraisal." _Amer J of Psychiatry_, 109:2 (1952-53), pp. 146-48.

840. Joly, R. "Philologie et psychanalyse: C. G. Jung et le 'Pasteur' d'Hermas." _Ant Class_, 32:2 (1953), pp. 422-29.

841. Kijm, J. M. "De katolieke godsdienst en de complexe psychologie van C. G. Jung." _Gawin_, 1 (1952-53), pp. 39-49.

842. Köckel, Elsa. "Freudsche und Jungsche Anschauungen in der Kasuistik." _Psyche_, 7 (1953), pp. 286-302.

843. Kriekemans, A. "De mens volgens C. G. Jung." _Vl opv Tijdschr_, 33 (1953), pp. 257-71.

844. Laszlo, Violet de. "The goal in Jungian psychotherapy." _BJMP_, 26 (1953), pp. 3-14. (see 787 above)

845. Leonard, A. "Incertitudes et perspective en psychologie religieuse." _Supp de la Vie Spirituelle_, 7 (1953), pp. 215-42.

846. Mallet, C. H. "Analyse des Grimm'schen Märchens 'Der starke Hans'." _Praxis Kinderpsychologie und Kinderpsychiatrie_, 2:2-3 (1953), pp. 53-62.

847. Meier, Carl Alfred. "Ancient incubation and modern psychotherapy." _Spring_ 1953, pp. 59-74.

848. Mucchielli, Roger. "Introversion et extraversion selon Kretschmer, Jung et Rorschach." _Etudes philosophiques_, 8 (1953), pp. 267-78.

849. Neumann, Erich. "Die Bedeutung des Erdarchetypes für die Neuzeit." _EJ_, 22 (1953), pp. 11-56.

*850. _____. _Kulturentwicklung und Religion_. Zurich: Rascher, 1953.

851. _____. "Die psychologischen Stadien der weiblichen Entwick-

lung." In <u>Weiblichen</u> (see *853 below). (see 1603 below for English edition)

852. _____. "Über den Mond und das matriarchale Bewußtsein." <u>Ibid.</u> (see 655 above for German and 942 and 1263 below for English editions)

853. _____. <u>Zur Psychologie des Weiblichen</u>. Zurich: Rascher, 1953.

854. _____. "Zu Mozarts Zauberflöte." In <u>Weiblichen</u> (see *853 above).

855. Pannwitz, Rudolf. "C. G. Jung's Wissenschaft von der Seele." <u>Merkur</u>, 7 (1953), pp. 418-38. (see 947 below)

856. Perry, John Weir. <u>The self in psychotic process: its symbolization in schizophrenia</u>. Forw. by C. G. Jung. Berkeley: University of Calif. Press, 1953.
    Rev. Werner H. Engel. <u>Amer J of Psychotherapy</u>, 9:4 (1955), pp. 754-56.

857. Pinillos, J. F. "La investigación científica de la personalidad." <u>Arbor</u>, 26:69 (1953), pp. 343-63.

858. Plaut, A. B. J. "On the clinical importance of the hermaphrodite." <u>BJMP</u>, 26:2 (1953), pp. 133-39.

859. Pobers, Michel. "The new universe of Carl Jung." <u>Tomorrow</u>, 1:2 (Win. 1952-53), pp. 20-30.

860. Portmann, Adolf. "Die Erde als Heimat des Lebens." <u>EJ</u>, 22 (1953), pp. 473-94.

861. Progoff, Ira. <u>Jung's psychology and its social meaning</u>. New York: Julian Press, 1953; London: Routledge & Kegan Paul, 1953. (see 2503 below for Spanish edition)
    Rev. Joseph Bram. <u>Library J</u>, 78 (1 April 1953), p. 596.
        Rollo May. <u>Sat Rev Lit</u>, 36 (15 Aug.1953), pp. 15-17.
        Unsigned. <u>Catholic World</u>, 177 (Sum. 1953), p. 478.
        Unsigned. <u>Kirkus</u>, 21 (1 Feb. 1953), p. 94.
        Unsigned. <u>US Q Book Rev</u>, 9 (Sum. 1953), p. 333.

862. Quispel, Gilles. "Der gnostische Anthropos und die jüdische Tradition." <u>EJ</u>, 22 (1953), pp. 195-234.

863. Scholem, Gershom G. "Die Vorstellungen vom Golem in ihren tellurischen und magischen Beziehungen." <u>Ibid.</u>, pp. 235-90.

864. Schwartz, Charlene. "Jung and Freud." <u>Integrity</u>, 7 (July 1953), pp. 20-24.

865. Shentoub, S. A. <u>Introduction historico-critique à la théorie de l'inconscient collectif de Jung</u>. (Complementary thesis).

Paris, March 1953.

866. Stern, Karl. "Jung and the Christians." Commonweal, 58 (1953), pp. 229-31.

867. Suzuki, Daisetz T. "The role of nature in Zen Buddhism." EJ, 22 (1953), pp. 291-323.

868. Tucci, Guiseppe. "Earth in India and Tibet." Ibid., pp., 323-64.

869. Van den Bergh van Eysinga, Gustav Adolf. "Jung en Job et cetera." In his Godsdienstwetenschappelijke Studiën XIV. Haarlem: H. D. Tjeenk Willink en Zoon, 1953, pp. 34-44.

870. Walder, Peter. "Zu einer Auseinandersetzung mit der Psychologie C. G. Jungs." Psyche, 7 (1953), pp, 26-33.

871. Werblowsky, R. J. Zwi. "God and the Unconscious." The Listener, 49 (1953), pp. 758-59.

872. _____. "Psychology and Religion." Ibid., pp. 677-79.

*873. White, Victor. God and the Unconscious. London: Collins, 1952/1967; Chicago: 1953. (see 1419 below for German edition)
    Rev. Michael Fordham. BJMP, 26:3-4 (1953), pp. 319-22.
    Stanley Leavy. Biblio for the Guild of Scholars, 14 (1953), pp. 1-3.
    George Stevens. Theological Studies, 14 (1953) pp. 409-505.

*874. Wickes, Frances G. Von der inneren Welt des Menschen. Forw. by C. G. Jung, R. Wurzel, trans. Zurich: Rascher, 1953. (see *217 and *519 above for English editions)

875. Zacharias, Gerhard Paulus. "Die Bedeutung der Psychologie C. G. Jungs für die christliche Theologie." Zeit für Religions- und Geistesgeschichte, 5 (1953), pp. 257-69. (see 1197 below for French edition)

876. "Portrait of C. G. Jung." New York Times Magazine, (4 Oct. 1953), p. 20.

1954

877. Allenby, Amy I. Relationship and Healing. London: GofPP Lecture # 84, Dec. 1954.

378. Allwohn, Adolf. "Carl Gustav Jung. Aus dem Werk." Gestalten
unserer Zeit (Oldenburg), 1 (1954), pp. 247-58.

379. Bash, Karl W. "Begriff und Bedeutung des Archetypus in der Psychologie C. G. Jung." In W. Canziani, ed. Psychologia-Jahrbuch 1955. Zurich: Rascher, 1954, pp. 84-95. (see 596
above)

380. Beirnaert, Louis. "Jung et Freud au regard de la foi chrétienne." Dieu Vivant, 26 (1954), pp. 93-100.

381. Bennet, Edward Armstrong. "The collective unconscious." Proc
of the Royal Soc of Medicine, 47 (1954), pp. 639-41.

382. Benz, Ernst. "Theogonie und Wandlung des Menschen bei Friedrich
Wilhelm Joseph Schelling." EJ, 23 (1954), pp. 305-66. (see
2120 below for English edition.)

383. Bitter, Wilhelm. "Zur Psychologie der Angst und Schuld bei
Freud Adler und Jung. Praktische Hinweise für das Studium
der Tiefenpsychologie." In his Psychotherapie und Seelsorge.
Stuttgart: Ernst Klett, 1954.

384. Brock, P. van den. "De relatie tussen het begrip 'belevingstype'
van Rorschach en de 'instellings'-typologie van Jung." Ned
Tijschr Psychol, 9 (1954), pp. 517-25.

385. Buonaiuti, Ernesto. "Ecclesia Spiritualis." PEY I (see *886 below), pp. 213-250. (see 188 above for German edition)

386. Campbell, Joseph, ed. Papers from the Eranos Yearbooks I. Spirit and Nature. Princeton, N.J.: Princeton University Press
(Bollingen Series XXX), 1954.

387. Christou, Evangelos. Complex psychology and the occidentalized
Easterner; an essay in clarification. (Diploma thesis).
CGJIZ, Jan. 1954.

388. Cogni, Giulio. "Psychologie de la volupté." Psyché, 9 (1954),
pp. 24-34.

389. Corbin, Henry. "Epiphanie divine et naissance spirituelle dans
la Gnose Ismaélienne." EJ, 23 (1954), pp. 141-250. (see 2133
below for English edition)

390. Corman, L. "Les types primaires et les types secondaires en car-
actérologie." Connaissance Homme, 3 (Nov. 1954), pp. 71-78.

391. Daim, Wilfred. Tiefenpsychologie und Erlösung. Vienna: Herold,
1954.

392. Daniélou, Jean. "La colombe et la ténèbre dans la mystique
Byzantine ancienne." EJ, 23 (1954), pp. 389-418. (see 2136
below for English edition)

893. De Haas, Clement H. "Psychology and Religion." <u>Cross Currents</u>, 4 (1954), pp. 70-75.

894. Delamain, M. "Sur les correspondances entre les types Jung et Le Senne." <u>Connaissance Homme</u>, 2 (Oct. 1954), pp. 49-58.

895. Dellaert, René. "L'apport de la psychologie analytique de Jung à l'orthopédagogie." <u>Acta psychotherapie et psychosomatique orthopédagogie</u>, 2 (1954), pp. 127-40.

896. De Sauvage Nolting, W. J. J. "Over menselijke relaties." <u>Ned Tijdschr Psychol</u>, 9 (1954), pp. 241-63.

897. Donnington, Robert. "Music as an unconscious force." <u>Harv</u>, 1 (1954), pp. 3-12.

898. Duchêne, H. "A propos de la guérison psychologique de C. G. Jung." <u>Evolution psychiatrique</u>, 4 (1943), pp. 771-77.

899. Eliade, Mircea. "Mystère et régéneration spirituelle dans les religions extraeuropéennes." <u>EJ</u>, 23 (1954), pp. 57-98. (see 2141 below for English edition)

900. Evans, Erastus. <u>Assessment of Jung's 'Answer to Job'</u>. London: GofPP Lecture # 78, Jan. 1954.

901. _____. <u>A pilgrim's way between psychotherapy and religion</u>. London: GofPP Lecture # 79, Feb. 1954.

902. Fierz-Monnier, Heinrich Karl. "Die Assimilation des incompatibilen Komplexes in der akuten Psychose." <u>Psyche</u>, 8 (1954), pp. 525-45.

903. _____. "Methodik und Technik in der Praxis der analytischen Psychologie." <u>Ibid.</u>, pp. 37-50.

*904. Firkel, Eva. <u>Schicksalsfragen der Frau</u>. Vienna: Herder, 1954.

905. Fox, Jack. "The Freudian and Jungian approaches to development of ego and self." In Bruno Klopfer, et al., <u>Development in the Rorschach Technique, Vol I</u>. Yonkers: World Book, 1954.

906. Frank, W. "Psychology and religion." <u>Nation</u>, 178 (16 Jan. 1954) pp. 54-56.

907. Franz, Marie-Louise von. "The dream of Socrates." <u>Spring</u> 1954, pp. 16-38.

908. Frühmann, Edmund. "Archetypus und auslösendes Schema als Determinanten des Verhaltens." <u>Jahr Psychologie und Psychotherapie</u>, 2 (1954), pp. 190-205.

*909. Glover, Edward. <u>Freud ou Jung</u>? L. Jones, trans. Paris: P.U.F., 1954. (see *540 above for English and *709 for Spanish edi-

tion)

910. Haberlandt, H. "Archetypus und Psyche; Gedanken über ein neues Buch von C. G. Jung." Archive für Psychologie Psychiatrie und Neurologie (Vienna), 4:3 (1954), pp. 161-66.

911. Haendler, Otto. "Unbewußte Projectionen auf das christliche Gottvaterbild und ihre seelsorgerliche Behandlung." In Vorträge über das Vaterproblem in Psychotherapie, Religion und Gesellschaft. Wilhelm Bitter, ed. Stuttgart: Hippokrates, 1954, pp. 187-212.

912. Hannah, Barbara. "Hugh de St. Victor's conversation with his anima." Harv, 1 (1954), pp. 23-44.

913. _____. "Victims of the creative spirit: a contribution to the psychology of the Brontës from the Jungian point of view." Spring 1954, pp. 65-82. (see 630 above)

914. Hayes, Dorsha. "Our relationship to the artist." Ibid., pp. 52-65.

915. Heinemann, F. H. "Survey of recent philosophical and theological literature. I. Philosophy." Hibbert J, 52:206 (1954), pp. 293-96.

916. Heydt, Vera von der. "Loneliness." Harv, 1 (1954), pp. 15-22.

917. _____. Psychology and the cure of souls: standards and values. London: GofPP Lecture # 81, June 1954.

*918. Hostie, Raymond. Analytische psychologie en godsdienst. Antwerp: Standaard-Boekhandel; Utrecht: Het Spectrum, 1954.

919. _____. "Psychologische kroniek. Publicaties van en over C. G. Jung." Bijdr philos theol Fac N Z Nederl Jeg, 15 (1954), pp. 417-20.

920. Hurwitz, Siegmund. "The God-image in the Cabbala." G. Dreifuss and H. Nagel, trans. Spring 1954, pp. 39-51.

921. Hutin, Serge. "L'art et l'alchimie." Rev Métapsychologie, 27 (Jan.-Feb. 1954), pp. 55-59.

922. Jacoby, Marianne. "Symbolism in Handwriting." Harv, 1 (1954), pp. 64-81.

923. Kaegi, Werner. "The transformation of the spirit in the Renaissance." PEY I (see *886 above), pp. 251-87. (see 412 above for German edition)

924. Kerényi, Carl. "Apollo Epiphanies." Ibid., pp. 49-74. (see 368 above for German edition)

925. _____. "Mythologische Epilegomena." In P. Radin, C. Kerényi, and C. G. Jung. Der Göttliche Schlem der indianischer Mythem-Zyklus. Zurich: Rhein, 1954.

926. Laiblin, Maria. "Zur Psychologie von C. G. Jung." In Psychotherapie und Seelsorge. Wilhelm Bitter, ed. Stuttgart: Ernst Klett, 1954, pp. 55-68.

927. Laiblin, Wilhelm. "Einführung in die Urbildlehre von C. G. Jung." Ibid., pp. 69-85.

928. Landers, J. J.; MacPhail, D. S., and Simpson, R. C. "Group therapy in H. M. Prison Wormwood Scrubs. The application of analytical psychology." J of Mental Science, 100 (1954), pp. 953-60.

929. Layard, John. "The sacrifice of tusked boars in Malekula." Harv, 1 (1954), pp. 90-97.

930. Mairet, Philip. "Dr. Jung and the alchemists." Fortnightly, 181 (NS 175) (Jan. 1954), pp. 55-61.

931. Masson-Oursel, Paul. "The Indian conception of psychology." and "Indian techniques of salvation." PEY I (see *886 above), pp. 204-12. (see 194 above for German edition)

932. Meier, C. Alfred. "Le concept de synchronicité selon C. G. Jung." Rev Métapsychologie, 29-30 (1954), pp. 173-78.

933. _____. "Jung's 'Meaningful coincidences'." Tomorrow, 2:3 (1954), pp. 3-7.

934. _____. "Projection, Übertragung und Subjekt-Objektrelation in der Psychologie." Dialectica (Neuchatel), 8:4 (1954), pp. 301-21. (see 1596 below for English edition)

935. Meier, Fritz. "The problem of nature in the esoteric monism of Islam." PEY I (see *886 above), pp. 149-203. (see 420 above for German edition)

936. _____. "Die Wandlung der Menschen in mystichen Islam." EJ, 23 (1954), pp. 99-140. (see 2195 below for English edition)

937. Meseguer, Pedro. "Psicología compleja (Jung)." Razón y fe, 149 (1954), pp. 87-90.

938. Metman, Philip. "Astrology and synchronicity." Harv, 1 (1954), pp. 48-58.

939. Michaelis, Edgar. "Satan -- die vierte Person der Gottheit? Zu C. G. Jungs Deutung des Buches Hiob." Zeitwende, 25 (1954), pp. 368-77.

*940. Neumann, Erich. Dieptepsychologie en de ontwikkeling der religie.

F. Dutric and C. L. de Ligt-Van Possem, trans. Arnhem: Van Loghum Slaterus, 1954. (see *503 above for German and *2726 below for English editions)

*941. _____. Kunst und Schopferisches Unbewußtes. Zurich: Rascher, 1954. (see *1600 below for English edition)

942. _____. "On the moon and matriarchal consciousness." H. Nagel, trans. Spring 1954, pp. 83-100. (see 655 above for German and complete list of other editions)

*943. _____. The origins and history of consciousness. Forw. by C. G. Jung, R. F. C. Hull, trans. New York: Pantheon, 1954; Princeton, New Jersey: Princeton University Press, 1970 (Bollingen Series XLII). (see *573 above for German edition)

944. _____. "Der schöpferische Mensch und die Wandlung." EJ, 23 (1954), pp. 9-56. (see 1503 below for English edition)

945. Niel, Henri. "Psychoanalyse et religion d'après C. G. Jung." Critique, 10:91(94) (1954), pp. 1056-66.

946. Pannwitz, Rudolf. "C. G. Jung's Wissenschaft von der Seele." In his Beiträge zu einer europäischen Kultur. Nürnberg: Hans Carl, 1954, pp. 104-31. (see 855 above)

947. Pauli, Wolfgang. "Naturwissenschaftliche und erkenntnisstheoretische Aspekte der Ideen von Unbewußten." Dialectica, 8:4 (1954), pp. 283-301.

948. Pokorny, R. Raphael. "Zum Problem der Jungschen Archetypen." SZP, 13 (1954), pp. 175-87; 14, pp. 61-62.

949. Portmann, Adolf. "Biology and the phenomenon of the spiritual." In: PEY I (see *886 above), pp. 342-70. (see 422 above for German edition)

950. _____. "Metamorphose der Tiere." EJ, 23 (1954), pp. 419-54. (see 2205 below for English edition)

951. Priestley, J. B. "Analytical psychology." New Statesman, 48 (30 Oct. 1954), p. 541.

952. _____. "Jung and the writer." Times Literary Supp, (6 Aug. 1954), np.

953. Pulver, Max. "The experience of the pneuma in Philo." PEY I (see *886 above), pp. 107-21. (see 377 above for German edition)

954. Rahner, Hugo. "Earth spirit and divine spirit in Patristic theology." Ibid., pp. 122-48. (see 378 above for German edition)

*955.   Roth, Paul. _Anima_ und _Animus_ in der _Psychologie_ C. G. _Jungs_.
        Winterthur: P. G. Keller, 1954.

 956.   Savage, D. S. "Jung, alchemy and self." _Explorations_, 2 (1954),
        pp. 14-37.

 957.   Schmidt, Ernst Walter. "Hiob, Jung und Bultmann." _Neue Deutsche
        Hefte_, 1 (1954), pp. 699-705.

 958.   Schrödinger, Erwin. "The spirit of science." _PEY I_ (see *886
        above), pp. 322-41. (see 426 above for German edition)

 959.   Seifert, Friedrich. "C. G. Jung's Lehre vom Unbewußten und den
        Archetypen." _Universitas_, 9 (1954), pp. 867-77.

*960.   Stein, Leopold and Alexander, __. _Loathsome Women_. London:
        Wingenfeld & Nicolson, 1954.
            Rev. Amy I. Allenby. _Harv_, 5 (1959), pp. 94-96.

 961.   Stocker, Arnold. "L'anima nelle dottrine psicologichie contem-
        poranee." In _L'anima_. Michele Federico Sciacca, ed. Brescia:
        Morcelliana, 1954, pp. 293-329.

 962.   Strauss, F. H. "Interpretation of thematic test material: a
        Jungian approach." _Brit Bull Psychology and Society_, 23 (In-
        set) (1954), pp. 12-13.

 963.   Suzuki, Daisetz T. "The awakening of a new consciousness in
        Zen." _EJ_, 23 (1954), pp. 275-304. (see 2227 below)

 964.   Tillich, Paul. "Das neue Sein als Zentralbegriff einer christ-
        lichen Theologie." _Ibid._, pp. 251-74. (see 2228 below for
        English edition)

 965.   Toynbee, Arnold. "I owe my thanks." _Sat Rev Lit_, (2 Oct. 1954),
        pp. 13-16, 51-55.

 966.   Vinchon, J. "Les formes et les éléments de la psyché dans la
        conception de Jung." _Rev Métapsychologie_, 27 (Jan.-Feb. 1954),
        pp. 41-50.

 967.   Whyte, Lancelot Law. "The growth of ideas." _EJ_, 23 (1954), pp.
        367-88. (see 2233 below)

 968.   Wildberger, H. "Das Hiobsproblem und seine neueste Deutung."
        Reformatio, 3 (1954), pp. 355-63, 439-48.

 969.   Wili, Walter. "The history of the spirit in antiquity." _PEY I_
        (see *886 above), pp. 75-106. (see 390 above for German edi-
        tion)

 970.   Wurm, Alois. "Zu dem Thema: C. G. Jungs Stellung zum Christen-
        tum." _Die Seele_, 30 (1954), pp. 148-50.

*971. Zacharias, Gerhard Paulus. Psyche und Mysterium. Die Bedeutung der Psychologie C. G. Jungs für die christliche Theologie und Liturgie. Zurich: Rascher, 1954.
    Rev. W. Nölle. Philos Lit Anzeig, 9:1 (1956), pp. 34-35.

972. _____, et al. "Aussprache über den Vortrag von Professor Haendler." (see 911 above), pp. 213-23.

*973. Zimmer, Heinrich. Der Weg zum Selbst. Zurich: Rascher, 1954.
    Rev. F. Schöll. Philos Lit Anzeig, 9:1 (1954), pp. 25-27.

974. "Big wise old man." Newsweek, 44 (16 Aug. 1954), p. 78.

1955

975. Abegg, E. "Jung und Indien." Asiatische Studien, 1-4 (1955), pp. 6-8.

976. Adler, Gerhard. "The archetypal content of transference." In International Congress of Psychotherapy, Zurich: 1954. M. Boss, H. K. Fierz and B. Stokvis, eds. Basel and New York: Karger, 1955, pp. 285-92.

977. _____. "Le dynamique du soi." DV, (1955), pp. 62-78. (see 590 above for German and complete list of other editions)

978. _____. "The logos of the unconscious." St CGJ I (see *984 above), pp. 229-46.

979. _____. "Der transpersonale Aspekt der Übertragung." Psyche, 9 (1955), pp. 241-60.

980. Aigrisse, Gilberte. "Une interprétation jungienne de Van Gogh." DV, (1955), pp. 321-29.

981. Allenby, Amy I. "The father archetype in feminine psychology." JAP, 1:1 (1955), pp. 79-92.

982. _____. "The nature of personality." Harv, 2 (1955), pp. 2-12.

983. Altizer, Thomas J. J. A critical analysis of C. G. Jung's understanding of religion. (Doctoral dissertation). University of Chicago, 1955.

*984. Aylward, James, et al., eds. Studien zur analytischen Psychologie C. G. Jungs. Festschrift zum 80. Geburtstag von C. G.

Jung. Vol I. Beiträge aus Theorie und Praxis. Zurich: Rascher, 1955.

*985. _____. Studien (see *984 above). Vol II. Beiträge zur Kul-
turgeschichte.

986. Barth, T. "Der 13. Kongress der 'Vereinigung deutscher Franzis-
kaner-Academien'." Wissenschaft und Weisheit, 18:1 (1955), pp.
51-59.

987. Bash, Karl W. "Carl Gustav Jung zum achtzigsten Geburtstag (26
Juli 1955)." SZP, 14 (1955), pp. 169-70.

988. _____. "Einstellungstypus und Erlebnistypus: C. G. Jung und
Herman Rorschach." J Projective Techniques, 19 (1955), pp.
236-42.

989. _____. "Über Präyantraformen und ein lineares Yantra." St
CGJ I (see *984 above), pp. 205-28.

990. Baudouin, Charles. "Jung, homme concret." DV, (1955), pp. 344-
51.

991. Baum, Julius. "Symbolic representations of the Eucharist." PEY
II (see *1011 below), pp. 261-73. (see 322 above for German
edition)

992. Baumann, Carol. "Psychological experiences connected with child-
birth." St CGJ I (see *984 above), pp. 336-70.

*993. Baynes, Helton Goodwin. Mythology of the Soul. New York: Hu-
manities Press, 1955. (see 246 above and 2663 below)

*994. Beit, Hedwig von. Symbolik des Märchens. Bern: Francke Verlag,
1955-67.

995. Bennet, Edward Armstrong. "The double." St CGJ I (see 984 a-
bove), pp. 384-96.

996. Benz, Ernst. "Der Mensch und die Sympathie aller Dinge am Ende
der Zeiten." EJ, 24 (1955), pp. 133-98.

*997. Bernet, Walter. Inhalt und Grenze der religiösen Erfahrung.
Eine Untersuchung der Problem der religiösen Erfahrung in Aus-
einandersetzung mit der Psychologie C. G. Jungs. Bern: Paul
Haupt, 1955.

998. Bertine, Eleanor. "La grande contribution de C. G. Jung à son
époque." DV, (1955), pp. 368-90. (see 433 above for English
edition)

999. Bertrand, R. "Jung et les nombres." Ibid., pp. 320-30.

1000. Binswanger, Kurt. "Psychologische und psychiatrische Fragen zum

Problem Van Gogh." St CGJ II (see *985 above), pp. 364-78.

1001. Bitter, Wilhelm. "Über die Verdrängung bei S. Freud und den Schatten bei C. G. Jung." Zeit psychosom Medizin, 1:3 (1955), pp. 200-06.

1002. Bodamer, Joachim. Gesundheit und technische Welt. Stuttgart: Ernst Klett, 1955.

1003. Böhler, Eugen. "Jungs Bedeutung für Geisteswissenschaft und Menschenbildung." Neue Zürcher Zeitung, 1965 (24 July 1955), p. 37.

1004. Bohm, Ewald. "Über experimentalle Tiefenpsychologie." SZP, 14 (1955), pp. 61-62.

1005. Bonime, Walter. "The psychic energy of Freud and Jung." Amer J of Psychiatry, 121 (1955), pp. 372-74.

1006. Brunner, A. "Tiefenspychologische Deutung der Religionsgeschichte." Stimmen der Zeit, 154 (1955), pp. 390-92.

1007. Cahen-Salabelle, Roland. "Jung, l'empiriste." DV, (1955), pp. 40-41.

1008. _____. "Psychothérapie de C. G. Jung." Encyclopédie Medico-Chururgicale. Paris: 1955, np.

1009. _____. "Transfert et intuition." St CGJ I (see *984 above), pp. 161-69.

*1010. Camerling, Elizabeth. Inleiding tot het denken van Jung. Assen: Born, 1955.

*1011. Campbell, Joseph, ed. Papers from the Eranos Yearbooks II. The Mysteries. Princeton, New Jersey: Princeton University Press (Bollingen Series XXX), 1955.
Rev. Robert F. Hobson. JAP, 2:1 (1957), pp. 102-05.

1012. Carp, Eugene A. D. E. "The theoretical foundations of catharsis," Folia psychiat neurol neurochirurg neerl, 58:4 (1955), pp. 224-30.

1013. Castillejo, Irene de. "The animus: friend or foe?" Harv, 2 (1955), pp. 38-58. (see 3072 below)

1014. Cazeneuve, J. A propos de quelques traditions récentes." DV, (1955), pp. 317-20.

1015. _____. "Archétypes et ethnographie." Synthèses, 10:115 (1955), pp. 373-80.

1016. Chang, Chung-Yuan. "Tao and the sympathy of all things." EJ. 24 (1955), pp. 407-32.

1017. Clark, Robert A. "Buber and Jung." Inward Light, 49 (Fall 1955), pp. 29-32.

1018. _____. "Freudian super ego and Jungian self." Ministry and medicine in human relations. New York: International Universities Press, 1955, pp. 119-25.

1019. _____. "Jung and Freud: a chapter in psychoanalytic history." Amer J of Psychotherapy, 9 (1955), pp. 605-11.

1020. Corbin, Henry. "Del'Iran à Eranos." Du, 15:4 (1955), np.

1021. _____. "Le symbolisme dans les recits visionaires d'Avicenne." Synthèses, 10:115(1955), pp. 462-82.

1022. _____. "Sympathie et théopathie chez les Fidèles d'Amour en Islam." EJ, 24 (1955), pp. 199-302.

1023. Corti, Walter Robert. "Vingt ans d'Eranos." DV, (1955), pp. 228-97.

1024. Crehan, J. H. "Maria paredros." Theological Studies, 16 (1955), pp. 414-23.

1025. Dam, René. "Pour sauver Andromède." DV, (1955), pp. 270-87.

1026. Demos, R. "Jung's thought and influence." Rev Metaphysics, 9 (Sum. 1955), pp. 71-89.

1027. Dierkens, Jean. "De la psychologie freudienne aux théories de Jung." DV, (1955), pp. 302-16.

*1028. Dillistone, F. W. Christianity and symbolism. London: Collins, 1955.

1029. Durtain, Luc. "Jung, Frued, réalités du rêve." DV, (1955), pp. 267-69.

1030. Edinger, Edward F. "Archetypal patterns in schizophrenia." Amer J of Psychiatry, 112:5 (1955), pp. 354-57.

1031. _____. "The collective unconscious as manifested in psychosis." Amer J of Psychotherapy, 9:4 (1955), pp. 624-29.

1032. Eliade, Mircea. "Note sur Jung et l'alchemie." DV, (1955), pp. 97-109.

1033. _____. "Symbolisme et rituels metallurgiques Babyloniens." St CGJ II (see *985 above), pp. 42-46.

1034. _____. "Terra Mater and cosmic hierogamies." J. A. Pratt, trans. Spring 1955, pp. 15-40. (see 825 above for French edition)

1035. Fierz-Monnier, Heinrich Karl. "Les aspects positifs et négatifs du problème du père dans la psychologie analytique de C. G. Jung." Synthèses, 10:115 (1955), pp. 414-43.

1036. Fordham, Michael. "Jung's contribution to social psychiatry." Int J of Social Psychiatry, 1:1 (1955), pp. 14-21. (see 1464 below)

1037. _____. "Note on a significance of archetypes for the trans- ference in childhood." Acta psychothera psychosom orthopaedag, 3 (supp) (1955), pp. 90-105. (see 1335 below)

1038. _____. "On the origins of the ego in childhood." St CGJ I (see 984 above), pp. 80-105. (see 1337 below)

1039. _____. "Reflections on the archetypes and synchronicity." Harv, 2 (1955), pp. 14-28. (see 1338 below)

1040. Franz, Marie-Louise von. "Bei der Schwarzen Frau." St CGJ II (see *985 above), pp. 1-41.

1041. _____. "Saint-Exupéry's 'Little Prince'." Harv, 2 (1955), pp. 74-102.

1042. Frei, Gebhard. "Aus der Traumserie eines Theologen." St CGJ I (see *984 above), pp. 371-83.

1043. Frey, Liliane. "Die Anfänge der Tiefenpsychologie von Mesmer bis Freud (1780-1900)." St CGJ I (see *984 above), pp. 1-79.

*1044. Gemelli, Agostino. Psychoanalysis today. New York: P. J. Ke- nedy and Sons, 1955.
        Rev. J. van der Veldt. Amer Eccl Rev, 134 (Feb. 1956), pp. 139-42.

*1045. _____. Psicologia e religione nella concezione analitica di C. G. Jung. Milan: Vita e Pensiero, 1955.

1046. Gerster, Georg. "Seelenarzt und Gottesglaube. Eine Stunde mit Prof. Dr. med. C. G. Jung." Die Weltwoche (Zurich), 23:1116 (1 April 1955), p. 7.

*1047. Goldbrunner, Josef. Holiness is wholeness. London: Burns and Oates; New York: Pantheon, 1955, (see 541 above for German and 2164 below for English editions)

*1048. _____. Individuation: a study of the depth psychology of C. G. Jung. S. Godman, trans. London: Hollis and Carter, 1955; New York: Pantheon, 1956. (see 542 above for German and com- plete list of other editions)
        Rev. L. Stein. JAP, 2:1 (1957), p. 112.

*1049. _____. Personale Seelsorge, Tiefenpsychologie und Seelsorge. Freiburg: 1955. (see 2163 below for English edition)

1050. Graber, Gustav Hans. "Individuation und Übertragung." Die Heilkunst, 68:7 (1955), pp. 227-29.

1051. _____. "Individuation und Übertragung." Der Psychologe, 7: 7 (1955), pp. 273-78.

1052. Grill, S., "Psychoanalytiker als Exegeten." Der Seelsorger, 25 (1955), pp. 322-26.

1053. Hammerschlag, Heinz E. "C. G. Jung und die Parapsychologie." Der Psychologe, 7:7 (1955), pp. 286-91.

1054. Hannah, Barbara. "All's well that ends well." St CGJ II (see *985 above), pp. 344-63. (see 1231 below)

1055. _____. Ego and shadow. London: GofPP Lecture # 85, March 1955.

1056. Harding, M. Esther. "Jung et la recherche de la santé mentale." DV, (1955), pp. 159-79.

1057. _____. "The psyche and the symbols of religion." Inter Record of Medicine and General Practice Clinics, 168:12 (1955), pp. 749-53.

*1058. _____. Woman's mysteries; ancient and modern, 2nd ed. New York: Pantheon, 1955. (see *148 above for complete list of other editions)
        Rev. Anthea Lahr. Sat Rev Lit, (6 May 1972), pp. 85-86.
        Robert Moody. JAP, 1:2 (1956), pp. 210-11.

1059. Hellens, F. "C. G. Jung, écrivain." Synthèses, 10:115 (1955), pp. 433-37.

1060. Henderson, James. Analytical psychology and education. London: GofPP Lecture # 87, May 1955.

1061. Henderson, Joseph L. "Analysis of transference in analytical psychology." Amer J of Psychiatry, 9:4 (1955), pp. 640-56.

1062. _____. "The inferior function." St CGJ I (see *984 above), pp. 134-40.

1063. _____. "Resolution of the transference in the light of C. G. Jung's psychology." Acta psychotherapeutica, 2 (1955), pp. 267-83.

1064. Heydt, Vera von der. "Individuation of the personality." Davidson Clinic Bull, 38 (1955), pp. 1-6.

1065. Heyer-Grote, Lucy. "Leben und Werk von C. G. Jung." Der Psychologe, 7:7 (1955), pp. 262-65.

1066. Hobson, Robert F. "Archetypal themes in depression." JAP, 1:1

(1955), pp. 33-47.

1067.   Hoch, Dorothee. "Von der 'prophetische Sendung' C. G. Jungs
        für Kirche und Theologie." <u>Kirchenblatt für die reformierte
        Schweiz</u>, 111 (1955), pp. 197-201.

1068.   Hoffmann, Hans. "Real God and real man." <u>Christian Century</u>,
        72 (1955), pp. 452-53.

*1069. Hostie, Raymond. <u>Du mythe à la religion</u>. Bruges and Paris:
        Desclée de Brouwer, 1955/1968. (see below, *1361 for German,
        *1362 for English, and *1799 for Spanish editions)
                Rev. L. Gernet. <u>Année Sociologique</u>, 3rd series 3:4
                (1955), pp. 53-54.
                A. Roldán. <u>Pensamiento</u>, 13:51 (1957), pp. 356-59.

1070.   Hurwitz, Siegmund. "Sabbatai Zwi." <u>St CGJ II</u> (see *985 above),
        pp. 239-63.

1071.   Illing, Hans A. "Jung und die moderne Tendenz in der Gruppen-
        psychotherapie." <u>Heilkunst</u>, 68:7 (1955), pp. 77-80.

1072.   Jaccard, Pierre. "L'oeuvre psychologique de C. G. Jung; hommage
        à un grand savant suisse, à l'occassion de son 80e anniver-
        saire." <u>L'Illustré</u>, 35:30 (24 July 1955), pp. 43-44.

1073.   Jacobi, Jolande. "Aus der Analyse eines jungen Akademikers."
        <u>St CGJ II</u> (see *985 above), pp. 262-308.

1074.   _____. "Le double nature de l'âme." <u>DV</u>, (1955), pp. 150-58.

1075.   _____. "Eranos -- vom Zuhörer aus Gesehen." <u>Du</u>, 15:4 (1955),
        pp. 51-57.

1076.   _____. "Pictures from the unconscious." <u>J of Projective
        Techniques</u>, 19:3 (1955), pp. 264-70.

1077.   _____. "Psychologie und Leben." <u>Die Heilkunst</u>, 68:7 (1955),
        pp. 219-21.

1078.   _____. "Der Traum vom Orakel." <u>St CGJ I</u> (see *984 above),
        pp. 264-308.

1079.   _____. "Versuch einer Abgrenzung der wichtigsten Konzeption
        C. G. Jungs von denen S. Freuds." <u>Psyche</u>, 9 (1955), pp. 261-
        78.

1080.   Jacobsohn, Helmuth. "Dieu et homme dans l'Egypte ancienne." <u>DV</u>,
        (1955), pp. 253-66.

1081.   _____. "Das Gegensatzproblem in alt-ägyptischen Mythos." <u>St
        CGJ II</u> (see *985 above), pp. 171-98.

1082.   Jaeger, Martha. "Reflections on the work of Jung and Rank. <u>J</u>

71

of Psychotherapy as a Religious Process, 2 (1955), pp. 47-57.

1083. Jaffé, Aniela. "Carl Gustav Jung." Du, 15:4 (1955), pp. 22-24.

1084. _____. "Hermann Broch: Der Tod des Vergil." St CGJ II (see
*985 above), pp. 288-344. (see 1490 below for English edition)

1085. _____. "La synchronicité." DV, (1955), pp. 110-18.

1086. Journet, C. "Sur Carl Gustav Jung et la 'psychologie des profondeurs'." Nova et Vetera, 4:30 (1955), pp. 299-304.

1087. Jung, Albert. "Grundsätzliches zum psychosomatischen Medizin
im Lichte der komplexen Psychologie von C. G. Jung." St CGJ I
(see *984 above), pp. 170-204.

1088. Jung, Emma. "Die Anima als Naturwesen." St CGJ II (see *985
above), pp. 78-120. (see below, 1367 and 2716 for English editions)

1089. Keller, Adolf. "Aus den Anfangen der Tiefenpsychologie." Neue
Zürcher Zeitung, Sunday ed. # 1965 (37), (24 July 1955), np.

1090. Kerényi, Carl. "C. G. Jung oder die Durchgeistigung der Seele."
Inter Bodensee-Zeitschrift für Literatur, Bildende Kunst, Musik
und Wissenschaft, 4:6 (1955), pp. 81-96.

*1091. _____. Geistiges Weg Europas. 5 Vorträge. Zurich: Rhein,
1955.

1092. _____. "The mysteries of the Kabeiroi." PEY II (see *1011
above), pp. 32-61. (see 328 above for German edition)

1093. _____. "Les mystères de naissance." DV, (1955), pp. 42-49.

1094. _____. "Perseus." St CGJ II (see *985 above), pp. 199-208.

1095. _____. "Was bedeutet der name Eranos?" Du, 15:4 (1955), pp.
39-40.

1096. Kirsch, James. "'Journey to the moon' a study in active imagination." St CGJ I (see *984 above), pp. 319-35.

1097. _____. "'The red one' psychological interpretation of a story by Jack London." Los Angeles: APCLA, 1955.

1098. Klopfer, Bruno. "Analytische Psychologie, Ich-Psychologie und
projective Methoden." St CGJ I (see *984 above), pp. 151-60.

1099. _____. "C. G. Jung and projective techniques. Introduction."
J of Projective Techniques, 19:3 (1955), p. 225.

1100. Knoll, Max. "Endogene Rythmen und biologische Zeit." EJ, 24
(1955), pp. 433-84.

1101. Künzli, Arnold. "Carl Gustav Jung." Deutsche Rundschau, 81 (1955), pp. 942-44.

1102. Lambilliotte, M. "Connaissance et vie." Synthèses, 10:115 (1955), pp. 341-53.

1103. Lancksweirt, F. "C. G. Jung et la métamorphose du moi." Ibid., 10:108-09 (1955), pp. 142-46.

1104. Layard, John. "Boar-sacrifice." JAP, 1:1 (1955), pp. 7-32.

1105. _____. "Identification with the sacrificial animal." EJ, 24 (1955), pp. 341-406.

1106. Lebois, André. "Réflexions sur les archétypes." DV, (1955), pp. 205-19.

1107. LeComte, M. "La mandala dans la création d'une conscience complète." Synthèses, 10:115 (1955), pp. 456-61.

1108. Leibbrand, Werner. "Das tiefenpsychologische Werk C. G. Jungs." Hochland, 47 (1954-55), pp. 441-51.

1109. Leisgang, Hans. "The mystery of the serpent." PEY II (see *1011 above), pp. 194-260. (see 231 above for German edition)

1110. LeLay, Yves. "Aux confines de la psychologie et de la philosophie." DV, (1955), pp. 50-61.

1111. Lemke, Gertrude. "Life's relation to death." H. Nagel, trans. Spring 1955, pp. 41-62.

1112. Link, Margaret Schevill. "Mythology of the Navajo Indians." St CGJ II (see *985 above), pp. 121-45.

1113. Lyddiatt, E. M. "The song of a bird; notes on spontaneous painting and modeling." Harv, 2 (1955), pp. 30-36.

1114. Mahla-Helwig, Rotraut. "Das Gorgomotiv in Mythos und Traum." Der Psychologe, 7:7 (1955), pp. 292-301.

1115. Mailhiot, B. "Achievement of Jung." Tablet, 203:103 (30 July 1955), np.

1116. Marcuse, Ludwig. "Der Fall C. G. Jung." Aufbau, 21:52 (1955), pp. 13-15.

*1117. Martin, Percival William. Experiment in depth: a study of the work of Jung, Eliot, and Toynbee. London: Routledge and Kegan Paul; New York: Pantheon, 1955.
          Rev. Louis Barron. Library J, 80 (15 Oct. 1955), p. 2239.
               Mary Scrutton. New Statesman and Nation, 50 (17 Sept. 1955), p. 336.
               Unsigned. Times Lit Supp, (2 Sept. 1955), p. 513.

1118. Massignon, Louis. "L'expérience mussulmane de la compassion, ordonée à l'universel; à propos de Fâtima et de Jallâj." EJ, 24 (1955), pp. 119-32.

1119. Masson-Oursel, Paul. "The Indian theories of redemption in the frame of the religions of salvation." PEY II (see*1011 above), pp. 3-14. (see 180 above for German edition)

1120. Masui, J. "Notes sur C. G. Jung et l'Orient." Synthèses, 10:115 (1955), pp. 450-55.

1121. Mauron, Charles. "Jung et la psychocritique." DV, (1955), pp. 190-204.

1122. McGlashan, Alan. "Fairy tale world." Harv, 2 (1955), pp. 59-62.

1123. Meier, Carl Alfred. "Blick aur ein Lebenswerk." Neue Zürcher Zeitung, Sunday ed. # 1965 (37), (24 July 1955), np.

1124. _____ "Incubation antique et psychotherapie moderne." DV, (1955), pp. 119-37.

1125. Meier, Fritz. "The mystery of the Ka'ba; symbol and reality in Islamic mysticism." PEY II (see *1011 above), pp. 149-68. (see 334 above for German edition)

1126. Menasce, Jean de. "The mysteries and the religion of Iran." Ibid., pp. 135-48. (see 335 above for French edition)

1127. Meseguer, P. "La psicologîa profunda explica los sueños." Razon y Fe, 151:685 (1955), pp. 149-66.

1128. Michel, Heinz. "Versuch einer vergleichenden Darstellung der Neurose bei Freud und Jung am Beispeil einer lieb-seelische Erkrankung." Schweizer ANP, 76 (1955), pp. 91-109.

1129. Mindess, Harvey. "Analytical psychology and the Rorschach test." J of Projective Techniques, 19 (1955), pp. 243-52.

1130. Moody, Robert. "On the function of counter-transference." JAP, 1:1 (1955), pp. 49-58.

1131. Morawitz-Cadio, Alice von. "Die psychologie Jungs als Methode Geister Führung." Die Heilkunst, 68:7 (1955), pp. 221-27.

1132. Mountford, Gwen. "The Shakespearian dream." Harv, 2 (1955), pp. 64-73.

1133. Nagel, Georges. "The 'mysteries' of Osiris in ancient Egypt." PEY II (see *1011 above), pp. 119-34. (see 336 above for French edition)

1134. Neumann, Erich. "Arts et temps; remarques sur Marc Chagall."

DV, (1955), pp. 138-49. (see 728 above for German, and 1392 below for English editions)

1135. _____. "Dank an Jung." Der Psychologe, 8:7 (1955), pp. 257-61.

1136. _____. "Die Erfahrung der Einheitswirklichkeit und die Sympathie der Dinge." EJ, 24 (1955), pp. 11-54.

1137. _____. "My thanks to Dr. Jung." Bull APCNY, 17:6 (1955), pp. 17-24.

*1138. _____. The Great Mother; an analysis of the archetype. R. Manheim, trans. London: Routledge and Kegan Paul; New York: Pantheon (Bollingen Series XLVII), 1955/1972.
Rev. M. Esther Harding. JAP, 2:1 (1957), pp. 97-101.

1139. _____. "Narzissmus, Automorphismus und Urbeziehung." St CGJ I (see *984 above), pp. 106-33. (see 2388 below for English edition)

1140. Otto, Walter F. "The meaning of the Eleusinian mysteries." PEY II (see *1011 above), pp. 14-31. (see 236 above for German edition)

1141. _____. "Der ursprüngliche Mythos im Lichte der Sympathie von Mensch und Welt." EJ, 24 (1955), pp. 303-40.

1142. Pauli, Wolfgang. "The influence of archetypal ideas on the scientific theories of Keppler." In C. G. Jung and W. Pauli, The interpretation of nature and the psyche. New York: Pantheon (Bollingen Series LI), 1955. (see 793 above for German edition)

1143. Percheron, Maurice. "La guérison psychologique." DV, (1955), pp. 180-89.

1144. Plaut, Alfred B. J. "Research into transference phenomena." Acta Psychotherapeutica, 2 (1955), pp. 557-62.

1145. Pontvik, Aleks. "Begegnung mit C. G. Jung." Die Heilkunst, 68 (1955), pp. 218-19.

1146. Portmann, Adolf. "Eranos." Du, 15:4 (1955), pp. 8-10.

1147. _____. "Der Lebendige als vorbereitete Beziehung." EJ, 24 (1955), pp. 485-506.

1148. Pratt, Jane Abbott. "The symbolism of the mountain in time of flood." Spring 1955, pp. 64-82.

1149. Priestley, J. B. "Wise old man." Sunday Times (London), (24 July 1955), p. 3.

1150. Progoff, Ira. "The power of the archetypes in modern civilization." St CGJ II (see *985 above), pp. 379-97.

1151. Pulver, Max. "Jesus' round dance and crucifixion according to the Acts of St. John." PEY II (see *1011 above), pp. 169-93.

1152. Radin, Paul. "The dreams of an American Indian: their meaning and function." St CGJ II (see *985 above), pp. 146-70.

1153. Rahner, Hugo. "The Christian mystery and the pagan mysteries." PEY II (see *1011 above), pp. 337-405.

1154. Read, Herbert. "An eightieth birthday." New Statesman, 50 (23 July 1955), p. 94.

1155. Riklin, Franz. "Jung's association test and dream interpretation." J of Projective Techniques, 19:3 (1955), pp. 226-35.

1156. Roth, G. "Die zerebralen Anfallsleiden im Elektroenzefhalogramm und im Jungschen Assoziationstest." Archiv für Psychologie, Psychiatrie und Neurologie (Vienna), 5:4 (1955), pp. 206-12.

1157. Sands, Frederick. "Men, women and God: an interview with Dr. C. G. Jung of Zurich." Daily Mail (London), (25-29 April 1955), p. 6 of each issue.

1158. Saurat, Denis. "Le rôle historique et l'avenir des idées de Jung." DV, (1955), pp. 220-30.

1159. Sborowitz, Arië. "Eine religiöse Konzeption in der Nachfolge C. G. Jungs." Psyche, 8 (1955), pp. 22-31.

1160. Schär, Hans. "C. G. Jungs Bedeutung für die gegenwartige Religiöse Lage." Der Psychologe, 7:7 (1955), pp. 279-83.

1161. _____. "Gott und Mensch in der Psychologie C. G. Jungs." Basler Nachrichten, (24 July 1955), np.

1162. _____. "Religiöse Erfahrung zu einer theologischen Auseinandersetzung mit der Psychologie C. G. Jungs." Ibid.

1163. _____. "Die Religion in der Psychologie C. G. Jungs." Psychologia-Jahrbuch, (1955), pp. 96-110.

1164. _____. "Vie spirituelle saine et maladive dans la religion." DV, (1955), pp. 236-52.

1165. _____. "Wirkungen und Grenzen religiöser Wandlung." St CGJ II (see *985 above), pp. 264-87.

1166. Schärf-Kluger, Rivkah. "Satan, un archétype." Synthèses, 10:115 (1955), pp. 391-413.

1167. _____. "Saul und der Geist Gottes." St CGJ II (see *985 above), pp. 209 - 38. (see 466 and 511 above for English editions)

1168. Scharpff, Wilhelm. "Der Tiefenspychologie C. G. Jung und die Religion." Wort und Tat, 9 (1955), pp. 76-79.

*1169. Schmaltz, Gustav. Komplexe Psychologie und Körperliches Symptom. Stuttgart: Hippokrates, 1955.

1170. Schmitt, Paul. "The ancient mysteries in the society of their time, their transformation and most recent echoes." PEY II (see *1011 above), pp. 93-118. (see 342 above for German edition)

1171. Scholem, Gershom G. "Seelenwandlung und Sympathie der Seelen in der jüdischen Mystik." EJ, 24 (1955), pp. 55-115.

1172. Schweizer, Lina. "Gespräch um die Erforschung der Seele." Der Kleine Bund, 338 (22 July 1955), p. 6.

1173. Seifert, Friedrich. "Geistesgeschichtliches zu dem Begriff der objektiv-psychischen Realität." Der Psychologe, 7:7 (1955), pp. 265-72.

*1174. _____. Tiefenpsychologie. Die Entwicklung der Lehre vom Unbewußten. Dusseldorf and Cologne: Eugen Diederichs, 1955.

1175. Spiegelman, Marvin. "Jungian theory and the analysis of thematic tests." J of Projective Techniques, 19 (1955), pp. 253-63.

1176. Steffen, Uwe. "Tiefenpsychologie und Theologie. Zum 80. Geburtstag von C. G. Jung am 26 Juli 1955." Monatsschrift für Pastoraltheologie, 44 (1955), pp. 416-30.

1177. Stein, Leopold. "Loathsome women." JAP, 1:1 (1955), pp. 59-68.

1178. Storr, Anthony. "A note on cybernetics and analytical psychology." Ibid., pp. 93-96.

1179. Stumper, E. "Le contenu de la psychose." DV, (1955), pp. 298-301.

1180. Suares, Carlo. "Jung et l'experience religieuse." Ibid., pp. 339-45.

1181. Sury, Kurt von. "Aus dem Werk C. G. Jung." Der Psychologe, 7:7 (1955), pp. 301-04.

1182. Teillard, Ania. "L'essence du rêve." DV, (1955), pp. 359-67.

1183. Teirich, H. R. "Beiträge zum Synchronizitätsproblem." Die Heilkunst, 68:7 (1955), pp. 229-32.

1184. _____. "Übertragungs- und Rangordnungsproblem in der Gruppentheorie." Acta Psychotherapeutica, 2 (1955), pp. 687-91.

1185. Vestdijk, Simon. "La pensée de C, G, Jung." DV, (1955), pp. 231-35.

*1186. Victoria, Marcos. Freud, Jung y Adler; tres capítulos seguidos de un diálogo. Buenos Aires: Edit. Raigal, 1955.

1187. Waelhens, Alphonse de. "Phenomenologie et psychanalyse." DV (1955), pp. 79-96.

1188. Watkin, E. "Religion?" Dublin Rev, 229 (1955), pp. 337-40.

1189. White, Victor. "Charles Gustave Jung." Time and Tide, 36:36 (23 July 1955), pp. 962-63.

1190. _____. "Jung on Job." Blackfriars, 36 (March 1955), pp. 52-60.

1191. _____. "Kinds of opposites." St CGJ I (see *984 above), pp. 141-50.

1192. Wickes, Frances G. "Three illustrations of the power of the projected image." Ibid., pp. 247-63.

1193. Wili, Walter. "The orphic mysteries and the Greek spirit." PEY II (see *1011 above), pp. 64-92. (see 346 above for German)

*1194. Wingenfeld, Bernard. Die Archetypen der Selbstwerdung bei Carl Gustav Jung. Pfullendorf/Baden, Schmidt und Sohn, 1955.

1195. _____. "Das Menschbild C. G. Jungs." Pastoralblatt (Eichstatt), 56 (1955), pp. 341-42.

1196. Witt, Gerhard. "The outlook for analytical psychology." Psychoanalysis, 3:4 (1955), pp. 60-72.

1197. Zacharias, Gerhard Paulus. "Signification de la psychologie de C. G. Jung pour la théologie chrétienne." Synthèses, 10: 115 (1955), pp. 381-90. (see 875 above for German edition)

1198. _____. "Die Symbolik des klassischen Tanzes." St CGJ II (see *985 above), pp. 47-77.

1199. Zueblin, W. "Die Aktive Imagination in der Kinderpsychotherapie." St CGJ I (see *984 above), pp. 309-18.

1200. "C. G. Jung - 80 Jahre." Aufbau, 21:31 (1955), p. 15.

1201. "Communication." New Republic, 132 (21 Feb. 1955), pp. 30-31.

1202. "Confession is good for the soul." Ave, 81 (26 Feb. 1955), p. 4.

203. "A little Jung is a dangerous thing." *America*, 92 (12 March 1955), p. 612.

204. "Old wise man." *Time*, 65 (14 Feb. 1955), pp. 62-64.

1956

205. Abenheimer, Karl M. "Notes on the spirit as conceived by dynamic psychology." *JAP*, 1:2 (1956), pp. 113-31.

206. Adler, Gerhard. "The dynamics of the self." In *Dynamic aspects of the psyche; selections from past Springs*. New York: APCNY, 1956, pp. 3-20. (see 590 above for German and a complete list of other editions)

207. Allen, Clifford. "Of myths and men. Symbols of transformation." *Nature*, 179:4565 (1956), p. 837.

208. Allenby, Amy I. "The gas company." *Harv*, 3 (1956), pp. 72-76.

209. _____. *Jung's contribution to the religious problem of our time*. London: GofPP Lecture # 91, 1956.

210. Bannerju, Samiran. "Prof. Dr. C. G. Jung." *Psychotherapie* (Calcutta), 1 (1956), p. 14.

211. Benz, Ernst. "Creatur Spiritus. Die Geistlehre des Joachim von Fiore." *EJ*, 25 (1956), pp. 285-356.

212. Binswanger, Kurt. "Der Heilweg der analytischen Psychologie C. G. Jungs." In *Heilwege der Tiefenpsychologie*. L. Szondi, ed. Bern: Hans Huber, 1956, pp. 35-48.

213. Bleuel, Josef. "Der trinitarische Urglaube. Bemerkungen zu einer Veröffentlichung C. G. Jungs." *Natur und Kultur*, 48 (1956), pp. 37-42.

214. Castillejo, Irene C. de. *What do we mean by love?* London: Gof PP Lecture # 89, April 1956.

215. Chamberlin, J. Maxwell and Hiltner, Seward. "Jung and Christianity." *Pastoral Psychology*, 7 (1956), pp. 53-56.

216. Chang, Chung-Yuan. "Creativity as process in Taoism." *EJ*, 25 (1956), pp. 391-416.

217. Corbin, Henry. "Imagination créatrice et prière créatrice dans le soufism d'Ibn 'Arabî. *Ibid.*, pp. 121-241.

1218. Crowley, T. "Jung and religion." Irish Theological Q, 23 (1956), pp. 73-79.

1219. Danielli, Mary. "Geometric diagrams as observed in the villages of Imerina, Madagascar." Harv, 3 (1956), pp. 52-69.

1220. Davies, D. V. An investigation of the attitude of abnormal personalities towards the idea of God. (Doctoral dissertation). King's College, London, 1956.

1221. Eliade, Mircea. "La vertu créatrice du mythe." EJ, 25 (1956), pp. 59-86.

1222. Evans, Erastus. "The phases of psychic life." In Christian essays in psychiatry. Philip Mairet, ed. London: SCM Press, 1956, pp. 109-26. (see 1329 below)

1223. Fordham, Michael. "Active imagination and imaginative activity." JAP, 1:2 (1956), pp. 207-08.

1224. _____. "Symposium on Jung's contribution to analytical thought and practice. I. The evolution of Jung's researches." BJMP, 29 (1956), pp. 3-8.

*1225. Franz, Marie-Louise von. The psychological meaning of redemption. Zurich: Privately printed, 1956.

1226. Frei, Gebhard. "Zur Darstellung Wingenfelds über C. G. Jung." Arzt und Seelsorger, 7:3 (1956), pp. 5-7.

*1227. Fromm-Reichmann, Frieda, and Moreno, J. Progress in psychotherapy. New York: Grune & Stratton, 1956.

1228. Futrell, William. "Exploring the soul: the approach of Jung's analytical psychology to religion." Dialogue, 1:1 (1956), pp. 13-22.

1229. Gemelli, Agostino. "La psychologie analytique de C. G. Jung." C. Busnelli, trans. Supp de la Vie Spirituelle, 9:36 (1956), pp. 44-80.

1230. Haendler, Otto. "Tiefenpsychologie." In Religion in Geschichte und Gegenwart. VI. Tübingen: J. C. B. Mohr, 1956--. pp. 886-95.

1231. Hannah, Barbara. "All's well that ends well." Spring 1956, pp. 26-42. (see 1054 above)

*1232. Harding, M. Esther. Journey into self. New York: Longmans, 1956. (see *1352 below for German edition)
        Rev. Kenneth Lambert. JAP, 3:1 (1958), pp. 79-80.
             Robert C. Leslie. Pastoral Psychology, 7:70 (1957), pp. 83-84.
             Elizabeth Swayzee. Inward Light, (1958), pp. 45-47.

1233. Harding, M Esther. "The psyche and the symbols of religion."
In Werner Wolff, _Psychiatry_ _and_ _Religion_. New York: M.D.
Publications, 1956, pp. 3-7.

1234. _____. "The visions at the house of the interpreter." _Harv_,
3 (1956), pp. 14-30.

1235. Hayes, Dorsha. "Heart of darkness." _Spring_ 1956, pp. 43-57.

1236. Henderson, James. "The way of the teacher - the core of Jung's
contribution." _The_ _New_ _Era_, 37:1 (1956), np.

1237. Henderson, Joseph L. "Psychological commentary." In Margaret
Schevill, _Pollen_ _Path_. _A_ _collection_ _of_ _Navaho_ _myths_. Stanford:
Stanford University Press, 1956, pp. 125-40.

1238. _____. "Stages of psychological development exemplified in
the poetical works of T. S. Eliot." _JAP_, 1:2 (1956), pp. 133-
44.

1239. Hill, Denis. "Movement and people." _Harv_, 3 (1956), pp. 1-13.

1240. Hiltner, Seward. "Carl Gustav Jung. _Pastoral_ _Psychology_, 6:60
(Jan. 1956), pp. 78-81.

1241. _____. "Man of the Month: Carl Gustav Jung." _Ibid._, 7
(1956), pp. 1-3.

1242. _____., et al. "Jung and Symbols." _Ibid._, pp. 53-56.

1243. Hodin, J. P. "The future of surrealism." _J_ _of_ _Aesthetics_, 14
(1956), pp. 475-84.

1244. Howes, Elizabeth Boyden. _Analytical_ _psychology_ _and_ _the_ _synoptic_
gospels. London: GofPP Lecture # 88, March 1956.

1245. Hutin, Serge. "Note sur C. G. Jung et l'astrologie." _La_ _Tour_
_St._ _Jacques_, 4 (1956), pp. 124-25.

1246. Illing, Hans A. "Eighty years of Carl Jung." _Guide_ _to_ _Psychia-_
tric _Literature_, 2 (1956), pp. 6-8.

1247. Jacobi, Jolande. "Freud and Jung -- meeting and parting." _Swiss_
Rev _of_ _World_ _Affairs_, 6:5 (1956), pp. 18-23. (see below, 1248
for German, 1484 for Spanish, and 3410 for French editions)

1248. _____. "Freud und Jung. Begegnung und Trennung." _NZZ_, (6
May 1956), np. (see 1247 above for English and list of other
editions)

1249. _____. "La psychologie analytique de C. G. Jung." _Bull_ _Psy-_
chologique, 9:3 (1956), pp. 130-36.

1250. Kerényi, Carl. "Archetype and culture types in the religion of

Greece and Rome." Inward Light, 19:50 (1956), pp. 9-15.

*1251. _____. Der Göttliche Arzt; Studien über Asklepios und seine
Kultstätten, 2ns ed. Darmstadt: Hermann Gentner, 1956. (see
*495 above for list of other editions)

1252. Kotschnig, Elined. "C. G. Jung." Inward Light, 19:50 (1956),
pp. 1-3.

*1253. Kranefeldt, Wolfgang M. Therapeutische psychologie: Ihr Weg
durch die psychoanalyse. Berlin: de Gruyter, 1956. (see *63
above for list of other editions)

1254. Krauss, Rudolf. "Carl Gustav Jung und sein psychologisches
Werk." Westdeutsche Schulzeitung, 65 (1956), pp. 4-6.

1255. Lossen, H. "Freud, Adler, Jung." Psychologische Hefte, 6
(1956), pp. 129-34.

1256. Mace, C. A. "On the eightieth birthday of C. G. Jung." JAP,
1:2 (1956), pp. 189-92.

1257. Mairet, Philip. "Presuppositions of psychological analysis."
In his Christian essays in psychiatry. London: SCM Press,
1956, pp. 61-72.

*1258. Malinine, Michel; Puech, Henri-Charles, and Quispel, Gilles,
eds. Evangelium Veritas. St ad CGJIZ, VI. Zurich: Rascher,
1956.

1259. Marcus, Kate. "The stranger in women's dreams." Los Angeles:
APCLA, Paper # 7, 1956. (see 3002 below)

1260. Moody, Robert. "Symposium: II. On Jung's concept of the symbol." BJMP, 29 (1956), pp. 9-14.

*1261. Neumann, Erich. Amor and Psyche. London: Routledge and Kegan
Paul; New York: Pantheon (Bollingen Series LIV), 1956. (see
*790 above for German edition)
Rev. Frieda Fordham. JAP, 3:1 (1956), pp. 83-84.

1262. _____. "In honor of the centenary of Freud's birth." JAP,
1:2 (1956), pp. 195-202. (see 1393 below)

1263. _____. "The moon and matriarchal consciousness." In Dynamic
aspects of the psyche. (see 1206 above). (see 655 above for
German and complete list of other editions)

1264. _____. "The psyche and the transformation of the reality
planes." Spring 1956, pp. 81-111. (see 791 above for German
edition)

1265. _____. "Der Schöpferische Mensch und die 'Große Erfahrung'."
EJ, 25 (1956), pp. 11-58.

1266. Palter, R. "Operations and the occult." Philosophy of Science, 23:4 (1956), pp. 297-314.

1267. Paulsen, Lola. "Transference and projection." JAP, 1:2 (1956), pp. 203-06.

1268. Perry, John Weir. "A Jungian formulation of schizophrenia." Amer J of Psychotherapy, 10 (1956), pp. 54-65.

1269. Phelps, Edith. "Kristine Mann Library." Stechert-Hofner Book News, 11:3 (1956), pp. 25-26.

1270. Plaut, Albert B. J. "Symposium: III. The transference in analytical psychology." BJMP, 29 (1956), pp. 15-19.

1271. Pope, Saxton T. "Jungian mystery." Contemporary Psychology, 1:7 (1956), pp. 198-200.

1272. Portmann, Adolf. "Erleuchtung und Erscheinung im Lebendigen." EJ, 25 (1956), pp. 477-504.

1273. Post, Laurens van der. "The creative pattern in primitive Africa." Ibid., pp. 417-54.

*1274. Progoff, Ira. The death and rebirth of psychology. New York: Julian Press, 1956.
          Rev. Unsigned. Time, 68 (24 Dec. 1956), pp. 51-52.

*1275. Radin, Paul. The trickster: a study in American Indian mythology. New York and London: 1956.
          Rev. John Layard. JAP, 2:1 (1957), pp. 106-11.

1276. Read, Herbert. "Poetic consciousness and creative experience." EJ, 25 (1956), pp. 357-90.

1277. Reinhardt, Karl. "Prometheus." Ibid., pp. 241-84.

1278. Roth, G. "Die Lehre C. G. Jungs in der Kritik ihrer Hilfswissenschaften." Wissenschaft und Weltbild, 9:1 (1956), pp. 39-44.

1279. Saburovitsh, A. "The notion of religion according to the ideas of C. G. Jung." (in Hebrew) Iyyum (Israel), 7:2 (1956), pp. 86-95.

1280. Salfield, D. J. "Freud oder Jung?" SZP, 15 (1956), pp. 169-84.

1281. Sargent, James O'Connor. "Critique of Dr. Jung's new astrology." Astrology Guide (New York), (Sept.-Oct. 1956), pp. 10-11, 92-94; (Nov.-Dec. 1956), pp. 11-12, 91-92; (Jan.-Feb. 1957), pp. 12-13, 93-94; (Mar.-April 1957), pp. 22-23, 96.

*1282. Sborowitz, Arie. Beziehung und Bestimmung. Die Lehren von Martin Buber und C. G. Jung in ihrem Verhältnis zueinander. Darmstadt: Gentner, 1956.

1283. Schär, Hans. "C. G. Jung." Inward Light, 19:50 (1956), pp. 4-8.

1284. Scholem, Gershom G. "Shöpfung aus Nichts und Selbstverschränk-ung Gottes." EJ, 25 (1956), pp. 87-120.

1285. Scott, R. D. "Notes on the body image and schema." JAP, 1:2 (1956), pp. 145-60.

1286. Shentoub, S. A. "Le problème du transfert chez Jung." Rev Fran-cais Psychoanalytique, 20 (1956), pp. 549-52.

1287. _____. "Le problème du transfert chez Jung ou la 'Guérison psychologique'." Bull Assoc Psychoanalytique Belgique, 24 (1956), np.

1288. Storr, Anthony. "Projection and individual development." Harv, 3 (1956), pp. 34-49.

1289. Strunk, Orlo. "Psychology, religion and C. G. Jung: a review of periodical literature." J of Bible and Religion, 24 (1956), pp. 106-13.

1290. Tourney, Garfield. "Empedocles and Freud, Heraclitus and Jung." Bull of the History of Medicine, 30 (1956), pp. 109-23.

1291. Toynbee, Arnold. "The value of C. G. Jung's work for histori-ans." JAP, 1:2 (1956), pp. 193-94.

1291. Vasavada, Arvind U. Tripura-Rahasya, or a comparative study of the process of individuation. (Diploma-thesis). Carl Gustav Jung-Institute, Zurich, 1956.

1293. Victoria, Marcos. "La crisis contemporánea según Jung 'Imago Mundi'." Preface to Jung's Conflictos del alma infantil. Buenos Aires: Paidos, 1956.

1294. Weizsäcker, Victor von. "Reminiscences of Freud and Jung." Amer J of Psychoanalysis, 7 (1956), pp. 33-34.

1295. Welch, Paul and Illing, Hans. "Jung's empiricism reconsidered." Amer J of Psychiatry, 112 (1955-56), pp. 71-72.

1296. Werblowsky, R. J. Zwi. "Some psychological aspects of Kabbalah." Harv, 3 (1956), pp. 77-96.

1297. Wheelwright, Joseph. "Jung's psychological concepts." In Pro-gress in Psychotherapy (see *1227 above), pp. 126-35.

1298. Whitmont, Edward C. "The magic levels of the unconscious." Spring 1956, pp. 58-80.

1299. Wilhelm, Helmut. "Das schöpferische Prinzip im Buch der Wandlungen." <u>EJ</u>, 25 (1956), pp. 455-76.

1300.   Williams, Mary. "A study of hysteria in women." <u>JAP</u>, 1:2
        (1956), pp. 177-88.

1301.   Wingenfeld, Bernard. "Zur Psychologie C. G. Jungs." <u>Arzt und
        Seelsorger</u>, 7:3 (1956), pp. 3-4.

1302.   Wolff, Toni. "Structural Forms of the Feminine Psyche." P.
        Watzlewicz, trans. Zurich: Students' Assoc. of the CGJI,
        1956. (see 747 above and 1633 below for German editions)

1303.   Zaehner, Robert Charls. "The religious instinct." In <u>The new
        outline of modern knowledge</u>, Alan Pryce-Jones, ed. London:
        Victor Gollancz, 1956, pp. 64-85.

1304.   "Briefe für und gegen C. G. Jung." <u>Aufbau</u>, 22:17 (1956), pp.
        20-21.

1305.   "Portrait of C. G. Jung." <u>Time</u>, 67 (23 April 1956), p. 72.

                              1957

*1306. Adler, Gerhard. <u>Studies in analytical psychology</u>. New York:
        G. P. Putnam's Sons for the C. G. Jung Foundation, 1957. (see
        *475 above for English and *1307 below for French editions)

*1307. _____. <u>Etudes de psychologie jungienne</u>. L. Fearn and J. Le-
        clercq, trans. Geneva: Georg; Paris: Albin Michel, 1957.
        (see *475 and *1306 above for English editions)

*1308. Affemann, Rudolf. <u>Psychologie und Bibel: eine Auseinandersetz-
        ung mit C. G. Jung</u>. Stuttgart: Ernst Klett, 1957.

 1309. Barker, Culver M. "Some observations on the spirit of C. G.
        Jung." <u>Harv</u>, 4 (1957), pp. 66-78.

*1310. Baudouin, Charles. <u>Psychoanalyse du symbole religieux</u>. Paris:
        Fayard, 1957.

 1311. Bertine, Eleanor. "Analytic relationship." <u>Amer J of Psychoan-
        alysis</u>, 17:1 (1957), pp. 45-57.

*1312. _____. <u>Menschliche Beziehungen. Eine psychologische Studie</u>.
        I. Krämer, trans. Zurich: Rhein, 1957.

 1313. Beyme, F. "Analyse eines schizofrenen Schwangerschaftswahns im
        Lichte der Forschungen von Bachofen, C. G. Jung und E. Neumann."

Schweizer <u>ANP</u>, 80:1-2 (1957), pp. 38-99.

1314. Böhler, Eugen. "Ethik und Wirtschaft." <u>Industriel Organisation</u>, 4 (1957), pp. 1-12.

1315. _____. "Der Mensch in der modernen Wirtschaft." <u>Gewerblichen Rundschau</u>, (June-July 1957), pp. 52-65.

1316. _____. "Der Mensch und die Kollectiven Mächte." <u>Schweizer Monatshefte</u>, (Sept. 1957), pp. 425-37.

1317. _____. "Der Mensch zwischen Kollektivität und Individualität." <u>Industriel Organisation</u>, 7 (1957), pp. 1-8.

1318. Cahen, Roland. "Psychothérapie de C. G. Jung. Problèmes de psychanalyse." <u>Recherches et débats</u>, 21 (Nov. 1957), pp. 83-106.

*1319. Campbell, Joseph, ed. <u>Papers from the Eranos Yearbooks III. Man and Time</u>. Princeton, New Jersey: Princeton University Press (Bollingen Series XXX), 1957.
Rev. Kenneth Lambert. <u>JAP</u>, 4:1 (1959), pp. 85-86.

1320. _____. "The symbol without meaning." <u>EJ</u>, 26 (1957), pp. 415-76.

*1321. Caruso, Igor. <u>Bios, Psyche, Person</u>. Freiburg: Karl Alber, 1957.

1322. Corbin, Henry. "Cyclical time in Mazdaism and Ismailism." <u>PEY III</u> (see *1319 above), pp. 115-72. (see 699 above)

1323. _____. "L'intériorisation du sens en herméneutique soufi iranienne." <u>EJ</u>, 26 (1957), pp. 57-188.

1324. Corti, Walter Robert. "Die Platonische Akademie im Wandel der Geschichte und als Aufgabe unsere Zeit." <u>Ibid</u>., pp. 387-414.

1325. Dupront, A. "Introduction à l'étude d'une archétype." <u>La Table Ronde</u>, (Dec. 1957), pp. 120 ff.

1326. Edinger, Edward F. "Some aspects of the transference phenomenon." <u>Spring</u> 1957, pp. 32-44.

1327. Eliade, Mircea. "Significations de la 'lumiere intérieure'." <u>EJ</u>, 26 (1957), pp. 189-242.

1328. _____. "Time and eternity in Indian thought." <u>PEY III</u> (see *1319 above), pp. 173-200. (see 703 above for French edition)

1329. Evans, Erastus. "The phases of psychic life." <u>Pastoral Psychology</u>, 8 (1957), pp. 33-46. (see 1222 above)

1330. Fierz-David, Linda. "Psychological reflexions on the fresco
series of the villa of the mysteries in Pompeii. An essay."
G. Phelan, trans. Zurich: Psychologischer Club, Zürich, 1957.
(see 1456 below for German edition)

1331. Fordham, Michael. "Biological theory and the concept of the
archetype." New developments (see *1334 below), pp. 1-34.

1332. _____. "Child analysis." Ibid., pp. 155-80.

1333. _____. "A child guidance approach to marriage." Ibid., pp.
188-98. (see 828 above)

*1334. _____. New developments in analytical psychology. London:
Routledge and Kegan Paul, 1957.
        Rev. Bruno Klopfer. JAP, 3:2 (1958), pp. 167-71.

1335. _____. "Notes on a significance of archetypes for the transference in childhood." New developments (see *1334 above), pp.
181-87. (see 1037 above)

1336. _____. "Notes on the transference." Ibid., pp. 62-103.

1337. _____. "The origins of the ego in childhood." Ibid., pp.
104-30. (see 1038 above)

1338. _____. "Reflections on the archetypes and synchronicity."
Ibid., pp. 35-50. (see 1039 above)

1339. _____. "Reflections on image and symbol." Ibid., pp. 51-61.

1340. _____. "Reflections on image and symbol." JAP, 2:1 (1957),
pp. 85-92.

1341. _____. "Some observations on the self and the ego in childhood." New developments (see *1334 above), pp. 131-54. (see
706 above)

*1342. Franz, Marie-Louise von. The dreams and visions of St. Niklaus
von der Flüe. Zurich: Privately printed, 1957.

*1343. _____. Mysterium Coniunctionis Vol III. Zurich: Rascher,
1957.

*1344. _____. Problem of the shadow in fairy tales. Zurich: Pri-
vately printed, 1957.

*1345. Froböse-Thiele, Felicia. Träume: eine Quelle religiöser Er-
fahrung? Göttingen: Vandenhoeck und Ruprecht, 1957. (see
2561 below)

1346. Gerster, Georg. "C. G. Jung und der Weihnachtsbaum." Weltkultur, 25:1259 (1957), p. 7.

1347. Harding, M. Esther. "Afterthoughts on The Pilgrim." Spring 1957, pp. 10-31.

1348. _____. "Afterthoughts on The Pilgrim." Paps APCNY Vol 7. New York: APCNY, 1956-57.

1349. _____. "Bunyan's pilgrimage in modern terms." Pastoral Psychology, 7:70 (Jan. 1957), pp. 67-82.

1350. _____. "Dr. Jung's contribution to the search for mental health." Paps APCNY Vol 7. New York: APCNY, 1956-57.

1351. _____. "Dynamic approach to psychotherapy." J of the South Carolina Medical Assoc, 53:10 (1957), pp. 387-88.

*1352. _____. Selbsterfahrung. Eine psychologische Deutung von Bunyans Pilgerreise. Zurich: Rhein, 1957. (see *1232 above for English edition)

1353. _____. "Why a psychological understanding of Bunyan's 'Pilgrims Progress' is essential for the American minister." Pastoral Psychology, 7:70 (Jan 1957), pp. 74-75.

1354. Havemann, E. "Where does psychology go from here.?" Life, 42 (4 Feb. 1957), pp. 68-70.

1355. Henderson, Joseph L. "Stages of psychological development exemplified in the poetical works of T. S. Eliot (continued)." JAP, 2:1 (1957), pp. 33-50.

1356. Hentschel, __. "Die Jungsche Typologie als Arbeitshypothese in der Motivationsdiagnostik." FORFA--Briefe, 6 (1957), pp. 74-76.

1357. Hepburn, Ronald W. "Poetry and religious belief." In Hepburn et al., Metaphysical beliefs. London: SCM Press, 1957, pp. 85-166.

1358. Heydt, Vera von der. On the parent archetype. London: GofPP Lecture # 92, Jan. 1957.

1359. Hobson, Robert F. "Prayer and the integration of the personality." Harv, 4 (1957), pp. 44-64.

1360. Hostie, Raymond. "Een antwoord aan Job?" Kath cult Tijdsch, 6: 10 (1957), pp. 302-12.

*1361. _____. C. G. Jung und die Religion. J. Tenzler, trans. Freiburg and Munich: Alber, 1957. (see *1069 above for French and list of other editions)
        Rev. Albert Jung. Anima, 4 (1957), pp. 374-75.

*1362. _____. Religion and the Psychology of Jung. G. R. Lamb, trans. London and New York: Sheed and Ward, 1957. (see *1069 above for French and list of other editions)

Rev. Wm. C. Bier. Pastoral Psychology, (Feb. 1959), pp. 52-54.
Robert F. Hobson. JAP, 3:1 (1958), pp. 64-69.
Alfred Torrie. Ibid., pp. 69-71.
Victor White. Ibid., pp. 59-64.

1363. Illing, Hans A. "C. G. Jung on the present trends in group therapy." Human Relations (London), 10:1 (1957), pp. 77-83. (see
1071 above for German edition)

1364. _____. "Jung and the Jews." Chicago Jewish Forum, 14 (1957),
pp. 200- 02.

1365. _____. "Jung's theory of the group as a tool in therapy."
Inter J of Group Psychotherapy, 7 (1957), pp. 392-97.

1366. Jacobi, Jolande. Komplex/Archetypus/Symbol in der Psychologie
C. G. Jungs. Zurich and Stuttgart: Rascher, 1957. (see *1584
below for English edition)
Rev. R. Battegay. Schweizer ANP, 81:1-2 (1957), p. 383.
Bernard Wingenfeld. Theologie und Glaube, 49
(1957), p. 49.

1367. Jung, Emma. "The anima as an elemental being." In Animus and
anima (see *1368 below), pp. 45-87. (see 1088 above for German
and list of other editions)

1368. _____. Animus and anima. C. F. Baynes and H. Nagel, trans.
New York: APCNY, 1957. (see *2717 below)

1369. _____. "On the nature of the animus." In Animus and anima
(see *1368 above), pp. 1-44. (see 119 above for German and
list of other editions)

1370. Kalff, Dora M. "The significance of the hare in 'Reynard the
Fox'." JAP, 2:2 (1957), pp. 183-94.

1371. Kerényi, Carl. La religion antique; ses lignes fondamentales.
Y. Le Lay, trans. Geneva: Georg, 1957.

1372. Kirsch, James. "The role of the analyst in Jung's psychotherapy." Conference on Psychoanalysis and Zen, Cuernavaca, Mex.,
1957.

1373. Klopfer, Bruno, et al. Developments in the Rorschach technique.
London: George G. Harrop, 1957.
Rev. F. H. Strauss. JAP, 3:1 (1958), pp. 81-82.

1374. _____. "Jungian modification of Freudian ego psychology."
In Developments (see *1373 above), pp. 565-75.

1375. Kluger, H. Yechezkel. "Ruth: a contribution to the development
of the feminine principle in the Old Testament." Spring 1957,
pp. 52-86.

1376. Knoll, Max. "Transformations of science in our age." PEY III (see *1319 above), pp. 263-307. (see 719 above for German edition)

1377. Köberle, Adolph. "Problem of Guilt." Pastoral Psychology, 70 (1957), np.

1378. Kraemer, William. "Success and failure in analysis." Harv, 4 (1957), pp. 30-42.

1379. Lachot, W. "La pensée du psychologue Erich Neumann de Tel-Aviv. A la recherche du centre mystérieux de l'homme." Rev de Théologie et Philosophie Suisse, 6:2 (1957), pp. 111-26.

1380. Leeuw, Gerardus van der. "Primordial time and final time." PEY III (see *1319 above), pp. 324-52. (see 567 above for German edition)

1381. Léonard, A. "Bulletin de psychologie de la religion." Vie Spirituelle, 41 (1957), pp. 240-64.

1382. Lewis, Aubrey. "Jung's early work." JAP, 2:2 (1957), pp. 119-36.

1383. Macavoy, Joseph. "Direction spirituelle et psychologie." In Dictionnaire de Spiritualité. 3. Charles Baumgartner et al. eds. Paris: Beauchesne, 1957, pp. 1143-73.

*1384. Maeder, Alphonse. Der Psychotherapist als Partner. Zurich and Stuttgart, Rascher, 1957.

1385. Marcus, Kate. "On initial dreams." Inward Light, 21:53 (1957), pp. 5-21.

1386. Massignon, Louis. "Time in Islamic thought." PEY III (see *1319 above), pp. 108-14. (see 724 above for French edition)

1387. Meier, Carl Alfred. "C. G. Jung's contributions to theory and therapy of schizophrenia." Congress report of the 2nd Inter Congress for Psychiatry, Zurich, 10 (1957), pp. 16-21.

1388. Metman, Philip. "The ego in schizophrenia (Part I)." JAP, 1:2 (1957), pp. 161-76.

1389. _____. "The ego in schizophrenia (Part II)." Ibid., 2:1 (1957), pp. 51-72.

1390. _____. "Religion and the psychology of the unconscious." Harv, 4 (1957), pp. 1-12.

*1391. Munroe, Ruth Leonard. Schools of psychoanalytic thought. New York: Dryden Press, 1955.
    Rev. Murray Jackson. JAP, 3:2 (1958), pp. 178-79.

1392. Neumann, Erich. "Art and time." PEY III (see *1319 above), pp. 3-37. (see above, 728 for German and 1134 for French editions)

1393. _____. "In honor of the centenary of Freud's birth." Spring 1957, pp. 45-51. (see 1262 above)

1394. _____. "Die Sinnfrage und das Individuum." EJ, 26 (1957), pp. 11-56.

1395. Perry, John Weir. "Acute catatonic schizophrenia." JAP, 2:2 (1957), pp. 137-52.

1396. Plessner, Helmuth. "On the relation of time to death." PEY III (see *1319 above), pp. 233-63. (see 730 above for German edition)

1397. Portmann, Adolf. "Sinndeutung als biologisches Problem." EJ, 26 (1957), pp. 477-510.

1398. _____. "Time in the life of the organism." PEY III (see *1319 above), pp. 308-24. (see 732 above for German edition)

1399. Progoff, Ira. "An evolutionary psychology of wholeness." Main Currents in Modern Thought, 15:2 (1957), pp. 27-31.

1400. Puech, Henri-Charles. "Gnosis and time." PEY III (see *1319 above), pp. 38-84. (see 733 above for French edition)

1401. Pye, Faye. "Some analytical problems encountered in South Afirca." JAP, 2:2 (1957), pp. 167-82.

1402. Quispel, Gilles. "Time and history in Patristic Christianity." PEY III (see *1319 above), pp. 85-107. (see 734 above for French edition)

1403. Ramakrishna Rao, K. "A note on Jung's conception of the psyche." Philosophical Q, 29 (1956-57), pp. 259-63.

1404. Read, Herbert. "The creative nature of humanism." EJ, 26 (1957), pp. 315-50.

1405. Reinhardt, Karl. "Die Sinneskrise bei Euripides." Ibid., pp. 279-314.

1406. Rychner, Max. "C. G. Jung zu seinem 80. Geburtstag." In Arachne: Aufsätze zur Literatur. Zurich: Manesse, 1957, pp. 206-17.

1407. Scholem, Gershom G. "Religiöse Autorität und Mystik." EJ, 26 (1957), pp. 243-78.

1408. Scoti, Michael. "Carl Gustav Jung." The Mirror, 3:4 (1957), pp. 6-8.

*1409. Scott-Maxwell, Florida. Women and sometimes men. London: Rout-
ledge and Kegan Paul, 1957
    Rev. Amy I. Allenby. JAP, 3:1 (1958), pp. 85-86.

1410. Servadio, Emilio. "Jung, Carl Gustav." In Dizionario biografi-
co degli autori. II. Bompiani, 1957, pp. 353-54.

1411. Soares Leites, Octavio. "O principio de sincronicidade acausal
de C. G. Jung." Bol Inst Psicol, 7:9-10 (1957), pp. 1-13.

1412. Stein, Leopold. "What is a symbol supposed to be?" JAP, 2:1
(1957), pp. 73-84. (see 3309 below)

1413. Stein, William Bysshe. "Melville's poetry: its symbols of individuation." Literature and Psychology, 7:2 (1957), pp. 21-
26.

1414. Storr, Anthony. "The psychopathology of fetishism and transves-
tism." JAP, 2:2 (1957), pp. 153-66.

1415. Thiry, A. "Jung et la religion." Nouvelle Rev Théologique, 79
(1957), pp. 248-76.

*1416. Vogel, Gustav. Tiefenpsychologie und Nächstenliebe. Mainz:
Matthias Grünewald, 1957.

*1417. Walker, Nigel. A short history of psychotherapy. London: Rout-
ledge and Kegan Paul, 1957.
    Rev. Murray Jackson. JAP, 3:2 (1958), p. 177.

1418. White, Victor. "Dogma and mental health." In Conducta religiosa y salud mental: VII congrese católico internacional de
psicotherapia y psicología clínica. Madrid, 1957, pp. 97-101.

*1419. _____. Gott und das Unbewußte. W. Schiesser, trans. Zur-
ich and Stuttgart: Rascher, 1957. (see *873 above)

1420. _____. "Two theologians on Jung's psychology. Cross Currents, 7 (1957), pp. 283-87.

1421. Whitmont, Edward. "Magic and the psychology of compulsive states."
JAP, 2:1 (1957), pp. 3-32.

1422. Wilhelm, Helmut. "The concept of time in the Book of Changes."
PEY III (see *1319 above), pp. 221-32. (see 746 above for German edition)

1423. _____. "The sacrifice, idea and attitude." Harv, 4 (1957),
pp. 14-28.

1424. _____. "Der Sinn des Geschens nach dem Buch der Wandlungen."
EJ, 26 (1957), pp. 351-86.

1425. Williams, Mary. "An example of synchronicity." JAP, 2:1 (1957),

pp. 93-96.

1426. Wyrsch, J. "Von Freud zu Jung." <u>Schweizer Rundschau</u>, 57:1 (1957), pp. 23-27.

*1427. Zaehner, Robert Charles. <u>Mysticism: sacred and profane. An inquiry into some varieties of preternatural experience</u>. Oxford: Clarendon, 1957.

1428. Zilboorg, G. "The abuse of the psychological in present-day clinical psychology." <u>Bull New York Academy of Medicine</u>, 33:2 (1957), pp. 89-97.

1429. "God, the devil, and the human soul." <u>Atlantic</u>, 200 (1957), pp. 57-63.

1430. "Jung and God." <u>Humanist World Digest</u>, 29 (1957), p. 21.

1431. "Meeting on the mind." <u>Time</u>, 70 (16 Sept. 1957), pp. 55-56.

1432. "Portrait of Jung." <u>Sat Rev Lit</u>, 40 (9 Feb. 1957), p. 19.

1433. "The self." <u>Cross Currents</u>, 7 (Sum. 1957), pp. 263-71.

1434. "Theology and Jung." <u>Religion Digest</u>, 5 (1957), pp. 34-35.

1958

1435. Allen, Clifford. "Advances in Jungian psychology." <u>Nature</u>, 181:4605 (1957), p. 298.

1436. Aylward, James C. <u>Lourdes and its mystery</u>. (Diploma thesis). C. G. Jung-Institute, Zurich, 1958.

1437. Benz, Ernst. "Der Friedensgedanke in der gegenwärtigen Auseinandersetzung zwischen Buddhismus und Christentum." <u>EJ</u>, 27 (1958), pp. 359-404.

1438. _____. "Über die Schwierigkeit des Verstehens fremder Religionen. Erfahrungen und Betrachtungen." <u>Geist und Werk</u> (see *1512 below), pp. 245-66.

*1439. Bertine, Eleanor. <u>Human relationships; in the family, in friendship, in love</u>. Forw. C. G. Jung. New York: Longmans, Green and Co., 1958. (see 1312 above for German edition)
        Rev. Michael Fordham. <u>JAP</u>, 4:2 (1959), p. 183.
             Elined Kotschnig. <u>Inward Light</u>, 22:56 (1958), pp. 41-44.

1440. _____. "The Jungian approach to religion: an introductory paper." Spring 1958, pp. 33-48. (see 1544 below)

1441. Blum, Ernst. "Freud und das Gewissen." Gewissen (see *1446 below), pp. 167-84. (see 2768 below for English edition)

1442. Böhler, Eugen. "Das Gewissen im Wirtschaftsleben." Ibid., pp. 53-88. (see 2769 below for English edition)

1443. _____. "Ideologie und Ideal." Industriel Organisation, 10 (1958), pp. 1-8. (see 1646 below for English edition)

1444. _____. "Ist die techniche Entwicklung zwangsläfig?" Ibid., 10:3 (1958), pp. 1-8.

1445. Brantmay, H. "Regards sur la psychologie abyssale dissidente." Praxis, 47 (1958), pp. 170-71.

*1446. C. G. Jung-Institute, Zürich, eds. Das Gewissen. Zurich and Stuttgart: Rascher, 1958. (see *2772 below)

1447. Campbell, Paul. Depth psychology and marriage. London: GofPP Lecture # 100, Dec. 1958.

1448. Castillejo, Irene C. de. Levels of responsibility. London: G ofPP Lecture # 99, Sept. 1958.

1449. Chang, Chung-Yuan. "Self-realization and the inner process of peace." EJ, 27 (1958), pp. 405-24.

1450. Corbin, Henry. "Eranos-Zeit." Geist und Werk (see *1512 below), pp. 197-208.

1451. _____. Quiétude et inquiétude de l'âme dans le soufisme de Rûzbehân Baglî de Shîrâz." EJ, 27 (1958), pp. 51-194.

1452. Corti, Walter Robert. "Der Mensch in der Sinnunruhe; 'cor nostrum inquietam'." Geist und Werk (see *1512 below), pp. 281-302.

1453. Dreifuss, Gustav. Die Opferung Isaaks in der judischen Legende; Versuch einer psychologischen Deutung. (Diploma thesis). C. C. Jung-Institute, Zürich, 1958.

1454. Eliade, Mircea. "La coincidentia oppositorum et le mystère de la totalité." EJ, 27 (1958), pp. 195-236.

1455. Ferand, Ernst. "Begegnung mit Béla Bartók." Geist und Werk (see *1512 below), pp. 87-124.

1456. Fierz-David, Linda. "Psychologische Betrachtungen zu der Freskenfolge der Villa dei Misteri. Zurich: Psych Club Zür, 1958.

1457. Fordham, Michael. "Analytical psychology and psychotherapy."

Objective Psyche (see *1465 below). pp. 168-79. (see 534 above)

1458. _____. "Analytical psychology and religious experience." Ibid., pp. 113-29. (see 440 above)

1459. _____. "The concept of the objective psyche." Ibid., pp. 32-48. (see 705 above)

1460. _____. "The dark night of the soul." Ibid., pp. 130-48. (see 355 above)

1461. _____. "The development and status of Jung's researches." Ibid., pp. 4-31.

1462. _____. "Individuation and ego development." JAP, 3:2 (1958), pp. 115-30.

1463. _____. "Individuation and ego development." Objective Psyche (see *1465 below), pp. 49-66.

1464. _____. "Jung's contribution to social psychiatry." Ibid., pp. 81-90. (see 1036 above)

*1465. _____. The objective psyche. London: Routledge and Kegan Paul, 1958.
Rev. John Layard. JAP, 5:1 (1960), pp. 65-72.

1466. _____. "Problems of active imagination." Objective Psyche (see *1465 above), pp. 67-80.

1467. _____. "Reflections on individual and collective psychology." Ibid., pp. 91-112. (see 483 above)

1468. _____. "Repression in Christian practices." Ibid., pp. 149-67. (see 484 above)

1469. _____. "A suggested centre for analytical psychology." Ibid., pp. 180-96.

1470. Franz, Marie-Louise von. "Die aktive Imagination in der Psychologie C. G. Jungs." In Meditation in Religion und Psychotherapie. Wilhelm Bitter, ed. Stuttgart: Ernst Klett, 1958.

*1471. _____. Problems of feminine psychology in fairy tales. Zurich: Privately printed, 1958-59. (see *3097 below)

*1472. _____. A psychological interpretation of the Golden Ass of Apuleius. Zurich: Privately printed, 1958. (see *2793 below)

1473. Galdston, Iago. "Job, Jung and Freud: an essay on the meaning of life." Bull New York Academy of Medicine, 34:12 (1958), pp. 769-84.

1474. Gerster, Georg. "C. G. Jung deutet die Fliegenden Teller." Weltwoche, 26:1269 (1958), p. 7.

1475. Grapp, Fritz. "Pädagogische Reflexionen über Carl Gustav Jungs Typenlehre." Praxis der Kinderpsychologie und Kinderpsychiatrie. 7:7 (1958), pp. 177-80.

1476. Harding, M. Esther. "Das Problem der Anima in Bunyans 'Pilgerfahrt.' Ein Nachtrag zu 'Selbsterfahrung'." Geist und Werk (see *1512 above), pp. 35-64.

1477. _____. "What makes the symbol effective?" Inter Record of Medicine, 172:12 (1958), pp. 732-36. (see 1792 below)

1478. Hauser, E. O. "He probes the human soul." Sat Evening Post, 230 (24 May 1958), pp. 30 ff.

1479. Henderson, James L. "Jung and the living past." Brit J of Educational Studies, 6:2 (1958), pp. 128-39.

1480. Hildebrand, H. P. "A factorial study of introversion-extraversion." Brit J of Psychology, 49:1 (1958), pp. 1-11.

1481. Hochheimer, Wolfgang. "Die Psychotherapie Carl Gustav Jung." Psyche, 11:10 (1957-58), pp. 561-639.

*1482. Hurwitz, Siegmund. Die Gestalt des sterbenden Messias. St ad C GJIZ VIII. Zurich: Rascher, 1958.

1483. Illing, Hans A. "A theory of the group according to C. G. Jung." Acta Psychotherapeutica, 6:2 (1958), pp. 137-44.

1484. Jacobi, Jolande. "Freud y Jung: Encuentro y separación." Rev Psicologia general aplicada, 13 (1958), pp. 723-38. (see 1247 above for English and complete list of other editions)

1485. _____. "On the frontiers of religion and psychology." Times (London), (23 May 1958), np.

1486. _____. "The process of individuation." JAP, 3:2 (1958), pp. 95-114.

*1487. _____. Two essays on Freud and Jung. Zurich: Students' Assoc, CGJ-I, Zür, 1958.

1488. Jaffé, Aniela. "Flying saucers, a modern myth, according to C. G. Jung." Swiss Rev of World Affairs, 8:2 (1958), pp. 17-19.

*1489. _____. Geistererscheinungen und Vorsichen. Eine psychologische Deutung. Zurich and Stuttgart: Rascher, 1958. (see *20-36 below for English edition)

1490. _____. "Hermann Broch: The death of Virgil." Spring 1958, pp. 65-120.

1491. Kayser, Hans. "Die Harmonie der Welt." EJ, 27 (1958), pp. 425-52.

1492. Kerényi, Carl. "Das ℗ von Samothrake." Geist und Werk (see *1512 below), pp. 125-38.

1493. Kiesow, Ernst-Rüdiger. "Der Protestantismus in der Sicht C. G. Jungs. Monatsschrift für Pastoraltheologie, 47 (1958), pp. 445-50.

1494. Kirsch, James. "The enigma of Moby Dick." JAP, 3:2 (1958), pp. 131-48.

1495. Kraemer, William P. "The dangers of unrecognized counter-transference." Ibid., 3:1 (1958), pp. 29-42.

1496. _____. Neurotic Alternative. London: GofPP Lecture # 98, May 1958.

1497. Layard, John. "The four-hundred-year-old kinship dream of a Pacific Islander." Geist und Werk (see *1512 below), pp. 65-86.

1498. _____. "Notes on the autonomous psyche and the ambivalence of the trickster concept." JAP, 3:1 (1958), pp. 21-28.

1499. Martin, Berhard. "Fliegende Untertassen und so weiten. Carl Gustav Jung: Ein Moderner Mythus." Die Neue Schau (Kassel), 19 (1958), pp. 192-93.

1500. Metman, Philip. "The trickster figure in schizophrenia." JAP, 3:1 (1958), pp. 5-20.

*1501. Morawitz-Cadio, Alice von. Spirituelle Psychologie. Zur Psychologie Jungs als Notwendigkeit der Gegenwart. Vienna: Amandus, 1958.

1502. Neumann, Erich. "Aus dem ersten Teil des Kafka-Kommentars: 'Das Gericht'." Geist und Werk (see *1512 below), pp. 175-97.

1503. _____. "Creative man and transformation." R. Manheim, trans. Spring 1958, pp. 1-32.

1504. _____. "Frieden als Symbol des Lebens." EJ, 27 (1958), pp. 7-50.

1505. Perrot, C. "L'épreuve d'association de Jung dans l'examen psychiatrique." These Fac Médicin et Pharmacie de Lyon, 176 (1958), np.

1506. Portmann, Adolf. "Kampf und Frieden als biologisches Problem." EJ, 27 (1958), pp. 453-84.

1507. _____. "Selbstdarstellung als Motiv der lebendigen." Geist und Werk (see *1512 below), pp. 139-74.

*1508. Progoff, Ira. <u>Depth psychology and modern man</u>. New York:
        Julian Press, 1958.

1509.   Read, Herbert. "C. G. Jung." In <u>The Tenth Muse</u>. New York:
        Grove Press, 1958, pp. 197 ff.

1510.   _____. "The flower of peach." <u>EJ</u>, 27 (1958), pp. 299-332.

1511.   _____. "The prehistoric artist." <u>Geist und Werk</u> (see *1512
        below), pp. 225-44.

*1512. Rhein Verlag, ed. <u>Geist und Werk</u>. Zurich: Rhein, 1958.

1513.   Rudin, Josef. "Das Gewissen in katholischer Sicht." <u>Gewissen</u>
        (see *1446 above), pp. 139-66. (see 2869 below for English edi-
        tion)

1514.   _____. "Das kranke Gottesbild." <u>Orientierung</u>, 22 (1958),
        pp. 155-72 (?).

1515.   Schär, Hans. "Das Gewissen in protestantischer Sicht." <u>Gewis-
        sen</u> (see *1446 above), pp. 119-38. (see 2871 below for English
        edition)

1516.   Schneider, Herbert W. "Peace as a scientific problem and as
        personal experience." <u>EJ</u>, 27 (1958), pp. 333-58.

1517.   Scholem, Gershom G. "Die Lehre von 'Gerechten' in der jüdischen
        Mystik." <u>Ibid</u>., pp. 237-98.

1518.   _____. "Zehn unhistorische Sätze über Kabbala." <u>Geist und
        Werk</u> (see *1512 above), pp. 209-16.

1519.   Schulz, Günther. "Die Gnosis im Urteil von Martin Buber, C. G.
        Jung, und Rudolf Pannwitz." In <u>Der Festgabe für Georg Poensgen</u>.
        Marianne Weber-Kreis, ed. Heidelberg: 1958, pp. 37-39.

1520.   Spiegelman, J. Marvin. <u>An essay on Utopia</u>. (Diploma thesis).
        C. G. Jung-Institute, Zurich, 1958.

1521.   Stein, Leopold. "Analytical psychology: a 'modern' science."
        <u>JAP</u>, 3:1 (1958), pp. 43-50. (see 3308 below)

1522.   Strauss, F. H. "A Jungian approach to the interpretation of
        thematic test material." <u>Acta Psychotherapeutica</u>, 6:4 (1958),
        pp. 336-47.

1523.   Sykes, G. "Dialogue of Freud and Jung." <u>Harpers</u>, 216 (Mar.
        1958), pp. 66-71. Discussion, <u>Ibid</u>., (May 1958), p. 4.

1524.   Tate, Dorothy. "On ego development." <u>JAP</u>, 3:2 (1958), pp. 149-
        56.

1525.   Tatlow, __. "Research into personality: the horns of a dilemma."

JAP, 3:1 (1958), pp. 51-58.

1526. Werblowsky. R. I. Zwi. "Das Gewissen in jüdischer Sicht." Gewissen (see *1446 above), pp. 89-119. (see 2887 below for English edition)

1527. Whitmont, Edward C. "Religious aspects of life problems in analysis." Spring 1958, pp. 49-64.

1528. Wilhelm, Helmut. "The stockades of the soul. Some Chinese post-Classical songs." Geist und werk (see *1512 above), pp. 217-24.

1529. Williams, Mary. "The fear of death." JAP, 3:2 (1958), pp. 157-66.

1530. Zbinder, Hans. "Das Gewissen in unserer Zeit." Gewissen (see *1446 above), pp. 9-52. (see 2893 below for English edition)

1531. "Doctor Jung and the Saucers." Time, 72 (11 Aug 1958), p. 38.

1532. "Dr. Jung." New Magazine, 1:3 (1958), pp. 33-38.

1533. "Jungian togetherness." Time, 72 (16 Sept. 1958), pp. 55-56.

1534. "Portrait of Jung." Cosmopolitan, 145 (Dec. 1958), pp. 145 ff.

1959

1535. Adler, Gerhard. "Ego integration and patterns of coniunctio." JAP, 4:2 (1959), pp. 153-59. (see 1749 below)

1536. Aldridge, M. "The birth of the black and white twins." Ibid., 4:1 (1959), pp. 55-62.

1537. Altizer, Thomas J. J. "Science and Gnosis in Jung's psychology." The Centennial Rev, 3 (1959), pp. 304-20.

1538. Backhaus, Wilhelm. "Das Unbewußte in der Politik. Ein Gespräch mit Prof. C. G. Jung." Die Kultur, 7:123 (1958-59), p. 3.

1539. Bash, Karl W. "The mental health problems of ageing and the aged." Bull of the W. H. O. # 21 (1959), pp. 563 ff.

1540. Bender, Hans. "Zur Psychologie der Ufo-Phänomene." Zeit für Parapsychologie und Grenzgebiete der Psychologie, 3 (1959), pp. 32-58.

*1541. Benedetti, Gaetano. "Die Angst in psychiatrischer Sicht."
Angst (see *1547 below), pp. 147-74.

1542. Benz, Ernst. "Die Angst in der Religion." Ibid., pp. 189-221.

1543. _____. "Der dreifache Aspekt der Übermenschen." EJ, 28
(1959), pp. 109-92.

1544. Bertine, Eleanor. "Jung's approach to religion. An introductory paper." Paps APCNY Vol 8. New York: APCNY, 1959.

1545. _____. "Jung's psychology and religion." Religion in Life,
28 (1959), pp. 365-75.

*1546. Bitter, Wilhelm, ed. Magie und Wunder in der Heilkunde: Ein
Tagungsbericht. Stuttgart: Ernst Klett, 1959.

*1547. CGJIZ, ed. Die Angst. St ad CGJIZ X. Zurich: Rascher, 1959.

1548. Campbell, Joseph. "Renewal myths and rites of the primitive
hunters and planters." EJ, 28 (1959), pp. 407-58.

1549. Castillejo, Irene C. de. Dilemma of levels. London: GofPP
Lecture # 101, May 1959.

1550. Champernowne, H. Irene. "Woman and the community." Harv, 5
(1959), pp. 50-70.

1551. Clark, James M. "C. G. Jung and Meister Eckhart." Modern Language Rev, 54 (1959), pp. 239-44.

*1552. Cope, Gilbert F. Symbolism in the Bible and the Church. London:
SCM Press, 1959.

1553. Corbin, Henry. "L'Imân chaché et la rénovation de l'homme en
théologie Shî 'ite." EJ, 28 (1959), pp. 47-108.

1554. Corti, Walter Robert. "Der Mensch als Organ Gottes." Ibid.,
pp. 377-406.

*1555. Cossa, P. Approches pathogéniques des troubles mentaux. Paris:
Masson et Cie., 1959.

*1556. Cox, David. Jung and St. Paul: the doctrine of justification by
faith and its relation to individuation. New York: 1959.
                Rev. N. K. Burger. NY Times Book Rev, (20 Sept. 1959),
                        p. 40.
                        Michael Fordham. JAP, 5:2 (1960), pp. 166-69.
                        George S. Gun. Scottish J of Theology, 13 (1960),
                        pp. 192-94
                        Harold Lancour. Library J, 84 (15 Oct. 1959), p.
                        3138.
                        Alasdair MacIntyre. Guardian, 6 (1959), p. 7.
                        G. S. Spinks. Hibbert J, 57 (1959), p. 414.

D. A. Walker. Christian Century, 76 (14 Oct. 1959), p. 1184.
Unsigned. Kirkus, 27 (1 May 1959), p. 348.
Unsigned. TLS, (15 April 1960), p. xvi.

1557. _____. "Jung and St. Paul." Pastoral Psychology, (April 1959), pp. 35-42.

1558. Dale-Green, Patricia. "Apis Mellifica." Harv, 5 (1959), pp. 30-48.

1559. Dawson, Eugene, E. The religious implications of Jung's psychology. (Doctoral dissertation). University of Wisconsin, 1959. (see 532 above)

1560. Dillistone, F. W. "The Christian doctrine of man and modern psychological theories." Hibbert J, 54 (1959), pp. 154-60.

1561. Eliade, Mircea. "Dimensions religieuses de renouvellement cosmique." EJ, 28 (1959), pp. 241-76.

*1562. _____. Naissance mystiques: essai sur quelques types d'initiation. Paris: Librairie Gallimard, 1959.

1563. Elkin, Henry. "On the origin of the self." Psychoanalysis and the Psychoanalytic Rev, 45:4 (1958-59), pp. 57-76.

1564. Fierz, Heinrich Karl. "Die klinische Bedeutung von Extraversion und Introversion." Acta Psychotherapeutica, 7:4 (1959), pp. 247-57. (see 1780 below for English and German editions)

1565. Fordham, Frieda. "Dr. Jung on life and death." The Listener, 62:1596 (29 Oct. 1959), pp. 722-25.

*1566. _____. Eine Einführung in die Psychologie C. G. Jungs. T. Meier-Fritsche, trans. Zurich and Stuttgart, 1959. (see *827 above for English and complete list of other editions)

1567. Fraenkel, E. "Contribution à l'étude de l'analité. Remarques relative à la nature du problème en général." Psyché, 19:1 (1959), pp. 1-47.

*1568. Franz, Marie-Louise von. Introduction to the symbolism of alchemy. Zurich: Privately printed, 1959.

*1569. _____. The problem of the puer aeternus. Zurich: Privately printed, 1959. (see *2792 below)

*1570. _____. Die Visionen des Niklaus von Flüe. St ad CGJIZ IX. Zurich: Rascher, 1959.

1571. Frey, Liliane. "The beginning of depth psychology from Mesmer to Freud." P. Watzlewicz, trans. Zurich: CGJIZ, 1959.

1572. Grütter, Emil. 'Psychoanalytische Bemerkungen zur Jungschen Heilsmethode." Psyche, 13 (1959). pp. 536-53.

1573. Haendler, Otto. "C. G. Jung." Theologische Literaturzeitung, 84 (1959), pp. 561-88.

1574. Hagger, James. "Dr. Jung." Psychology, 3:4 (1959), pp. 54-61.

1575. Harding, M. Esther. "Jung's contribution to religious symbolism." Spring 1959, pp. 1-16.

1576. _____. "Jung's influence on contemporary thought." Paps APCNY Vol 8. New York: APCNY, 1958-59. (see 1900 below)

1577. Harner, Gloria. "Jung and analytical psychology." Psychology, 3:4 (1959), pp. 62-70.

1578. Hartman, John Francis. "Carl G. Jung's point of view as a guide to counseling." (Doctoral dissertation). University of Wisconsin, 1959.

1579. Hayes, Dorsha. "Consideration of the dance from a Jungian viewpoint. JAP, 4:2 (1959), pp. 169-81.

1580. Hediger, H. "Die Angst des Tieres." Angst (see *1547 above), pp. 7-34.

1581. Heyer, Gustav Richard. "Garl Gustav Jung." In K. Kalle, Große Nervenärzte. Stuttgart: Thieme, 1959, pp. 153-74.

1582. _____. "Komplexe psychologie (C. G. Jung)." In Handbuch der Neurosenlehre und Psychotherapie. V. E. Frankl et al., eds. Munich and Berlin: Urban and Schwarzenberg, 1957-59.

1583. Hobson, Robert F. "An approach to group analysis." JAP, 4:2 (1959), pp. 139-52. (see 1796 below)

*1584. Jacobi, Jolande. Complex/Archetype/Symbol in the psychology of C. G. Jung. R. Manheim, trans. London: Routledge and Kegan Paul; New York: Pantheon (Bollingen Series LVII), 1959. (see *1366 above for German and complete list of other editions)
        Rev. Michael Fordham. JAP, 5:1 (1960), pp. 73-74.
        J. N. Hartt. Yale Rev, n.s. 49 (March 1960), p. 436.
        Unsigned. TLS, (30 Dec. 1960), p. 850.

*1585. _____. Die Psychologie von C. G. Jung; eine Einführung. 4th rev. ed. Zurich: Rascher, 1959. (see *255 above for German and complete list of other editions)

1586. Jacobson, Rebecca. "Some aspects of the mother-in-law relationship as an instrument of transformation." Spring 1959, pp. 47-62.

*1587. Johnson, Paul E. Psychology of Religion. New York: Abingdon,

1959.

*1588. Kerényi, Carl. Asklepios: archetypal image of the physician's existence. R. Manheim, trans. New York: Pantheon (Bollingen Series LXV), 1959. (see *495 above for German and list of other editions)

*1589. _____. Prometheus; die menschliche Existenz in griechischer Deutung. Hamburg: Rowohlt, 1959. (see *2039 above for English edition)

1590. Layard, John. "Homo-eroticism in primitive society as a function of the Self." JAP, 4:2 (1959), pp. 101-116. (see 1817 below)

1591. _____. "On psychic consciousness." EJ, 28 (1959), pp. 277-344.

1592. Londero, Carissimo. Il simbolismo religioso nel pensiero de C. G. Jung. (Doctoral dissertation). Pontificio Ateneo Antoniano, Rome, 1959.

1593. Mackworth, Joan. Some reflections on the self and God in sickness and in maturity. London: GofPP Lecture # 102, June 1959.

1594. Meier, Carl Alfred. "Einige Konsequenzen der Neueren Psychologie." Studia Philosophica, 19 (1959), pp. 157-72.

*1595. _____. Jung and analytical psychology. Newton Center, (Mass): Andover Newton Theological School, 1959.

1596. _____. "Projection, transference, and the subject-object relation." JAP, 4:1 (1959), pp. 21-34. (see 934 above for German edition)

1597. Munroe, Ruth Leonard. "Other psychoanalytic approaches (Adler, Jung, Rank)." In The Amer Handbook of Psychiatry. New York: Basic Books, 1959, pp. 1453-65.

1598. Neumann, Erich. "Die Angst vor dem Weiblichen." Angst (see *1547 above), pp. 67-112.

*1599. _____. The archetypal world of Henry Moore. R. F. C. Hull, trans. London: Routledge and Kegan Paul; New York: Pantheon (Bollingen Series LXVIII), 1959.

*1600. _____. Art and the creative unconscious. R. Manheim, trans. New York: Pantheon (Bollingen Series LXI), 1959. (see 941 above for German edition)
Rev. N. Meyer. JAP, 5:2 (1960), pp. 177-78.

1601. _____. "Das Bild des Menschen in Krise und Erneuerung." EJ, 28 (1959), pp. 7-46.

1602. _____. "Leonardo da Vinci and the mother archetype." In Creative Unconscious (see *1600 above), pp. 3-80.

1603. _____. "The psychological stages of feminine development."
R. Jacobson, trans. Spring 1959, pp. 63-97. (see 851 above
for German edition)

1604. _____. "The significance of the genetic aspect for analytical psychology." JAP, 4:2 (1959), pp. 125-38. (see 1827 below for English and German editions)

1605. Paulsen, Lola. "The shadow: this thing of darkness I acknowledge mine." Harv, 5 (1959), pp. 3-16.

1606. Philipson, Morris H. C. G. Jung's theory of symbolism as a contribution to aesthetics. (Doctoral dissertation). Columbia U-
niversity, 1959.

*1607. Philp, Howard L. Jung and the problem of evil. London: Rock-
cliff; New York: R. M. McBride Co. 1959.
     Rev. Kenneth Lambert. JAP, 5:2 (1960), pp. 170-76.

1608. Plaut, Albert B. J. "A case of tricksterism illustrating ego
defences." JAP, 4:1 (1959), pp. 35-54.

1609. _____. "Hungry patients: reflections on ego structure."
Ibid., 4:2 (1959), pp. 161-68. (see 1835 below)

1610. Portmann, Adolf. "Der biologische Beitrag zu einem neuen Bild
des Menschen." EJ, 28 (1959), pp. 459-92.

1611. Prelle, R. de. "Regard sur le monde de C. G. Jung." Synthèses,
14:157 (1959), pp. 226-37.

1612. Prince, G. Stewart. "The therapeutic function of the homosexual
transference." JAP, 4:2 (1959), pp. 117-24. (see 1838 below)

1613. Read, Herbert. "Nihilism and renewal in the art of our time."
EJ, 28 (1959), pp. 345-76.

*1614. Schmid, Karl. Hochmut und Angst. Zurich and Stuttgart: Rascher,
1959.

1615. Scholem, Gershom G. "Zum Verständnis der messianischen Idee im
Judentum." EJ, 28 (1959), pp. 193-240.

1616. Schwarz, Urs. "Die Angst in der Politik." Angst (see *1547 a-
bove), pp. 113-46.

1617. Schwermer, Josef. "Religiöse Termini bei C. G. Jung." Theologie
und Glaube, 49 (1959), pp. 386-74.

*1618. Seidmann, Peter. Der Weg der Tiefenpsychologie in geistesge-
schtlicher Perspective. Zurich and Stuttgart: Rascher, 1959.

1619. Seifert, Friedrich. "Psychologische Aspekte des Problems von Gut und Böse." In Gut und Böse in der Psychotherapie. Wilhelm Bitter, ed. Stuttgart: Ernst Klett, 1959, pp. 7-28.

*1620. Stein, Robert M. Analytical psychology and healing; a short study of some problems of modern psychotherapy. Zurich: CGJIZ, 1959.

*1621. Streatfield, D. A study of two worlds: Persephone. London: Routledge and Kegan Paul, 1959.

1622. Thorburn, John M. "Do the gods exist?" Harv, 5 (1959), pp. 72-87.

1623. Überwasser, Walter. "Die Angst in den Malerei des Abendlandes." Angst (see *1547 above), pp. 223-52.

1624. Westman, H. "What is Psychotherapy: a Jungian view?" Annals of Psychotherapy, 1 (1959), pp. 23-30.

1625. Whitmont, Edward C. "Religious aspects of life problems in analysis." Paps APCNY Vol 8. New York: APCNY, 1958-59.

*1626. Wienckel, Erna van de. De l'inconscient à Dieu. Ascèse chrétienne et psychologie de C. G. Jung. Paris: Montaignes, 1959.

1627. Wolff, Toni. "Christentum nach innen." Studien (see *1634 below), pp. 319-32. (see 429 above for English edition)

1628. _____. "Einege Prinzipien der Trauminterpretation." Ibid., pp. 231-56.

1629. _____. "Einfuhrung in die Grundlagen der Komplexen Psychologie." Ibid., pp. 15-230. (see 170 above)

1630. _____. "Gedanken zum Individuationsprozeß der Frau." Ibid., pp. 257-68. (see 285 above for English edition)

1631. _____. "Die Kulturelle Bedeutung der komplexen Psychologie." Ibid., pp. 214-31.

1632. _____. "Der psychologische Energiebegriff." Ibid., pp. 172-213.

1633. _____. "Strukturformen der weiblichen Psyche." Ibid., pp. 269-84. (see above, 747 for German and 1302 for English editions.)

*1634. _____. Studien zu C. G. Jungs Psychologie. Zurich: Rhein, 1959.

1635. _____. "Tantrische Symbolik bei Goethe." Studien (see *1634 above), pp. 285-318.

105

1636. Zaehner, Robert Charles. "A new Buddha and a new Tao." In Concise encyclopaedia of living faiths. London: Hutchinson, 1959.

1637. Zulliger, Hans. "Die Angst des Kindes." Angst (see *1547 above), pp. 35-66.

1960

1638. Angers, William P. "Jung's approach to religion." Downside Rev, 78 (1959-60), pp. 36-51.

1639. Arluck, Edward W. "Training facilities of the C. G. Jung-Institute, Zurich." Amer Psychologist, 15 (1960), pp. 626-29.

*1640. Baird, James. Ishmael; a study of the symbolic mode in primitivism. New York: Harper Bros (Harper Torchbooks), 1960.

1641. Baudouin, Charles. "The process of individuation in Blaise Pascal." JAP, 5:2 (1960), pp. 101-12.

1642. Beirnaert, Louis. Contribution to "Débat sur psychologie et religion." In L'armee et la nation. No. 30, Recherches et Débats. Paris: Fayard, 1960, pp. 200-06.

1643. Bernouli, Rudolf. "Spiritual development as reflected in alchemy and related disciplines." PEY IV (see *1650 below), pp. 305-40. (see 136 above for German edition)

1644. Bertine, Eleanor. "The perennial problem of good and evil." Spring 1960, pp. 21-33.

1645. Böhler, Eugen. "Die Grundgedanken der Psychologie von C. G. Jung." Industriel Organisation, 4 (1960), pp. 1-11.

1646. _____. "Ideologies and ideals." Spring 1960, pp. 87-105.

1647. Boss, Medard. "Le problème du moi dans la motivation." Evolution Psychiatrique, 25 (1960), pp. 481-89.

1648. Buber, Martin. "Symbolic and sacramental existence in Judaism." PEY IV (see *1653 below), pp. 168-85. (see 109 above for German edition)

1649. Byles, Marie B. "Vipassana meditation and psychologist Jung." Maha-Bodi, 68 (1960), pp. 362-66.

1650. C. G. Jung-Institute, Zurich. "A report on the first twelve years." Zurich: 1960.

1651. Cahen, Roland. Contribution to "Débat sur psychologie et religion." (see 1642 above), pp. 149-88.

1652. Cammerloher, M. C. "The position of art in the psychology of our time." PEY IV (see *1653 below), pp. 424-50. (see 111 above for German edition)

*1653. Campbell, Joseph, ed. Papers from the Eranos Yearbooks IV. Spiritual disciplines. Princeton, New Jersey: Princeton University Press (Bollingen Series XXX), 1960.

1654. Castillejo, Irene C. de. Rainmaker ideal. London: GofPP Lecture # 107, Feb. 1960.

1655. Corbin, Henry. "Pour une morphologie de la spiritualité Shí 'ite." EJ, 29 (1960). pp. 57-108.

1656. Cowles, Ben Thomson. The ethical implications of a Christian estimate of man, with special reference to the anthropologies of Carl Jung and Paul Tillich. (Doctoral dissertation). University of Southern California, 1960.

1657. Cox, David. God and the self. London: GofPP Lecture # 112, July 1960.

1658. Dale-Green, Patricia. Symbolism of the toad. London: GofPP Lecture # 110, March 1960.

1659. Danzel, Theodor-Wilhelm. "The psychology of ancient Mexican symbolism." PEY IV (see *1653 above), pp. 102-14. (see 189 above for German edition)

1660. De La Croix, Michele-Marie. Contribution to "Débat sur psychologie et religion." (see 1642 above), pp. 206-14.

1661. Diekmann, Hans. "Die Differenz zwischen dem anschaulichen und abstrahierenden Denken in den Psychologien von C. G. Jung und Freud." Zeit Psychosomatische Medizin, 6:4 (1960), pp. 287-92; 7:1 (1960), pp. 58-65.

1662. Duplain, Georges. "An interview with C. G. Jung." Spring 1960, pp. 6-20.

1663. Edinger, Edward F. "The ego-self paradox." JAP, 5:1 (1960), pp. 3-18.

*1664. Eliade, Mircea. Myths, dreams and mysteries. The encounter between contemporary faiths and archaic realities. P. Mairet, trans. London: Harvill Press, 1960.

1665. _____. "Mythes et symboles de la courde." EJ, 29 (1960), pp. 109-38.

*1666. Farau, Alfred and Schaffer, H. La psychologie de profondeurs

107

des origines à nos jours. Paris: Payot, 1960.

1667. Fordham, Michael. "The development of analytical psychology in Great Britain." Harv, 6 (1960), pp. 1-17.

1668. _____. "Ego, self and mental health." BJMP, 33:4 (1960), pp. 249-53.

1669. _____. "The emergence of a symbol in a five-year-old child." JAP, 5:1 (1960), pp. 33-40. (see 1783 below)

1670. _____. "The relevance of analytical theory to alchemy, mysticism and theology." JAP, 5:2 (1960), pp. 113-28.

1671. Franz, Marie-Louise von. "Die alchemistische Nakrokosmos-Mikrokosmos-Idee im Lichte der Jungschen Psychologie." Symbolon, 1960, pp. 27-38.

1672. _____. "The problem of evil in fairy tales." Harv, 6 (1960), pp. 20-52.

1673. Freeman, J. "Interview with C. G. Jung." Bull APCNY, 22:5 (May 1960), pp. 1-17.

1674. Galdston, Iago. "Psychoanalysis 1959." Bull New York Academy of Medicine, 36:10 (1960), pp. 702-13.

1675. Gerster, Georg. "Zum 85. Geburtstag von Carl Gustav Jung." Sontagsblatt, 31 (1960), p. 7.

*1676. Gottschalk, Herbert. C. G. Jung. Berlin: Colloquium, 1960.

1677. Harms, Ernst. "How to understand Jung." Contemporary Psychology, (Feb. 1960), p. 61.

1678. Heiler, Friedrich. "Contemplation in Christian mysticism." PEY IV (see *1653 above), pp. 186-238.

1679. Heninger, S. K. "A Jungian reading of Kubla Khan." J of Aesthetics and Art Criticism, 18 (1960), pp. 358-67.

*1680. Herzog, Edgar. Psyche und Tod: Wandlungen des Todesbildes in Mythos und in den Träumen heutiger Menschen. St ad CGJIZ XI. Zurich and Stuttgart: Rascher, 1960. (see *2457 below for English edition)

*1681. Herzog-Dürch, J. Menschsein als Wagnis und Heilung im Sinne einer personalen Psychotherapie. Stuttgart: Ernst Klett, 1960.

1682. Heumann, Mathilde. Archetypische Träume eines jungen Manschen. (Diploma thesis). C. G. Jung-Institute, Zürich, 1960.

*1683. Hillman, James. Emotion: a comprehensive phenomenology of

theories <u>and their meaning for</u> therapy. London: Routledge
and Kegan Paul, 1960.
     Rev. Kenneth Lambert. <u>JAP</u>, 7:2 (1962), p. 168.

1684. Hiltner, Seward. "Archetypes and elections." <u>Pastoral Psycho-
logy</u>, (June 1960), pp. 7-9.

1685. Hostie, Raymond. "Carl Gustav Jung." <u>Lexikon für Theologie
und Kirche</u>. 5. J. Höfer & K. Rahner, eds. Freiburg: Herder, 1960, p. 1207.

1686. Howes, Elizabeth Boyden. <u>Son of Man -- Image of the self</u>. London: GofPP Lecture # 109, 1960.

1687. Jackson, Murray. "Jung's 'archetype': clarity or confusion?"
<u>BJMP</u>, 33 (1960), pp. 83-94.

1688. _____. "Jung's 'archetypes' and psychiatry." <u>J of Mental
Science</u>, 106:445 (1960). pp. 1518-26.

1689. Jacobi, Jolande. "Archétype et symbole dans la psychologie de
Jung." In <u>Polarité du symbole</u>. Bruges: Desclée de Brouwer,
1960.

1690. _____. "Dream books." <u>Spring</u> 1960, pp. 34-52. (see 367 a-
bove for German edition)

1691. Jaffé, Aniela. "C. G. Jung und die Parapsychologie." <u>ZPGP</u>, 4
(1960), pp. 8-23.

1692. Jones, W. M. "Eudora Welty's use of myth in 'Death of a travel-
ing Salesman.'" <u>Amer J of Folklore</u>, 73:287 (1960), pp. 18-23.

*1693. Jung, Emma and Franz, Marie-Louise von. <u>Graalslegende in psy-
chologischer Sicht</u>. St ad CGJIZ XII. Zurich and Stuttgart:
Rascher, 1960. (see *2827 below for English edition)

1694. Kerényi, Carl. "Man and Mask." <u>PEY IV</u> (see *1653 above), pp.
151-67. (see 497 above for German edition)

1695. Kirsch, James. "Affinities between Zen and analytical psychology." <u>Psychologia</u> (Kyoto), 3:2 (1960), pp. 85-91.

1696. Kluger, Harold Yechezkel. "Dreams and other manifestations of
the unconscious." Los Angeles: APCLA, 1960.

1697. Krauss, Rudolf. "Carl Gustav Jung und sein psychologisches
Werk." <u>Wegweiser</u> (Troisdorf), 11 (1960), pp. 323-27.

1698. Lambert, Kenneth. "Can theologians and analytical psychologists collaborate?" <u>JAP</u>, 5:2 (1960), pp. 129-46.

1699. Larson, C. A. "Science milestone." <u>Science Digest</u>, 48 (Nov.
1960), pp. 82-88.

*1700. Lauer, Hans Erhard. Die Rätsel der Seele. Tiefenpsychologie und Anthroposophie. Freiburg: die Kommended, 1960/1964.

1701. Layard, John. "The heroic encounter by Dorothy Norman, an annotation." JAP, 5:2 (1960), pp. 155-58.

1702. _____. "The Malekulan journey of the dead." PEY IV (see *1653 above), pp. 115-50. (see 192 above for German edition)

1703. Liran, Bernhard. Contribution to "Débat sur psychologie et religion." (see 1642 above), pp. 187-97.

1704. Marcus, Kate. "Separation dreams." Los Angeles: APCLA, 1960. (see 3001 below)

1705. Meier, Fritz. "The spiritual man in the Persian poet 'Attār." PEY IV (see *1653 above), pp. 267-304. (see 374 above for German edition)

1706. Metman, Eva. "Reflections on Samuel Beckett's plays." JAP, 5: 1 (1960), pp. 41-64.

1707. Neumann, Erich. "Die Psyche als Ort der Gestaltung." EJ, 29 (1960), pp. 13-56.

1708. Plaut, Albert B. J. "A concept of mental health." BJMP, 30:4 (1960), pp. 275-78.

1709. Pohier, J. M. "Psychologie et religion de Carl G. Jung." Rev des sciences philosophiques et théologiques, 44 (1960), pp. 639-45.

1710. Pope, A. R. The eros aspect of the eye; the left eye. (Diploma thesis). G. G. Jung-Institute, Zurich, 1960.

1711. Portmann, Adolf. "Gestaltung als Lebensvorgang." EJ, 29 (1960), pp. 327-69.

1712. Pruyser, Paul W. "Some trends in psychology of religion." J of Religion, 40 (1960), pp. 113-29.

1713. Pulver, Max. "The experience of light in the Gospel of St. John, in the 'Corpus hermeticum,' in Gnosticism, and in the Eastern Church." PEY IV (see *1653 above), pp. 239-66. (see 310 above for German edition)

1714. Pye, Faye. "Stages in the integration of the shadow." Harv, 6 (1960), pp. 54-71.

1715. Read, Herbert. "C. G. Jung und die Psychologie des 20. Jahrhunderts." Universitas, 15 (1960), pp. 1043-57.

*1716. _____. The forms of things unknown. New York: Horizon Press, 1960.

110

1717. _____. "The origins of form in art." _EJ_, 19 (1960), pp. 183-206.

1718. _____. "Zum 85. Geburtstag von Prof. Dr. Carl Gustav Jung 26. Juli 1960." Zurich: Rascher, 1960.

*1719. Reich, Heinrich. _Seelenbilder_. Rascher: Stuttgart, 1960.

1720. Rosenthall, Michael. "Jesus-in-reverse: some notes on the case of a compulsive Jew." _JAP_, 5:1 (1960), pp. 19-32.

1721. Rouselle, Erwin. "Spiritual guidance in contemporary Taoism." _PEY_ _IV_ (see *1653 above), pp. 59-101. (see 98 above for German edition)

1722. Rudin, Josef. "Das kranke Gottesbild." In _Psychotherapie_ und _Religion_. Olten: Walter, 1960/1964. (see 1514 above for German edition)

*1723. _____. _Psychotherapie_ und _Religion_: _Seele_, _Person_, _Gott_. Olten: Walter, 1960/1964. (see *2637 below for English edition)

1724. Salfield, D. J. "Considerations concerning the origin and phenomena of anxiety in children, its psychiatric diagnosis, differential diagnosis and treatment." _Acta paedopsychiatrie_, 26:1 (1960), pp. 10-17.

1725. Schärf-Kluger, Rivkah. "Psychology and religion." Los Angeles: APCLA, 1960.

1726. Schneider, Herbert W. "Historical construction and reconstruction." _EJ_, 29 (1960), pp. 243-64.

1727. Scholem, Gershom G. "Die mystische Gestalt der Gottheit in der Kabbala." _Ibid_., pp. 139-82.

*1728. _____. _Zur_ _Kabbala_ und _ihrer_ _Symbolik_. Zurich: Rhein, 1960. (see *2319 below for English edition)

*1729. Sierksma, Fokke. _The_ _gods_ _as_ _we_ _shape_ _them_. London: Routledge and Kegan Paul, 1960.

1730. Souza Monteiro, José Alfredo Pimenta de. "A psicología analitica de Jung." _Rev_ _Portug_ _Filos_, 16 (1960), pp. 48-72.

1731. Stansfield, James. _Art_ _and_ _the_ _integration_ _of_ _personality_: _a_ _philosophy_ _of_ _art_ _education_ _based_ _on_ _the_ _psychology_ _of_ _Carl_ _Gustav_ _Jung_. (Doctoral dissertation). Columbia University, 1960.

1732. Tillich, Paul. "The impact of psychotherapy on theological thought." New York: Academy of Religion and Mental Health, 1960.

1733. Uslar, D. von. "Begegnung des Unbewußten. Probleme der Para-psychologie." Merkur, 14:144 (1960), pp. 126-36.

1734. Végh, Sandor. "Musik als Erlebnis." EJ, 29 (1960), pp. 309-26.

1735. White, Victor. "Desafíos a la religión. La teología y S. Freud, Jung y la sobrenatural." Criterio (Buenos Aires), 32 (1960), pp. 131-33.

*1736. _____. Soul and Psyche. An enquiry into the relationship of psychotherapy and religion. London: Collins and Harvill, 1960.
             Rev. Kenneth Lambert. JAP, 6:2 (1961), p. 171.
             Doris Layard. Harv, 6 (1960), 76-77.

1737. _____. "Theological reflections." JAP, 5:1 (1960), pp. 147-54.

*1738. Wilhelm, Helmut. Change: eight lectures on the I Ching. C. F. Baynes, trans. New York: Pantheon (Bollingen Series LXII), 1960.
             Rev. Philip Metman. JAP, 6:2 (1961), pp. 177-78.

1739. _____. "Die 'Eigene Stadt' als Schauplatz der Gestaltung." EJ, 29 (1960), pp. 207-42.

1740. Winkler, Klaus. Dogmatische Aussagen in der neueren Theologie im Verhaltnis zu den Grundbegriffen der Komplexen Psychologie C. G. Jungs. (Doctoral dissertation). Berlin, 1960.

1741. Zeller, Max. "Some aspects of the individuation process." Los Angeles: APCLA, 1960.

1742. Zimmer, Heinrich. "The Indian world mother." Spring 1960, pp. 53-86.

1743. _____. "On the significance of the Indian Tantric Yoga." PEY IV (see *1653 above), pp. 3-58.

1744. Zuckerkandl, Victor. "Die Tongestalt." EJ, 29 (1960), pp. 265-308.

1745. "C. G. Jung zum 85. Geburtstag." ZPGP, 4 (1960), pp. 1-8.

1746. "Case for the razor?" TLS, 3022 (29 Jan. 1960), pp. 57-58.

1747. "How we add up." Newsweek, 56 (1 Aug. 1960), p. 79.

*1748. Adler, Gerhard, ed. Current trends in analytical psychology. Proceedings of the first international congress for analytical psychology. London: Tavistock, 1961.
      Rev. Ruth Strauss. JAP, 8:2 (1963), pp. 181-85.

1749. _____. "Ego integration and patterns of conjunctio." Ibid., pp. 160-68. (see 1535 above)

*1750. _____. The living symbol; a case study in the process of individuation. New York: Pantheon (Bollingen Series LXIII), 1961. (see *2764 below for German edition)
      Rev. M. Esther Harding. JAP, 7:2 (1962), pp. 162-65.
      Gwen Mountford. Harv, 8 (1962), pp. 99-100
      Albert B. J. Plaut. JAP, 7:2 (1962), pp. 165-67.

1751. Agoston, Tibor. "Theory and method of analytical psychology." Dept. of Mental Hygiene of Ohio, Monograph, 1961.

1752. Allenby, Amy I. "The church and the analyst." JAP, 6:2 (1961), pp. 137-55.

*1753. Assagioli, Roberto. Self-realization and psychological disturbances. Greenville, Del.: Psychosynthesis, 1961.

1754. Barker, Culver M. "Healing in depth: the conception and its application." Current trends (see *1748 above), pp. 138-49.

*1755. Bash, Karl W. Introduction to general clinical psychopathology. Zurich: OGJIZ, 1961.

1756. Baudouin, Charles. "D'un climat d'esprit ou se forma C. G. Jung." Action et Pensée, 4 (Dec. 1961), pp. 123-24.

1757. _____. "Dernieres vision de C. G. Jung." Ibid., 3 (Nov. 1961), pp. 65-66.

1758. _____. "De quelques couples d'opposes ou d'une philosophie implicite." Current trends (see *1748 above), pp. 54-66. "Some pairs of opposites: or reflections on an implicit philosophy." C. Rowland, trans. Ibid., pp. 67-79.

1759. Becka, R. "Jung, St. Thomas and the concrete conditions of human knowing." Amer Catholic Philosophical Assoc Proc, 35 (1961), pp. 141-50.

1760. Bennett, A. A. G. "The work of Jung." Maha Bodhi (Calcutta), 69:9 (1961), pp. 264-73.

*1761. Bennet, Edward Armstrong. C. G. Jung. London: Barrie and
        Rockliff, 1961. (see below, *1971 for German and 1878 for I-
        talian editions)
                Rev. G. Stewart Prince. JAP, 7:2 (1962), pp. 155-56.

 1762. Brand, Renée. "The resistance to Christian symbolism in the
        process of psychological development." Current trends (see
        *1748 above), pp. 198-213.

 1763. Brown, Brock. "Who's in among the analysts; from Freud forward;
        the search for truth." Esquire, 56:1 (July 1961), pp. 78-83.

 1764. Burchard, Edward M. L. "Mystical and scientific aspects of the
        psychoanalytic theories of Freud, Adler and Jung." Amer J of
        Psychotherapy, 14 (1961), pp. 289-307.

*1765. C. G. Jung-Institute, Zürich. Das Böse. St ad CGJIZ XIII.
        Zurich and Stuttgart: Rascher, 1961.

 1766. Castillejo, Irene C. de. The older woman. London: GofPP Lec-
        ture # 115, June 1961.

 1767. Clark, Robert Alfred. "Analytic psychology today." Amer J of
        Psychotherapy, 15 (1961), pp. 193-204.

 1768. _____. "Jungian and Freudian approaches to dreams." Ibid.,
        pp. 89-100.

 1769. Corbin, Henry. "Le combat spirituel du Shî 'isme." EJ, 30
        (1961), pp. 69-126.

*1770. Cox, David. History and Myth. London: Darton, Longman and
        Todd, 1961.

 1771. _____. "The self and God." Harv, 7 (1961), pp. 3-13.

 1772. Deich, Friedrich. "Abschied von C. G. Jung." Universitas, 16
        (1961), pp. 895-97.

*1773. Dry, Avis Mary. The psychology of Jung: a critical interpre-
        tation. London: Meuthen, 1961; New York: John Wiley and
        Sons, 1962.
                Rev. F. Plaut. JAP, 9:1 (1964), pp. 96-97.

 1774. Dunn, I. Jay. "Analysis of patients who meet the problems of
        the first half of life in the second." JAP, 6:1 (1961), pp.
        55-68.

 1775. Du Preez, Jan Petrus van Albertus. Opvoeding en die ombewuste-
        'n bydrae van die analitiese sielkundeskool von C. G. Jung tot
        opvoedkunde. (M. Ed. dissertation). University of South Afri-
        ca, Pretoria, 1961.

 1776. Eliade, Mircea. "Le créateur et son 'ombre'." EJ, 30 (1961),

pp. 211-40.

1777.   Eschenbach, Helmut. "Analytische Psychologie in ihrer Bedeutung
        für den Einzelnen und die Gemeinschaft." In Zur Rettung des
        Menschlichen in unserer Zeit. Wilhelm Bitter, ed. Stuttgart:
        Ernst Klett, 1961, pp. 116-34.

1778.   Falck, Colin. "Active imagination." Time and Tide, 42:48
        (1961), p. 2028.

1779.   Farau, A. "C. G. Jung: an Adlerian appreciation." J Individual
        Psychology, 17:2 (1961), pp. 135-41.

1780.   Fierz, Heinrich Karl. "Die klinische Bedeutung von Extraver-
        sion und Introversion." Current trends (see *1784 above), pp.
        80-88. "The clinical significance of extraversion and intro-
        version." C. Rowland, trans. Ibid., pp. 89-97. (see 1564 a-
        bove for German edition)

1781.   Fordham, Frieda. "Carl Gustav Jung." The Listener, 65:1681
        (15 June 1961), p. 1043.

1782.   Fordham, Michael. "Comment on the theory of the original self."
        JAP, 6:1 (1961), pp. 78-80.

1783.   _____. "The emergence of a symbol in a five-year-old child."
        Current trends (see *1748 above), pp. 98-107. (see 1669 above)

1784.   _____. "Suggestions toward a theory of supervision." With
        a comment by E. F. Edinger and a reply by the author. JAP, 6:
        2 (1961), pp. 107-17.

1785.   Franz, Marie-Louise von. "Das Problem des Bösen im Märchen."
        Das Böse (see *1765 above), pp. 91-129. (see 1672 above and
        2449 below for English editions)

1786.   Frey-Rohn, Liliane. "Das Böse in psychologischer Sicht." Ibid.,
        pp. 161-210. (see 2264 and 2450 below for English editions)

*1787. Goldbrunner, Josef. Individuação. A psicologia de profundidade
        de Carlos Gustavo Jung. São Paulo: Edit Herder, 1961. (see
        *542 above for German and complete list of other editions)

1788.   _____. "The structure of the psyche and the personalist view
        of man: a critical study of the depth-psychology of C. G.
        Jung." J of Psychological Researches, 5 (1961), pp. 97-102.

1789.   Gordon, Rosemary. "The death instinct and its relation to the
        self." JAP, 6:2 (1961), pp. 119-36.

1790.   Hannah, Barbara. The religious function of the animus in the
        book of Tobit. London: GofPP Lecture # 114, March 1961.

1791.   Harding, M. Esther. "The spiritual problem of woman." In Three

115

papers. Montreal: YWCA, 1961.

1792. _____. "What makes the symbol effective as a healing agent?"
Current trends (see *1748 above), pp. 1-18. (see 1477 above)

1793. Haynes, R. "Carl Gustav Jung: exploring uncharted territory."
Tablet, 215 (17 June 1961), pp. 577-78.

1794. Helbig, Gerhard. "Psychologie." Der Jungbuchhandel, 15:8
(1961), pp. 478-83.

1795. Hess, Gertrude. "Die analytische Psychologie von C. G. Jung."
Der Buchhändler, 42 (1961), pp. 143-49.

1796. Hobson, Robert F. "An approach to group analysis." Current
trends (see *1748 above), pp. 275-91. (see 1583 above)

1797. _____. "Psychological aspects of circumcision." JAP, 6:1
(1961), pp. 5-34.

1798. Hostie, Raymond. "Dromen van C. G. Jung." Streven, 14 (1960-
61), pp. 1048-55.

*1799. _____. El mito y la religión. La psicología analítica de
C. G. Jung y la religión. A. de Linera, trans. Madrid: Razón y Fe, 1961. (see 1069 above for German and list of other
editions)

1800. Jackson, Murray. "Chair, couch, and counter-transference."
JAP, 6:1 (1961), pp. 35-44.

*1801. Jacobs, Hans. Western psychotherapy and Hindu Sâdhanâ. A con-
tribution to comparative studies in psychology and metaphysics.
London: Allen and Unwin, 1961.

1802. Jacoby, Marianne and Edinger, Edward F. "The ego-self paradox."
JAP, 6:1 (1961), pp. 69-77.

1803. Jäger, Otto. "Ein Gespräch über C. G. Jung." Deutsches Pfarrer-
blatt, 61 (1961), pp. 83-85.

1804. Jorés, A. "Anxieties about life and death." Spring 1961, pp.
80-90.

1805. Jung, Albert. "Selbstverwirklichung." Current trends (see
*1748 above), pp. 292-303. "Self-realization." C. Rowland,
trans. Ibid., pp. 304-14.

1806. Kerényi, Carl. "Das Problem des Bösen in der Mythologie." Das
Böse (see *1765 above), pp. 9-24.

1807. Kettle, Martin. "C. G. Jung and religion." J of Religion, 14:3
(1961), pp. 154-63.

116

1808. Kirsch, Hilde. "An analyst's dilemma." Current trends (see *1748 above), pp. 169-75.

1809. Kirsch, James. "Active imagination as a method in the process of individuation." Fresno, Calif.: 1961.

1819. _____. "King Lear as a play of redemption." Harv, 7 (1961), pp. 25-45.

1811. _____. "The problem of dictatorship as represented in Moby Dick." Current trends (see *1748 above), pp. 261-74. (see 2041 below)

1812. Klopfer, Bruno. "Suicide: the Jungian point of view." In The cry for help. N. L. Faberlow and E. S. Schneiderman, eds. New York: McGraw Hill, 1961, pp. 193-203.

1813. Koch, M. "Über den Aufforderungscharakter optischer Schablonen." Zeit Psychotherapie und medizinische Psychologie, 11:4 (1961), pp. 142-52.

1814. Kouretas, Demetrios. "The scientific value of Carl Jung's work: a critique from a psychoanalytic angle." (in Greek) Nea Estia, (1961), pp. 816-902.

1815. Kunz, H. "Die eine Welt und die Weisen des in-der-Welt-Seins. Bemerkungen zu den Voraussetzungen der Daseinsanalytisch-anthropologischen Interpretationen psychopathologischer Phänomene." Psyche, 16:2 (1961), pp. 142-59.

1816. Lagravinese, N. "The collective unconscious disappeared with Carl Jung." (in Italian) Rassegna di clinica, terapia e scienze affini, 60 (1961), pp. 313-19.

1817. Layard, John. "Homo-eroticism in primitive society as a function of the self." Current trends (see *1748 above), pp. 241-60. (see 1590 above)

1818. Löwith, Karl. "Der philosophische Begriff des Gesten und Bösen." Das Böse (see *1765 above), pp. 211-36. (see 2484 below for English edition)

1819. Maag, Victor. "Der Antichrist als Symbol des Bösen." Ibid., pp. 63-90. (see 2485 below for English edition)

1820. McLeish, John. "Carl Jung, psychology and Catholicism." Wiseman Rev, 489 (1961), pp. 264-76; 490 (1961-62), pp. 313-18.

1821. Manuel, André. "C. G. Jung, gnostique et agnostique." La Nation, (3 Aug. 1961), np.

1822. Meissner, W. W. "Origen and the analytic psychology of symbolism." Downside Rev, 79 (1961), pp. 201-16.

117

1823. Mendaza, Rafael Tomas. "La vida y la obra de Carlos Gustavo Jung." Rev de Psicología General y Aplicada, 16:60 (1961), pp. 737-64.

1824. Moody, Robert. "A contribution to the psychology of the mother-child relationship." Current trends (see *1748 above), pp. 128-37.

1825. Morawitz-Cadio, Alice von. "Dem Andenken C. G. Jungs." Natur und Kultur, 53 (1961), pp. 211-13.

1826. Mountford, Gwen. "Modern fairy tales." Harv, 7 (1961), pp. 47-68.

1827. Neumann, Erich. "Die Bedeutung des genetischen Aspekts für die analytische Psychologie." Current trends (see *1748 above), pp. 19-36. "The significance of the genetic aspect for analytical psychology." R. F. C. Hull, trans. Ibid., pp. 37-53. (see 1604 above)

*1828. _____. Krise und Erneuerung. Zurich: Rascher, 1961.

1829. _____. "Mystical man." Spring 1961, pp. 9-49. (see 502 above for German and 2624 below for English editions)

1830. Neves, Flávio. "Jung e a experiencia religiosa." Kriterion, 14 (1961), pp. 316-25.

1831. Newton, Kathleen. "Personal reflections on training." JAP, 6:2 (1961), pp. 103-06.

1832. Oates, Wayne. Christ and Selfhood. New York: Association Press, 1961, pp. 230-33.

1833. Pinatel, Jean. "L'oeuvre de Jung devant la psychologie et la criminologie contemporaines." Rev de science criminelle et de droit pénal comparé, N. S. 16 (1961), pp. 623-30.

1834. Plaut, Albert B. J. "A dynamic outline of the training situation." JAP, 6:2 (1961), pp. 98-102.

1835. _____. "Hungry patients: reflections on ego structure." Current trends (see *1748 above), pp. 150-59. (see 1609 above)

1836. Portmann, Adolf. "Die Ordnung der Lebendigen in Deutungsversuch der Biologie." EJ, 30 (1961), pp. 285-332.

1837. Preetorius, Emil. "Vom Ordnungsgefüze der Kunst." Ibid., pp. 143-74.

1838. Prince, G. Stewart. "The therapeutic function of the homosexual transference." Current trends (see *1748 above), pp. 231-40. (see 1612 above)

1839. Pye, Faye. "Aspects of the psychology of South African women." Harv, 7 (1961), pp. 14-23.

1840. Quenétain, Tannegny de. "Carl Jung à la recherche des 4 piliers de la sagesse." Réalités, 183 (April 1961), pp. 22-28.

1841. _____. "What Carl Jung has left us." Ibid., pp. 18-22.

1842. Read, Herbert. "Beauty and the Beast." EJ, 30 (1961), pp. 175-210.

1843. Rochedieu, Edmond. "C. G. Jung a redonné à la psychologie ses dimensions spirituelles." La Vie Protestante, (16 June 1961), np.

1844. Rössler, Dietrich. "Tiefenpsychologie als theologisches Problem." Evangelische Theologie, 21 (1961), pp. 162-73.

1845. Rudin, Josef. "Gott und das Böse bei C. G. Jung." Arzt und Seelsorger, 12 (1961), pp. 4-8.

1846. _____. "Psychotherapie und religiöse Problematik." Rettung des Menschlichen (see 1777 above), pp. 230-47.

1847. _____. "Typ und Archetyp. Ein Versuch zu C. G. Jungs Werk." Orientierung, 25 (1961), pp. 154-57.

1848. Rudolph, Arthur W. Nietzsche's Influence on Jung. (Doctoral dissertation). University of Southern California, 1961.

1849. Sands, F. "Why I believe in God; an interview with C. G. Jung." Good Housekeeping, 153 (Dec. 1961), pp. 64 ff.

*1850. Schär, Hans. Seelsorge und Psychotherapie. Zurich: Rascher, 1961.

1851. _____. "Zum Gedächtnis von Carl Gustav Jung, 26. Juli 1875-6. Juni 1961." Freies Christentum, 13 (1961), pp. 111-13.

1852. Schlappner, Martin. "Das Böse und der Film." Das Böse (see *1765 above), pp. 127-60. (see 2511 above for English edition)

1853. Schmid, Karl. "Aspekte des Bösen im Schöpferischen." Ibid., pp. 237-60. (see 2512 below for English edition)

1854. Schmitt, Winfried. "C. G. Jung als persönliches Erlebnis." Der Lebensweiser, 28:8 (1961), pp. 29-33.

1855. Scholem, Gershom G. "Gut und Böse in der Kabbala." EJ, 30 (1961), pp. 29-68.

1856. Schwander, Otto. "C. G. Jung und die Phänomene der Parapsychologie." Natur und Kultur, 53 (1961), pp. 25-30.

119

1857. Seitz, Franz. "Dank an C. G. Jung." Die Bayrische Schule, 14
       (1961), pp. 360-61.

1858. Smith, Robert Carl. A critical analysis of religious and philo-
       sophic issues between Buber and Jung. (STD dissertation).
       Temple University, 1961.

1859. Speiser, Andreas. "Ton und Zahl." EJ, 30 (1961), pp. 127-42.

1860. Stickelberger, Rudolf. "Seelsorger als Arznei. Nach dem Tode
       Jungs." Reformatio, 10 (1961), pp. 295-99.

1861. Storr, Anthony. "The sage of Zurich." New Statesman, 61:1578
       (9 June 1961), p. 910.

1862. Suares, Carlo. "C. G. Jung. Le vieil homme de la terre." In
       De quelques apprentis-sorciers. Paris: Etre Libre, 1961, pp.
       113-34.

1863. Tate, Dorothy. "Invasion and Separation." JAP, 6:1 (1961), pp.
       45-54.

*1864. Trüb, Hans. Heilung aus der Begegnung. Eine Auseinandersetzung
       mit der psychologie C. G. Jungs. Stuttgart: Ernst Klett, 1961.

1865. Uhsadel, Walter. "Zum Problem der Transzendenz in der Psycholo-
       gie C. G. Jungs." In Forschung und Erfahrung im Dienst der
       Seelsorge. Göttingen, Vandenhoeck und Ruprecht, 1961, pp. 66-
       70.

1866. Velazquez, José M. "Jung: psicólogo de la religión." Universi-
       dad de la Habana, 25 (1961), pp. 140-44.

1867. Westman, Heinz. "From schizophrenia to art: excerpts from a
       case-history." Current trends (see *1748 above), pp. 214-30.

1868. Whitmont, Edward. "Individual and group." Spring 1961, pp.
       59-79.

1869. _____. "The magical dimension in transference and counter-
       transference." Current trends (see *1748 above), pp. 176-97.

1870. Wilhelm, Richard. "Circulation of events in the I Ching."
       Spring 1961, pp. 91-108.

1871. Windengren, Geo. "Das Prinzip des Bösen in den östlichen Reli-
       gionen." Das Böse (see *1765 above), pp. 25-62. (see 2522 be-
       low for English edition)

1872. Wren-Lewis, J. "How scientific was Jung?" Time and Tide, 42:24
       (1961), p. 972.

1873. Zuckerkandl, Victor. "Der singende und der sprechende Mensch."
       EJ, 30 (1961), pp. 241-84.

1874. Züblin, W. "Die Mutterfigur in den Phantasien eines frühver-
       wahrlosten Knaben." Current trends (see *1748 above), pp. 108-
       17. "The mother figure in the fantasies of a boy suffering
       from early deprivation." C. Rowland, trans. Ibid., pp. 118-
       27.

1875. "The old wise man." Time, 77 (16 June 1961), p. 49.

                              1962

1876. Aigrisse, Gilberte. "Character re-education and professional
       re-adaptation of a man aged forty-five." JAP, 7:2 (1962), pp.
       95-118.

1877. Bartning, Gerhard. "Hebräische wider griechische Psychologie?
       Zum Gespräch mit C. G. Jung." Quatember, 26 (1962), pp. 117-
       20.

*1878. Bennet, Edward Armstrong. C. G. Jung. T. Piceni, trans. Milan:
       Rizzoli, 1962. (see *1761 above for English and *1971 below
       for German editions)

1879. Benz, Ernst. "Vision und Führung in der christlichen Mystik."
       EJ, 31 (1962), pp. 117-70.

1880. Blake-Paliner, G. "Jung's influence on psychiatry and anthro-
       pology." New Zealand Medical J, 61 (1962), pp. 450-53.

1881. Corbin, Henry. "De la philosophie prophétique en Islam shî'ite"
       EJ, 31 (1962), pp. 49-116.

1882. Daniélou, Jean. "Les traditions secrètes des Apôtres." Ibid.,
       pp. 199-216.

1883. Dashiell, John F. "The unreliability of secondary sources with
       examples from Jung." Psychological Record, 12 (1962), pp. 331-
       34.

1884. Douglas, William. "The influence of Jung's work; a critical
       comment." With a comment by M. Esther Harding and a reply from
       the author. J of Religious Health, 1 (April 1962), pp. 260-72.

1885. Edinger, Edward F. "Symbols: meaning of life." Spring 1962,
       pp. 45-66.

*1886. Eliade, Mircea. The forge and the crucible. S. Corrin, trans.
       London: Rider and Co., 1962.

                              121

Engel, Werner H. "Reflections on the psychiatric consequences of persecution; an evaluation of restriction claimants." Amer J of Psychotherapy, 26:2 (1962), pp. 191-203.

1888. Fierz-Monnier, Heinrich Karl. "Die analytische psychotherapie (C. G. Jung) in der psychiatrischen Klinik." Acta psychotherapeutica, 10 (1962), pp. 219-32.

1889. Fordham, Michael. An evaluation of Jung's work. London: Gof PP Lecture # 119, Oct, 1962.

1890. _____. "An interpretation of Jung's thesis about synchronicity." BJMP, 35:2 (1962), pp. 205-10.

1891. _____. The self in Jung's writings. London: GofPP Lecture # 117, Mar. 1962.

1892. Fortmann, H. M. M. "De godsdienstpsychologie van Jung." Gawein, 10:5 (1962), pp. 265-74.

1893. Frey-Wehrlin, C. T. "Probleme der Traumdeutung." JAP, 7:2 (1962), pp. 119-31. (see 2011 and 2012 below)

1894. Funk, Melvin Frank. Moral Judgments and Neurosis. (Doctoral dissertation). University of Illinois, 1962.

*1895. Goetz, Bruno. Das Reich ohne Raum. With a commentary by M. L. von Franz. Zurich: Rascher, 1962.

*1896. Goldbrunner, Josef. Individuación. La psicología profonda de Carl Gustav Jung. Madrid: Fax, 1962. (see *542 above for German and complete list of other editions)

1897. Gordon, Rosemary. "Reflections on Jung's concept of synchronicity." Harv, 8 (1962), pp. 77-98.

1898. Haendler, Otto. "C. G. Jung in seinem Gesamtwerk." Wege zum Menschen, 14 (1962), pp. 8-13.

1899. _____. "C. G. Jung zum Gedächtnis." Ibid., pp. 1-2.

1900. Harding, M. Esther. "Jung's influence on contemporary thought." J of Religion and Health, 1:3 (1962), pp. 247-59. (see 1576 above)

1901. Harms, Ernst. "Carl Gustav Jung." Amer J of Psychiatry, (Feb. 1962), pp. 728-32.

1902. Henderson, James L. "The Jungian concept of the gifted child." Yearbook of Education, 1962, pp. 91-98.

1903. Hesse, Hermann. "Greetings on Jung's eightieth birthday." Spring 1962, p. 19.

1904. Heun, Eugene. "Zur analytischen Psychologie C. G. Jungs." Thorraduran Therapie, 33:10 (1962), pp. 256-68; 11, pp. 281-96; 12, pp. 309-19.

1905. Hillman, James. "Friends and enemies." Harv, 8 (1962), pp. 1-22.

1906. _____. "Training and the C. G. Jung Institute, Zürich." With comments by A. Plaut and Michael Fordham and a reply by the author. JAP, 7:1 (1962), pp. 3-28.

1907. Holton, Gerald. "Über die Hypothesen, welche der Naturwissenschaft zugruned liegen." EJ, 31 (1962), pp. 351-426.

1908. Jackson, Murray. "Jung's later work. The archetype." BJMP, 35 (1962), pp. 199-204.

1909. Jaffé, Aniela. "The psychic world of C. G. Jung." Tomorrow (New York), 9:2 (1962), pp. 7-21.

1910. _____. "Psychological aspects of spontaneous cases." Inter J of Parapsychology, 4:2 (1967), pp. 97-120.

1911. Kawai, H. "Professor Carl G. Jung and Japanese psychology." Psychologia (Kyoto), 5:1 (1962), pp. 8-9.

*1912. Kerényi, Carl. Die Mysterien von Eleusis. Zurich: Rhein, 1962. (see *2478 below for English edition)

1913. Kiesow, Ernst-Rüdiger. Katholizismus und Protestantismus bei Carl Gustav Jung. (Doctoral dissertation). Humboldt University of Berlin, 1962.

1914. Kijowski, A. "Archeologia myobrazni." Tworczocs, 18:5 (1962), pp. 124-27.

1915. Kirsch, James. "Hamlet, a drama of haunted man." Harv, 8 (1962), pp. 24-47.

1916. Knight, James A. "Some significant perspectives in the work of Carl Gustav Jung." J of Existential Psychiatry, 3:10 (1962), pp. 179-95.

1917. Knoll, Max et al. "Note on the spectroscopy of subjective light patterns." JAP, 7:1 (1962), pp. 55-70.

*1918. Köberle, Adolf. Christliches Denken: von der Erkenntnis zur Verwirklichung. Hamburg: Furche, 1962.

1919. Lambert, Kenneth. "Jung's later work. Historical studies." BJMP, 35:2 (1962), pp. 191-98.

1920. McCully, Robert S. "The phoenix and turtle: an interpretation." Harv, 8 (1962), pp. 50-56.

123

1921. McGlashan, Alan. "Psyche unbound." Ibid., pp. 58-70.

1922. Mann, Kristine. "In the shadow of death." Spring 1962, pp. 89-106. (see 258 above)

1923. Martins, D. "C. G. Jung: O homem à descoberta de sua alma." Rev Port Filos, 18:3 (1962), pp. 225-43.

1924. Mayne, Isobel. "Emily Brontë and the Magna Mater." JAP, 7:1 (1962), pp. 71-82.

1925. Meier, Carl Alfred. "Psychosomatik in Jungscher Sicht." Psyche, 15 (1962), pp. 625-38. (see 2051 below for English edition)

1926. Ormea, F. "The concept of the complex in depth psychology. Origin and significance of the term 'complex' in Jung's analytical (complex) psychology." (in Italian) Minerva Med, 53 (1962), pp. 689-94.

1927. Ostrowski-Sachs, Margaret. "Anima images in Spittler's poetry." Spring 1962, pp. 67-88.

1928. Penna, J. O. de Meira. "A psicología de C. G. Jung." Senhor, 4:2 (1962), pp. 31-34.

1929. Perry, John Weir. "Reconstitutive process in the psychopathology of the self." Annals of the New York Academy of Science, 96 (1962), pp. 853-76.

1930. Plaut, Albert B. J. and Bash, Karl W. "Training and Psychopathology." JAP, 7:2 (1962), pp. 149-52.

1931. Portmann, Adolf. "Freiheit und Bindung in biologischer Sicht." EJ, 31 (1962), pp. 427-52.

1932. Read, Herbert. "The poet and his Muse." Ibid., pp. 217-48.

1933. Rumpf, Louis. "C. G. Jung, déchiffreur de l'âme en souffrance." Rev de théologie et de philosophie, (1962), pp. 250-69.

1934. Scharfenberg, Joachim. "Zum theologischen Gespräch mit C. G. Jung." Quatember, 26 (1962), pp. 21-27.

1935. _____. "Zum theologischen Gespräch mit C. G. Jung." Wege zum Menschen, 14 (1962), pp. 3-8.

1936. Schoedel, W. R. "Rediscovery of Gnosis." Interpretation, 16 (Oce. 1962), pp. 387-401.

1937. Scholem, Gershom G. "Tradition und Kommentar als religiöse Kategorien im Judentum." EJ, 31 (1962), pp. 19-48.

1938. Simon, J. H. "A 'Weltanschauung' de Jung." Veritas (Porto Alegre), 7:1 (1962), pp. 1-11.

1939. Skard, Åse Grude. "Seks som gjekk bort." Norsk Pedagogisk
       Tidskrift, 46:1 (1962), pp. 1-5.

1940. Stein, Leopold. "An entity named ego." JAP, 7:1 (1962), pp.
       41-54.

1941. Storr, Anthony. "C. G. Jung." The Amer Scholar, 31:3 (1962),
       pp. 395-403.

1942. Strauss, Heinz Artur. "Anima als Projectionserlebnis, darge-
       stellt an Beispielen aus der Literatur." In Krisis und Zu-
       der Frau. Wilhelm Bitter, ed. Stuttgart: Ernst Klett, 1962,
       pp. 52-68.

1943. Strauss-Kloebe, Sigrid. "Erscheinungsweissen des Animus im
       weiblichen Seelenleben." In Krisis (see 1942 above), pp. 69-
       86.

1944. Syřištová, E. "Historical review of the psychotherapy of schi-
       zophrenia." Českosl Psychol, 6:1 (1962), pp. 79-94.

1945. Underwood, Richard Arnold. The possibility of the Word in the
       'Time of the World-Picture'--prolegomena to a study of the
       depth psychology of C. G. Jung in relation to contemporary the-
       ological interpretation. (Doctoral dissertation). Drew Uni-
       versity, 1962.

1946. Valett, Robert E. "Carl Gustav Jung: some contributions to
       modern psychology." J of Humanistic Psychology, 2:1 (1962),
       pp. 23-34.

1947. _____. "Jung's effect on psychology." Bull Brit Psychologi-
       cal Soc, 46 (1962), pp. 58-66.

1948. Washburn, D. E. Contributions of C. G. Jung's psychology to a
       general theory of communication. (Doctoral dissertation).
       University of Denver, 1962.

1949. Weidlé, Vladimir. "Vom Sinn des Mimesis." EJ, 31 (1962), pp.
       249-74.

1950. Werblowsky, R. J. Zwi. "Führe uns, Mutter: der Weg der
       Väter und das Finden des Sohnes." Ibid., 31 (1962), pp. 171-
       98.

1951. Wethered, Maud. "Some thoughts on abstract art." Harv, 8
       (1962), pp. 71-75.

1952. Wheelwright, Joseph B. "Freud and Jung revisited." New Repub-
       lic, 146 (23 April 1962), pp. 18-19.

1953. Wilhelm, Helmut. "Das Zusammenwirken von Himmel, Erde und
       Mensch." EJ, 31 (1962), pp. 317-50.

1954. Wilhelm, Richard. "Death and renewal." <u>Spring</u> 1962, pp. 20-44.

1955. Williams, Mary. "The fear of death. Part II: the fear of death in consciousness." <u>JAP</u>, 7:1 (1962), pp. 29-40.

1956. Ziegler, A. "A cardiac infarction and a dream as synchronous events." <u>Ibid</u>., 7:2 (1962), pp. 141-48.

1957. Zuckerkandl, Victor. "Vom Wachstum des Kunstwerks." <u>EJ</u>, 31 (1962), pp. 275-316.

1958. "Commonsense about Jung." <u>TLS</u>, 3142 (18 May 1962), p. 356.

1963

1959. Adler, Gerhard. "C. G. Jung." <u>Middlesex Hospital J</u> (London), 63:4 (1963), pp. 157-63.

1960. _____. "On the question of meaning in psychotherapy." <u>Spring</u> 1963, pp. 5-30. (see below, 1961 and 2114 for German and 2899 for English editions)

1961. _____. "Die Sinnfrage in der Psychotherapie." <u>Psyche</u>, 17 (1963), pp. 379-400. (see 1960 above for English and list of other editions)

1962. Alex, William. "A personal assessment." <u>Contact</u> (see *2007 below), pp. 168-71.

1963. Allenby, Amy I. "Angels as archetypal symbols." <u>Spring</u> 1963, pp. 46-53. (see 2117 below)

1964. _____. "A tribute to C. G. Jung." <u>Contact</u> (see *2007 below), pp. 67-70.

1965. Alm, Ivar. "C. G. Jungs Erfahrungen in theologischer Sicht." <u>Theologische Zeit</u>, 19 (1963), pp. 352-59.

*1966. Anrich, Ernst. <u>Moderne Physik und Tiefenpsychologie</u>. <u>Zur Einheit der Wirklichkeit und damit der Wissenschaft</u>. Stuttgart: Ernst Klett, 1963.

1967. Aumüller, Anneliese. "Personal stimulus of Jung." <u>Contact</u> (see *2007 below), pp. 190-93.

1968. Baudouin, Charles. "Le cheminement de C. G. Jung: de l'association au complexe." <u>Action et Penseé</u>, 39:1-2 (1963), pp. 1-20.

1969.   _____. "Instantanés de C. G. Jung 1945-1954." <u>Contact</u> (see *2007 below), pp. 144-47.

*1970.   _____. <u>L'oeuvre de Jung et la psychologie complexe</u>. Paris: Payot, 1963. (see *2424 below for Spanish edition)

*1971.   Bennet, Edward Armstrong. <u>C. G. Jung</u>. <u>Ein Blicke in Leben und Werk</u>. M. Borbely, trans. Zurich and Stuttgart: Rascher, 1963. (see *1761 above for English and list of other editions)

1972.   Bernhard, Ernst. "The tasks confronting analytical psychology in Italy." <u>Contact</u> (see *2007 below), pp. 97-107.

1973.   Beyme, F. "Archetypischer Traum (Todeshochzeit) und psychosomatisches Symptom (weibliche Impotenz) im Lichte der Forschungen von J. J. Bachofen, C. G. Jung und E. Neumann." <u>Schweiz</u> <u>ANP</u>, 92:1 (1963); 93:1 (1964); 94:1 (1964), np.

1974.   Binswanger, Hilde. "Positive aspects of the animus." <u>Spring</u> 1963, pp. 82-101.

1975.   Birkhäuser, Sibylle. "The figure of the spinning women in fairy tales." <u>Ibid.</u>, pp. 31-45.

1976.   Brand, Renée. "Thoughts about realization." <u>Contact</u> (see *2007 below), pp. 232-34.

*1977.   Brunner, Cornelia. <u>Die Anima als Schicksalsproblem des Mannes</u>. <u>St ad CGJIZ XIV</u>. Zurich: Rascher, 1963.
        Rev. Vera von der Heydt. <u>JAP</u>, 10:2 (1965), pp. 199-200.

1978.   Buder, H. "Der Zeitraum von 1933-1945 und die Zeit nach dem Kriege." <u>Contact</u> (see *2007 below), pp. 33-35.

1979.   Bügler, Käthe. "Die Entwicklung der analytischen Psychologie in Deutschland." <u>Ibid.</u>, pp. 23-33.

1980.   Burkhardt, H. "Die psychologischen Typen C. G. Jungs." <u>Monatschrifte für praktische Psychologie</u>, 17 (1963), pp. 215-19.

1981.   Cahen, Roland. "Vingt ans après." <u>Contact</u> (see *2007 below), pp. 3-9.

1982.   Carol, Hans. "Aus einem Gespräch mit C. G. Jung." <u>NZZ</u>, 58 (2 June 1963), np.

1983.   Castillejo, Irene C. de. <u>Inferior function, tranquilisers and Trafalgar Square</u>. London: GofPP Lecture # 123, Nov. 1963.

1984.   _____. "The second apple." <u>Harv</u>, 9 (1963), pp. 56-63.

*1985.   Christou, Evangelos. <u>The Logos of the Soul</u>. Intro. by J. Hillman, forw. by C. A. Meier. New York: Spring Pubs., 1963.

1986. Coleman, Elliott. "A note on Joyce and Jung." James Joyce Q, 1:1 (1963), pp. 11-16.

1987. Collins, Margaret. "The stimulus of Jung's concepts in child psychiatry." Contact (see *2007 below), pp. 79-81.

1988. Corbin, Henry. "Au pays de l'Imâm caché." EJ, 32 (1963), pp. 31-88.

*1989. Cox, David. How the mind works; a simple account of analytical psychology. London: Darton, Longman and Todd, 1963. (see *2135 and *2543 below)

1990. Dale-Green, Patricia. The archetypal cat: a bearer of both healing and dis-ease. London: GofPP Lecture # 124, Dec. 1963.

*1991. _____. The cult of the cat. London: William Heinman, Ltd., 1963.

1992. _____. "The golden eagle." Harv, 9 (1963), pp. 35-41.

*1993. Donnington, Robert. Wagner's 'Ring' and its symbols; the music and the myth. New York: St. Martin's Press, 1963.

1994. Donnot, Dudley. "Jung and religion." Believer, 3:6 (1963), p. 4.

1995. Duddington, Alexander. "Meeting the individual in the Russian." Harv, 9 (1963), pp. 1-12.

1996. Dunn, I. Jay. "Prospects for C. G. Jung's psychology in the United States." Contact (see *2007 below), pp. 164-67.

1997. Ebon, Martin. "The second soul of C. G. Jung." Inter J of Parapsychology, 5:4 (1963), pp. 428-58.

1998. Edinger, Edward F. "Inner life in an outer-space age." Sat Rev Lit, 46 (1 June 1963), pp. 23 ff.

*1999. Eliade, Mircea. Images and symbols; studies in religious symbols. P. Mairet, trans. New York: Sheed and Ward, 1963.

2000. _____. "Paradis et utopie: geographie mythique et eschatologie." EJ, 32 (1963), pp. 211-34.

2001. Elliott, Lucile. "Concerning Jung's influence in California." Contact (see *2007 below), pp. 207-09.

*2002. Fierz, Heinrich Karl. Klinik und analytische Psychologie. St ad CGJIZ XV. Zurich and Stuttgart: Rascher, 1963.
Rev. A. B. J. Plaut. JAP, 12:1 (1967), pp. 73-76.

2003. Fierz, Markus. "Symbole in der Wissenschaft, insbesondere in in der Physik." Traum (see *2052 below), pp. 9-34.

2004. _____. "Die Vier Elemente." Ibid., pp. 35-64.

2005. Fodor, Nandor. "Jung, Freud, and a newly discovered letter on the poltergeist theme." Psychoanalytic Rev, 50:2 (1963), pp. 119-28.

2006. Fordham, Frieda. "Myths, archetypes and patterns of childhood." Harv, 9 (1963), pp. 13-24.

*2007. Fordham, Michael. Contact with Jung; essays on the influence of his work and personality. London: Tavistock, 1963.
    Rev. Rosemary Gordon. JAP, 9:1 (1964), pp. 92-95.

2008. _____. "The empirical foundation and theories of the self in Jung's works." JAP, 8:1 (1963), pp. 1-24. (see 3219 below)

2009. Frank, Margit van Leight. "Reflections on spirit and pseudo spirit." Contact (see *2007 above), pp. 194-200.

2010. Franz, Marie Louise von. "Die Bibliothek C. G. Jungs in Küsnacht." Librarium (Zurich), 6 (1963), pp. 95-109. (see 2789 below for English edition)

2011. Frey-Wehrlin, C. T. "Problems of dream interpretation." JAP, 8:1 (1963), pp. 132-40. (see 1893 above and 2012 below for German editions)

2012. _____. "Probleme der Traumdeutung." Traum (see *2052 below), pp. 65-88. (see 1893 above for German edition)

2013. Frischknecht, Max. "Neue Begegnung mit C. G. Jung." Reformatio, 12 (1963), pp. 307-15,

2014. Froböse-Thiele, Felicia. "Was mich C. G. Jung gelehrt hat." Contact (see *2007 above), pp. 36-38.

2015. Gaffney, James. "Symbolism of the Mass in Jung's psychology." Rev de l'Université d'Ottawa, 33 (1963), pp. 214-31.

2016. Gordon, Rosemary. "Gods and the deintegrates." JAP, 8:1 (1963), pp. 25-44.

2017. Gross, Don Hargrave. A Jungian analysis of New Testament exorcism. (Doctoral dissertation). Harvard University, 1963.

2018. Hannah, Barbara. "Aion." Lecture, CGJIZ, April 1963.

2019. _____. "The most significant stimulus derived from C. G. Jung." Contact (see *2007 Above), pp. 129-31.

2020. Harding, M. Esther. "Critical appreciation of 'Symbol formation and the delusional transference'." JAP, 8:2 (1963), pp. 160-64.

129

2021. _____. "The early days." Contact (see *2007 above), pp. 179-84.

*2022. _____. Psychic energy: its source and its transformation. 2nd rev. ed. Princeton, New Jersey: Princeton University Press (Bollingen Series X), 1963/1973. (see *290 above for list of other editions)

2023. Henderson, Joseph L. "C. G. Jung: a personal evaluation." Contact (see *2007 above), pp. 221-23.

*2024. _____. and Oakes, Maud. The wisdom of the serpent; myths of death, rebirth, and resurrection. (Patterns of myth series). New York: George Braziller, 1963.
          Rev. Michael Fordham. JAP, 9:2 (1964), pp. 188-89.

2025. Hendrix, P. "'Garten' und 'Morgen' als Ort und Zeit für das Mysterium Paschale in der Orthodoxen Kirche." EJ, 32 (1963), pp. 147-72.

2026. Hess, Gertrude. "Die Überwindung des biologischen Kanons." Contact (see *2007 above), pp. 134-38.

2027. Hillman, James. "Introduction" to Logos of the Soul (see *1985 above), pp. iii-viii.

2028. _____. "Methodologische Probleme in der Traumforschung." Traum (see *2052 below), pp. 89-122. (see 3546 below for English edition)

2029. Himmelfarb, G. "Reply to Storr." Amer Scholar, 32 (Winter 1962-63). p. 160.

2030. Hoch, Dorothee. "Zum 'Credo' von C. G. Jung." Kirchenblatt für die Reformierte Schweiz, 119 (1963), pp. 66-68.

2031. Jackson, Murray. "Symbol formation and the delusional transference." With comments by M. Esther Harding and a reply by the author. JAP, 8:2 (1963), pp. 145-66. (see 2178 below)

2032. _____. "Technique and procedure in analytic practice with special reference to schizoid states." JAP, 8:1 (1963), pp. 51-64.

2033. Jacobi, Jolande. "Farbgestaltungen der unbewußten Psyche." Palette (Basel), 12 (1963), pp. 15-26.

*2034. _____. De Psychologie van C. G. Jung. M. Drukker, trans. Zeist, W. de Haan, 1963. (see *255 above for German and list of other editions)

2035. Jaeger, Marc A. "Die Psychologie C. G. Jungs und die Frage nach dem Lebenssinn in der Gegenwart." Universitas, 18 (1963), pp. 417-22.

*2036. Jaffé, Aniela. Apparitions and precognitions; a study from the point of view of C. G. Jung's psychology. Forw. by C. G. Jung. New Hyde Park, New York: University Books, 1963. (see *1489 above for German edition)

2037. _____. "The person and the experience." Apparitions (see *2036 above), pp. 17-46.

*2038. Kadinsky, David. Strukturelemente der Persönlichkeit. Bern and Stuttgart: Hans Huber, 1963.
        Rev. H. J. Wilke. ZAP, 2:4 (1971), pp. 257-58.

*2039. Kerényi, Carl. Prometheus: archetypal image of human existence. R. Manheim, trans. New York: Pantheon (Bollingen Series LXV-I), 1963. (see *1589 above for German edition)

2040. _____. "Ursinn und Sinnwandel des Utopischen." EJ, 32 (1963), pp. 9-30.

2041. Kirsch, James. "Le probleme de la dictature et sa symbolisation dans Moby Dick." Action et Pensée, 39:1-2 (1963), pp. 35-51.

2042. Kotschnig, Elined. "Jung on survival of consciousness." Inward Light, 24:64 (1963), pp. 28-49.

2043. Lambert, Kenneth. "A debt to C. G. Jung." Contact (see *2007 above), pp. 71-73.

*2044. Löwenich, Walther von. Luther und der Neuprotestantismus. Witten: Luther, 1963.

*2045. MacQuarrie, John. Twentieth-century religious thought. The frontiers of philosophy and theology. London: SCM Press, 1963.

2046. Mahler, Margaret Schoenberger. "Thoughts about development and individuation." The psychoanalytic study of the child. R. S. Eissler, et al., eds. New York: Inter Universities Press, 18, (1963), pp. 307-24.

2047. _____. and Feuer, M. "Certain aspects of the separation-individuation phase." Psychoanalytic Q, 32 (1963), pp. 1-14.

2048. Marjasch, Sonja. "Vom Ich im Traum." Traum (see *2052 below), pp. 123-42. (see 2385 below for English edition)

*2049. Marjula, Anna. The healing influence of active imagination in a specific case of neurosis. A human document. Intro. by B. Hannah. Zurich: Privately printed, 1963.

2050. Mead, John. "Technology and the unconscious victims." Harv, 9 (1963), pp. 43-53.

2051. Meier, C. A. "Psychosomatic medicine from the Jungian point of view." <u>JAP</u>, 8:2 (1963), pp. 103-22. (see 1925 above for German edition)

*2052. _____. <u>Traum und Symbol</u>. Zurich: Rascher, 1963.

2053. _____. "Der Traum im alten Griechenland." <u>Traum</u> (see *2052 above), pp. 143-70.

2054. Menasce, Adrien de. "The unpredictable image." <u>Harv</u>, 9 (1963), pp. 65-76.

2055. Nelson, Benjamin. "Hesse and Jung: two newly recovered letters." <u>Psychoanalytic Rev</u>, 50:3 (1963), pp. 361-66.

2056. Neumann, Erich. "Dank an Jung." <u>Contact</u> (see *2007 above), pp. 89-94.

*2057. _____. "Psikhologiat hamaamakim umusar hadash." Jerusalem: Schocken, 1963.

*2058. _____. <u>Das Kind</u>; <u>Struktur und Dynamik der werdenden Persönlichkeit</u>. Zurich: Rhein, 1963. (see *3284 below for English edition)

2059. Osterman, Elizabeth K. "C. G. Jung. A personal memoir." <u>Contact</u> (see *2007 above), pp. 218-20.

2060. Paulsen, Alma A. "Origins of analytical psychology in the New York area." <u>Ibid</u>., pp. 185-89.

2061. Paulsen, Lola. <u>The shadow</u>: <u>this thing of darkness I acknowledge mine</u>. London: GofPP Lecture # 122, 1963. (see 1605 above)

2062. Peavy, Richard Vance. <u>A study of C. G. Jung's concept of intuitive perception and the intuitive type</u>. (Ed. D. dissertation). University of Oregon, 1963.

2063. Perry, John Weir. "Jung's influence on my life and work." <u>Contact</u> (see *2007 above), pp. 214-17.

*2064. Petro, Carlo. <u>Le psicologie del profondo ed in particolare la psicologia analitica di C. G. Jung e l'igiene mentale</u>. Cremona: Mangiarotti, 1963.

*2065. Philipson, Morris H. <u>Outline of a Jungian aesthetics</u>. Evanston, Ill.: Northwestern University Press, 1963.
       Rev. David Gebhard. <u>Library J</u>, 89 (1 Jan. 1964), p. 94. Donald Weeks. <u>J of Aesthetics</u>, 22 (Sum. 1964), p. 475.

2066. Poeppig, Fred. "Carl Gustav Jung Bekenntnis. Das Abenteuer der Schelle." <u>Die Kommenden</u>, 17:11 (1963), pp. 19-21.

2067. Portmann, Adolf. "Utopisches in der Lebensforschung." EJ, 32
       (1963), pp. 311-46.

2068. Prince, G. Stewart. "Jung's psychology in Britain." Contact
       (see *2007 above), pp. 41-61.

2069. Progoff, Ira. "The dynamics of hope and the image of utopia."
       EJ, 32 (1963), pp. 89-146.

2070. Pye, Faye. The soul as a function of relationship in psychology
       and religion. London: GofPP Lecture # 121, June 1963.

2071. Riklin, Franz. "Some problems of interpretation." Contact (see
       *2007 above), pp. 111-28.

2072. Rochedieu, E. "Le collectif et l'individuel dans l'histoire des
       religions." Ibid., pp. 132-33.

*2073. Rolfe, E. The intelligent agnostic's introduction to Christi-
       anity. London: Arrow Books, 1963.

2074. Rorarius, Winfried. "C. G. Jungs Einsicht in die Seele und die
       Anrede des Evangeliums." Zeitwende, 34 (1963), pp. 225-39.

2075. Rosenthal, Michael. "Notes on envy and the contrasexual arche-
       type." JAP, 8:1 (1963), pp. 65-76.

2076. Rudin, Josef. "Misstrauen gegen das religiose Erleben." In his
       Religion und Erlebnis. Ein Weg zur Überwindung der religiösen
       Krise. Olten: Walter, 1963, pp. 15-29.

2077. Schär, Hans. "Bemerkungen zu Träumen der Bibel." Traum (see
       *2052 above), pp. 171-79.

2078. Schärf, Rivkah. "Dream and reality." Spring 1963, pp. 54-81.

2079. Schöler, J. P. "Carl Gustav Jung und die Parapsychologie."
       Metaphysik, 6 (1963), pp. 1-6.

2080. Schweizer, Erica. "Das Leben eines vollendeten Menschen." Con-
       tact (see *2007 above), pp. 139-43.

2081. Selesnick, Sheldon T. "C. G. Jung's contribution to psychoana-
       lysis." Amer J of Psychiatry, 120:4 (1963), pp. 350-56.

2082. Sestier, Jean. "Actualité de Jung." Contact (see *2007 above),
       pp. 10-13.

2083. Spiegelman, J. Marvin. "Analytical psychology in Los Angeles."
       Ibid., pp. 151-56.

2084. _____. "Progress in Jungian psychotherapy." In Progress in
       clinical psychology. B. Riess and L. E. Abt, eds. New York:
       Grune and Stratton, 5 (1963), pp. 149-58.

133

*2085. Spinks, R. Stehpen. _Psychology_ and _religion_: _an introduction_ _to_ _contemporary_ _views_. Boston: Beacon Press, 1963.

2086. Stein, Leopold. "Language and archetypes." _Contact_ (see *2007 above), pp. 75-78.

2087. Stein, Robert M. "Reflections on Jung's practice and concepts." _Ibid._, pp. 172-75.

2088. Stockfish, Thomas J. "Religious symbolism in the psychology of C. G. Jung." _Insight_, 2:2 (1963), pp. 36-40.

2089. Strauss, Ruth. "A personal recollection." _Contact_ (see *2007 above), p. 74.

2090. Strojnowski, Jerzy. "Psychologia religii K. G. Jung." _Zeszyty_ _Naukowe_ _Katol_ _Uniw_ _Lubelskiego_, 6 (1963), pp. 35-45. (variant, 1:21)

2091. Tenny, E. V. "The impact of Jung's ideas on American universities." _Contact_ (see *2007 above), pp. 157-63.

2092. Thompson, Claire. "Jung's contribution from the point of view of a psychologist." _Ibid._, pp. 212-13.

2093. Torrie, Alfred. "Schizophreniform illness as a therapeutic process." _Ibid._, pp. 82-86.

*2094. Vasavada, Arvind U. _Dr_. _C_. _G_. _Jung_ _ka_ _nislesanatmake_ _manovij-_ _ñan_. _Ek_ _samksipth_ _Paricay_. Varanasi: Chowkhamba Vidyabhawan, 1963.

2095. Verne, Georges. "A travers C. G. Jung: retour à l'authenticité." _Contact_ (see *2007 above), pp. 14-19.

2096. Wall, Richard J. "Yeats and Jung: an ideological comparison." _Literature_ _and_ _Psychology_, 13 (1963), pp. 44-52.

2097. Weiss, Joseph G. "Eine spätjüdische Utopie religiöse Freiheit." _EJ_, 32 (1963), pp. 235-80.

2098. Wheelwright, Jane. "A personal experience." _Contact_ (see *2007 above), pp. 226-28.

2099. Wheelwright, Joseph B. "An attempt at appreciation." _Ibid._, pp. 224-25.

2100. _____. "Jung's influence on the American scene." _Ibid._, pp. 210-12.

*2101. White, Steward Edward. _Das_ _uneingeschränkte_ _Weltall_. A. Hess, trans. Zurich: Origo, 1963.

2102. Whitmont, Edward C. "The symbolic view." _Contact_ (see *2007 above), pp. 201-04.

2103. Whitney, James G. "A personal experience of analytical psychology." Ibid., pp. 229-31.

*2104. Wickes, Frances G. The inner world of choice. Forw. by H. A. Murray. New York: Harper and Row, 1963.

2105. Williams, Mary. "The indivisibility of the personal and collective unconscious." JAP, 8:1 (1963), pp. 45-50. (see 3329 below)

2106. _____. "The poltergeist man." Ibid., 8:2 (1963), pp. 123-44.

*2107. Wisse, Stephen. Das religiöse Symbol. Versuch einer Wesendeutung. Essen: Ludgerus, 1963.

2108. Zaehner, R. C. "Utopia and beyond: some Indian views." EJ, 32 (1963), pp. 281-310.

2109. Zimmerman, Werner. "Lebensschau von C. G. Jung." Vivas Voco, 13 (1963), pp. 312-17.

2110. Zuckerkandl, Victor. "Die Wahrheit des Traumes und der Traum der Wahrheit." EJ, 32 (1963), pp. 173-210.

2111. "C. G. Jung: oneirologist par excellence." Christian Century, 80 (6 March 1963), p. 319.

2112. "Dark and light of dreams." Time, 81 (10 May 1963), p. 100.

2113. "Two faces of Jung." TLS, 3205 (2 Aug. 1963), p. 592.

1964

2114. Adler, Gerhard. "Die Sinnfrage in der Psychotherapie." Prob (see *2129 below), pp. 9-37. (see 1960 above for English and list of other editions)

2115. Aigrisse, Gilberte. "A Don Juan on the way to wisdom." JAP, 9:2 (1964), pp. 151-62.

*2116. _____. Psychanalyse de Paul Valéry. Paris: Editions Universitaires, 1964.
           Rev. Therese Raynal. JAP, 10:2 (1965), p. 199.

2117. Allenby, Amy I. "Angels as archetype and symbol." Archetype (see *2166 below), pp. 88-94. (see 1963 above)

2118. Aylward, James. "Archetype and natural law." _Ibid._, pp. 81-87.

2119. Baumann, Carol. "Time and Tao." _Harv_, 10 (1964), pp. 13-36.
       (see 693 above)

2120. Benz, Ernst. "Theogony and the transformation of man in Fried-
       rich Wilhelm Joseph Schelling." _PEY_ _V_ (see *2130 below), pp.
       202-41. (see 882 above for German edition)

2121. Binswanger, Kurt. "Hintergründe einer Impotenz." _Prob_ (see
       *2129 below), pp. 125-74.

2122. Bockus, Frank Mann. _The_ _self_ _and_ _Christ_: _a_ _study_ _of_ _Carl_
       Jung's _psychology_ _of_ _the_ _self_ _and_ _its_ _bearing_ _on_ _Christology_.
       (D. D. dissertation). University of Chicago, 1964.

2123. Bradway, Katherine. "Jung's psychological types: classifica-
       tion by test versus classification by self." _JAP_, 9:2 (1964),
       pp. 129-36.

2124. Brawer, Florence B. and Spiegelman, J. Marvin. "Rorschach and
       Jung: a study of introversion-extraversion." _Ibid._, pp. 137-
       50.

2125. Brooks, Henry Curtis. _The_ _concept_ _of_ _God_ _in_ _the_ _analytical_ _psy-_
       chology _of_ _Carl_ _Gustav_ _Jung_. (Doctoral dissertation). Boston
       University, 1964.

2126. Burns, Charles. "The Catholic psychotherapist and the future."
       Wiseman _Rev_, 498 (1963-64), pp. 383-94.

2127. Burt, Cyril. "Baudouin on Jung." _Brit_ _J_ _Psychology_, 55:4 (1964),
       pp. 477-84.

2128. Bychowski, Gustav. "Freud and Jung: an encounter." _Israel_ _An_
       Psychiatry, 2:2 (1964), pp. 129-43.

*2129. CGJI-Z., ed. _Psychotherapeutische_ _Probleme_. Zurich and Stutt-
       gart: Rascher, 1964.
            Rev. F. Strauss. _JAP_, 12:2 (1967), pp. 175-76.

*2130. Campbell, Joseph, ed. _Man_ _and_ _Transformation_. _Papers_ _from_ _the_
       Eranos _Yearbooks_ _V_. Princeton, New Jersey: Princeton Univer-
       sity Press (Bollingen Series XXX), 1964.

*2131. Caruso, Igor. _Existential_ _psychology_: _from_ _analysis_ _to_ _synthe-_
       sis. London: Darton, Longman and Todd, 1964. (see *765 a-
       bove for German edition)

2132. Castillejo, Irene C. de. "Man the hero." _Harv_, 10 (1964), pp.
       37-48.

2133. Corbin, Henry. "Divine epiphany and spiritual birth in Ismaili-
       an Gnosis." _PEY_ _V_ (see *2130 above), pp. 69-160. (see 889 a-

bove for German edition)

2134. _____. "Herméneutique spirituelle comparée (I. Swedenborg-II. Gnose ismaelienne). EJ, 33 (1964), pp. 71-176.

*2135. Cox, David. How the mind works. New York: Barnes & Noble, 1964. (Also titled: Teach yourself analytical psychology) (see *1989 above and *2543 below)

2136. Daniélou, Jean. "The dove and the darkness in ancient Byzantine mysticism." PEY V (see *2130 above), pp. 270-96. (see 892 above for French edition)

2137. Dicks-Mireaux, M. J. "Extraversion-introversion in experimental psychology: examples of experimental evidence and theoretical implications." JAP, 9:2 (1964), pp. 117-28.

2138. Durand, Gilbert. "Dualismes et dramatisation: régime antithétique et structures dramatiques de l'imaginaire." EJ, 33 (1964), pp. 245-84.

2139. Edinger, Edward F. "Trinity and quaternity." Archetype (see *2166 below), pp. 16-29.

2140. _____. "Trinity and quaternity." JAP, 9:2 (1964), pp. 103-16.

2141. Eliade, Mircea. "Mystery and spiritual regeneration in extra-European religions." PEY V (see *2130 above), pp. 3-36. (see 899 above for French edition)

*2142. _____. Shamanism-archaic techniques of ecstasy. W. R. Trask, trans. New York: Pantheon (Bollingen Series LXXVI), 1964.

2143. Ellenberger, Henri F. "La psychologie de Carl Gustav Jung. A propos de son autobiographie." Union Médicale du Canada, 93 (1964), pp. 993-1006.

*2144. Evans, Richard Isadore. Conversations with Carl Jung and reactions from Ernst Jones. Princeton, New Jersey: Van Nostrand, 1964. (see 2783 below for French edition)
        Rev. Mary Williams. JAP, 11:1 (1966), p. 79.

2145. Fierz, Heinrich Karl. "Besessenheit durch den Mutterarchetypus." Archetype (see *2166 below), pp. 128-39.

2146. _____. "Klinik und Psychotherapie des Schattens." Prob (see *2129 above), pp. 69-89.

2147. Fodor, Nándor. "Jung's sermons to the dead." Psychoanalytic Rev, 51 (1964), pp. 74-78.

2148. Fordham, Frieda. "The care of regressed patients and the child archetype." <u>JAP</u>, 9:1 (1964), pp. 61-74.

*2149. _____. <u>Inleiding</u> tot <u>de</u> <u>psychologie</u> <u>van</u> <u>Jung</u>. A. J. Blits, trans. Amsterdam: Wereldbibliotheek, 1964. (see 827 above)

2150. Fordham, Michael. "Ego and the self." <u>J</u> <u>of</u> <u>Psychology</u> (Lahore), 1:1 (1964), np.

2151. _____. "The theory of archetypes as applied to child development." <u>Archetype</u> (see *2166 below), pp. 48-62.

2152. _____. "Well-motivated parents: the importance of the environment in the therapy of a schizophrenic child." <u>JAP</u>, 9:2 (1964), pp. 163-70.

2153. Frank, Margit van Leight. "The adoration of the complex." <u>Archetype</u> (see *2166 below), pp. 209-19.

2154. Franz, Marie Louise von. "Conclusion: science and the unconscious." In C. G. Jung et al. <u>Man</u> <u>and</u> <u>his</u> <u>symbols</u>. New York: Doubleday, 1964, pp. 304-10.

*2155. _____. <u>Dealing</u> <u>with</u> <u>evil</u> <u>in</u> <u>fairy</u> <u>tales</u>. Zurich: 1964.

2156. _____. "Peter Birkhäuser: a modern artist who strikes a new path." <u>Spring</u> 1964, pp. 33-46.

2157. _____. "The process of individuation." In <u>Symbols</u> (see *2154 above), pp. 158-229.

2158. _____. "Religiöse oder magische Einstellung zum Unbewußten." <u>Prob</u> (see *2129 above), pp. 39-68.

2159. _____. "Über religiöse Hintergründe des Puer-Aeternus-Probleme." <u>Archetype</u> (see *2166 below), pp. 141-56. (see 2357 below for English edition)

2160. Fraser, Jessie E. "ARAS: Archive for Research in Archetypal Symbolism." <u>Spring</u> 1964, pp. 60-67.

2161. Friedman, Paul and Goldstein, J. "Comments on the psychology of C. G. Jung." <u>Psychoanalytic</u> <u>Q</u>, 33:2 (1964), pp. 194-225.

*2162. Gebsettel, Victor Emil. <u>Imago</u> <u>Hominis:</u> <u>Beiträge</u> <u>zu</u> <u>einer</u> <u>personalen</u> <u>Anthropologie</u>. Schweinfurt: Neues Forum, 1964.

*2163. Goldbrunner, Josef. <u>Cure</u> <u>of</u> <u>mind</u>, <u>cure</u> <u>of</u> <u>soul:</u> <u>depth</u> <u>psychology</u> <u>and</u> <u>pastoral</u> <u>care</u>. Notre Dame, Ind.: University of Notre Dame Press, 1964. (see *1049 above for German edition)

*2164. _____. <u>Holiness</u> <u>and</u> <u>wholeness</u> <u>and</u> <u>other</u> <u>essays</u>. Notre Dame, Ind.: University of Notre Dame Press, 1964. (see *541 above for German and list of other editions)

138

*2165. _____. Individuation: a study of the depth psychology of C.
G. Jung. S. Godman, trans. Notre Dame, Ind.: University of
Notre Dame Press, 1964. (see *542 above for German and list of
other editions)

*2166. Guggenbühl-Craig, Adolf, ed. Der Archetyp / The archetype.
Basel and New York: Karger, 1964.
        Rev. Mary Williams. JAP, 10:2 (1965), pp. 196-97.

2167. Hannah, Barbara. "The animus in Charlotte Brontë's 'Strange e-
vents'." Harv, 10 (1964), pp. 1-12.

2168. _____. "Regression oder Erneuerung im Alter." Prob (see
*2129 above), pp. 175-206.

2169. Hawkey, Lawry. "The therapeutic factor in child analysis." Archetype (see *2166 above), pp. 119-27.

2170. Henderson, Joseph L. "Ancient myths and modern man." Symbols
(see *2185 below), pp. 104-57.

2171. _____. "The archetype of culture." Archetype (see *2166 a-
bove), pp. 3-15.

2172. Heydt, Vera von der. On the animus. London: GofPP Lecture #
126, July 1964.

2173. Hillman, James. Betrayal. London: GofPP Lecture # 128, Dec.
1964. (see 2279 and 3543 below)

*2174. _____. Suicide and the soul. London: Hodder and Staughton,
1964; New York: Harper and Row, 1964/1965. (see below, *2369
for German and *3654 for English editions)
        Rev. Rosemary Gordon. JAP, 10:2 (1965), pp. 198-99.
        Gwen Mountford. Harv, 11 (1965), pp. 80-81.

2175. Hobson, Robert F. "Group dynamics and analytical psychology."
JAP, 9:1 (1964), pp. 23-50.

2176. Holton, Gerald. "Stil und Verwirklichung in der Physik." EJ, 33
(1964), pp. 319-65.

2177. Jackson, Murray. "The importance of depression emerging in a
therapeutic group." JAP, 9:1 (1964), pp. 51-60.

2178. _____. "Symbol formation and the delusional transference."
Archetype (see *2166 above), pp. 30-47. (see 2031 above)

2179. Jacobi, Jolande. "Ein Fall von Schreibkrampf." Prob (see *2129
above), pp. 89-124.

*2180. _____. La psychologie de C. G. Jung. V. Baillods, trans.
Geneva: Editions du Mont Blanc, 1964. (see *255 above for
German and list of other editions)

139

2181. _____. "Das Religiöse in den Malereien von seelischen Lei-
denden." In Neurose und Religion (see *2210 below), pp. 65-
94.

2182. _____. "Symbols in an individual analysis." Symbols (see
*2185 below), pp. 272-303.

2183. _____. "Symbolism in the visual arts." Ibid., pp. 230-71.
(see 2600 below for German edition)

2184. Jung, Albert. "Psychologie vegetativer Neurosen." Archetype
(see *2166 above), pp. 157-81.

*2185. Jung, Carl Gustav, et al. Man and his symbols. London: Aldus
books; New York: Doubleday, 1964.
Rev. William Kraemer. JAP, 11:1 (1966), p. 78.

*2186. Kadinsky, David. Die Entwicklung des Ich beim Kinde. Ein Bei-
trag zur analytischen Kinderpsychologie. Bern and Stuttgart:
Hans Huber, 1964.
Rev. H. J. Wilke. ZAP, 2:4 (1971), p. 253.

2187. Kalff, Dora M. "Archetypus als heilender Faktor." Archetype
(see *2166 above), pp. 182-200.

2188. Kawai, Hayao. The figure of the sun goddess in Japanese mythology. (Diploma thesis). CGJI, Zürich, 1964.

2189. Keppe, N. R. "Schools of clinical psychology. 3. Carl Gustav
Jung's analytical psychology." (in Portugese) Arquivos de
ciurgia clinical e experimental, 27 (1964), pp. 210-12.

2190. Kermode. F. "That time, this time." New Statesman, 68 (16
Oct. 1964), pp. 578-79.

2191. Kirsch, James. "The sleep-walking scene in Macbeth." Harv, 10
(1964), pp. 80-91.

2192. Kluger, H Yechezkel. "On the archetype as a prognostic factor."
Archetype (see *2166 above), pp. 95-103.

2193. Leeuw, Gerardus van der. "Immortality." PEY V (see *2130 a-
bove), pp. 353-70. (see 646 above for German edition)

2194. Marshak, Mildred D. "The significance of the patient in the
training of analysts: observations on Harold Stone's paper."
(see 2220 below) JAP, 9:1 (1964), pp. 80-84.

2195. Meier, Fritz. "The transformation of man in mystical Islam."
PEY V (see *2130 above), pp. 37-68. (see 936 above for German
edition)

2196. Melhado, Julian J. Exploratory studies in symbolism. (Doctoral
dissertation). University of Texas, 1964.

2197. Metman, Philip. "Chakra-symbolism and analytical therapy." Archetype (see *2166 above), pp. 220-24.

2198. Michel, Rudolf. "Pictures in analytical psychology." Spring 1964, pp. 68-73.

2199. Moreno, Mario. "The therapeutic factor in agoraphobia." Archetype (see *2166 above), pp. 201-08.

2200. Moscu, I. "Considérations sur la psychologie des profondeurs." Rev Psichol Rom, 10:4 (1964), pp. 331-43.

2201. Mountford, Gwen. "Love and power in personal relations." Harv, 10 (1964), pp. 66-79.

2202. O'Meara, Thomas Aquinas. "Marian theology and the contemporary problem of myth." Marian Studies, 15 (1964), pp. 127-56.

2203. Plaut, Albert B. J. "On some relations between psychotherapy and analysis." Archetype (see *2166 above), pp. 225-32.

2204. Portmann, Adolf. "Die Idee der Evolution als Schicksal von Charles Darwin." EJ, 33 (1964), pp. 365-406.

2205. _____. "Metamorphosis in animals: the transformation of the individual and the type." PEY V (see *2130 above), pp. 297-325. (see 950 above for German edition)

2206. Progoff, Ira. "The integrity of life and death." EJ, 33 (1964), pp. 201-44.

2207. Read, Herbert. "High noon and darkest night: some reflections on Ortega y Gasset's philosophy of art." Ibid., pp. 51-70.

2208. Rieff, Philip. "C. G. Jung's confession: psychology as a language of faith." Encounter, 22 (May 1964), pp. 45-50.

2209. Rudin, Josef. "C. G. Jung und die Religion." Orientierung, 28 (1964), pp. 238-42. (see 2315 below)

*2210. _____. Neurose und Religion. Krankheitsbilder und ihre Problematik. Olten: Walter, 1964.

2211. _____. "Psychotherapie und religiöse Glaube." In Neurose (see *2210 above), pp. 65-94.

2212. Rüsche, Franz. "Über ein bedeutsames Buch zum Thema 'C. G. Jung und die Religion'." Theologie und Glaube, 54 (1964), pp. 81-90.

*2213. Sas, Stephen. Der Hinkende als Symbol. St ad CGJIZ XV. Zurich: Rascher, 1964.

2214. Scholem, Gershom G. "Das Ringen zwischen dem biblischen Gott und dem Gott Plotins in der alten Kabbala." <u>EJ</u>, 33 (1964), pp. 9-50.

2215. Seifert, Friedrich. "Gut und Böse als Antinomie und als Polarität." <u>Archetype</u> (see *2166 above), pp. 63-80.

*2216. Serrano, Miguel. <u>El Circulo Hermético</u>. Santiago, Chile: Zig-Zag, 1964. (see *2404 below for English edition)

2217. Smith, G. M. "Dreams are messages from the other side." <u>Gateway</u>, 4:5 (1964), pp. 75-76, 83-85.

*2218. Spengler, Ernst. <u>Das Gewissen bei Freud und Jung, mit einer philosophisch-anthropologischen Grundlegung</u>. Zurich: Juris, 1964.

2219. Staerk, M. "Zurich; Jung's library at Küsnacht." <u>Critic</u>, 22 (Dec. 1963-Jan. 1964), p. 70.

2220. Stone, Harold. "Reflections of an ex-trainee on his training." <u>JAP</u>, 9:1 (1964), pp. 75-79.

2221. Strauss, Ruth. "The archetype of separation." <u>Archetype</u> (see *2166 above), pp. 104-12.

2222. Stricker, J. Lawrence, and Ross, John. "An assessment of some structural properties of the Jungian personality typology." <u>J of Abnormal Social Psychology</u>, 68:1 (1964), pp. 62-71.

2223. _____. "Some correlates of a Jungian personality inventory." <u>Psychological Reports</u>, 14:2 (1964), pp. 623-43.

2224. _____. "Some correlates of a Jungian personality inventory." In <u>Research in Clinical Assessment</u>. E. I. Megargee, ed. New York: Harper and Row, 1964, pp. 316-32.

2225. Suzuki, Daisetz T. "The awakening of a new consciousness in Zen." <u>PEY V</u> (see *2130 above), pp. 179-202. (see 963 above for German edition)

2226. Thorburn, John. "The horoscopes of Beethoven." <u>Harv</u>, 10 (1964), pp. 50-64.

2227. Tillich, Paul. "The importance of New Being for Christian theology." <u>PEY V</u> (see *2130 above), pp. 161-78. (see 964 above for German edition)

2228. Uchizono, Roy Saburo. <u>Science and metaphysics in the psychology of C. G. Jung: an interpretation</u>. (Doctoral dissertation). Claremont Graduate School, 1964.

2229. Vasavada, Arvind U. "The place of psychology in philosophy." Presidential address to the 38th session of the Indian Philosophical Congress of Madras, 1964.

2230. Whitmont, Edward C. "Group therapy and analytical psychology." JAP, 9:1 (1964), pp. 1-22.

2231. _____. "Guilt and responsibility." Spring 1964, pp. 4-32.

2232. _____. "The magic dimension of the unconscious." In Dynamic aspects of the psyche: selections from past Springs. New York: APCNY, 1964, pp. 21-49.

2233. Whyte, Lancelot Law. "The growth of ideas." PEY V (see *2130 above), pp. 250-69. (see 967 above)

2234. Wilhelm, Helmut. "Wanderungen des Geistes." EJ, 33 (1964), pp. 177-200.

*2235. Wilson, Katherine. The nightengale and the hawk. London: George Allen and Unwin, 1964.

2236. Zimmer, Heinrich. "Death and rebirth in the light of India." PEY V (see *2130 above), pp. 326-52. (see 244 above for German edition)

2237. _____. "The Hindu view of world history according to the Puranic myths." Spring 1964, pp. 74-96. (see 301 above)

2238. Zuckerkandl, Victor. "Kreis und Pfeil im Werk Beethovens." EJ, 33 (1964), pp. 285-318.

1965

2239. Aylward, James C. "Health and conscience." Spectrum (see *2266 below), pp. 109-30.

2240. Barberousse, Eleanor H. An investigation of the variability of eight-grade students' behavioral responses on creative criteria, intelligence, and sociometric choices in relation to their Jungian psychological types. (Ed. D. dissertation). Auburn University, 1965.

2241. Baroni, Christophe. "Dieu est-il mort? De Nietzsche à Jung." Syntheses, 19 (1965), pp. 328-43. (see 2340 below)

2242. Bartmeier, Leo H. "Psychoanalysis and religion." Bull of the Menninger Clinic, 29 (1965), pp. 237-44.

2243. Binswanger, Hilde. "Ego, anima and persona." Harv, 11 (1965), pp. 1-14.

2244. Brann, Henry Walter. "C. G. Jung und Schopenhauer." Schopen-hauer-Jahr, 46 (1965), pp. 76-87.

2245. Brooks, Henry Curtis. "Analytical psychology and the image of God." Andover Newton Q, 6:2 (Nov. 1965), pp. 35-55.

2246. Castillejo, Irene C. de. "Woman's role as mediator." Harv, 11 (1965), pp. 44-58.

2247. Cline, Ronald A. Psychological interpretation of the Theseus myth. (Diploma thesis). CGJI, Zurich, 1965.

2248. Conray, Franklin Melvin. An investigation of the variability of behavioral responses of Jungian psychological types to select educational variables. (Ed. D. dissertation). Auburn University, 1965.

2249. Corbin, Henry. "La configuration du temple de la Ka'ba comme secret de la vie spirituelle." EJ, 34 (1965), pp. 79-166.

2250. Davidson, Dorothy. "A problem of identity in relation to an image of a damaged mother." JAP, 10:1 (1965), pp. 67-76. (see 3208 below)

2251. De Rougemont, Denis. "Le Suisse moyen et quelques autres." Rev de Paris, 72 (1965), pp. 52-64.

2252. Deshaies, M. "Les significations de la psychotherapie." Bull de Psychologie, 18 (16:240) (1965), pp. 934-41; 18 (17:241) (1965), pp. 1063-67.

2253. Diekmann, Hans. "Integration process of the ego-complex in dreams." JAP, 10:1 (1965), pp. 49-66.

2254. Diem, Ernst. "Glossen zur Didaktik." Spectrum (see *2266 below), pp. 229-32.

2255. Dreifuss, Gustav. "A psychological study of circumcision in Judaism." JAP, 10:1 (1965), pp. 23-32.

2256. Durand, Gilbert. "Tâches de l'esprit et impératifs de l'être." EJ, 34 (1965), pp. 303-60.

2257. Edinger, Edward F. "Ralph Waldo Emerson: naturalist of the soul." Spring 1965, pp. 77-99.

*2258. Eliade, Mircea. The two and the one. London: Harvill Press, 1965.
        Rev. Gerhard Adler. JAP, 12:1 (1967), p. 84.

2259. Fernandes, M. A. "The contradictions in 'Jungian' psychotherapy in an informative review for dynamic psychiatry." (in Portu-gese) J Med, 57 (1965), pp. 741-46.

2260. Fierz, Heinrich Karl. "Die verbrecherische Zerstörung der Einheit (zu Emersons 'Uriel')." Spectrum (see *2266 below), pp. 53-58.

2261. Fierz, Markus. "Über den Zufall." Ibid., pp. 97-108.

2262. Fordham, Michael. "The importance of analysing childhood for assimilation of the shadow." JAP, 10:1 (1965), pp. 33-47. (see 3220 below)

2263. Franz, Marie Louise von. "The idea of the macro- and microcosmos in the light of Jungian psychology." Ambix, 13:1 (Feb. 1965), pp. 22-34.

2264. Frey-Rohn, Liliane. "Evil from the psychological point of view." Spring 1965, pp. 5-48. (see 1786 above for German and 2450 below for English editions)

2265. Frey-Wehrlin, C. T. "Ein prophetischer Traum." Spectrum (see *2266 below), pp. 249-52.

*2266. _____. Spectrum Psychologiae: eine Freundesgabe. Zurich: Rascher, 1965.
         Rev. Albert B. J. Plaut. JAP, 11:1 (1966), p. 77

2267. Goldbrunner, Josef. "Die Bedeutung der Tiefenpsychologie für das christliche Leben." In Sprechzimmer und Beichstuhl. Über Religion und Psychologie. Basel: Herder, 1965, pp. 47-56.

2268. Gordon, Rosemary. "The concept of projective identification: an evaluation." JAP, 10:2 (1965), pp. 127-50.

2269. Gregori, Ellen. "C. G. Jung. Absichten und menschliche Grundlagen seines Werkes." Wirklichkeit und Wahrheit, 1 (1965), pp. 12-24.

2270. Griffin, Graeme Maxwell. The self and Jesus Christ. (Doctoral dissertation). Princeton University, 1965.

2271. Guggenbühl-Craig, Adolf. "Youth in trouble and the problem of evil." Andover Newton Q, 57 (1965), p. 3.

*2272. Gut, Gottlieb. Schicksal in Freiheit. Freiburg, Alber, 1965.

2273. Han, Michael. "Jung and the East." Indian Art, (1965), p. 8.

*2274. Harding, M. Esther. The 'I' and the 'Not-I'. New York: Pantheon (Bollingen Series LXXIX), 1965/1973.
         Rev. Amy I. Allenby. JAP, 12:1 (1967), p. 78.

*2275. _____. The parental image, its injury and reconstruction. Forw. by F. Riklin. New York: G. P. Putnam's Sons for the C. G. Jung Foundation, 1965.
         Rev. Hans Diekmann. ZAP, 2:3 (1971), pp. 177-78.

Michael Fordham. <u>JAP</u>, 11:1 (1966), pp. 74-76.
James Kirsch. <u>Contemporary Psychology</u>, 3 (1968), np.
Ruth Tenny. <u>Harv</u>, 11 (1965), pp. 82-83.

2276. Hart, David L. "Owning." <u>Spectrum</u> (see *2266 above), pp. 207-14.

2277. Helwig, Paul. "Die großen Romantiker: Freud, Adler, Jung und ihre Bedeutung für die Tiefenpsychologie in kritischer Betrachtung." <u>Wirklichkeit und Wahrheit</u>, 1 (1965), pp. 24-27.

2278. Hess, Gertrud. "Fröbels mystische Beziehung zur Natur als Folge frükindlichen Verlassenseins." <u>Spectrum</u> (see *2266 above), pp. 71-90.

2279. Hillman, James. "Betrayal." <u>Spring</u> 1965, pp. 57-76. (see 2173 above and 3543 below)

2280. Holt, David. <u>Persona and actor</u>. (Diploma thesis). CGJI, Zurich, 1965.

2281. Holton, Gerald. "The metaphor of space-time events in science." <u>EJ</u>, 34 (1965), pp. 33-78.

2282. Hopper, Stanley Romaine. "Symbolic reality and the poet's task." <u>Ibid</u>., pp. 167-218.

*2283. Jacobi, Jolande. <u>Der Weg zur Individuation</u>. Zurich and Stuttgart: Rascher, 1965. (see *2466 below for English edition)
Rev. Marianne Jacoby. <u>JAP</u>, 12:2 (1967), p. 177.

2284. Jordan, Daniel C. <u>An experimental approach to the Jungian theory of the archetypes</u>. (Doctoral dissertation). University of Chicago, 1965.

2285. Kerényi, Carl. "Grund zur eleusinischen Vision." <u>Spectrum</u> (see *2266 above), pp. 13-16.

2286. Kiesow, Ernst-Rüdiger. "Bemerkungen zu C. G. Jungs Selbstdarstellungen." <u>Wege zum Menschen</u>, 17 (1965), pp. 146-50.

2287. Kirsch, James. "The birth of evil in 'Macbeth'." <u>Spectrum</u> (see *2266 above), pp. 31-52.

2288. Klopfer, Bruno and Spiegelman, J. Marvin. "Some dimensions of psychotherapy." <u>Ibid</u>., pp. 177-84.

2289. Knoll, Max. "Die Welt der inneren Lichterscheinungen." <u>EJ</u>, 34 (1965), pp. 361-98.

2290. Kyle, William. <u>The impact of psychology on pastoral work</u>. London: GofPP Lecture # 131, Aug. 1965.

146

2291. Lacombe, Pierre. "Halloween, the 50-megaton bomb, and the Cuban crisis." JAP, 10:1 (1965), pp. 97-108.

2292. _____. "A note on the acting out of the Halloween myth." Ibid., 10:2 (1965), pp. 187-88.

2293. Lehman, Margaret. Eine Interpretation von Ernst Barbachs Dramen Gestütztauf die Psychologie von C. G. Jung. (Doctoral dissertation). New York University, 1965.

2294. McGlashan, Alan. "Such stuff as dreams." Harv, 11 (1965), pp. 33-43.

*2295. Mc Pherson, Thomas. The philosophy of religion. New York: Van Nostrand, 1965.

2296. Mandler, George. "Subjects to think: a reply to Jung's comments." Psychological Rev, 72:4 (1965), pp. 323-26.

2297. Mann, Ulrich. "Tiefenpsychologie und Theologie." Lutheranische Monatshefte, 4 (1965), pp. 188-92.

2298. Markus, Kate. "Early childhood experiences remembered by adult analysands." JAP, 10:2 (1965), pp. 163-72.

2299. Marjasch, Sonja. "Der Puzelbaum." Spectrum (see *2266 above), pp. 91-96.

2300. Martin, Percival William. "Depth psychology and religious experience." Inward Light, 28:67 (1965), pp. 47-53.

2301. Mattoon, Mary Ann. The New Testament concept of sin as an approach to the shadow. (Diploma thesis). CGJI, Zurich, 1965.

2302. Merkelbach, Rhinhold. "Dis Kosmogonie der Mithrasmysterien." EJ, 34 (1965), pp. 219-58.

2303. Moreno, Mario. "Archetypal foundations in the analysis of women." JAP, 10:2 (1965), pp. 173-86.

2304. Morenz, Sigfried. "Ägyptischer Totenglaube in Rahmen der Struktur ägyptischer Religion." EJ, 34 (1965), pp. 399-446.

2305. Nagel, Hildegard. "That the scriptures might be fulfilled." Spring 1965, pp. 49-56.

2306. Newton, Kathleen. "Mediation of the image of infant-mother togetherness." JAP, 10:2 (1965), pp. 151-62. (see 3286 below)

2307. Nidever, Jack. Communication between ego and non-ego; an exploratory experiment. (Diploma thesis). CGJI, Zurich, 1965.

2308. Ostrowski-Sachs, Margaret. Aus Gesprächen mit C. G. Jung. Zurich: CGJIZ, 1965.

*2309. Pintacuda, Luigi. La psicologia analitica di Karl Jung. Rome: Paoline, 1965.

2310. Portmann, Adolf. "Gestalt als erstes und letztes Problem der Lebensforschung." EJ, 34 (1965), pp. 447-84.

2311. Progoff, Ira. "Form, time and opus: the dialectic of the creative psyche." Ibid., pp. 259-302.

2312. Pye, Faye. "Transformations of the persona." Harv, 11 (1965), pp. 70-79.

2313. Quispel, Gilles. "Das Lied von der Perle." EJ, 34 (1965), pp. 9-32.

2314. Rhally, Miltiade. "Varieties of paranormal cognition." Spectrum (see *2266 above), pp. 253-66.

2315. Rudin, Josef. "C. G. Jung und die Religion." In Psychotherapie und religiöse Erfahrung. Wilhelm Bitter, ed. Stuttgart: Ernst Klett, 1965/1968, pp. 73-86. (see 2209 above)

2316. Sborowitz, Arië. "Freud, Jung und die Möglichkeit einer christlichen Psychotherapie." In Der leidende Mensch: Personale Psychotherapie in anthropologischer Sicht. Darmstadt: Wissenschaftliche Buchgesellschaft, 1965, pp. 62-105.

2317. Schär, Hans. "Gotteserfahrung, Gotteserkenntnis und Seele." Schweiz Theologische Umschau, 35 (1965), pp. 16-28.

2318. Schmid, Karl. "Grundtrauer, und Freudefrömmigkeit." Spectrum (see *2266 above), pp. 59-70.

*2319. Scholem, Gershom G. On the Kabbalah and its symbolism. R. Manheim, trans. London: Routledge and Kegan Paul, 1965. (see *1738 above for German edition)
     Rev. Gerhard Adler. JAP, 12:1 (1967), pp. 84-85.

*2320. Seifert, Frederick and Seifert-Helwig, Rotraut. Bilder und Urbilder, Erscheinungsformen des Archetypus. Munich and Basel: Rienhardt, 1965.
     Rev. Vera von der Heydt. JAP, 12:1 (1967), p. 77.

2321. Seligman, Paul. "Some notes on the collective significance of circumcision and allied practices." JAP, 10:1 (1965), pp. 5-22.

2322. Smart, Frances. "Psychotherapy in men's prisons." Harv, 11 (1965), pp. 15-32.

2323. _____. "Reflections on psychotherapy among prisoners." Spectrum (see *2266 above), pp. 215-28.

2324. Spiegelman, J. Marvin. "Some implications of the transference"

Ibid., pp. 163-76.

2325. Stein, Robert M. "The Oedipus myth and the incest archetype." Ibid., pp. 17-30.

2326. Steiner, Gustav. "Erinnerungen an C. G. Jung." Basler Stadt-buch, 1965, np.

2327. Stone, Harold. "The child: his mind and his imagination." Spectrum (see *2266 above), pp. 185-206.

2328. Thornton, Edward. "Jungian psychology and the Vedanta." Ibid., pp. 131-42.

2329. Trevi, Mario. "L'edizione italiana di Jung." Il Veltro, 2 (1965), np.

2330. Vasavada, Arvind U. "Philosophical roots of the psychotherapies of the West." Spectrum (see *2266 above), pp. 143-54.

*2331. _____. Tripura-rahasya. Varanasi: Chowkhamba Sanskrit Offices, 1965.

2332. Walcott, William O. "The paternity of James Joyce's Stephen Dedalus." JAP, 10:1 (1965), pp. 77-96.

2333. Walter, Emil J. "Das System der Psychologie C. G. Jungs im Lichte seiner 'Autobiographie'." SZP, 24:2 (1965), pp. 123-33.

2334. Wethered, Audrey. "The enigmatic oneness of living being." Harv, 11 (1965), pp. 59-68.

2335. Zacharias, Gerhard. "Zur Rolle des Wiederstandes in der Psycho-therapie." Spectrum (see *2266 above), pp. 155-62.

2336. Zeller, Max. "The phenomenon of a poltergeist in a dream." Ibid., pp. 233-48.

1966

2337. Adler, Gerhard. "A psychological approach to religion." In Studies (see *2338 below), pp. 176-216.

*2338. _____. Studies in analytical psychology. London: Hodder and Stoughton, 1966; New York: G. P. Putnam's Sons for the C. G. Jung Foundation, 1969.

2339. Allenby, Amy I. "The individual in historical perspective."

The Seeker, (Aut. 1966), np.

2340. Baroni, Christophe. "Dieu est-il mort? De Nietzsche à Jung." In Introduction à la psychologie des profondeurs. Lausanne: L'Homme sans Masque, 1966, pp. 76-80. (see 2241 above)

2341. Bennette, Graham. "Some ideas towards an interpretation of cancer in psychological terms." Harv, 12 (1966), pp. 35-70.

2342. Benz, Ernst. "Psychologie et religion chez C. G. Jung." SZP, 25 (1966), pp. 230-35.

2343. Bernet, Walter. "C. G. Jung." In Tendenzen der Theologie im 20. Jahrhundert. Eine Geschichte in Porträts. Stuttgart: Krenz, 1966, pp. 150-55.

2344. Bishop, John Grahm. Jung and Christianity. (Christian Knowledge Booklets, 34). London: Society for Promoting Christian Knowledge, 1966.

*2345. Böhler, Eugen. Der Mythus im Wirtschaft und Wissenschaft. Freiburg: 1966.

2346. Castillejo, Irene C. de. "Difficulties of communication." Harv, 12 (1966), pp. 72-83.

2347. Champernowne, Irene and Lewis, E. "Psychodynamics of therapy in a residential group." JAP, 11:2 (1966), pp. 163-80.

2348. Corbin, Henry. "De l'epopée heroïque a l'epopée mystique." EJ, 35 (1966), pp. 177-241.

*2349. Dale-Green, Patricia. Dog. London: Rupert Hart-Davis, 1966.

2350. Davidson, Dorothy, "Transference as a form of active imagination." JAP, 11:2 (1966), pp. 135-46.

*2351. Diekmann, Hans. Märchen und Träume als Helfer des Menschen. Stuttgart: 1966.

2352. Durand, Gilbert. "La création artistique comme configuration dynamique des structures." EJ, 35 (1966), pp. 57-98.

2353. Edinger, Edward F. "Christ as paradigm of the individuating ego." Spring 1966, pp. 5-23.

*2354. _____. Christ as paradigm of the individuating ego. New York: Spring Pubs., 1966.

2355. Fordham, Michael. "Is God supernatural? Freud, Jung and the theologian." Theology, 69 (1966), pp. 386-96.

*2356. Franz, Marie Louise von. Arora consurgens; a document attributed to Thomas Aquinas on the problem of opposites in alchemy.

R. F. C. Hull and A. S. B. Glover, trans. New York: Pantheon
(Bollingen Series LXXVII), 1966.
Rev. P. Seligman, _JAP_, 13:1 (1968), pp. 77-80.

2357. _____. "Religious aspects in the background of the puer aeternus problem." _Harv_, 12 (1966), pp. 4-15. (see 2159 above)

2358. _____. "Time and synchronicity in analytic psychology." In
Voices of time. Jessie T. Fraser, ed. New York: George Braziller, 1966, pp. 218-32.

2359. Fraser, Jessie E. "Heracles: an introduction with illustrations." _Spring_ 1966, pp. 24-38.

2360. Friedman, Maurice. "Jung's image of psychological man." _Psy-
choanalytic Rev_, 53 (1966), pp. 595-608. (see 2451 below)

2361. Frye, Northrup. "Archetypes of literature." In _Myth and literature. Contemporary theory and practice_. Lincoln, Neb.: University of Nebraska Press, 1966, pp. 87-97.

2362. Gantner, Joseph. "'L'immagine de Cuor.' Die vorgestaltenden
Formen der Phantasie und ihre Auswirkung in der Kunst." _EJ_,
35 (1966), pp. 267-302.

*2363. Goldbrunner, Josef. _Individuation_. Freiburg: Erich Wewel Ver-
lag, 1966. (see *542 above for complete list of other editions)

*2364. _____. _Realization: anthropology of pastoral care_. Notre
Dame Ind.: University of Notre Dame Press, 1966.

2365. Gorlow, Leon; Simonson, Norman R. and Krauss, Herbert. "An empirical investigation of Jungian typology." _Brit J of Social
and Clinical Psychology_, 5:2 (1966), pp. 108-17.

2366. Herzog, Edgar. "Der Beitrag der Tiefenpsychologie zum Verstehen
frümenschlichen religiösen Erlebens." In _Transzendenz als Er-
fahrung_. M. Hippius, ed. Wielheim Obb.: Otto Wilhelm, 1966.

2367. Heydt, Vera von der. _Modern myth_. London: GofPP Lecture #
135, Aug. 1966.

2368. Hillman, James. "On psychological creativity." _EJ_, 35 (1966),
pp. 349-410.

*2369. _____. _Selbstmord und seelische Wandlung_. H. Binswanger,
trans. Zurich: Rascher, 1966. (see *2174 above for English
edition)

2370. _____. "Towards the archetypal model for the masturbation
inhibition." _JAP_, 11:1 (1966), pp. 49-77. (see 2585 and 3555
below)

*2371. Hochheimer, Wolfgang. _Die Psychotherapie von C. G. Jung_. Bern

and Stuttgart: Huber, 1966. (see *2703 above for English edition)
Rev. Marianne Jacoby. JAP, 12:2 (1967), p. 179.

2372. Howes, E. B. "Contribution of Dr. C. G. Jung to our religious situation and the contemporary scene." Pastoral Psychology, 17:161 (Feb. 1966), pp. 35-46.

2373. Hubback, Judith. "VII sermones ad mortuos." JAP, 11:1 (1966), pp. 95-111.

2374. Jacobi, Jolande. "Jungs analytische Psychologie." In Handbuch der Psychologie. David and Rosa Katz, eds. Stuttgart: Bruno Schwabe, 1966, pp. 451-62.

2375. Kellogg, Rhoda. "Stages in the development of pre-school art." In Child art: the beginnings of self-affirmation. H. P. Lewis, ed. Berkeley, Calif.: Deablo Press, 1966, pp. 19-24.

*2376. Kirsch, James. Shakespeare's royal self. New York: G. P. Putnam's Sons for the C. G. Jung Foundation, 1966.
Rev. Ruth Tenny. Harv, 12 (1966), p. 84.

2377. Kling, L. C. "Archetypische Symbolik und Synchronizitäten im aktuellen Weltgesehen." Verborgene Welt, 4 (1965-66), np.

2378. Koplik, Irwin, Jay. Jung's psychology in the plays of O'Neill. (Doctoral dissertation). New York University, 1966.

2379. Kraemer, William P. Psychology and religion. GofPP Lecture # 136, July 1966.

2380. Lebovici, S. "Freud et Jung." La psychiatrie de l'enfant, 9:1 (1966), pp. 223-49.

2381. Looser, Günther. "Jung's childhood dream." Spring 1966, pp. 76-80.

2382. McGlashan, Alan. "Dreams: dark messenger of light." Harper's Bazaar, (Jan. 1966), pp. 120, 159.

*2383. Mahoney, Maria F. The meaning in dreams and dreaming; the Jungian viewpoint. New York: Citadel Press, 1966.
Rev. Ruth Tenny. Harv, 13 (1967), p. 82.

2384. Marjasch, Sonja. "On the dream psychology of C. G. Jung." In The dream and human societies. G. E. von Grunegaum, ed. Berkeley and Los Angeles: University of California Press, 1966, np.

2385. _____. "The 'I' in dreams." Spring 1966, pp. 60-75. (see 2048 above)

2386. Meier, Carl Alfred. "The dream in ancient Greece and its use

152

in temple cures." (see 2384 above)

2387. Merkelbach, Reinhold. "Inhalt und Form in symbolischen Erzäh-
       lungen der Antike." EJ, 35 (1966), pp. 145-76.

2388. Neumann, Erich. "Narcissism, normal self-formation, and the
       primary relation to the mother." Spring 1966, pp. 81-106.
       (see 1139 above for German edition)

2389. Paulsen, Alma A. "The spirit Mercury in relation to the indivi-
       duation process." Ibid., pp. 107-20. (see 2626 below)

*2390. Perry, John Weir. Lord of the Four Quarters; myths of the
       royal father. New York: George Braziller, 1966.
              Rev. Gerhard Adler. JAP, 12:2 (1967), p. 178.

2391. _____. "Reflections on the nature of the kingship archetype."
       JAP, 11:2 (1966), pp. 147-62.

2392. Portmann, Adolf. "Ursprung und Entwicklung als Problem der Bi-
       ologie." EJ, 35 (1966), pp. 411-40.

2393. Progoff, Ira. "The man who transforms consciousness: the inner
       myths of Martin Buber, Paul Tillich, and C. G. Jung." Ibid.,
       pp. 99-144.

2394. Quispel, Gilles. "Faust: symbol of Western man." Ibid., pp.
       241-66.

2395. Read, Herbert. "Art as a unifying principle in education." In
       Child art (see 2375 above), pp. 1-18.

2396. Redfearn, J. W. T. "The patient's experience of his 'mind'."
       JAP, 11:1 (1966), pp. 1-20.

2397. Rorarius, Winfried. "Der archetypische Gott. Über Verhältnis
       von Glauben und Psychotherapie bei Freud und Jung." Zeitwende,
       37 (1966), pp. 368-81.

2398. Ross, John. "The relationship between a Jungian personality in-
       ventory and tests, ability, personality and interest." Austra-
       lian J of Psychology, 18:1 (1966), pp. 1-17.

2399. Sambursky, Schmuel. "Phänomen und Theorie. Das Physikalische
       Denken der Antike im Licht der modernen Physik." EJ, 35 (1966),
       pp. 303-48.

*2400. Sanford, John A. Gottes vergessene Sprache. St ad CGJIZ XIII.
       Zurich and Stuttgart: Rascher, 1966. (see *2639 below for
       English edition)

*2401. Schär, Hans. Religion and the cure of souls in Jung's psycholo-
       gy. New York: Schocken Books, 1966. (see *423 above for Ger-
       man and *670 for English editions)

2402. Scholem, Gershom G. "Martin Bubers Auffassung des Judentums."
EJ, 35 (1966), pp. 9-56.

2403. Scott, Thomas A. "Jung and Piaget: a study in relationships."
In Contemporary studies in social psychology and behavioral
change. J. L. Philbrick, ed. New York: Selected Academic
Readings, 1966.

*2404. Serrano, Miguel. C. G. Jung and Hermann Hesse. A record of two
friendships. F. McShane, trans. London: Routledge and Kegan
Paul; New York: Schocken Books, 1966. (see *2216 above for
Spanish edition)
        Rev. Unsigned. Choice, 4 (March 1976), p. 30
             Unsigned, N Y Times Book Rev, (12 June 1966), p.
             29.

2405. Stansfiel, James D. The Jungian typology, neuroticism and
field-dependence. (Doctoral dissertation). Duke University,
1966.

2406. Stein, Leopold. "In pursuit of first principles." With comments by Rosemary Gordon, Michael Fordham, and John Layard.
JAP, 11:1 (1966), pp. 21-48.

2407. Swinn, Richard M. "Jungian personality typology and color dreaming." Psychiatric Q, 40:4 (1966), pp. 659-66.

*2408. Uhsadel, Walter. Evangelische Seelsorge. Heidelberg: Quelle
und Meyer, 1966.
        Rev. G. Hummel, ZAP, 1:2 (1970), p. 48.

2409. Vidal, Guillermo. "Individuación y alienación." Proc IV World
Congress of Psychiatry, 1966, pp. 1522-24.

*2410. Wallace, Anthony F. C. Religion: an anthropological view. New
Nork: Random House, 1966.

2411. White, Victor. "Good and evil." Harv, 12 (1966), pp. 16-34.

2412. Whitmont, Edward C. "The role of the ego in the life drama."
Spring 1966, pp. 39-59.

*2413. Wickes, Frances G. The inner world of childhood: a study in
analytical psychology. Intro. by C. G. Jung. New York: Ap-
pleton-Century-Crofts, 1966. (see *48 above for list of other
editions)

2414. Ziegler, A. "Der Beitrag der analytischen Psychologie C. G.
Jungs zur Psychosomatik." Therapeutische Umschau und Medizinische Bibliographie, 23 (1966), pp. 251-55.

*2415. Zunini, Giorgio. Homo religiosus. Milan: Il Saggiatore, 1966.
(see *2762 below for English edition)

2416. Adler, Gerhard. "Methods of treatment in analytical psychology." In Psychoanalytic techniques. Benjamin B. Wolman, ed. New York: Basic Books, 1967, pp. 338-78. (see 2526 below)

*2417. Aigrisse, Gilberte. Psychothérapie analytique. Paris: Editions Universitaires, 1967.
    Rev. M. J. Dicks-Mireaux. JAP, 13:2 (1968), p. 173.

2418. Alex, William. An analytic approach to schizophrenia. (Diploma thesis). CGJI, Zurich, 1967.

2419. Allenby, Amy I. "The life of the spirit and the life of today." Harv, 13 (1967), pp. 18-29.

2420. Assagioli, Roberto. "Jung and psychosynthesis." Psychosynthesis research foundation, 1967, no. 19. (see 3341 below)

2421. Ball, Espy Daniel. A factor analytic investigation of the personality typology of C. G. Jung. (Doctoral dissertation). Pennsylvania State University, 1967.

2422. Barz, Helmut. Die altkirchliche Taufe: Versuch einer psychologischen Interpretation. (Diploma thesis). CGJI, Zurich, 1967.

2423. _____. "Fragen der Tiefenpsychologie an die Kirche." In Was weiss man von der Seele? Hans Jürgen Schultz, ed. Stuttgart, Krenz, pp. 186-94.

*2424. Baudouin, Charles. La obra de Jung y la psicología de los complejos. B. Garces, trans. Madrid: Gredos, 1967. (see *1970 above for French edition)

2425. Beach, Brewster, Y. Jung and Tillich; a critical appraisal. (M. A. thesis). Drew University, 1967.

*2426. Bennet, Edward Armstrong. Che cosa ha veramente detto Jung. F. Cardelli, trans. Rome: Ubaldini, 1967. (see below, *2427 for English and *2533 for French editions)

*2427. _____. What Jung really said. New York: Schocken Books, 1967, (see *2426 above for Italian and *2533 below for French editions)
    Rev. George Adelman. Library J, 92 (15 Sept. 1967), p. 3049.
    Unsigned. Choice, 46 (Feb. 1968), p. 1446.

2428. Bennette, Graham. "A psychological interpretation of cancer: psychological aspects." Harv, 13 (1967), pp. 1-17.

2429. Bernet, Walter. "Fragen der Theologie an der Tiefenpsychologie." In Seele (see 2423 above), pp. 195-202.

2430. Beyme, F. "Archetypal dreams and frigidity." With comments by A. B. J. Plaut and C. B. Blakemore and replies by the author. JAP, 12:1 (1967), pp. 3-22.

2431. Broadribb, Donald. "An analytic approach to biblical mythology." Milla wa-Milla; the Australian Bull of Comparative Religion, (7 Dec. 1967), pp. 31-40.

*2432. Brome, Vincent. Freud and his early circle. New York: William Morrow, 1967.

*2433. CGJIZ, ed. Evil. R. Manheim and H. Nagel, trans. Evanston, Ill.: Northwestern University Press, 1967.

2434. Campbell, Ruth. "Violence in adolescence." JAP, 12:2 (1967), pp. 161-74.

2435. Corbin, Henry. "Face de Dieu et face de l'homme." EJ, 36 (1967), pp. 165-228.

2436. Cox, David. Psychology and Christianity. London: GofPP Lecture # 141, June 1967.

2437. Delfgaauw, Bernard. "Gregor von Nazianz: Antiker und christlicher Denken." EJ, 36 (1967), pp. 113-64.

2438. Diekmann, Hans. "Zum Aspekt des Grausamen im Märchen." Praxis Kinderpsychologie, 16 (1967), p. 8.

2439. Drake, C. C. "Jung and his critics." J Amer Folklore, 80 (Oct. 1967), pp. 321-33.

2440. Duddington, Alexander. "Group-relationship and the transcendent." Harv, 13 (1967), pp. 61-79.

2441. Durand, Gilbert. "Les structures polarisantes de la conscience psychique et de la culture." EJ, 36 (1967), pp. 269-300.

2442. Edinger, Edward F. "On being an individual." Spring 1967, pp. 65-85.

2443. Eliade, Mircea. "Mythes de combat et de repos. Dyads et polarités." EJ, 36 (1967), pp. 59-112.

2444. Eschenbach, Helmut W. "Studie zur Psychologie C. G. Jungs: ein Erfassungsmodell." Landarzt, 43:28 (1967), pp. 1353-61.

*2445. Fabricius, Johannes. Drommens virkelighed. Freud og Jung. Copenhagen: Arnold Busck, 1967.

*2446. _____. The unconscious and Mr. Eliot. Copenhagen: Arnold

Busck, 1967.

2447. Fordham, Michael. "Active imagination--deintegration or disintegration." _JAP_, 12:1 (1967), pp. 51-66.

2448. _____. _Psychiatry: its definition and its practice._ London: GofPP Lecture # 140, May 1967.

2449. Franz, Marie Louise von. "The problem of evil in fairy tales." _Evil_ (see *2433 above), pp. 83-121. (see 1672 above)

2450. Frey-Rohn, Liliane. "Evil from the psychological point of view." _Ibid._, pp. 151-200. (see 1786 above for German and 2264 below for English editions)

2451. Friedman, Maurice. "Jung's image of psychological man." In _To deny our nothingness: contemporary images of man._ London: Victor Gollancz, 1967, pp. 146-67. (see 2360 above)

2452. Gilen, Leonhard. "Das Unbewußte und die Religion nach C. G. Jung. Zugleich ein Beitrag zur Religionspsychologie des Modernismus." _Theologie und Philosophie_, 42 (1967), pp. 481-506.

2453. Gordon, Rosemary. "Symbols: content and process." _JAP_, 12:1 (1967), pp. 23-34. (see 2563 and 3231 below)

*2454. Hanna, Charles Bartruff. _The face of the deep: the religious ideas of C. G. Jung._ Philadelphia: Westminster, 1967.
     Rev. Shildes Johnson. _Library J_, 92 (15 March 1967), p. 1163.
     M. Welch. _JAP_, 13:2 (1968), p. 172.
     Unsigned. _Choice_, 5 (March 1968), p. 38.

2455. Hannah, Barbara. "The healing influence of active imagination in 9 specific cases of neurosis." Zurich: Privately printed, 1967.

*2456. Henderson, Joseph L. _Threshholds of initiation._ Middletown, Conn.: Wesleyan University Press, 1967.
     Rev. Michael Fordham. _JAP_, 13:2 (1968), pp. 161-63.

*2457. Herzog, Edgar. _Psyche and death._ D. Cox and E. Rolfe, trans. New York: G. P. Putnam's Sons for the C. G. Jung Foundation, 1967. (see *1680 above for German edition)

2458. Heuscher, Julius E. "Mythologic and fairy tale themes in psychotherapy." _Amer J of Psychotherapy_, 21:3 (1967), pp. 655-65.

*2459. Hillman, James. _Insearch: psychology and religion._ London: Hodder and Stoughton; New York: Scribner's, 1967.
     Rev. Kenneth Lambert. _JAP_, 13:2 (1968), pp. 164-65.

2460. _____. "Preface ." _Evil_ (see *2433 above).

2461.   _____. "Preface." Satan (see *2510 below).

2462.   _____. "A psychological commentary." The evolutionary energy in man. Gopi Krishna. New Delhi and London: Watkins; Berkeley: Shambala, 1967/1970.

2463.   _____. "Senex and puer: an aspect of the historical and
psychological present." EJ, 36 (1967), pp. 301-61. (see 3111
below)

2464. Hoffman, Helmut. "Die Polaritätslehre des späten Buddhismus."
Ibid., pp. 361-78.

2465. Izutsu, Toshihiku. "The absolute and the perfect man in Taoism."
Ibid., pp. 379-442.

*2466. Jacobi, Jolande. The way of individuation. R. F. C. Hull, trans.
London: Hodder and Stoughton; New York: Harcourt, Brace and
World, 1967. (see *2283 above for German and list of other e-
ditions)
          Rev. Edward F. Edinger. Library J, 92 (15 March 1967),
               p. 1169.
               Unsigned. N. Y. Times Book Rev, (20 Aug. 1967), p.
               16.

2467. Jacoby, Mario. "Das Tier im Traum." Studium Generale, 20:3
(1967), pp. 139-48.

2468. Jaffé, Aniela. "C. G. Jung and parapsychology." In Science
and ESP. J. R. Smythies, ed. London: Routledge and Kegan
Paul; New York: Humanities Press, 1967. (see 1691 above for
German edition)

2469.   _____. "The influence of alchemy on the work of C. G. Jung."
Spring 1967, pp. 7-25.

*2470.   _____. Der Mythus vom Sinn. Zurich: Rascher, 1967. (see
*2825 for Dutch and *2977 for English editions)
          Rev. M. Jacoby. JAP, 13:1 (1968), p. 80.

2471. Jahoda, G. "Jung's meaningful coincidences." Philosophical J,
4:1 (1967), pp. 35-42.

2472. Johnston, William. "Zen and Christian mysticism: a comparison
in psychological structure." Inter Philosophical Q, 7 (1967),
pp. 441-69.

2473. Jordens, J. "Prana and libido." J Indian Academy of Philosophy, 6 (1967), pp. 32-44.

2474. Jung, Emma. "Interpreting animus images." Inward Light, 30:72
(Fall 1967), pp. 27-29.

*2475. Kalff, Dora M. Sandspiel: seine therapeutische Wirkung auf die

158

Psyche. Zurich and Stuttgart: Rascher, 1967. (see *2982 below for English edition)
      Rev. Marianne Jacoby. JAP, 12:2 (1967), p. 179

2476. Kalsched, Donald E. Hesse's Demian as an example of the individuation process. (B. Div. dissertation). Union Theological Seminary, 1967.

*2477. Kaune, Fritz Jürgen. Selbstverwicklung: eine Konfrontation der Psychologie C. G. Jungs mit der Ethik. Munich and Basel: Ernst Reinhardt, 1967.

*2478. Kerényi, Carl. Eleusis: archetypal image of mother and daughter. R. Manheim, trans. New York: Pantheon (Bollingen Series LXV), 1967. (see *1912 above for German edition)
      Rev. Joseph L. Henderson. JAP, 13:2 (1968), p. 171.

2479. _____. "The problem of evil in mythology." Evil (see *2433 above), pp. 1-18. (see 1806 above for German edition)

2480. Kirsch, Thomas B. "Psychiatry and religion." J of Religion and Health, 6 (1967), pp. 74-79.

2481. Kraemer, William P. "Guilt--a reality." Harv, 13 (1967), pp. 49-60.

2482. _____. et al. "Symposium on Jung's greatest contribution." Ibid., pp. 36-48.

*2483. Lecourt, Jacques. Carl Gustav Jung et Pierre Teilhard de Chardin: leur combat pour la santé de l'âme. Dammartin-en-Goele: Institut Coue, 1967/1970.

2484. Löwith, Karl. "The philosophical concept of good and evil." Evil (see *2433 above), pp. 227-50. (see 1818 above for German edition)

2485. Maag, Victor. "The antichrist as a symbol of evil." Ibid., pp. 57-82. (see 1819 above for German edition)

2486. McGlashan, Alan. "Man and his bomb." Harv, 13 (1967), pp. 30-34.

2487. Mahler, Margaret Schoenberger. "On human symbiosis and the vicissitudes of individuation." J Amer Psychoanalytic Assoc, 15 (1967), pp. 740-63.

2488. Mann, Ulrich. "Quaternität bei C. G. Jung." Theologische Literatur-Zeitung, 92 (1967), pp. 331-36.

2489. _____. "Symbole und tiefenpsychologische Gestaltungsfaktoren der Religion." In Grenzfragen des Glaubens. Charlotte Hörgl and Fritz Rauh, eds. Zurich: Benzinger, 1967, pp. 153-75.

2490. Marshall, I. N. "Extraversion and libido in Jung and Cattell."
       JAP, 12:2 (1967), pp. 115-36.

*2491. Meier, Carl Alfred. Ancient incubation and modern psychotherapy.
        M. Curtius, et al., trans. Evanston, Ill.: Northwestern Uni-
        versity Press, 1967. (see *569 above for German edition)
                Rev. Michael Fordham. JAP, 15:2 (1970), pp. 192-94.

2492. Meyerhoff, Hilde. "Klee and the pine tree." Spring 1967, pp.
       55-64.

2493. Moreno, Antonio. "Jung's collective unconscious." Laval Théo-
       logique Philosophique, 23 (1967), pp. 175-96.

2494. _____. "Jung's ideas on religion." Thomist, 31 (1967), pp.
       282-320.

*2495. Moreno, Mario. Conscio collettivo e inconscio collettivo.
        Rome: Centro Italiano di Psicologia Analitico, 1967.

2496. _____. "Collective conscious and collective unconscious in
       the genesis of neurosis." Psychotherapeutica Psychosomatica,
       15 (1967), p. 48.

2497. _____. "Il problema della donna nel mondo contemporaneo."
       Clin Psichiat, 1 (1967), np.

2498. _____. "Prospettive della psicologia analitica per una psi-
       coterapia breve." Riv Psichiatria, 2 (1967), pp. 488-91.

2499. Paulsen, Alma A. "Introduction." Jung's contribution to our
       time. New York: C. P. Putnam's Sons for the C. G. Jung Foun-
       dation, 1967.

2500. Paulsen, Lola. "The unimaginable touch of time." JAP, 12:1
       (1967), pp. 35-50. (see 3292 below)

2501. Portmann, Adolf. "Dualität der Geschlechten: Einheit und Viel-
       falt." EJ, 36 (1967), pp. 443-78.

*2502. Pratt, Jane Abbott. Consciousness and sacrifice: an interpreta-
        tion of two episodes in the Indian myth of Manu. New York:
        APCNY, 1967.

*2503. Progoff, Ira. La psicologia de C. G. Jung y su significacion.
        Buenos Aires: Paidós, 1967. (see *861 above for English edi-
        tion)

2504. _____. "The psychology of Lee Harvey Oswald: a Jungian ap-
       proach." J of Individual Psychology, 23:1 (1967), pp. 37-47.

2505. Quispel, Gilles. "Das ewige Ebenbild des Menschen. Zur Begeg-
       nung mit dem Selbst in der Gnosis." EJ, 36 (1967), pp. 9-30.

2506. Read, Herbert. "C. G. Jung und seine Psychologie." Universitas, 22:2 (1967), pp. 133-41.

2507. Riukas, Stanley. God: myth, symbol and reality. A study of
Jung's psychology. (Doctoral dissertation). New York University, 1967.

2508. Sager, Nejama. "Inmutabilidad y mutabilidad del símbolo: plan-
teo para una comprehensión semilógica del simbolo de Jung."
Rev de Psicología, 4 (1967), pp. 93-104.

2509. Sambursky, Schmuel. "Antithetische Elemente in Natur und Natur-
erkenntnis." EJ, 36 (1967), pp. 229-68.

*2510. Schärf-Kluger, Rivkah. Satan in the Old Testament. Evanston,
Ill.: Northwestern University Press, 1967.
Rev. Rosemary Gordon. JAP, 13:2 (1968), p. 173.

2511. Schlappner, Martin. "Evil in the cinema." Evil (see *2433 a-
bove), pp. 121-50. (see 1852 above for German edition)

2512, Schmid, Karl. "Aspects of evil in the creative." Ibid., pp.
227-50. (see 1853 above for German edition)

2513. Singer, June. "William Blake's 'Proverbs of Hell': a Jungian
commentary." Spring 1967, pp. 26-54.

2514. Stein, Leopold. "Introducing not-self." JAP, 12:2 (1967), pp.
97-114.

2515. Tenzler, Johannes. "Lebenswende und Individuationsprozeß. Das
Problem der Lebensmitte nach C. G. Jung." JPP, 15:3-4 (1967).
pp. 313-37.

*2516. Thornton, Edward. The diary of a mystic. London: Allen and
Unwin, 1967.

2517. Ulanov, Ann Belford. A consideration of C. G. Jung's psychology
of the feminine and its implications for Christian theology.
(Th. D. dissertation). Union Theological Seminary, 1967.

2518. Vergote, Antoine, "Interpretazioni psicologiche dei fenomeni
religiosi nell'ateismo contemporaneo." In L'ateismo contemporaneo. Ed. by the Faculty of Philosophy of the Pontificia Uni-
versita Salesiana, Rome. Turin: Societa Editrice Internazio-
nale, 1967, Vol I, pp. 327-80.

2519. Whitmont, Edward C. "Carl Jung." In Comprehensive Textbook of
Psychiatry. A. M. Freedman and H. I. Kaplan, eds. Baltimore:
Williams and Wilkins, 1967, pp. 366-72.

2520. Wilhelm, Helmut. "The interplay of image and concept in the
book of changes." EJ, 36 (1967), pp. 31-58.

2521. Willeford, William. "Group psychotherapy and symbol formation."
       JAP, 12:2 (1967), pp. 137-60.

2522. Windengren, Geo. "The principle of evil in the Eastern reli-
       gions." Evil (see *2433 above), pp. 19-56. (see 1871 above
       for German edition)

2523. Ziegler, Alfred T. "Psychosomatische und psychotherapeutische
       Strömungen in der Medizin unserer Zeit. Konzepte und kritische
       Reflexion. 2. Die Lehre Jungs." Hippokrates, 38 (1967), pp.
       855-58.

*2524. The collective unconscious in literature: selections from past
       Springs. New York: APCNY, 1967.

                                  1968

2525. Abenheimer, Karl M. "The ego as subject." Reality (see *2655
       below), pp. 61-73.

2526. Adler, Gerhard. "Methods of treatment in analytical psychology."
       Spring 1968, pp. 8-45. (see 2416 above)

2527. Adolf, Helen. "Wrestling with the angel: Rilke's 'gazing eye'
       and the archetype." In Perspectives in literary symbolism.
       Joseph Strelka, ed. University Park, Pa.: Pennsylvania State
       University Press, 1968, pp. 29-39.

2528. Amann, A. "Der Traum als diagnostischer und therapeutischer
       Faktor." "The dream as a diagnostic and therapeutic factor."
       Reality (see *2655 below), pp. 85-97.

2529. Bamberger, J. E. "The psychic dynamisms in the ascetical theo-
       logy of St. Basil." Orient christ period, 34:2 (1968), pp.
       233-51.

2530. Barefield, R. S. The realization of the self: a comparison of
       self-actualization in the writings of Carl Jung and Carl Rogers.
       (Ed. D. dissertation). Florida State University, 1968.

2531. Beach, B. Y. "Jung on metaphysics." New York: APCNY, 1968.

2532. Beit, Hedwig von. "Concerning the problem of transformation in
       the fairy tale." In Perspectives (see 2527 above), pp. 48-71.

*2533. Bennet, Edward Armstrong. Ce que Jung a vraiment dit. __. de
       Monique, trans. Paris: Stock, 1968. (see *1968 above for
       Italian and *2427 below for English editions)

                                  162

*2534. Bertine, Eleanor. Jung's contribution to our time. New York:
G. P. Putnam's Sons for the C. G. Jung Foundation, 1968.
      Rev. Amy I. Allenby. JAP, 14:2 (1969), p. 194.
          Ross Hainline. Library J, 93 (1 Feb. 1968), p. 561.
          June K. Singer. Quad, 1 (1968), p. 26.
          Unsigned. Choice, 5 (Oct. 1968), p. 1046.

2535. Bockus, Frank M. "The archetypal self: theological values in
Jung's psychology." In The dialogue between theology and psychology. Peter Homans, ed. University of Chicago Press,
1968, pp. 221-47.

2536. Braybrooke, Neville. "C. G. Jung and Teilhard de Chardin: a
dialogue." Month, 225 (1968), pp. 96-104. (see below, 2671
for Spanish and 2672 for Egnlish editions)

2537. Buonaiuti, Ernesto. "Christ and St. Paul." "Christology and
ecclesiology in St. Paul." "Symbols and rites in the religious
life of certain monastic orders." PEY VI (*2540), pp. 120-209.
(see 110 and 267 above for German editions)

*2538. OGJIZ, ed. Timeless documents of the soul. Evanston, Ill.:
Northwestern University Press, 1968.
      Rev. Michael Fordham. JAP, 15:2 (1970), p. 195.

*2539. Campbell, Joseph. The masks of god: creative mythology. New
York: Viking Press, 1968.
      Rev. Joseph L. Henderson. JAP, 14:2 (1969), p. 193.

*2540. _____., ed. The mystic vision. Papers from the Eranos Year-
books VI. Princeton, New Jersey: Princeton University Press
(Bollingen Series XXX), 1968.

2541. Cannon, A. "Transference as creative illusion." JAP, 13:2
(1968), pp. 95-108.

2542. Citroen, Paul. "Wir Mahler heute und die Kunsttradition." EJ,
37 (1968), pp. 133-60.

*2543. Cox, David. Modern psychology. The teachings of Carl Gustav
Jung. New York: Barnes and Noble, 1968. (see 1989 and 2135
above)

2544. D'Agostino, E. and Trevi, M. "Struttura e tensione dialettica:
note sulla concezione del Selbst nella psicologia dell'indivi-
duazione." Clin Psichiatr, 6 (1968), np.

2545. Diekman, Hans. "Das Lieblingsmärchen der Kindheit als therapeutische Faktor in der Analyse." Praxis Kinderpsychologie, 17:8
(1968), np. (see 2921 and 2922 below for English and German
editions)

*2546. _____. Probleme der Lebensmitte. Stuttgart: Adolf Bonz,
1968.

Rev. R. Blomeyer. _ZAP_, 1:1 (1969), pp. 47-48.
E. Seligman. _JAP_, 14:1 (1969), p. 86.

*2547. Di Forti, Filippo. Il contrasto Freud/Jung e le nuove direzioni della psicoanalisi. Rome: Silva, 1968.

2548. Dunn, I. Jay. "Social and community psychiatry and individual social consciousness." _JAP_, 13:2 (1968), pp. 146-54.

2549. Durand, Gilbert. "Structure et fonction récurrentes de la figure de Dieu ou la conversion herméneutique." _EJ_, 37 (1968), pp. 449-522.

2550. Edinger, Edward F. "An outline of analytical psychology." _Quad_, 1 (1968), pp. 8-19.

2551. Fierz, Heinrich Karl. "Plastiken in der Therapie von Psychosen." "Plastic work of art in the therapy of psychoses." _Reality_ (see *2655 below), pp. 28-41.

2552. _____. "Utbildningen i psykoterapi i Schweiz." _Svenska Föringen för Medicinsk Psykologi_, 11 (1968), np.

*2553. Fordham, Frieda. Introduzione a Carl Gustav Jung. V. Nozzoli, trans. Florence: Editrice universitaria, 1968. (see *827 above for English and list of other editions)

2554. Fordham, Michael. "Individuation in childhood." _Reality_ (see *2655 below), pp. 54-60.

*2555. Fortmann, H. M. M. Als ziende de Onsienlijke. Een cultuurpsychologische studie over de religieuze waarneming en de zogenaamde religieuze projectie. Hilversum, Paul Brand, 1968.

2556. _____. "Jung en de godsdienstpsychologie." _Dienstpsychologie_, (1968), pp. 21-31.

2557. Franz, Marie Louise von. "The dream of Descartes." _Timeless_ (see *2538 above). (see 744 above for German edition)

2558. _____. "Der Individuationsprozeß." _Symbole_ (see *2602 below), pp. 158-220.

2559. _____. "Symbole des 'Unus Mundus'." "Symbols of the 'Unus Mundus'." _Realtiy_ (see *2655 below), pp. 179-207.

2560. _____. "Zum Abschluss: das Unbewußte und die Wissenschaften." _Symbole_ (see *2602 below), pp. 304-10.

2561. Froböse-Thiele, Felicia. "Träume: eine Quelle religiöser Erfahrung?" _Bedeutung_ (see *2565 below), pp. 298-320. (see 1345 above)

2562. Goldbrunner, Josef. "Dialog zwischen Tiefenpsychologie und katolischer Theologie." In Festschrift für Wilhelm Bitter. Stuttgart: Ernst Klett, 1968.

2563. Gordon, Rosemary. "Symbols: content and process." Reality (see *2655 below), pp. 293-304. (see 2453 above and 3231 below)

2564. _____. "Transference as a fulcrum of analysis." JAP, 13:2 (1968), pp. 109-17.

*2565. Gravenitz, Jutta von. Bedeutung und Deutung des Traumes in der Psychotherapie. Darmstadt: Wissenschaftliche Buchgesellschaft, 1968.

2566. Guggenbühl-Craig, Adolf. "Medicine and power; the wounded healer." Harv, 14 (1968), pp. 1-14.

2567. _____. "Der Schatten des Psychotherapeuten." "The psychotherapist's shadow." Reality (see *2655 below), pp. 235-57.

2568. Hadot, Pierre. "L'apport du Néoplatonism à la philosophie de la nature en occident." EJ, 37 (1968), pp. 91-132.

2569. Hall, Calvin Springer. "The dreams of Freud and Jung." Psychology Today, 2:1 (1968), pp. 42-45, 64-65.

2570. Haendler, Otto. "Theologische Einleitung." Bedeutung (see *2565 above), pp. 5-18.

*2571. Hannah, Barbara. Possession and exorcism; 'polarities of the psyche'. Zurich: Privately printed, 1968.

2572. Harding, M. Esther. "The coming dawn." Quad, 2 (1968), pp. 5-13.

2573. _____. "The reality of the psyche." Reality (see *2655 below), pp. 1-13.

2574. Hayes, Dorsha. "Religion: an individual search." Harv, 14 (1968), pp. 35-50.

2575. Heiler, Friedrich. "The Madonna as religious symbol." PEY VI (see *2540 above), pp. 348-74. (see 114 above for German edition)

*2576. Henderson, James L. Education for world understanding. New York: Pergamon Press, 1968.
      Rev. Anne Allee. Quad, 5 (1969), p. 12.

2577. Henderson, Joseph L. "Der moderne Mensch und die Mythen." Symbole (see *2602 below), pp. 104-57.

2578. Hendrickson, Marion Vaux. "A paper on Dante Alighiere." In The collective unconscious in literature. Selections from past Springs. New York: APCNY, 1968. (see 364 above)

*2579. Hess, Gertrude. Biology--psychology: two ways of research into life. Zurich: Rascher, 1968.
        Rev. E. Rüf. JAP, 15:2 (1970), pp. 199-200.

2580. Heydt, Vera von der. On psychic energy. London: GofPP Lecture # 144, May 1968.

2581. Hillman, James. "C. G. Jung on emotion." In The nature of emotion. M. B. Arnold, ed. Harmondsworth: Penguin, 1968.

2582. _____. "The language of psychology and the speech of the soul." EJ, 37 (1968), pp. 249-365.

2583. _____. "Preface." In C. A. Meier. Ancient Incubation and modern psychotherapy. Evanston, Ill.: Northwestern University Press, 1968.

2584. _____. "Preface." Timeless (see *2538 above).

2585. _____. "Towards the archetypal model for the masturbation inhibition." Reality (see *2655 below), pp. 114-27. (see 2370 above and 3555 below)

2586. Hinkelman, Emmet Arthur and Alderman, Morris. "Apparent theoretical parallels between G. Stanley Hall and C. G. Jung." J of the History of the Behavioral Sciences, 4:3 (1968), pp. 254-57.

2587. Holt, David. Hypocrites and analyst. London: GofPP Lecture # 145, May 1968.

2588. _____. "Money and power." Harv, 14 (1968), pp. 16-33.

2589. Holton, Gerald. "The roots of complementarity." EJ, 37 (1968), pp. 45-90.

2590. Hostie, Raymond. "Jung: theorie en therapie." Dienstpsychologie, (1968), pp. 101-45.

*2591. Howes, Elizabeth Boyden. Die Evangelien im Aspekt der Tiefenpsychologie. Zurich: Origo, 1968.

2592. Hurwitz, Siegmund. "Psychological aspects in early Hasidic literature." Timeless (see *2538 above), pp. 149-239. (see 780 above for German edition)

2593. Iandelli, C. L. "The serpent symbol." Reality (see *2655 below), pp. 98-113.

*2594. Jacobi, Jolande. Frauenprobleme, Eheprobleme. Zurich and Stuttgart: Rascher, 1968.
        Rev. E. Krauss. ZAP, 1:1 (1969), p. 48.

*2595. _____. The psychology of C. G. Jung: an introduction. 7th
ed. R. Manheim, trans. New Haven, Conn.: Yale University
Press, 1968. (see *255 above for German and list of other
editions)

2596. _____. "Symbole auf dem Weg der Reifung." Symbole (see
*2602 below), pp. 272-303.

2597. Jacobsohn, Helmuth. "Der altägyptische, der christliche und
der moderne Mythos." EJ, 37 (1968), pp. 411-48.

2598. _____. "The dialogue of a world-weary man with his Ba."
Timeless (see *2538 above). (see 781 above for German edition)

*2599, Jaffé, Aniela. Aus Leben und Werkstatt von C. G. Jung. Zurich
and Stuttgart: Rascher, 1968. (see *2976 below for English
edition)

2600. _____. "Bildene Kunst als Symbol." Symbole (see *2602 below), pp. 221-71. (see 2183 above for English edition)

2601. Jung, Albert. "Die Beziehungen zum eigenen Körper." Civitas,
23:4 (1967-68), np.

*2602. Jung, Carl Gustav et al. Der Mensch und seine Symbole. Olten:
Walter, 1968.

*2603. Kelsey, Morton T. Dreams: the dark speech of the spirit. A
Christian interpretation. Garden City, New York: Doubleday,
1968.

2604. Kiener, Hélène. "L'apport de C. G. Jung au débat théologique
actuel." Problème (see *2605 below), pp. 19-38.

*2605. _____. Le problème religieux dans l'oeuvre de C. G. Jung.
Fontainebleau, Ferrière, 1968.

2606. _____. "Le problème religieux dans l'oeuvre de C. G. Jung."
Problème (see *2605 above), pp. 1-17.

2607. _____. "Réponse à quelques critiques sur la portée religieuse de l'oeuvre de C. G. Jung." Ibid., pp. 39-58.

2608. Kirsch, Thomas B. "The relation of the REM state to analytical
psychology." Amer J of Psychiatry, 194 (1968), pp. 1459-63.

2609. Klopfer, Bruno. "Jungian analysis and professional psychology."
Reality (see *2655 below), pp. 258-61.

2610. Koppers, Wilhelm. "On the origin of the mysteries in the light
of ethnology and Indiology." PEY VI (see *2540 above), pp.
32-69. (see 329 above for German edition)

2611. Lewis, Eve. "The archetypes during the years of middle child-hood." _Harv_, 14 (1968), pp. 51-61.

2612. Mann, Harriet; Siegler, M., and Osmond, H. "The many worlds of time." _JAP_, 13:1 (1968), pp. 33-56.
Rev. H. J. Wilke. _ZAP_, 1:1 (1969), p. 48.

2613. Marcoen, A. "Carl Gustav Jung en Sigmund Freud. Ontmoeting, onenigheid un breuk." _Tijdschrift voor Filosofie_, 30:3 (1968), pp. 439-93.

2614. Marshak, M. D. "A psychological approach to mythology. II." _Didaskalos_, 2:3 (1968), np.

2615. Marshall, I. N. "The four functions: a conceptual analysis." _JAP_, 13:1 (1968), pp. 1-32.

2616. Massignon, Louis. "Nature in Islamic thought." "The idea of the spirit in Islam." _PEY VI_ (see *2540 above), pp. 315-23. (see 418 above for German edition)

*2617. Matthews, H. _The hard journey: the myth of man's rebirth_. London: Chatto and Windus, 1968.
Rev. Mary Williams. _JAP_, 15:1 (1970). pp. 110-11.

*2618. Meier, Carl Alfred. _Lehrbuch der komplexen Psychologie C. G. Jungs, I: Die Empirie des Unbewußten_. Zurich and Stuttgart: Rascher, 1968.
Rev. H. K. Fierz. _JAP_, 15:1 (1970), pp. 109-10.
E. Jung. _ZAP_, 1:1 (1969), p. 47.

2619. _____. "Forgetting of dreams in the laboratory." _Perceptual Motor Skills_, 26 (1968), pp. 551-57.

2620. Menasce, Jean de. "The experience of the spirit in Christian mysticism." _PEY VI_ (see *2540 above), pp. 324-47. (see 375 above for German edition)

2621. Mendelsohn, J. "Die Phantasie vom weissen Kind." "The fantasy of the white child." _Reality_ (see *2655 below), pp. 128-64.

2622. Mus, Paul. "Traditions asiennes et Bouddhisme moderne." _EJ_, 37 (1968), pp. 161-276.

2623. Nagel, Hildegard. "Goethe's Mephistopheles." In _Collective_ (see 2578 above). np. (see 571 above)

2624. Neumann, Erich. "Mystical man." _PEY VI_ (see *2540 above) pp. 375-418. (see above, 502 for German and 1829 for English editions)

2625. Osterman, Elizabeth K. "The tendency toward patterning and order in matter and in the psyche." _Reality_ (see *2655 below), pp. 14-27.

2626. Paulsem, Alma A. "The spirit Mercury as related to the individuation process." Ibid., pp. 74-84. (see 2389 above)

2627. Portmann, Adolf. "Im Kampf um die Auffassung vom Lebendigen." EJ, 37 (1968), pp. 523-48.

2628. Puech, Henri-Charles. "The concept of redemption in Manicheism." PEY VI (see *2540 above), pp. 247-314. (see 183 above for German edition)

2629. Quispel, Gilles. "C. G. Jung und die Gnosis." EJ, 37 (1968), pp. 277-98.

2630. _____. "Gnostic man: the doctrine of Basilides." PEY VI (see *2540 above), pp. 210-46. (see 508 above for German edition)

2631. Raine, Kathleen. "Poetic symbols as a vehicle of tradition: the crisis of the present in English poetry." EJ,37 (1968), pp. 357-410.

2632. Rhally, Miltiade. "Schwierigkeiten in der therapeutischen Begegnung." "Difficulties in the therapeutic encounter." Reality (see *2655 below), pp. 208-34.

2633. Richek, H. G. and Brown, O. H. "Phenomenological correlates of Jung's typology." JAP, 13:1 (1968), pp. 57-66.

2634. Riklin, Franz. "Shakespeares 'A Midsummer Night's Dream': Ein Beitrag zum Individuationsprozeß." "Shakespear's 'A Midsummer Night's Dream': a contribution to the process of individuation." Reality (see *2655 below), pp. 262-92.

2635. Rouselle, Erwin. "Dragon and mare, figures of primordial Chinese mythology." PEY VI (see *2540 above), pp. 103-19.

2636. Rudin, Josef. "The defective image of God." In Psychotherapy (see *2637 below), pp. 135-54.

*2637. _____. Psychotherapy and religion. E. Reinecke and P. C. Bailey, trans. Notre Dame, Ind.: Notre Dame University Press, 1968. (see *1723 above for German edition)

2638. _____. "Das Schuldproblem in der tiefenpsychologie von C. G. Jung." In Schuld und religiöse Erfahrung. J. Rudin et al., eds. Freiburg, Herder, 1968, pp. 61-71.

*2639. Sanford, John A. Dreams: God's forgotten language. Philadelphia: J. B. Lippincott, 1968. (see *2400 above for German edition)

2640. Schärf-Kluger, Rivkah. "Flood dreams." Reality (see *2655 below), pp. 42-53.

2641. Schechter, David E. "Identification and individuation." J Amer Psychoanalytic Assoc, 16 (1968), pp. 48-80.

2642. Scholem, Gershom G. "Die Krise der Tradition im jüdischen Messianismus." EJ, 37 (1968), pp. 9-44.

*2643. Scott-Maxwell, Florida. The measure of my days. New York: Alfred A. Knopf, 1968.

2644. Seligman, Paul. "Concern with death and eternity." Harv, 14 (1968), pp. 63-79.

*2645. Silveira, Nise da. Jung, vida e obra. Rio de Janeiro: 1968.

2646. Solie, Pierre. "Psychologie analytique et imagerie mentale." Action et Pensée, 44 (March-June 1968), pp. 1-2.

2647. Spare, Geraldine H. A study of the law of enantiadromia as it relates to the attitudes of introversion and extraversion. (Doctoral dissertation). Washington State University, 1968.

*2648. Spiti, Alessandro. Il simbolismo in Carl Gustav Jung. Pistoia: Tip-Bugiani, 1968.

2649. Tenzler, Johannes. "C. G. Jungs Phantasieauffassung im strukturpsychologischer Sicht." In Wirklichkeit der Mitte. Beiträge zu einer Strukturanthropologie. Freiburg and Munich: 1968, pp. 252-91.

2650. Ulanov, Ann Belford. "Where depth psychology and theology meet." Union Seminary Q Rev, 23:2 (1968), pp. 159-67.

2651. Urban, Peter. "Philosophische und empirische Aspekte der Synchronizitätstheorie." Grenzgebiete der Wissenschaft, 17:4 (1968), pp. 347 ff.

2652. Vasavada, Arvind U. "Jungs analytische Psychologie und indische Weisheit." In Abendländische Therapie und östliche Weisheit. Wilhelm Bitter, ed. Stuttgart: Ernst Klett, 1968, pp. 236-44.

2653. _____. "Jung's analytical psychology and Indian wisdom." JAP, 13:2 (1968), pp. 131-45.

3654. Welch, M. "Confusion and the search for identity." Ibid., pp. 118-30.

*2655. Wheelwright, Joseph B. The reality of the psyche. New York: G. P. Putnam's Sons for the C. G. Jung Foundation, 1968.

2656. Wheelwright, Philip. "The archetypal symbol." In Perspectives (see *2527 above), pp. 214-43.

2657. Wilson, John Richardson. Psychodynamic structure and trinitarian foundations. (Doctoral dissertation). University of Edinburgh, 1968.

2658. Wysheslawzeff, Boris. "Two ways of redemption: redemption as a solution of the tragic contradiction." PEY VI (see *2540 above), pp. 3-31. (see 186 above for German edition)

2659. Zimmer, Heinrich. "The Indian world mother." Ibid., pp. 70-103. (see 219 above for German edition)

2660. _____. "Notes on the Kundalini Yoga." Spring 1968, pp. 49-52.

1969

2661. Anghinetti, Paul William. Alienation, rebellion, and myth: a study of the works of Nietzsche, Jung, Yeats, Camus and Joyce. (Doctoral dissertation). Florida State University, 1969.

2662. Barker, Culver M. "The child within." Harv, 15 (1969), pp. 56-67.

*2663. Baynes, Helton Goowin. Mythology of the soul. 2nd ed. London: Rider and Co., 1969. (see *246 and *993 above)

2664. Beck, Irene. "Franz von Sales und C. G. Jung. Aktuelle psychologische Aspekte der salesianischen Theologie." Jahr für salasianische Studien, (1969), pp. 5-16.

2665. Benoit, Ray. "Whitman, Teilhard and Jung." In The continuous flame: Teilhard in the great traditions. Harry J. Cargas, ed. St. Louis, Mo.: B. Herder, 1969, pp. 79-89.

2666. Benz, Ernst. "Der Mensch als Imago Dei." EJ, 38 (1969), pp. 297-330.

*2667. Bernhard, Ernst. Mitobiografia. Milan: Biblioteca Adelphi, 1969.
          Rev. Helen Shipway. JAP, 17:2 (1972), pp. 223-24.

2668. Billinsky, John M. "Jung and Freud." Andover Newton Q, 10 (1969), pp. 39-43.

2669. Bitter, Wilhelm. "Psychotherapie im Strafwesen." ZAP, 1:1 (1969), pp. 5-23.

*2670. _____. Der Verlust der Seele. Freiburg, Basel and Vienna: Herder, 1969.
          Rev. G. Adler. ZAP, 1:2 (1970), p. 46.

171

2671. Braybrooke, Neville. "C. G. Jung y Teilhard de Chardin. Un diálogo." Arbor, 72 (1969), pp. 345-62. (see 2536 above for English edition)

2672. _____. "C. G. Jung and Teilhard de Chardin: a dialogue." J of General Education, 20 (1969), pp. 272-80. (see 2536 above)

2673. Broadribb, Donald. "Myth and development." Abr-Nabrein (Melbourne), 8 (1968-69), np.

2674. Cairns, Huntington. "The Bollingen adventure; a toast to J. D. B. and V. G." Princeton, New Jersey: Princeton University Press, 1969.

*2675. Calluf, Emir. Sonhos, complexos e personalidade. A psicologia analítica de C. G. Jung. Sao Paolo: Mestre Jou, 1969.

*2676. Campbell, Joseph. The flight of the wild gander; explorations in the mythological dimension. New York: Viking Press, 1969.

*2677. Carp, Eugene A. D. E. Teilhard, Jung en Sartre over evolutie. Utrecht: Het Spectrum, 1969.

2678. Cooley, R. "Jung, Lévy-Strauss and the interpretation of myth." The Critic, 8 (Aut-Win 1968-69), pp. 12-16.

2679. Corbin, Henry. "Le récit du nuage blanc." EJ, 38 (1969), pp. 195-260.

2680. Diekman, Hans. "Magie und Mythos in menschlichen Unbewußten." Wege zum Menschen, 21:6 (1969), np.

2681. _____. "Vergleichende Untersuchung über die Initialträume von 90 Patienten." ZAP, 1:1 (1969), pp. 24-38.

3682. _____. "Über das Bewußtsein der Frau im 20. Jahrhundert." Niedersächsische Ärzte-Blatt, 42:4 (1969).

2683. Drake, C. C. "Jungian psychology and its uses in folklore." J of Amer Folklore, 82:342 (1969), pp. 122-31.

2684. Dreifuss, Gustav. "The analyst and the damaged victim of Nazi persecution." With comments by G. Tedeschi, J. Mendelsohn, D. Kutzinski and M. Williams and a reply by the author. JAP, 14: 2 (1969), pp. 163-75. (see 2927 below for English and German editions)

2685. Durand, Gilbert. "Défiguration philosophique et figure traditionnelle de l'homme en Occident." EJ, 38 (1969), pp. 45-93.

2686. Edinger, Edward F. "Metaphysics and the unconscious." Spring 1969, pp. 101-28.

2687. Fordham, Frieda. "Some views on individuation." _JAP_, 14:1
       (1969), pp. 1-12. (see 3218 below)

2688. Fordham, Michael. "Technique and counter-transference." _JAP_,
       14:2 (1969), pp. 95-118.

2689. _____. "Theorie und Praxis der Kinderanalyse auf der Sicht
       der analytischen Psychologie C. G. Jungs." In _Handbuch der
       Kinderpsychotherapie_. Munich and Basel: Reinhardt, 1969, pp.
       168-85.

2690. Frantz, K. E. "The analyst's own involvement with the process
       and the patient." _JAP_, 14:2 (1969), pp. 143-51. (see 2940
       below)

2691. Franz, Marie Louise von. "C. G. Jung and the problem of our
       time." _Quad_, 5 (1969), pp. 4-11. (see 3514 below)

2692. _____. "Das Symbol des Anthropos als Zeitbild des Individu-
       ationsprozesses und der Menschheitsentwicklung." _ZAP_, 1:1
       (1969), pp. 39-44.

*2693. Frei, Gebhard. _Imago Mundi_. A. Rensch, ed. Panderborn, 1969.

*2694. Frey-Rohn, Liliane. _Von Freud zu Jung_. _St ad CGJIZ XIX_. Zur-
       ich and Stuttgart: Rascher, 1969. (see *3378 below for Eng-
       lish edition)
            Rev. R. Blomeyer. _ZAP_, 2:3 (1971), pp. 179-81.
                  Marianne Jacoby. _JAP_, 16:1 (1971), p. 115.

2695. Gillibert, Jean. "Le muertre de l'imago et le processus d'indi-
       viduation." _Rev Fr Psychanalytique_, 33 (1969), pp. 375-414.

2696. Giorgioni, Claudio. "Due saggi sull'arte di Carl Gustav Jung."
       Riv di Estetica, 14 (1969), pp. 413-26.

2697. Hallman, Ralph J. "The archetypes in _Peter Pan_." _JAP_, 14:1
       (1969), pp. 65-73.

2698. Hannah, Barbara. "The beyond." _Harv_, 15 (1969), pp. 68-89.

2699. _____. "The beyond." _Quad_, 3 (1969), pp. 12-23.

*2700. Herwig, Hedda J. _Therapie der Menschheit_. _Studien zur Psycho-
       analyse Freuds und Jungs_. Munich: Paul List, 1969.

*2701. Herzog-Dürck, Johanna. _Probleme menschlicher Reifung_. Stutt-
       gart: Ernst Klett, 1969.

2702. Hillman, James. "First Adam, then Eve: fantasies of female in-
       feriority in changing consciousness." _EJ_, 38 (1969), pp. 349-
       412. (see 2811 below)

*2703. Hochheimer, Wolfgang. _The psychotherapy of C. G. Jung_. H. Na-

173

gel, trans. New York: G. P. Putnam's Sons for the C. G. Jung
Foundation, 1969. (see *2371 above for German edition)
  Rev. K. E. Frantz. Quad, 4 (1969), p. 5.
     Ross Hainline. Library J, 94 (15 April 1969), p.
     1642.
     Unsigned. Choice, 7 (Oct. 1970), p. 1142.

*2704. _____. La psicoterapia de C. G. Jung. Madrid: Herder,
     1969.

2705. Homans, Peter. "Psychology and hermeneutics: Jung's contribu-
     tion." Zygon, 4 (1969), pp. 333-55.

2706. Hubback, Judith. "The symbolic attitude in psychotherapy." JA
     P, 14:1 (1969), pp. 36-47.

2707. Izutsu, Toshihiko. "The structure of selfhood in Zen-Buddhism."
     EJ, 38 (1969), pp. 95-150.

2708. Jacobi, Jolande. "A case of homosexuality." JAP, 14:1 (1969),
     pp. 48-64.

2709. _____. "Depth psychology and self-knowledge. A conversa-
     tion with Jung." Spring 1969, pp. 129-39.

*2710. _____. Vom Bilderreich der Seele; Wege und Umwege zu sich
     Selbst. Olten and Freiburg: Walter, 1969.
       Rev. Marianne Jacoby. JAP, 15:1 (1970), p. 111.

2711. Jacobsohn, Helmuth. "Gestaltwandel der Götter und des Menschen
     im alten Ägypten." EJ, 38 (1969), pp. 9-43.

2712. Jacoby, Mario. "The analytical psychology of C. G. Jung and
     the problem of literary evaluation." In Problems of literary
     evaluation. Joseph Strelka, ed. University Park, Pennsylvania:
     Pennsylvania State University, 1969.

2713. Jacoby, Mario. "A contribution to the phenomenon of transfer-
     ence." JAP, 14:2 (1969), pp. 133-42. (see 2975 below for Eng-
     lish and German editions)

2714. Jacoby, Mario. "The individual and the community." Harv, 15
     (1969), pp. 1-55.

*2715. Jaffé, Aniela. Jung over parapsychologie en alchemie. Jungs
     laatste jaren. Rotterdam: Lemniscott, 1969.

2716. Jung, Emma. "The anima as an elemental being." In Animus (see
     *2717 below), pp. 45-87. (see above, 1088 for German and 1367
     for English editions)

*2717. _____. Animus and anima. Zurich and New York: Spring Pub-
     lications, 1969. (see *1368 above)
       Rev. G. Wehr. Zeit für Religions- und Geistesgeschichte,

174

21:3 (1969), p. 287.

*2718. Kadinsky, David. Der Mythos der Maschine. Aus der Praxis ana-
lytische Psychotherapie. Bern Stuttgart and Vienna: Hans Huber, 1969.
Rev. E. Jung. ZAP, 2:4 (1971), pp. 253-57.

2719. Kerényi, Carl. "A mythological image of girlhood." Spring
1969, pp. 93-100. (see 561 above for German edition)

2720. Kyle, William. The uniqueness of pastoral psychotherapy. London: GofPP Lecture # 150, March 1969.

2721. Lorenzo, Silvia. "Il metodo dell'imaginazione attiva nella pra-
tica della psicologia analytica." Clin Psichiat, 7 (1969), np.

*2722. Mahler, Margaret Schoenberger. On human symbiosis and the vi-
cissitudes of individuation. Vol. I. Infantile psychosis.
London: Hogarth Press, 1969.
Rev. Michael Fordham. JAP, 17:2 (1972), p. 216.

2723. _____., et al. "The mother's reaction to her toddler's de-
sire for individuation." In Parenthood. E. J. Anthony and T.
Bonedeck, eds. Boston: Little Brown, 1969, pp. 257-74.

2724. Merlin, E. A. "Faith and psyche: a role for Jung in theology."
Catholic World, 209:1252 (1969), pp. 172-75.

*2725. Moreno, Mario. Psicodinamica della contestazione. Turin: ERI,
1969.
Rev. Helen Shipway. JAP, 16:1 (1971), p. 116.

*2726. Neumann, Erich. Depth psychology and a new ethic. E. Rolfe,
trans. New York: G. P. Putnam's Sons for the C. G. Jung Foundation, 1969. (see above, *503 for German and *940 for Dutch
editions)
Rev. James C. Aylward. Quad, 10 (1971), pp. 26-27.
Faye Pye. JAP, 15:2 (1970), p. 196.
Ruth Tenny. Harv, 15 (1969), pp. 90-91.

2727. Nowak, Antoni J. "Ekssawersja i intrawersja wujecus C. G.
Junga i R. B. Cattella." Studia philosophiae christianae,
5:1 (1969), pp. 251-59.

2728. Ombach, Elzbieta. "Analytical psychology of C. G. Jung." (in
Polish) Ibid., pp. 159-66.

2729. Pauson, Marian L. "C. G. Jung and the a-priori." Tulane Studies in Philosophy, 18 (1969), pp. 93-103.

2730. Plaut, Albert B. J. Analyst at the crossroads. London: GofPP
Lecture # 154, Nov. 1969.

2731. Pontius, Anneliesa A. "Easter Island's stone giants: a neuro-

175

psychiatric view." <u>Perceptual</u> <u>and</u> <u>Motor</u> <u>Skills</u>, 28 (1969), pp. 207-12.

2732. Portmann, Adolf. "Vom Urmenschenmythos zur Theorie der Menschwerdung." <u>EJ</u>, 38 (1969), pp. 413-39.

2733. Quispel, Gilles. "Gnosis and the new sayings of Jesus." <u>Ibid</u>., pp. 261-96.

*2734. Rauhala, Lauri. <u>Intentionality</u> <u>and</u> <u>the</u> <u>problem</u> <u>of</u> <u>the</u> <u>uncon</u><u>scious</u>. Helsinki: Academic Bookshops, 1969.
       Rev. P. Seligman. <u>JAP</u>, 15:1 (1970), p. 108.

2735. Redfearn, J. W. T. "Several views of the self." <u>JAP</u>, 14:1 (1969), pp. 13-25.

2736. Riklin, Franz. "C. G. Jung--ein Porträt." In <u>Was</u> <u>weiss</u> <u>man</u> <u>von</u> <u>der</u> <u>Seele</u>? Stuttgart: 1969.

2737. _____. "Joan of Arc." <u>Quad</u>, 4 (1969), pp. 6-20.

2738. Ritchey, Melvin S. <u>Light</u> <u>from</u> <u>the</u> <u>darkness</u>: <u>modern</u> <u>man</u> <u>in</u> <u>search</u> <u>of</u> <u>a</u> <u>meaningful</u> <u>Church</u>. (Diploma thesis), CGJI, Zurich, 1969.

2739. Rosinska, Zofia. "Antropologia analityczna Junga a humanizm." <u>Studia</u> <u>Filozoficzne</u> <u>Supplement</u>, (1969), pp. 249-58.

2740. Sänger, Annemarie. "Kinderpsychotherapie in der Sicht der analytischen Psychologie C. G. Jungs." <u>Praxis</u> <u>der</u> <u>Kinderpsycho</u><u>gie</u>, 18:8 (1969), pp. 282-85. (see 3021 below for English and German editions)

2741. Sambursky, Schmuel. "Die Willenfreiheit im Wandel des physikalischen Weltbildes." <u>EJ</u>, 38 (1969), pp. 151-93.

2742. Santis, Maria Isabella de. "A integração do animus na metanóia e o relaxamento." <u>Bol</u> <u>de</u> <u>psicologia</u>, 21:57-8 (1969), pp. 25-35.

2743. Schmidbauer, Wolfgang. "Mythos und Psychologie." <u>Studium</u> <u>Ge</u><u>nerale</u>, 22 (1969), pp. 890-912.

2744. Scholem, Gershom G. "Three types of Jewish piety." <u>EJ</u>, 38 (1969), pp. 331-48.

2745. Schulze, W. A. "Die Himmelfahrt Mariens bei C. G. Jung." <u>The</u><u>ologische</u> <u>Zeit</u>, 25 (1969), pp. 215-18.

2746. Schwartz, Nathan. <u>Entropy</u>, <u>negentropy</u> <u>and</u> <u>the</u> <u>psyche</u>. (Diploma thesis). CGJI, Zurich, 1969.

2747. Schwartzbaugh, R. "The 'collective' soul. Essays in philosophical anthropology. I." <u>Mandkind</u> <u>Q</u>, 10:1 (1969), pp. 22-44.

2748. Scott, R. D. and Ainsworth, P. L. "The shadow of the ancestor: a historical factor in the transmission of schizophrenia." BJM P, 42:1 (1969), pp. 13-32.

2749. Sherrard, Philip. "An introduction to the religious thought of C. G. Jung." Studies in Comparative Religion, 111:1 (1969), pp. 33-49.

2750. Singer, June K. "Religion and the collective unconscious; common ground of psychology and religion." Zygon, 4 (1969), pp. 315-32.

2751. Spiegelman, J. Marvin. "A Jungian contribution to the future of psychotherapy." Inter Psychiatry Clinics, 6:3 (1969), pp. 29-53.

2752. Tedeschi, Gianfranco. "Analytical psychotherapy with schizophrenic patients." JAP, 14:2 (1969), pp. 152-62. (see 3031 below for Italian and English editions)

2753. Towers, Bernard. "Jung and Teilhard." In Flame (see 2662 above), pp. 79-87.

2754. Vásquez, Francisco. "Ideas anthropologicas de Jung." Arbor, 74:288 (1969), pp. 305-21.

2755. Verne, Georges. "Individuation and the emergence of the unexpected." JAP, 14:1 (1969), pp. 26-35.

*2756. Wehr, Gerhard. C. G. Jung in Selbstzeugnissen und Bilddokumenten. Reinbek bei Hamburg: Rowohlt, 1969. (see *3038 below for English edition)

2757. Whitmont, Edward C. "The destiny concept in psychotherapy." Spring 1969, pp. 73-92. (see 3043 below)

*2758. _____. The symbolic quest: basic concepts of analytical psychology. New York: G. P. Putnam's Sons for the C. G. Jung Foundation, 1969.
        Rev. Lola Paulsen. JAP, 16:1 (1971), pp. 110-11.

*2759. Willeford, William. The fool and his scepter. Evanston, Ill.: Northwestern University Press, 1969.
        Rev. Alma A. Paulsen. Quad, 7 (1970), pp. 20-21.
             Albert B. J. Plaut. JAP, 16:1 (1971), p. 115.

2760. Wolff, Hanna. Anima Jesu. (Diploma thesis). CGJI, Zurich, 1969.

2761. Zinkin, L. "Flexibility in analytic technique." JAP, 14:2 (1969), pp. 119-32.

*2762. Zunini, Giorgio. Man and his religion: aspects of religious psychology. London: Geoffrey Chapman, 1969. (see *2415

177

above for Italian edition)

1970

2763. Adler, Gerhard. "Analytical psychology and the principle of complementarity." Harv, 16 (1970), pp. 1-11. (see 2897 below)

*2764. _____. Das Lebendige Symbol--Darstellung eines analytischen Individuationsprozesses. H. Binswanger, trans. Munich: Urban and Schwarzenberg, 1970. (see *1750 above for English edition) Rev. Hans Diekman. ZAP, 2:2 (1971), pp. 128-30.

2765. Altizer, Thomas J. J. "Response I." In John B. Cobb Jr. The theology of Altizer: critique and response. Philadelphia: Westminster, 1970, pp. 194-98.

2766. Barker, Ian F. "LSD 25 and analytical psychology." Zurich: Clinic and Research center for Jungian Psychology, 1970.

2767. Benz, Ernst. "Die Schöpferische Bedeutung des Wortes bei Jacob Boehme." EJ, 39 (1970), pp. 1-40.

2768. Blum, Ernst. "Freud and conscience." Conscience (see *2772 below), pp. 159-78. (see 1441 above for German edition)

2769. Böhler, Eugen. "Conscience in economic life." Ibid., pp. 41-78. (see 1442 above for German edition)

2770. Bosanquet, C. "Getting in touch." JAP, 15:1 (1970), pp. 42-58.

2771. Brooks, Henry Curtis. "C. G. Jung's view of religion." Andover Newton Q, 11:2 (1970), pp. 94-99.

2772. CGJI, Z, ed. Conscience. Evanston, Ill.: Northwestern University Press, 1970. (see *1446 above for German edition) Rev. Faye Pye. JAP, 16:2 (1971), p. 218.

2773. Campbell, Joseph. "Mythological themes in creative literature and art." In Myths, dreams and religion. New York: Dutton, 1970, pp. 138-75.

2774. Carlsson, Allan. "Jung on meaning and symbols in religion." J of General Education, 22 (1970), pp. 29-40.

2775. Chouinard, T. "The symbol and the archetype in analytical psychology and literary criticism." JAP, 15:2 (1970), pp. 155-64.

2776. Cook, David Alan. Is Jung's typology true? A theoretical and experimental study of some assumptions implicit in a theory of personality types. (Doctoral dissertation). Duke University, 1970.

*2777. Corbin, Henry. Creative imagination in the Sufism of Ibn 'Arabī. R. Manheim, trans. London: Routledge and Kegan Paul, 1970.

2778. _____. "L'initiation ismaélienne ou l'ésotérism et le verbe." EJ, 39 (1970), pp. 41-142.

2779. Dossetor, Frank. Plato's influence on analytical psychology. London: GofPP Lecture # 161, July 1970.

2780. Durand, Gilbert. "Linguistique et métalanguages." EJ, 39 (1970), pp. 341-96.

2781. Elkind, D. "Freud, Jung and the collective unconscious." NY Times Magazine, (Oct, 1970), pp. 23-25 ff.

*2782. Ellenberger, Henri F. The discovery of the unconscious. The history and evolution of dynamic psychiatry. London: Allen Lane The Penguin Press; New York: Basic Books, 1970.

*2783. Evans, Richard Isodore. Entretiens avec C. G. Jung. P. P. Coussy, trans. Paris: Payot, 1970. (see *2144 above for English edition)

2784. Farrington, Lorna Dishington. 'Empedocles on Etna': a Jungian perspective. (D. A. dissertation). Carnegie Mellon University, 1970.

*2785. Fordham, Frieda. Introduccion a la psicología de Jung. L . Izquierdo, trans. Madrid: Ed. Morata, 1970. (see *827 above for English and list of other editions)

*2786. Fordham, Michael. Children as individuals. New York: G. P. Putnam's Sons for the C. G. Jung Foundation, 1970. (see *352 above)
        Rev. Dorothy Davidson. JAP, 16:2 (1971), p. 212.
        Dora Kalff. JAP, 16:2 (1971), p. 211.

2787. _____. "Reflections on training analysis." JAP, 15:1 (1970), pp. 59-71. (see 2936 below)

2788. _____. "Reply to Plaut's comment." Ibid., pp. 177-81.

2789. Franz, Marie Louise von. "C. G. Jung's Library." Spring 1970, pp. 190-95. (see 2010 above for German edition)

*2790. _____. An introduction to the interpretation of fairy tales. New York: Spring Pubs., 1970.

2791. _____. "Der komische Mensch als Zeitbild des Individuations-

prozesses." In Evolution. Wilhelm Bitter, ed. Stuttgart:
Ernst Klett, 1970, pp. 94-114.

*2792. _____. The problem of the puer aeternus. New York: Spring
Pubs., 1970. (see 1569 above)

*2793. _____. A psychological interpretation of the Golden Ass of
Apuleius. New York: Spring Pubs., 1970. (see 1472 above)

*2794. _____. Zahl und Zeit. Stuttgart: Ernst Klett, 1970. (see
*3376 below for English edition)

2795. Friedman, Maurice. "Religion and psychology: the limits of the
psyche as touchstone of reality." Quaker Religious Thought,
12:1 (1970), pp. 1-48.

*2796. Furrer, Walter. Objektivierung des Unbewußten. Bern, Stuttgart
and Vienna: Hans Huber, 1970.
Rev. E. Jung. ZAP, pp. 46-48.

*2797. Giehrl, H. E. Volkmärchen und Tiefenpsychologie. Munich:
1970.

2798. Grinnell, Robert. "Reflections on the archetype of consciousness: personality and psychological faith." Spring 1970, pp.
15-39.

2799. Guggenbühl-Craig, Adolf. "Must analysis fail through its destructive aspect?" Ibid., pp. 133-45.

2800. Hall, Richard Charles. The symbolic relationship: its nature
and manifestations in the works of Freud, Jung, Cassirer, Urban and Tillich. (Doctoral dissertation). Claremont Graduate
School, 1970.

2801. Harding, M. Esther. "The Christmas message from the point of
view of analytical psychology." Concern, 12:16 (1970), pp.
15-20.

*2802. _____. The way of all women; a psychological interpretation.
rev. ed. New York: G. P. Putnam's Sons for the C. G. Jung
Foundation, 1970; London: Rider, 1971. (see *90 above for
a complete list of other editions)
Rev. Amy I. Allenby. JAP, 17:1 (1972), pp. 89-92.

2803. Hawkey, M. Lawry. "Case study of an adolescent girl." JAP,
15:2 (1970), pp. 138-47.

2804. Hayes, Dorsha. "A Child's phantasy." PP, 1:2 (1970), pp. 122-
37.

2805. Heisler, Verda. "Individuation through marriage." Ibid., pp.
104-15.

2806. Helwig, Werner. "Streifzug durch das Werk des Schweizer Psychologen C. G. Jung." Neue deutsche Hefte, 17:2 (1970), pp. 62-82.

2807. Henderson, Joseph L. "An archetypal theme in three films." PP, 1:1 (1970), pp. 69-74.

2708. _____. "Transcendence: symbols of man's search for self." Ibid., pp. 34-42.

2809. Heydt, Vera von der. "The treatment of Catholic patients." JAP, 15:1 (1970), pp. 72-80.

2810. Hillman, James. "C. G. Jung's contribution to 'Feelings and Emotions': synopsis and implications." In Feelings and emotions. M. B. Arnold, ed. New York: Academic Press, 1970.

2811. _____. "First Adam, then Eve: fantasies of female inferiority in changing consciousness." Art Inter (Lugano), 14:7 (1970), pp. 40-43. (see 2702 above)

2812. _____. "An imaginal ego." Inscape, 2 (1970).

2813. _____. "An introductory note--C. G. Carus and C. G. Jung." In Psyche (Part one). C. G. Carus. New York and Zurich: Spring Pubs., 1970.

2814. _____. "The problem of fantasies and the fantasy of problems." Lecture. London: Centre for Spiritual and Psychological Studies, 1970. (mimeographed)

2815. _____. "Preface." Conscience (see *2772 above).

2816. _____. "On senex consciousness." Spring 1970, pp. 146-65.

2817. _____. "Why 'archetypal' psychology?" Ibid., pp. 212-17. (see 3556 below)

2818. Holt, David. Idolatry and work in psychology. London: GofPP Lecture # 155, June 1970.

*2819. Hoop, J. H. van der. Character and the unconscious; a critical exposition of the psychology of Freud and Jung. College Pk. Md.: Mc Grath, 1970. (see *31 above)

2820. Hubback, Judith. "The assassination of Robert Kennedy: patients' and analysts' reactions." JAP, 15:1 (1970), pp. 81-87.

2821. Hull, R. F. C. "A prefatory note to two posthumous papers by C. G. Jung." Spring 1970, pp. 166-69.

2822. Hurwitz, Siegmund. "Psychologische Aspekte der messianischen Idee im Judentum." ZAP, 1:2 (1970), pp. 37-41. (see 2971 below for English edition)

2823. Izutsu, Toshihiko. "Sense and nonsense in Zen Buddhism." EJ, 39 (1970), pp. 183-215.

2824. Jacobsohn, Helmuth. "Das göttliche Wort und der göttliche Stein im alten Ägypten." EJ, 39 (1970), pp. 217-41.

*2825. Jaffé, Aniela. Jung over de zin van het leven. H. A. Schreuder, trans. Rotterdam: Lemniscaat, 1970. (see *2470 above for German and list of other editions)

2826. Jenkins, E. S. "A creative force in John Donne's 'Holy Sonnets'." PP, 1:2 (1970), pp. 139-51.

*2827. Jung, Emma and Franz, Marie Louise von. The Grail legend. A. Dykes, trans. New York: G. P. Putnam's Sons for the C. G. Jung Foundation, 1970. (see *1693 above for German edition)
          Rev. J. Lawrence. Front, 14 (May 1971), pp. 111-14.
          Gwen Mountford. Harv, 17 (1971), pp. 63-66.

2828. Kadinsky, David. "The meaning of technique." JAP, 15:2 (1970), pp. 165-76.

2829. Kalff, Dora. "Sandplay. A Jungian contribution to child psychotherapy." In Handbuch der Kinderpsychotherapie. Munich and Basel: Ernst Reinhardt, 1970.

2830. Kelsey, Morton T. "God, education and the unconscious." Religious Education, 65 (1970), pp. 227-34.

2831. Kolaříková, O. "About dimensional conception possibilities of Kretschmer's tempermental variants." (in Czech) Československá Psychologie, 14:6 (1970), pp. 535-43.

2832. Kopp, Sheldon B. "A time for priests, a time for shamans." PP, 1:1 (1970), pp. 9-16.

2833. Kraemer, William P. "What is life from the point of view of a psychiatrist?" Harv, 16 (1970), pp. 53-57.

2834. Krippner, Stanley and Easton, Harry K. "The essential theme in Jungian psychology." J of Contemporary Psychotherapy, 3:1 (1970), pp. 19-26.

*2835. Laiblin, Wilhelm. Märchenforschung und Tiefenpsychologie. Darmstadt: 1970.

2836. Lambert, Kenneth. "Some notes on the process of reconstruction." JAP, 15:1 (1970), pp. 23-41.

*2837. Lauterborn, Eleonore. Swami Omkaranda und C. G. Jung. Der psychologische Schatten und das überpsychologische Selbst. Zurich: ABC, 1970.

2838. McClintock, J. I. "Jack London's use of Carl Jung's psychology of the unconscious." Amer Literature, 42 (Nov. 1970), pp. 336-47.

2839. McCully, Robert S. "Archetypal qualities underlying the Rorschach experience." In Rorschach proceedings. A. Friedmann et al., eds. Bern: Hans Huber, 1970, pp. 30-39.

*2840. Mann, Ulrich. Theogonische Tage. Die Entwicklungsphasen des Gottesbewußtseins in der altorientalischen und biblischen Religion. Stuttgart: Ernst Klett, 1970.
      Rev. K. Lüthi. ZAP, 2:3 (1971), pp. 175-77.

2841. Marshak, Mildred D. "Observations of the treatment of adolescents." JAP, 15:2 (1970), pp. 123-37.

2842. Martins, Diamantino. "Pisição analítico-existencial do problema de Deus." Rev Port de Filosofia, 32 (1970), pp. 110-20.

2843. Mattoon, Mary A. The theory of dream interpretation according to C. G. Jung: an exposition and analysis. (Doctoral dissertation). University of Minnesota, 1970.

2844. Meier, C. A. "Individuation und psychologische Typen." ZAP, 1:2 (1970), pp. 6-19.

2845. Merwin, W. S. "The remembering machines of tomorrow." PP, 1:2 (1970), pp. 118-21.

2846. Mindess, Harvey. "The possibilities of humor." Ibid., pp. 94-103.

*2847. Moon, Shiela. A magic Dwells. Middletown, Conn.: Weslyan University Press, 1970.

*2848. Moreno, Antonio. Jung, gods and modern man. London: University of Notre Dame Press, 1970.
      Rev. C. A. Meier. AP, 6:1 (1975), pp. 85-87.

2849. Mountford, Gwen. "What is a snob?" Harv, 16 (1970), pp. 58-65.

*2850. Mueller, Fernand-Lucien. L'irrationalism contemporain. Schopenhauer, Nietzsche, Freud, Adler, Jung, Sartre.... Paris: Payot, 1970.

2851. Neumann, Erich. "Stages of religious experience and the path of depth psychology." Israel An of Psychiatry and related Disciplines, 8:3 (1970), pp. 232-54.

2852. Noel, Daniel C. "Thomas Altizer and the dialectic of regression." (see 2765 above), pp. 147-63.

2853. Oeri, Albert. "Some youthful memories of C. G. Jung." L. R. Kaufman, trans. Spring 1970, pp. 182-89. (see 160 above for

German edition)

2854. Pauson, Marion L. "Structures in art media." Tulane Studies in Philosophy, 19 (1970), pp. 65-78.

2855. Perry, John Weir. "Emotions and object relations." JAP, 15:1 (1970), pp. 1-12. (see 3009 below)

2856. Plaut, Albert B. J. "Analysis analysed." Theoria to Theory, 4:4 (1970), np.

2857. _____. "Comment: on not incarnating the archetype." JAP, 15:1 (1970), pp. 88-94.

2858. _____. "Developments in analytical psychology." Harv, 16 (1970), pp. 13-30.

2859. _____. "'What do you actually do?' Problems in communicating." JAP, 15:1 (1970), pp. 13-22.

2860. Portmann, Adolf. "Der Weg zum Wort: Stuffen lebendiger Kommunikation." EJ, 39 (1970), pp. 397-424.

2861. Pye, Faye. "An interpretation of Jung." Harv, 16 (1970), pp. 31-51.

2862. Quispel, Gilles. "From Mythos to Logos." EJ, 39 (1970), pp. 323-40.

2863. Rauhala, Lauri . "Man--the philosophical conception and empirical study." JAP, 15:2 (1970), pp. 148-54.

2864. Ricketts, M. L. "Nature and extent of Eliade's Jungianism." Union Seminary Q Rev, 25 (Win. 1970), pp. 211-34.

2865. Riklin, Franz. "The crisis in middle life." Spring 1970, pp. 6-14.

2866. Ritsema, Rudolf. "Notes for differentiating some terms in the I Ching." Ibid., pp. 111-25.

*2867. Rochedieu, Edmond. C. G. Jung et l'individu dans le monde d'aujourd'hui. (Philosophes de tous les temps, # 63) Paris: Seghers, 1970.

2868. Rosińska, Z. "The importance of art in the theory of C. G. Jung." Stud Estet Pol, 7 (1970), pp. 211-23.

2869. Rudin, Josef. "A Catholic view of conscience." Conscience (see *2772 above), pp. 131-58. (see 1513 above for German edition)

2870. Sambursky, Schmuel. "Wort und Begriff in der Wissenschaft." EJ, 39 (1970), pp. 143-82.

2871. Schär, Hans. "A Protestant view of conscience." Conscience (see *2772 above), pp. 111-30. (see 1515 above for German edition)

2872. Scholem, Gershom G. "Der Name Gottes und die Sprachtheorie der Kabbala." EJ, 39 (1970), pp. 243-99.

2873. Schwartz, Nathan J. and Sandra Ross. "On the concept of psychic entropy and negentropy." Spring 1970, pp. 67-90.

2874. Sellery, J'nan and Vickery, J. B. "Ritual in the streets: a study of Pritchett's 'The Scapegoat'." PP, 1:1 (1970), pp. 57-68.

2875. Sellner, Timothy Frederick. Novalis' Heinrich von Ofterdingen: "Erfullung" as "Individuation." An interpretation of the novel based on the psychology of C. G. Jung. (Doctoral dissertation). University of Michigan, 1970.

2876. Singer, June K. "The collective unconscious, Jung's most misunderstood concept." Quad, 7 (1970), pp. 4-13.

*2877. _____. The unholy bible. New York: G. P. Putnam's Sons for the C. G. Jung Foundation, 1970.
           Rev. James C. Aylward. Quad, 10 (1971), pp. 27-28.
                B. Butler. JAP, 17:1 (1972), pp. 99-100.

2878. Skublics, E. "Psychologically living symbolism and liturgy." Eglise et Théologie, 1 (May 1970), pp. 205-28.

2879. Smith, Ronald Aubrey. The relationship between the type theory and the personality growth theory of Carl Jung and the helping relationship theory of Carl Rogers. (Doctoral dissertation). University of Calif. at Los Angeles, 1970.

2880. Spero, Richard Henry. The Jungian world of Tennessee Williams. (Doctoral dissertation). University of Wisconsin, 1970.

2881. Spiegelman, J. Marvin. "Notes from the underground." Spring 1970, pp. 196-211.

2882. _____. "A view of love and religion from a psychotherapist's cave." Loc. cit.

2883. Stein, Robert M. "Animus and impersonal sexuality." Ibid., pp. 126-32.

2884. Stone, Harold. "The problem of good and evil in the development of the child." PP, 1:1 (1970), pp. 43-56.

2885. Uesküll, Thure von. "Körperwelt: Grenze und Kommunikation." EJ, 39 (1970), pp. 301-22.

2886. Walcott, William. "Carl Jung and James Joyce: a narrative of three encounters." <u>PP</u>, 1:1 (1970), pp. 21-31.

2887. Werblowsky, R. J. Zwi. "The concept of conscience in Jewish perspective." <u>Conscience</u> (see *2772 above), pp. 79-110. (see 1526 above for German edition)

2888. Whitmont, Edward C. "On aggression." <u>Spring</u> 1970, pp. 40-66.

2889. Wilhelm, Helmut. "The creative principle in the <u>Book of Changes</u> (<u>I Ching</u>)." <u>Ibid.</u>, pp. 91-110.

2890. Wilke, H. J. "Die Empfindungsfunktionen in der analytischen Arbeit." <u>ZAP</u>, 1:2 (1970), pp. 20-36.

2891. Yandell, James. "No hands: the balancing act of today's youth." <u>PP</u>, 1:1 (1970), pp. 17-20.

*2892. Zaehner, Robert Charles. <u>Concordant discord: the interdependence of faith</u>. Oxford: Clarendon, 1970.

2893. Zbinder, Hans. "Conscience in our time." <u>Conscience</u> (see *2772 above), pp. 1-40. (see 1530 above for German edition)

2894. Zeller, Max. "Jung and the unconscious." <u>PP</u>, 1:2 (1970), pp. 89-92.

1971

2895. Abenheimer, Karl M. "Lou Andreas-Salomé's main contributions to psycho-analysis." <u>Spring</u> 1971, pp. 22-37.

2896. Abood, Edward. "Genet: an underground man." <u>PP</u>, 2:2 (1971), pp. 113-25.

2897. Adler, Gerhard. "Analytical psychology and the principle of complementarity." <u>Process</u> (see *3039 below), pp. 110-21. (see 2763 above)

2898. _____. "C. G. Jung after ten years." <u>PP</u>, 2:2 (1971), pp. 91-96.

2899. _____. "On the question of meaning in psychotherapy." <u>Tree</u> (see *2986 below), pp. 159-83. (see 1960 above for list of other editions)

*2900. Alex, William. <u>Dreams, the unconscious and analytical therapy</u>. San Francisco: CGJISF, 1971. (see *3189 below)

2901. _____. "When old gods die." Tree (see *2986 below), pp. 33-47.

2902. Allchin, William H. "Archetypes and the adolescent unit." Harv, 17 (1971), pp. 34-48.

2903. Amman, Peter. "Fellini's 'Satyicon': reflections on crisis and development in the life of an artist." Spring 1971, pp. 186-92.

2904. Aurigemma, Luigi. "Symboles de transformation dans la tradition astrologique." "Transformation symbols in the astrological tradition." Process (see *3039 below), pp. 18-37.

2905. Benko, S. "Religionless Christianity." J of the Amer Assoc of Religion, 39 (Mar. 1971), pp. 43-47.

2906. Benz, Ernst. "Die ewige Jugend in der christlichen Mystik von Meister Eckhart bis Schleiermacher." EJ, 40 (1971), pp. 1-50.

2907. Bernhard, Dora. "Excerpts from Ernst Bernhard's autobiography." Tree (see *2986 below), pp. 278-83.

2908. _____. "The transcendent function in dreams." "Die transcendente Funktion im Traum." Process (see *3039 below), pp. 85-109.

2909. Bertram, Gerda. "Hippocrates--ein archetypisches Bild ärtzlicher Individuation." "Hippocrates--an archetypal image of the individuation way of the physician." Ibid., pp. 199-214.

2910. _____. "Hippokrates, ein archetypisches Bild ärztlicher Individuation." ZAP, 2:3 (1971), pp. 165-74.

2911. Blomeyer, Rudolf. "Die Konstellierung der Gegenübertragung beim Auftreten archetypischer Träume (Kasuistik)." Ibid., 3:1 (1971), pp. 29-40. (see 3349 below for English and German editions)

2912. _____. "Über weniger beachtete Motive in der Auseinandersetzung zwischen Freud und Jung." Ibid., 2:2 (1971), pp. 105-22.

*2913. Böhme, Wolfgang, ed. C. G. Jung und die Theologen: Selbsterfahrung, Gotteserfahrung bei C. G. Jung. Stuttgart: Radius, 1971.

2914. Cahen, Roland. "Tentatives d'accélération du processus analytique et leurs conséquences cliniques." "An attempt to accelerate the analytic process and its clinical consequences." Process (see *3039 below), pp. 215-44.

2915. Champernowne, H. Irene. "Art and therapy: an uneasy partnership." Harv, 17 (1971), pp. 49-61.

2916.   Chouinard, Timothy. "Eliot's Oeuvre, Bradley's 'finite centres', and Jung's anima concept." JAP, 16:1 (1971), pp. 48-68.

2917.   Clift, Wallace B. Psychological and Biblical theological perspectives on hope from the viewpoint of C. G. Jung and John Knox. (Doctoral dissertation). University of Chicago, 1971.

2918.   Corbin, Henry. "Juvénilité et chevalerie en Islam iranien." EJ, 40 (1971), pp. 311-56.

2919.   Covitz, Joel. "A Jewish myth of a priori knowledge." Spring 1971, pp. 50-63.

2920.   Danielius, Gerhard. "Ovid's Metamorphosis: the great poem of neurotic suffering." Tree (see *2986 below), pp. 351-63.

2921.   Diekmann, Hans. "The favourite fairy-tale of childhood." JAP, 16:1 (1971), pp. 18-30. (see 2545 above for German edition)

2922.   _____. "Das Lieblingsmärchen der Kindheit als therapeutischer Faktor in der Analyse." "The favorite fairy tale from childhood as a therapeutic factor in analysis." Process (see *3039 above), pp. 68-84. (see 2545 above)

2923.   _____. "Die Konstellierung der Gegenübertragung beim Auftreten archetypischer Träume (Untersuchungsmethoden und -ergebnisse)." ZAP, 3:1 (1971), pp. 11-28.

2924.   _____. "Symbols of active imagination." With comments by V. v. d. Heydt and E. Jung and a reply by the author. JAP, 16:2 (1971), pp. 127-48.

2925.   Doyle, Eric. "God and the feminine." The Clergy Rev, NS 56 (1971), pp. 866-77.

2926.   Draghi, Gianfranco. "Rapporti tra sui luppo individuale e collettivo." "The relationship between individual and collective development." Process (see *3039 below), pp. 257-75.

2927.   Dreifuss, Gustav. "Der Analytiker und der Verfolgungsgeschädigte." "The analyst and the damaged victim of Nazi persecution." Ibid., pp. 245-57. (see 2684 above for English edition with comments and reply)

2928.   _____. "Issac, the sacrificial lamb (a study of some Jewish legends)." JAP, 16:1 (1971), pp. 69-78.

2929.   Duddington, A. "Jung in our time." Harv, 17 (1971), pp. 8-20.

2930.   Durand, Gilbert. "Exploration of the imaginal." R. Horine, trans. Spring 1971, pp. 84-100.

2931.   Engel, Werner H. "Slave and slave-driver: an active therapeutic phase with archetypal meaning." Tree (see *2986 below),

pp. 220-34.

2932. Fabricius, Johannes. "The individuation process as reflected by 'The rosary of the philosophers' 1550." JAP, 16:1 (1971), pp. 31-47.

2933. Ranning, Esther. "Selections from a shorthand notebook." Tree (see *2986 below), pp. 382-88.

2934. Fierz-Monnier, Heinrich Karl. "The Lambspring figures." Ibid., pp. 143-58.

2935. Fordham, Michael. "Primary self, primary narcissism and related concepts." With comments by J. Jubback and H. J. Wilke and a reply by the author. JAP, 16:2 (1971), pp. 168-87. (see 3092 below for German edition)

3936. _____. "Reflections on training analysis." Process (see *3039 below), pp. 172-84. (see 2787 above)

2937. _____. "Religious experience in childhood." Tree (see *2986 below), pp. 79-89.

2938. _____. "Über die Entwicklung des Ichs in der Kindheit." ZAP, 2:4 (1971), pp. 207-30.

2939. Foy, Glenn A. "Reflections on 'The corn king and the Spring queen'." Tree (see *2986 below), pp. 328-50.

2940. Frantz, Kieffer E. "The analyst's own involvement with the process and the patient." Process (see *3039 below), pp. 148-56. (see 2690 above)

2941. _____. "The fallacy of peace of mind." Tree (see *2986 below), pp. 70-78.

2942. Franz, Marie Louise von. "The inferior function." Lectures (see *2946 below).

2943. _____. "Die Selbsterfahrung bei C. G. Jung." In Theologen (see *2913 above), pp. 25-45.

2944. _____. "Die Sinnfindung im Individuationsprozeß." ZAP, 3:1 (1971), pp. 41-59.

2945. _____. "Zur Psychologie der Gruppe." Die Zeitwende, (July 1971).

*2946. _____., and Hillman, James. Lectures on Jung's typology. New York: Spring Pubs., 1971.

2947. Frey, Liliane. "The shadow revealed in the works of Friedrich Nietzsche." Tree (see *2986 below), pp. 300-27.

2948. Frey-Wehrlin, C. T. "Tiefenpsychologie und Ethik." Zeit Evangelische Ethik, 15 (July 1971), pp. 196-205.

2949. Grønbek, William. "Jung og religionspsykologien." Dansk Teologisk Tidsskrift, 34:1 (1971), pp. 40-57.

*2940. Guggenbühl-Craig, Adolf. Macht als Gefahr beim Helfer. Basel: Karger, 1971.
        Rev. Hans Diekmann. JAP, 18:1 (1971), pp. 70-71.
                      ZAP, 4:1 (1972), pp. 68-70.

*2951. _____. Power in the helping professions. New York: Spring Pubs., 1971.

*2952. Haendler, Otto. Tiefenpsychologie, Theologie und Seelsorge. Göttingen: 1971.

*2953. Hannah, Barbara. Striving toward wholeness. New York: G. P. Putnam's Sons for the C. G. Jung Foundation, 1971.
        Rev. Faye Pye. JAP, 17:2 (1972), p. 224.
        Ruth Tenny. Harv, 18 (1972), pp. 75-77.

2954. Harada, Hermógenes. "Christologia e psicologia de C. G. Jung." Rev Eclesiástica Brasileira, 31:121 (1971), pp. 119-44.

2955. Harding, M. Esther. "The burning bush." Tree (see *2986 below), pp. 1-13.

2956. _____. "The cross as an archetypal symbol." Quad, 11 (1971), pp. 5-14.

2957. Heidland, Hans-Wolfgang. "Die Bedeutung der analytischen Psychologie für die Verkündigung der Kirche." In Theologen (see *2913 above), pp. 46-59.

2958. Heisig, James. "La nozione de Dio secondo Carl Gustav Jung." Humanitas, 26 (1971), pp. 777-802.

2959. Henderson, Joseph L. "The artist's relation to the unconscious." Process (see *3039 below), pp. 309-16.

2960. _____. "Symbolism of the unconscious in two plays of Shakespears." Tree (see *2986 below), pp. 284-99.

2961. Hillman, James. "Abandoning the child." EJ, 40 (1971), pp. 357-407. (see 3541 below)

2962. _____. "Avant propos." to the Catalogue of Cecil Collins: Recent paintings. London: Arthur Tooth and Sons, 1971.

2963. _____. "The feeling function." In Lectures (see *2946 below).

2964. _____. "Guidelines for the future." Lecture. Malvern,

Great Britain: Centre for Spiritual and Psychological Studies,
1971. (mimeographed)

2965. _____. "Psychology: monotheistic or polytheistic?" Spring
1971, pp. 193-208.

2966. Hobson, Robert F. "Imagination and amplification in psychotherapy." JAP, 16:1 (1971), pp. 79-105.

2967. Hough, Graham. "W. B. Yeats, a study in poetic integration."
EJ, 40 (1971), pp. 51-83.

2968. Hull, R. F. C. "Biographical notes on active imagination in the
works of C. G. Jung." Spring 1971, pp. 115-21.

2969. Humbert, Elie G. "Active imagination: theory and practice."
J. A. Pratt, trans. Ibid., pp. 101-14.

2970. _____. "Die Frage nach dem Sinn." ZAP, 2:3 (1971), pp. 141-
52.

2971. Hurwitz, Siegmund. "Some psychological aspects of the messianic
idea in Judaism." Tree (see *2986 below), pp. 130-42. (see
2822 above for German edition)

2972. Huyghe, René. "Les thèmes-clef et l'évolution de l'artiste:
Vermeer, Rembrandt, Delacroix." EJ, 40 (1971), pp. 159-200.

2973. Jacobi, Jolande. "Pictures from the unconscious in four cases
of obsessional neurosis." Process (see *3039 below), pp. 146-
47.

*2974. _____. Die Seelenmaske. Olten and Freiburg: Walter, 1971.
Rev. D. Baldus. ZAP, 4:4 (1973), pp. 393-94.

2975. Jacoby, Mario. "Kasuistischer Beitrag zum Phänomen der Übertragung." "A contribution to the phenomenon of transference."
Process (see *3039 below), pp. 1-17.

*2976. Jaffé, Aniela. From the life and work of C. G. Jung. R. F. C.
Hull, trans. New York: Harper and Row, 1971. (see *2599 a-
bove for German edition)

*2977. _____. The myth of meaning in the work of C. G. Jung. Lon-
don: Hodder and Stoughton; New York: G. P. Putnam's Sons for
the C. G. Jung Foundation, 1971. (see *2470 above for German
edition)
Rev. Ross Hainline. Library J, 96 (Oct. 1971), p. 3145.
Lola Paulsen. JAP, 17:1 (1972), p. 98.
Unsigned. Choice, 8 (Oct. 1971), p. 1094.

2978. _____. "Die schöpferischen Phasen im Leben von C. G. Jung."
EJ, 40 (1971), pp. 85-122. (see 3122 below for English edition)

2979. Jung, Eberhard. "Der Großinquisitor, ein Beitrag zum Archetyp des Großenvaters." ZAP, 2:2 (1971), pp. 79-104.

2980. Kadinsky, M. "Kindliches Ich-Erleben." Ibid., 2:4 (1971). pp. 191-206.

2981. Kalff, Dora M. "Experiences with Far Eastern philosophies." Process (see *3039 below), pp. 56-67.

*2982. _____. Sandplay: mirror of a child's psyche. San Francisco: Browser Press, 1971. (see *2475 above for German edition)

2983. Katz, Walter. "Birthday letter to a friend my age." Tree (see *2986 below), pp. 389-90.

2984. Kelsey, Morton T. "Jung as philosopher and theologian." Ibid., pp. 184-96.

2985. Kirk, Geoffrey S. "Old age and maturity in ancient Greece." EJ, 40 (1971), pp. 123-58.

*2986. Kirsch, Hilde, ed. The well-tended tree: essays into the spirit of our time. New York: G. P. Putnam's Sons for the C. G. Jung Foundation, 1971.
　　　　　　　Rev. Hans Diekmann. ZAP, 4:4 (1973), p. 293.
　　　　　　　William Willeford. JAP, 18:1 (1973), p. 78.

2987. Kirsch, James. "The symbol of the cloud in European literature of the 19th and 20th centuries." Quad, 10 (1971), pp. 4-16. (see 3129 below for German edition)

2988. Kirstein, Peter T. "On the (ir)relevance of technology on analitical therapy." Tree (see *2986 above), pp. 269-72.

2989. Korolko, Miroslav. "Karola Gustavo Junga psychologia religii." Nowe ksiazki, 512 (1971), pp. 811-13.

2990. Kraemer, William P. "Reflections on past and present events." BJMP, 44:3 (1971), pp. 197-210.

2991. Kraft, Werner. "Three stories." Tree (see *2986 above), pp. 363-78.

2992. Kreinheder, Albert. "The jealous father syndrome." PP, 2:1 (1971), pp. 43-50.

2993. Krogmann, Angelica E. "Ödipus contra Freud. Nach der 10. Wiederkehr des Todestages von Carl Gustav Jung (6 Juni 1961). Die Christengemeinschaft, 43 (1971), pp. 286-89.

2994. Lynch, Thomas A. "Corroboration of Jungian psychology in the biblical story of Abraham." Psychotherapy: Theory, Research and <u>Practice</u>, 8:4 (1971), pp. 313-18.

2995. McCully, Robert S. "Changing concepts and a new theory about Rorschach's plates." <u>Rorschachiana Japonica</u>, (1971), pp. 205-09.

2996. _____. "The rorschach in a new key." <u>Projective Psychology</u> <u>J</u>, 17 (Dec. 1971).

*2997. _____. <u>Rorschach theory and symbolism. A Jungian approach</u>. Edinburgh: Churchill Livingstone; Baltimore: Williams and Wilkins, 1971.
            Rev. J. E. Fraser. <u>Quad</u>, 12 (1972), pp. 21-24.
                 R. Gordon. <u>JAP</u>, 18:2 (1973), p. 181.

2998. Malamud, René. "The amazon problem." M. Stein, trans. <u>Spring</u> 1971, pp. 1-21.

2999. Mance, Joan. <u>A comparison between counselling and analysis</u>. London: GofPP Lecture # 159, Feb. 1971.

3000. Mann, Ulrich. "Die Gotteserfahrung des Menschen bei C. G. Jung." In <u>Theologen</u> (see *2913 above), pp. 7-24.

3001. Marcus, Kate. "Separation dreams." <u>PP</u>, 2:1 (1971), pp. 11-23. (see 1704 above)

3002. _____. "The stranger in women's dreams." <u>Tree</u> (see *2986 above), pp. 204-19. (see 1259 above)

3003. Meier, Carl Alfred. "Der Jung'sche Gesichtspunke in der neueren experimentallen Schlaf- und Traumforschung." <u>ZAP</u>, 2:3 (1971), pp. 153-64.

3004. _____. "The psychological parameters of the examination situation." <u>Tree</u> (see *2986 above), pp. 48-57.

3005. _____. "Psychological types and individualism: a plea for a more scientific approach in Jungian psychology." <u>Process</u> (see *3039 below), pp. 276-90.

3006. Moon, Shiela. "Friend and foe as mirror of oneself." <u>PP</u>, 2:1 (1971), pp. 30-41.

3007. Nowak, Antoni J. "The symbol as seen by Igor A Caruso." (in Polish) <u>Roczniki Filozoficzne</u>, 19:4 (1971), pp. 175-81.

3008. Paulsen, Lola. "Dreams and fantasies of falling." <u>JAP</u>, 16:1 (1971), pp. 1-17.

3009. Perry, John Weir. "Emotions and object relations." <u>Process</u> (see *3039 below), pp. 297-308. (see 2855 above)

3010. _____. "Societal implications of the renewal process."

Spring 1971, pp. 153-67.

3011. Plaut, Albert B. J. "What do we actually do? Learning from ex-
       perience." With comments by K. Newton and V. Zielen and a re-
       ply by the author. JAP, 16:2 (1971), pp. 188-203.

3012. _____. "Was tun wir wirklich? Wir lernen aus Erfahrung!"
       ZAP, 2:4 (1971), pp. 231-43.

3013. Pontius, Anneliese A. "Die Subject-Object-Beziehung in Begrif-
       fen von Kant und Jung." Kantstudien, 62 (1971), pp. 121-25.

3014. _____. "Philosophischer Überblick über die Entwicklung von
       Jungs Begriff des objectiv Psychischen." ZAP, 2:2 (1971), pp.
       69-78.

3015. Portmann, Adolf. "Die Autonomie der Lebensphasen im der orga-
       nischer Natur." EJ, 40 (1971), pp. 409-42.

3016. Post, Laurens van der. "The feminine principle." Bull APCNY,
       33:3 (March 1971), pp. 5 ff.

2317. Pye, Faye. "Some ethical factors in the analytical process."
       Process (see *3039 below), pp. 290-96.

3018. Quispel, Gilles. "The birth of the child, some Gnostic and
       Jewish aspects." EJ, 40 (1971), pp. 285-309.

3019. Rappaport, Leon. "A psychological perspective on Vietnam." PP,
       2:1 (1971), pp. 25-29.

3020. Ritsema, Rud. "Notes for differentiating terms in the I Ching."
       Spring 1971, pp. 141-52.

3021. Sänger. Annemarie. "Kinderpsychotherapie in der Sicht der ana-
       lytischen psychologie C. G. Jungs." "Child psychology based
       on the analytical psychology of C. G. Jung." Process (see
       *3039 below), pp. 157-71. (see 2740 above)

3022. Sambursky, Schmuel. "Von Keppler bis Einstein: Das Genie in
       der Naturwissenschaft." EJ, 40 (1971), pp. 201-38.

3023. Sanford, John A. "Analytical psychology: science or religion?
       An explanation of the epistemology of analytical psychology."
       Tree (see *2986 above), pp. 90-105.

3024. Schweizer, Erica. "Individuationsprozeß und Therapie." "The
       process of individuation and therapy." Process (see *3039 be-
       low), pp. 122-45.

3025. Servier, Jean. "Aspects et causes de la non-créativité chez
       quelques margineaux d'Europe." EJ, 40 (1971), pp. 239-84.

3026. Silber, James R. "The experience of Zen: Oxherding stories."

Tree (see *2986 above), pp. 106-22.

3027. Simon, Ernst. "On the meaning of tradition." Ibid., pp. 14-32.

3028. Stein, Robert M. "Transference and individuation: reflections on the process and future of analysis." Spring 1971, pp. 38-49.

3029. Stone, Harold. "The enigma of Yurii Zhivago." PP, 2:1 (1971), pp. 52-63.

3030. Sullwold, Edith. "Eagle eye." Tree (see *2986 above), pp. 235-52.

3031. Tedeschi, Gianfranco. "Psicoterapiea analitica con pazienti schizofrenici." "Analytical psychotherapy with schizophrenic patients." Process (see *3039 below), pp. 38-56. (see 2752 above)

3032. Tenny, Ruth. "Tribute for an anniversary." Tree (see *2986 above), pp. 378-82.

3033. Thornton, Edward. "Some reflections on the nature of entelechy." Ibid., pp. 123-29.

3034. Traux, Lee. "On avoiding bullshit." PP, 2:2 (1971), pp. 127-45.

*3035. Ulanov, Ann Belford. The feminine in Jungian psychology and in Christian theology. Evanston Ill.: Northwestern University Press, 1971.
　　　　Rev. T. A. Greene. Library J, 97 (June 1972), p. 2106.
　　　　　　 J'nan Sellery. PP, 4:2 (1973), pp. 200-05.
　　　　　　 Unsigned. Choice, 9 (June 1972), p. 581.

3036. Vlaikovič, Stefan. Biologie des Träumens in tiefenpsychologischer Sicht. (Diploma thesis). CGJI, Zurich, 1971.

3037. Walcott, William. "On the beginning of the Aquarian age." PP, 2:2 (1971), pp. 98-111.

*3038. Wehr, Gerhard. Portrait of Jung. W. A. Hargreaver, trans. New York: Herder and Herder, 1971. (see *2756 above for German edition)

*3039. Wheelwright, Joseph B., ed. The analytic process: aims, analysis, training. New York: G. P. Putnam's Sons for the C. G. Jung Foundation, 1971.
　　　　Rev. Judith Hubback. JAP, 17:2 (1972), pp. 220-23.

3040. _____. "Reflections on marriage in the second half of life." Quad, 8-9 (1970-71), pp. 26-31.

3041. _____. "A tribute and some comments on the etiology of the animus and anima." Tree (see *2986 above), pp. 197-203.

3042. Whitehouse, Mary. "Reflections on a metamorphosis." Ibid., pp. 272-77.

3043. Whitmont, Edward C. "The destiny concept in psychotherapy." Process (see *3039 above), pp. 185-98. (see 2757 above)

3044. _____. "Nature, symbol and imaginal reality." Spring 1971, pp. 64-83.

3045. Wilke, H. J. "Problems in heart neurosis." With comments by J. Redfearn and R. Blomeyer and a reply by the author. JAP, 16:2 (1971), pp. 149-67.

3036. Williams, Jay G. "Other-worldly Christianity: some positive considerations." Theology Today, 28 (1971), pp. 328-36.

3047. _____. "You have not spoken truth of me; mystery and irony in Job." Zeit für die Alttestamentische Wissenschaft, 83:2 (1971), pp. 231-55.

3048. Williams, Mary. "The archetypes in marriage." Harv, 17 (1971), pp. 21-33.

*3049. Winski, Norman. Understanding Jung. Los Angeles: Sherbourn Press, 1971.

3050. Zeller Max. "Psychological interpretation of myth in religion." PP, 2:2 (1971), pp. 146-59.

3051. _____. "Sickness, suffering and redemption in the human and archetypal world. Tree (see *2986 above), pp. 58-69.

3052. "Der Wort-Assoziationstest nach C. G. Jung. Ein Beitrag zur Diagnostik psychogener Erkrankungen." Medizinische Welt, 7 (1971), pp. 233-37.

1972

3053. Allenby, Amy I. "Die Göttin Athene." ZAP, 3:3 (1972), pp. 161-76.

*3054. Aronson, Alex. Psyche and symbol in Shakespeare. Bloomington, Ind. and London: Indiana University Press, 1972.
            Rev. Ruth Gordon. JAP, 19:2 (1974), p. 215.
            James Kirsch. Quad, 14 (1973), pp. 19-21.

3055. Bach, Hans I. "Der archetypische Komplex 'Seines Vaters Sohn'." ZAP, 3:2 (1972), pp. 69-84. (see 3194 below for English edi-

tion)

3056. _____. "Der archetypische Komplex 'Seines Vaters Sohn', II. Teil." Ibid., 3:3 (1972), pp. 129-44. (see 3194 below for English edition)

3057. _____. "Jung's relation to synchronicity." Harv, 18 (1972), pp. 17-21.

3058. _____.; Duddington, A. and Whitehouse, R. "Synchronicity." Harv, 18 (1972), pp. 17-32.

3059. Bachant, Janet Lee. Process of transformation in the strucure of the ego during emotion within the theoretical framework of C. G. Jung. (Doctoral dissertation). New School for Social Research, 1972.

*3060. Balmer, H. H. Der Archetypentheorie von C. G. Jung: Eine Kritik. Berlin, Heidelberg and New York: Springer, 1972. Rev. R. Blomeyer. ZAP, 4:3 (1973), pp. 211-18.

3061. Bancroft, Henrietta, comp. "References to Nietzsche; taken from the writings of Prof. C. G. Jung." Zurich: 1972. (unpublished typescript)

*3062. Barker, Culver M. Healing in depth. H. I. Bach, ed. London: Hodder and Stoughton, 1972. Rev. J. E. Fraser. Quad, 12 (1972), pp. 24-27. Faye Pye. JAP, 18:1 (1973), p. 77. Unsigned. Harv, 18 (1972), pp. 78-79.

3063. Barz, Helmut. "Die Bedeutung von Symbolen für die Psychotherapie." ZAP, 3:2 (1972), pp. 103-10.

3064. Benz, Ernst. "Die Farbe im Erlebnisberich der christlichen Vision." EJ, 41 (1972), pp. 265-325.

*3065. Bitter, Wilhelm. Freud--Adler--Jung. Kindler-Taschenbücher, 1972. (see *695 above)

3066. Black, Roland Allen. Existentialism of dialogue and dialogue with the absurd in the psychology of C. G. Jung. (Doctoral dissertation). Temple University, 1972.

3067. Blomeyer, Rudolf. "Übertragung und Gegenübertragung in der Kindertherapie unter Gesichtspunkten der analytischen Psychologie." ZAP, 3:4 (1972), pp. 207-18.

3068. Brown, Eric Donald. Archetypes of transformation: a Jungian analysis of Chaucer's 'Wife of Bath's Tale' and 'Clerk's Tale'. (Doctoral dissertation). Pennsylvania State University, 1972.

3069. Carloni, G. and Nobili, D. "Filicide: II. Filicide in myth and art." Rev Sperimentali de Freniatria, 96:5 (1972), pp.

1337-80.

3070. Carpintero, F. J. "Freud, Adler y Jung. Estudio comparativo de sua ideas." _Franciscanum_, 14:40 (1972), pp. 57-107.

3071. _____. "Freud, Adler, Jung II." _Ibid_., 14:41 (1972), pp. 177-99.

3072. Castillejo, Irene C. de. "The animus: friend or foe." _PP_, 3:1 (1972), pp. 19-36. (see 1013 above)

*3073. Cirlot, J. E. _A dictionary of symbols_. J. Sage, trans, forw. by Herbert Read. London: Routledge and Kegan Paul, 1972.

3074. Corbin, Henry. "Mundus imaginalis: or the imaginary and the imaginal." _Spring_ 1972, pp. 1-19.

3075. _____. "Réalism et symbolism des coulerus in cosmologie shî-'ite." _EJ_, 41 (1972), pp. 109-75.

3076. Cowan, Thomas. "On Finnegans Wake." _Spring_ 1972, pp. 43-59.

3077. Detloff, Wayne K. "'Psychological types': fifty years after." _PP_, 3:1 (1972), pp. 62-73.

*3078. Diekmann, Hans. _Traum als Sprache der Seele, Einführung in die Traumdeutung der Analytischen Psychologie C. G. Jungs_. Stuttgart: Adolf Bonz, 1972.
        Rev. E. Jung. _ZAP_, 4:1 (1972), p. 72.
        Lola Paulsen. _JAP_, 19:1 (1974), p. 114.

3079. _____. "Das Traumsymbol in der Analytischen Psychologie." _ZAP_, 3:2 (1972), pp. 85-102.

3080. Dreifuss, Gustav. "The figures of Satan and Abraham." _JAP_, 17:2 (1972), pp. 166-78.

3081. Dreistadt, Roy. "A unifying theory of dreams, a new theory of nightmares, and the relationship of nightmares to psychopathology, literature, and collective social panic behavior." _Psychology_, 9:4 (1972), pp. 19-30.

3082. Dronke, Peter. "Tradition and innovation in medieval Western colour-imagery." _EJ_, 41 (1972), pp. 51-107.

*3083. Edinger, Edward F. _Ego and archetype: individuation and the religious function of the psyche_. New York: G. P. Putnam's Sons for the C. G. Jung Foundation, 1972.
        Rev. E. C. M. Begg. _PP_, 5:1 (1974), pp. 74-77.
        Sidney Handel. _Quad_, 13 (1973), pp. 18-21.
        A. B. J. Plaut. _JAP_, 18:2 (1973), pp. 173-75.

3084. Edson, Cynthia J. _Animus: man of many masks; a compilation of writings about and a personal confrontation with animus devel-_

opment <u>in</u> <u>feminine</u> <u>psychology</u>. (D. Min. dissertation). Andover Newton Theological School, 1972.

3085. Edwards, Alan. "Fantasy and early phases of self-representation." <u>JAP</u>, 17:1 (1972), pp. 17-30.

3086. Fardon, Nina. <u>Socrates</u> <u>and</u> <u>the</u> <u>analysand</u>. London: GofPP Lecture # 165, April 1972.

*3087. Fierz, Heinrich Karl. <u>Methodik</u>, <u>Theorie</u>, <u>und</u> <u>Ethik</u> <u>in</u> <u>der</u> <u>analytischen</u> <u>Psychotherapie</u>. Zurich: Klinik und Forschungsstätte für Jung'sche Psychologie, 1972. (see 3511 below)

3088. _____. "Psychotherapie der Depression." <u>ZAP</u>, 4:1 (1972),pp. 5-18.

*3089. Fodor, Nandor. <u>Freud</u>, <u>Jung</u> <u>and</u> <u>Occultism</u>. New York: Lyle Stuart, 1972.

3090. Fordham, Michael. "The interrelation between patient and therapist." <u>JAP</u>, 17:2 (1972), pp. 179-83.

3091. _____. "Notes on psychological types." <u>Ibid</u>., 17:2 (1972), pp. 111-15.

3092. _____. "Primäres Selbst, primäres Narzißmus und verwandte Theorien." <u>ZAP</u>, 3:4 (1972), pp. 189-206. (see 2935 above for English edition)

3093. Fossum. J. "Kristus og anti-krist; en studie pe bakgrunn av C. G. Jungs laere om selvets arketyp." <u>NTTid</u>, 73:1 (1972), pp. 27-34.

3094. Franz, Gilda. "An approach to the center: interview with Mary Whitehouse." <u>PP</u>, 3:1 (1972), pp. 37-46.

*3095. Franz, Marie Louise von. <u>C</u>. <u>G</u>. <u>Jung</u>: <u>sein</u> <u>Mythos</u> <u>in</u> <u>unserer</u> <u>Zeit</u>. Frauenfeld: Huber, 1972. (see *3515 below for English edition)
   Rev.   David Holt. <u>Harv</u>, 18 (1972), pp. 66-74.
   Eberhart Jung. <u>AP</u>, 5:1 (1974), pp. 70-71.

*3096. _____. <u>Patterns</u> <u>of</u> <u>creativity</u> <u>mirrored</u> <u>in</u> <u>creation</u> <u>myths</u>. New York: Spring Pubs., 1972.

*3097. _____. <u>Problems</u> <u>of</u> <u>the</u> <u>feminine</u> <u>in</u> <u>fairy</u> <u>tales</u>. New York: Spring Pubs., 1972. (see *1471 above)

3098. Frenkle, Norbert J. <u>Konfessionalismus</u> <u>und</u> <u>Religion</u> <u>aus</u> <u>der</u> <u>Sicht</u> <u>einiger</u> <u>analytischer</u> <u>Prozesse</u>. (Dibploma thesis). CGJI, Zurich, 1972

3099. Goldberg, Jonathan. <u>Aspects</u> <u>of</u> <u>eros</u>, <u>with</u> <u>a</u> <u>focus</u> <u>on</u> <u>homosexuality</u>. (Diploma thesis). CGJF, New York, 1972.

3100. Gordon, Rosemary. "Students and the new ethic." _Harv_, 18 (1972), pp. 37-42.

3101. Guggenbühl-Craig, Adolf. "Analytical rigidity and ritual." _Spring_ 1972, pp. 34-42.

3102. _____. "Reply to Schwartz." _Ibid._, pp. 223-25.

3103. Hart, David L. "The path to wholeness." _PP_, 3:2 (1972), pp. 150-60.

3104. Heisig, James W. "The _VII Sermones_: play and theory." _Spring_ 1972, pp. 206-18.

3105. Henderson, Joseph L. "The psychic activity of dreaming." _PP_, 3:2 (1972), pp. 99-111.

3106. Hillman, James. "Dionysos in Jung's writings." _Spring_ 1972, pp. 191-205.

3107. _____. "An essay on Pan." In _Pan_ (see *3109 below).

*3108. _____. The _myth_ _of_ analysis--three _essays_ _in_ archetypal psy-chology. Evanston, Ill.: Northwestern University Press, 1972. Rev. Ean Begg. _Harv_, 21 (1975), pp. 116-17.

*3109. _____. _Pan_ and _nightmare_. New York: Spring Pubs., 1972.

3110. _____. _Schism_ as differing visions. London: GofPP Lecture # 126, Jan. 1972. (see 3552 below)

3111. _____. "Senex and puer: an aspect of the historical and psychological." _Art_ _Inter_ (Lugano), 15:1 (1972), pp. 69-82. (see 2463 above)

3112. _____. "Three ways of failure and analysis." _JAP_, 17:1 (1972), pp. 1-6. (see 3398 and 3554 below)

3113. Horia, V. "Las memorias del siglo." _Arbor_, 82:321-22 (1972), pp. 31-43.

3114. Hubback, Judith. "Envy and the shadow." _JAP_, 17:2 (1972), pp. 152-65.

*3115. Hummel, Gert. Theologische Anthropologie und die Wirklichkeit der _Psyche_. Darmstadt: Wissenschaftlische Buchgesellschaft, 1972.

3116. Huyghe, René. "La couleur et l'expression de la dureé interi-eure in Occident." _EJ_, 41 (1972), pp. 217-63.

3117. Izutsu, Toshihiko. "The elimination of color in Far eastern art and philosophy." _Ibid._, pp. 429-64.

3118. Jacobi, Jolande. "Von den Tieren bei der Christgeburt." ZAP, 4:1 (1972), pp. 59-62.

3119. Jacoby, Marianne. "Psychotherapy in a nonhuman cosmos." Spring 1972, pp. 20-33.

3120. Jacoby, Mario. "Religious problems encountered by the analyst." Lecture, APC London, 19 Oct. 1972.

3121. Jaffé, Aniela. "Carl Gustav Jung." Psychology Today, 6:7 (1972), pp. 74-75.

3122. _____. "The creative phases in Jung's life." M. Stein, trans. Spring 1972, pp. 162-90. (see 2978 above for German edition)

3123. Keen, Sam. "Jung passes the electric kool-aid acid test." Psychology Today, 6:7 (1972), p. 64.

3124. Keller, Tina. "C. G. Jung: some memories and reflections." Inward Light, 35:81 (1972), pp. 6-25.

3125. Kelsey, Morton. Section on Jung in Encounter with God: a theology of Christian experience. Minneapolis: Bethany Fellowship, 1972, pp. 102-21.

3126. _____. "Rediscovering the priesthood through the unconscious." J of Pastoral Counseling, 7 (1972), pp. 26-36.

*3127. Kerényi, Carl. Zeus und Hera. Leiden: E. J. Brill, 1972. (see *3569 below for English edition)

3128. Kim, C. "Can men find the meaning of 'meaning'." Etcetera, 29:3 (1972), pp. 251-55.

3129. Kirsch, James. "Das Symbol der Wolke in der Europäischen Literatur des 19. und 20. Jahrhunderts." ZAP, 3:3 (1972), pp. 145-60. (see 2987 above for English edition)

3130. Kirsch, Thomas. "Psychodelic drug imagery in dreams." PP, 3:1 (1972), pp. 47-59.

*3131. Koestler, Arthur. The roots of coincidence. London: Hutchinson, 1972.
Rev. Gerhard Adler. JAP, 18:1 (1973), p. 81.

3132. Kolaříková, O. "Extraversion-introversion as types and as a factor of personality." (in Czech) Československá Psychologie, 16:1 (1972), pp. 15-26.

3133. Kopp, Sheldon B. "The discontented disciple." PP, 3:2 (1972), pp. 161-66.

3134. Kraemer, William P. and Gordon, Rosemary. "Student unrest."

<u>Harv</u>, 18 (1972), pp. 33-42.

3135. Lambert, Kenneth. "Transference/counter-transference: talion law and gratitude." <u>JAP</u>, 17:1 (1972), pp. 31-50.

3136. Laney, John H. "The peyote movement: an introduction." <u>Spring</u> 1972, pp. 110-31.

*3137. Layard, John. <u>The virgin archetype</u>. New York: Spring Pubs., 1972.

3138. Maguire, Anne. "The relation between the unconscious psyche and the organ of the skin." <u>Harv</u>, 18 (1972), pp. 43-54.

3139. Mann, Harriet, et al. "Four types of personalities and four ways of perceiving time." <u>Psychology Today</u>, 6:7 (1972), pp. 76-84.

3140. Marcus, Kate. "Childhood dreams and experiences: intimations of the future." <u>PP</u>, 3:2 (1972), pp. 135-47.

*3141. Meier, Carl Alfred. <u>Die Bedeutung des Traumes</u>. Olten and Freiburg: Walter, 1972.
　　　　　Rev. E. Krause. <u>ZAP</u>, 4:3 (1973), pp. 221-22.
　　　　　Lola Paulsen. <u>JAP</u>, 19:1 (1974), p. 114.

3142. Mitroff, Ian I. "The mythology of methodology: an essay on the nature of a feeling science." <u>Theory and Decision</u>, 2 (1972), pp. 274-90.

3143. Moore, N. "Counter-transference, anxiety and change." <u>JAP</u>, 17:1 (1972), pp. 51-65.

3144. Musial, T. J. and Pleasants, J. R. "Mendelian evolution and mandalian involution: speculations about the foundations of cultural change." <u>Rev Politics</u>, 34:4 (1972), pp. 154-71.

3145. Newman, Jeffrey. "Aspects of woman in Judaism." <u>Harv</u>, 18 (1972), pp. 55-65.

3146. O'Byrne, Margaret M. and Angers, William P. "Jung's concept of self-actualization and Teilhard de Chardin's philosophy." <u>J of Religion and Health</u>, 11:3 (1972), pp. 241-51.

*3147. Olney, James. <u>Metaphors of self</u>. Princeton, New Jersey: Princeton University Press, 1972.
　　　　　Rev. Carolyn Grant Fay. <u>Quad</u>, 14 (1973), pp. 22-24.

2148. Osgood, Judith Anne. <u>The relation between friendship bonds and Jung's psychological types</u>. (Doctoral dissertation). Arizona State University, 1972.

3149. Palmiere, L. "Intro-extra-version as an organizing principle in fantasy production." <u>JAP</u>, 17:2 (1972), pp. 116-31.

3150. Peerbolte, L. "Synchronicity and complementarity with regard to life." Systematics, 10:3 (1972), pp. 186-201.

3151. Perry, John Weir. "The messianic hero." JAP, 17:2 (1972), pp. 184-98.

3152. Peterson, Kenneth Vernon. The self in Carl Gustav Jung's analytical psychology and its relationship to perception. (Doctoral dissertation). University of North Dakota, 1972.

3153. Plaut, Albert B. J. "Analytical psychologists and psychological types: comment on replies to a survey." JAP, 17:2 (1972), pp. 137-51.

3154. _____. "Lerntheorie und Analytische Psychologie." ZAP, 4:1 (1972), pp. 19-40.

3155. Pontius, Anneliese A. "Spiel, Vermittler zwischen Gegensätzen-- seine Konkretisierung in Feuersetzen." Ibid., 3:4 (1972), pp. 219-32.

3156. Portmann, Adolf. "Farbensinn und Bedeutung der Farben in biologischer Sicht." EJ, 41 (1972), pp. 465-92.

3157. Redfearn, J. W. T. Parting, clinging, individuation. London: GofPP Lecture # 166, May 1972.

3158. Riedl, Peter Anselm. "Vom Orphismus zur Optical Art." EJ, 41 (1972), pp. 397-427.

3159. Ritsema, Rud. "The corrupted: a study of the 18th hexagram in the I Ching." Spring 1972, pp. 90-109.

*3160. Rogers, Barrie. Human personality: towards a unified theory. New York: Vantage Press, 1972.

3161. Romano, P. "Some considerations on Jungian psychology as a topical question in the current cultural situation." (in Italian) Riv Sperimentale di Ferniatria, 96:5 (1972), pp. 1381-89.

3162. Rossi, Ernest Lawrence. "Dream in the creation of personality." PP, 3:2 (1972), pp. 122-34.

*3163. _____. Dreams and the growth of personality. Elmsford, NY: Pergamon Press, 1972.
        Rev. William Willeford. Quad, 14 (1973), pp. 24-27.

3164. Rowe, Christopher. "Conceptions of colour and colour symbolism in the ancient world." EJ, 41 (1972), pp. 327-64.

3165. Rude, Jorge. "Arquetipos analiticos in 'Sobrehéros y tumbas'." Reflexion, 2:1 (1972), np.

3166. Rutting, H. "Alchemy and homo faber." (in Danish) Catolica,

29:3 (1972), pp. 135-41.

3167. Sambursky, Schmuel. "Lichte und Farbe in dem physikalischen Wissenschaften und in Goethes Lehre." EJ, 41 (1972), pp. 177-215.

3168. Sander, Donald F. "Healing symbolism in Navaho religion." Spring 1972, pp. 132-43.

3169. Scholem, Gershom G. "Farben und ihre Symbolik in der jüdischen Überlieferung und Mystik." EJ, 41 (1972), pp. 1-49.

3170. Schwartz, Nathan. "Drugs: the devil with the golden hair." Quad, 12 (1972), pp. 17-20.

3171. _____. and Sandra Ross. "A note on the so-called destructive aspect of psychotherapy." Spring 1972, pp. 219-22.

3172. Seifert, Theodore. "Allgemeine Grundlagen der Gruppentherapie. Gruppentherapie im Rahmen der Analytische Psychologie." ZAP, 4:1 (1972), pp. 41-58.

3173. Shapiro, Kenneth J. "A critique of introversion." Spring 1972, pp. 60-73.

*3174. Singer, June K. Boundaries of the soul. Garden City, NY: Doubleday, 1972.
            Rev. P. G. Dimmett. Christian Century, 90 (27 June 1972), p. 707.
            Thayer A. Greene. Quad, 16 (1974), pp. 39-40.
            Kenneth Lambert. JAP, 19:1 (1974), pp. 107-09.
            P. C. Lynn. Library J, 98 (15 Jan. 1973), p. 172.

3175. _____. "Individuation: discovery or disaster." Harv, 18 (1972), pp. 3-14.

3176. Smith, Edward W. "Personality growth through the presentification of personal symbols." Inter J of Symbology, 3:2 (1972), pp. 1-3.

3177. Stewart, Kilton. "Dream theory in Malaya." PP, 3:2 (1972), pp. 112-21.

*3178. Storr, Anthony. The dynamics of creation. London: Secker and Warburg, 1972.
            Rev. R. Gordon. JAP, 18:2 (1973), p. 176.

3179. Strauss, F. H. "Comment on Lucille Palmiere's study." JAP, 17:2 (1972), pp. 132-36.

*3180. Wehr, Gerhard. C. G. Jung und Rudolf Steiner--Konfrontation und Synopse. Stuttgart: Ernst Klett, 1972.
            Rev. M. Laiblin. ZAP, 4:3 (1972), pp. 219-20.

3181. _____. "Rudolf Steiner and C. G. Jung." Inward Light, 38:82 (1972), pp. 35-40.

3182. Whitmont, Edward C. "Body experience and psychological aware-ness." Quad, 12 (1972), pp. 5-16.

2183. _____. "Jungian analysis today." Psychology Today, 6:7 (1972), pp. 63-72.

3184. Wilhelm, Helmut. "On sacrifice in the I Ching." Spring 1972, pp. 74-89.

3185. Williams, Mary. "Success and failure in analysis: primary envy and the fate of the good." JAP, 17:1 (1972), pp. 7-16. (see 3472 below)

3186. Wolfe, Judith. "Jungian aspects of Jackson Pollock's imagery." Artform, 11:3 (1972), pp. 65-73.

3187. Zahan, Dominique. "White, red and black: colour symbolism in Black Africa." EJ, 41 (1972), pp. 365-96.

1973

*3188. Aigrisse, Gilberte. Psychogènese d'un poème: La route du sel (Roger Bodart). Brussels: De Rache, 1973.
      Rev. Juddith Hubback. JAP, 20:1 (1975), p. 83.

*3189. Alex, William. Dreams; the unconscious and analytical therapy. San Francisco: Lodestar Press, 1973. (see 2900 above)

3190. Allen, James Lovic. "The road to Byzantium: archetypal criti-cism and Yeats." J of Aesthetics and Art Criticism, 32 (Fall 1973), pp. 53-64.

3191. Arens, R. "C. G. Jung and some Far Eastern parallels." Cross Currents, 23:1 (1973), pp. 73-91.

3192. Aurigemma, Luigi. "Carl Gustav Jung." An Economies, Sociétés, Civilizations, 28:2 (1973), pp. 343-67.

3193. Avendano, Fausto. Jung, la figura del anima y la narrativa La-tino Americano. (Doctoral dissertation). University of Ari-zonz, 1973.

3194. Bach, Hans I. "On the archetypal complex: his father's son." Quad, 15 (1973), pp. 4-31. (see 3055-56 above for German edi-tion)

3195. Bambrough, Renford, et al. "The presence of eternity: a dis-
       cussion." _Harv_, 19 (1973), pp. 60-73.

3196. Benz, Ernst. "Die Signatur der Dinge. Aussen und Innen in der
       analytischen Kosmologie und Schriftauslegung." _EJ_, 42 (1973),
       pp. 517-80.

3197. Berry, Patricia. "On reduction." _Spring_ 1973, pp. 67-84.

3198. Blomeyer, Rudolf. "Der Gottmensch-Komplex bei Freud und seine
       Darstellung bei Jones." _ZAP_, 4:4 (1973), pp. 248-70.

3199. Bomar, P. H. "Golden pill: a Jungian archetype of creativity."
       Texas Q, 16 (Spring 1973), pp. 124-35.

3200. Bowan, James. "C. G. Jung." _Renewal_, 5:3 (1973). pp. 15-28.

3201. Cahen, Roland. "Der Gesetz der spezifischen Verplendung." _ZAP_,
       4:2 (1973), pp. 95-104.

3202. Carlson, Rae and Levy, Nissim. "Studies of Jungian typology: I.
       Memory, social perception, and social action." _J of Personali-
       ty_, 41:4 (1973), pp. 559-76.

*3203. Castillejo, Irene C. de. _Knowing woman: a feminine psychology_.
       New York: G. P. Putnam's Sons for the C. G. Jung Foundation,
       1973; Harper and Row, 1974.
              Rev. Marian Reith. _Quad_, 14 (1973), pp. 16-19.
                    Ruth Tenny. _Harv_, 19 (1973), pp. 74-75.
                    Deborah Wesley. _PP_, 4:2 (1973), pp. 195-99.

3204. Clark, Gary. "The truly sapient hominid: Jung and the uncon-
       scious." _Philosophy Today_, 17 (Fall 1973), pp. 205-12.

3205. Corbin, Henry. "Mysticism and humor." C. E. Schroeder, trans.
       Spring 1973, pp. 24-34.

3206. _____. "La science de la balance et les correspondances
       entre les mondes." _EJ_, 42 (1973), pp. 79-162.

3207. Davidson, Dorothy. "Invasion and separation." _Science_ (see
       *3223 below), pp. 162-72.

3208. _____. "A problem of identity in relation to the image of a
       damaged mother." _Ibid._, pp. 150-61. (see 2250 above)

*3209. Davis, Robert William, ed. _Toward a discovery of the person_.
       Burbank, Calif.: Society for Personality Assessment, 1973.

3210. Diekmann, Hans. "Übertragung--Gegenübertragung--Beziehung."
       ZAP, 4:3 (1973), pp. 169-80.

3211. Dreifuss, Gustav. "Can we evaluate analysis in terms of success
       and failure?" _JAP_, 18:2 (1973), pp. 165-72. (see 3366 below)

3212. Durand, Gilbert. "Similitude hermétique et science de l'homme." EJ, 42 (1973), pp. 427-515.

3213. Engel, Werner H. "Psychotherapeutic prophylaxis in a changing world." Amer J of Psychotherapy, 27:2 (1973), pp. 178-86.

3214. Fabricius, Johannes. "The symbol of the self in the alchemical 'proiectio'." JAP, 18:1 (1973), pp. 47-58.

3215. Faivre, Antoine. "Mystische Alchemie und geistige Hermeneutik." EJ, 42 (1973), pp. 323-60.

3216. Faye, Lawrence J. The role of Jungian psychology in the training of counselors. (Doctoral dissertation). University of Notre Dame, 1973.

3217. Fierz, Markus. "Wege der Wissenschaft und Religion." ZAP, 4:4 (1973), pp. 235-47.

3218. Fordham, Michael. "Some views on individuation." Science (see *3223 below), pp. 110-26. (see 2687 above)

3219. _____. "The empirical foundation and theories of the self in Jung's works." Ibid., pp. 12-38. (see 2008 above)

3220. _____. "The importance of analysing childhood for assimilation of the shadow." Ibid., pp. 95-109. (see 2262 above)

3221. _____. "Maturation of ego and self in infancy." Ibid., pp. 83-94.

3222. _____. "Reflections on child analysis." Riv Psicologica, 14:2 (1973), np.

*3223. _____., et al., eds. Analytical psychology a modern science. LAP I. London: Heinemann, 1973.
    Rev. Joseph L. Henderson. PP, 6:2 (1975), pp. 197-203.
    Marianne Jacoby. JAP, 20:1 (1975), p. 81.
    E. Lewis. JAP, 19:1 (1974), p. 122.

*3224. _____. Techniques in Jungian analysis. LAP II. London: Heinemann, 1973.
    Rev. Joseph L Henderson. PP, 6:2 (1975), pp. 197-203.
    P. King. JAP, 19:2 (1974), pp. 220-21.
    June K. Singer. JAP, 19:2 (1974), p. 222.

3225. Foy, Glenn A. "Individual growth in the family." PP, 4:1 (1973), pp. 44-59.

3226. Franz, Marie Louise von. "On group psychology." Quad, 13 (1973), pp. 4-11.

3227. _____. "Über einige Aspekte der Übertragung." ZAP, 4:3 (1973), pp. 157-68.

3228. Gammon, Mary R. "Window into eternity." _JAP_, 18:1 (1973), pp. 11-24.

3229. Goldstein, David. "Authority and conscience in Judaism." _Harv_, 19 (1973), pp. 13-20.

3230. Gomes, F. Soares. "O eros e o logos como ambivalencia do instinto de alteridade." _Rev Port Filosofia_, 29 (Jan.-June 1973), pp. 169-201.

3231. Gordon, Rosemary. "Symbols: content and process." _Science_ (see *3223 above), pp. 52-65. (see 2453 and 2563 above)

*3232. Grinnell, Robert. _Alchemy in a modern woman_. New York: Spring Pubs., 1973.

*3233. Hall, Calvin Springer, and Nordby, Vernon J. _A primer of Jungian psychology_. New York: Taplinger, 1973.
         Rev. M. E. Monbeck. _Library J_, 99 (15 Jan. 1973), p. 143.
         Unsigned. _Choice_, 11 (Oct. 1974), p. 1218.

*3234. Harding, M. Esther. _I misteri della donna; un'interpretazione psicologica del principio femminile come e raffigurato nel mito, nella storia è nei sogni_. A. Giuliani, trans. Rome: Astrolabio, 1973. (see *148 above for English and list of other editions)

3235. Hart, David L. "Classic man-woman models in fairy tales." _Quad_, 13 (1973), pp. 12-18.

3236. Heisig, James W. "Jung and theology: a bibliographical essay." _Spring_ 1973, pp. 204-55.

3237. Heisler, V. "The transpersonal in Jungian theory and therapy." _J of Religion and Health_, 12 (1973), pp. 337-40.

3238. Henderson, Joseph L. "The picture method in Jungian psychotherapy." _Art Psychotherapy_, 1:2 (1973), pp. 135-40.

3239. Heydt, Vera von der. "On the father in psychotherapy." In _Fathers and mothers_. New York: Spring Pubs., 1973, pp. 128-42.

3240. Hillman, James. "Anima. I." _Spring_ 1973, pp. 97-132.

3241. _____. "The dream and the underworld." _EJ_, 42 (1973), pp. 237-321.

3242. _____. "The great mother, her son, her hero, and the puer." In _Fathers_ (see *3335 below).

3243. _____. "Pathologizing (or falling apart)." _Art Inter_, 17:6 (1973), pp. 120-31.

3244.   _____. "Psychologizing (or seeing through). _Ibid._, 17:8
(1973), pp. 68-79.

3245.   Hobson, Robert F. "The archetypes of the collective unconscious." _Science_ (see *3223 above), pp. 66-75.

3246.   Hollis, James R. "Convergent patterns in Yeats and Jung." _PP_,
4:1 (1973), pp. 60-68.

3247.   Holt, David. "Jung and Marx." _Spring_ 1973, pp. 52-66.

3248.   _____. "Projection." _Harv_, 19 (1973), pp. 47-59.

3249.   Hough, Graham. "Nature and spirit in Shakespeare's last plays."
_EJ_, 42 (1973), pp. 43-77.

3250.   _____. "Poetry and the anima." _Spring_ 1973, pp. 85-96.

3251.   Hubback, Judith. "Uses and abuses of analogy." _JAP_, 18:2
(1973), pp. 91-104.

3252.   Izutsu, Toshihiko. "The interior and exterior in Zen Buddhism."
_EJ_, 42 (1973), pp. 581-618.

3253.   Jacoby, Mario. "Authority and revolt: the archetypal foundation." _Harv_, 19 (1973), pp. 21-33. (see 3564 below)

3254.   _____. "Zum Berufsbild des Jung'schen Analytikers." _ZAP_, 4:
4 (1973), pp. 282-92.

3255.   _____. "Zur Unterscheidung von Beziehung und Übertragung in
der analytischen Situation." _Ibid._, 4:3 (1973), pp. 181-92.

3256.   Jaffé, Aniela. "Synchronizität und Kausalität in Parapsychologie." _EJ_, 42 (1973), pp. 1-42.

3257.   Jung, Eberhard. "Über den Beitrag der Analytischen Psychologie
C. G. Jungs zur psychiatrischen Forschung." _ZAP_, 4:2 (1973),
pp. 105-16.

3258.   _____. "Zur Gruppendynamik in einem Psychotherapeuten-For-
schungsteam." _Ibid._, 4:3 (1973), pp. 193-210.

3259.   Kelm, Donald Roger. _Abreactionary elements in the plays and
selected paintings, prints and drawings of Oskar Kokoschka as
related to the ego-anima conflict as discussed in the psychology of C. G. Jung._ (Doctoral dissertation). Ohio University,
1973.

3260.   Kelsey, Morton T. "Aggression and religion: the psychology and
theology of the punitive element in man." _Religious Education_,
68:3 (1973), pp. 366-86.

3261.   _____. "Confronting inner violence." _J of Pastoral Counsel-_

ing. 8:1 (1973), pp. 11-22.

3262. King, P. "The therapist-patient relationship." JAP, 18:1 (1973), pp. 1-8.

3263. Kirsch, Hilde, and Kluger, Rivkah. "A bath-mitzva feast." PP, 4:2 (1973), pp. 177-81.

*3264. Kirsch, James. The reluctant prophet. Los Angeles: Sherborne Press, 1973.
Rev. A. and A. S. Herman. JAP, 19:2 (1974), p. 208.
Ruth Tenny. Harv, (1974), pp. 126-27.
William Walcott. PP, 5:2 (1974), pp. 185-88.

3265. _____. "Woman's changing image of self." PP, 4:2 (1973), pp. 151-68.

3266. Koestler, Arthur. "Physik und Synchronizität." ZPGP, 15:1 (1973), pp. 1 ff.

3267. Kreinheder, Albert. "Art in Jungian analysis." PP, 4:1 (1973), pp. 69-79.

3268. Lambert, Kenneth. "Agape as a therapeutic factor in analysis." JAP, 18:1 (1973), pp. 25-46.

3269. _____. "Facilitating elements in analysis." BJMP, 46 (1973), pp. 303-16.

3270. _____. The problem of authority in the early development of the individual. London: GofPP Lecture # 170, Feb. 1973.

3271. Lee, C. "The influence of Chinese philosophy on Western psychology." Chinese Culture, 14:3 (1973), pp. 17-24.

3272. Lockhart, Russell A. "The forgotten psyche of behavioral therapy." PP, 4:1 (1973), pp. 22-41.

3273. McCully, Robert S. "The interlacing of genius: Herman Rorschach and Carl G. Jung." Rorschachiana, 10 (1973), pp. 252-60.

3274. Mason, Bertha S. "Woman: image or individual." PP, 4:2 (1973), pp. 115-21.

3275. Mehren-Thomas, Helga. "Der Einvelne und die Gesellschaft im Werke C. G. Jungs." Zeit für Kultur und Politik, 28:7 (1973), pp. 522-25.

3276. Micklem, Niel. "Symbols and the process of healing." Harv, 19 (1973), pp. 34-45.

3277. Miller, David L. "Achelous and the butterfly: toward an archetypal psychology of humor." Spring 1973, pp. 1-23.

3278. Miller, Frank. "Eine Beispiele schöpferischer Eingebung aus dem Unbewußten." ZAP, 4:2 (1973), pp. 117-24.

3279. Mindell, Arnold. "The psychoid nature of the transference." Quad, 14 (1973), pp. 5-16.

3280. Moore, Ralph W., and Rojcewicz, Stephen. "Are all dreams Freudian?" Amer J of Psychoanalysis, 33:2 (1973), pp. 207-10.

*3281. Moreno, Mario. La dimensione simbolica. Padua: Marsilio Editori, 1973.
        Rev. Helen Shipway. JAP, 19:1 (1974), p. 116.

3282. Mosak, Harold H., and Kopp, Richard R. "The early recollections of Adler, Freud and Jung." J of Individual Psychology, 29:2 (1973), pp. 157-66.

*3283. Munz, Peter. When the Golden Bough breaks. London: Routledge and Kegan Paul, 1973.

*3284. Neumann, Erich. The child. New York: G. P. Putnam's Sons for the C. G. Jung Foundation, 1973. (see *2058 above for German edition)
        Rev. Faye Pye. JAP, 19:2 (1974), p. 218.
        Deborah Wesley. PP, 5:1 (1974), pp. 78-80.

3285. _____. "The moon and matriarchal consciousness." In Fathers (see *3335 below). (see 655 above for German and list of other editions)

3286. Newton, Kathleen. "Mediation of the image of infant-mother togetherness." Science (see *3223 above), pp. 173-86. (see 2306 above)

3287. Nichols, Sallie. "La papesse: high priestess of tarot." PP, 4:2 (1973), pp. 135-49.

3288. Nightingale. John A. The relationship of Jungian type to death concern and time perspective. (Doctoral dissertation). University of South Carolina, 1973.

3289. Odajnyk, Walter. "The political ideas of C. G. Jung." Amer Political Science Rev, 67:1 (1973), pp. 142-52.

3290. Olney, James. "Powerful emblem: the towers of Yeats and Jung." South Atlantic Q, 72 (Autumn 1973), pp. 494-515.

3291. Ormerod, J. P. "Authority and law." Harv, 19 (1973), pp. 3-12.

3292. Paulsen, Lola. "The unimaginable touch of time." Science (see *3223 above), pp. 187-204.

3293. Plaut, Albert B. J. "Reflections on not being able to imagine." Ibid., pp. 127-49.

3294. _____. "The ungappable bridge." JAP, 18:2 (1973), pp. 105-26.

3295. Portmann, Adolf. "Homologie und Anologie. Ein Grundproblem der Lebensdeutung." EJ, 42 (1973), pp. 619-49.

*3296. Progoff, Ira. Jung, synchronicity and human destiny. New York: Julian Press, 1973.
        Rev. B. Y. Beach. Library J, 99 (1 Feb. 1974), p. 370.
        Joan Carson. Quad, 17 (1974), p. 54.
        Unsigned. Choice, 11 (1974), p. 1028.

*3297. _____. The symbolic and the real. New York: McGraw-Hill, 1973.

3298. Pye, Faye. "Feminine images of success." PP, 4:2 (1973), pp. 169-76.

3299. Rauhala, Lauri. "The basic views of C. G. Jung in the light of hermeneutic metascience." Human Context, 5 (Sum. 1973), pp. 245-66.

3300. _____. "Wissenschaftsphilosophie der Tiefenpsychologie." ZAP, 4:2 (1973), pp. 79-94.

3301. Redfearn, J. W. T. "The nature of archetypal activity." JAP, 18:2 (1973), pp. 127-45.

3302. Ritsema, Rud. "The pit and the brilliance: hexagrams 29 and 30 in the I Ching." Spring 1973, pp. 142-70.

3303. Sambursky, Schmuel. "Wahrnemungen, Theorien und reale Aussen-welt." EJ, 42 (1973), pp. 163-203.

3304. Sanford, John A. "Jesus, Paul, and depth psychology." Religious Education, 68:6 (1973), pp. 673-89.

3305. _____. "Jesus, Paul and the shadow." PP, 4:1 (1973), pp. 9-21.

3306. Scott-Maxwell, Florida. "Early memories of Jung." Inward Light, 36:83 (1973), pp. 30-34.

3307. Seifert, Theodor. "Kritische Reflexionen zur Praxis der Analytischen Psychologie." ZAP, 4:4 (1973), pp. 271-82.

3308. Stein, Leopold. "Analytical psychology: a modern science." Science (see *3223 above), pp. 3-11. (see 1521 above)

3309. _____. "What is a symbol supposed to be?" Ibid., pp. 39-51. (see 1412 above)

3310. Stein, Murray. "The devouring father." In Fathers (see *3335 below).

3311. _____. "Hephaistos: a pattern of introversion." _Spring_ 1973, pp. 35-51.

*3312. Stein, Robert M. _Incest and human love; the betrayal of the soul in psychotherapy._ New York: The Third Press, 1973.
Rev. B. Y. Beach. _Quad_, 16 (1974), pp. 40-42.
T. B. Kirsch. _JAP_, 20:2 (1975), p. 237.

3313. _____. "The incest wound." _Spring_ 1973, pp. 133-41.

*3314. Storr, Anthony. _C. G. Jung._ New York: Viking Press, 1973.
Rev. Robertson Davies. _NY Times Book Rev_, (25 Feb. 1973), p. 31.
Rosemary Gordon. _JAP_, 18:2 (1973), p. 176.
James A. Hall. _Quad_, 16 (1974), p. 42.
Faye Pye. _Harv_, 19 (1973), p. 78.
Unsigned. _Choice_, 10 (Sept. 1973), p. 1085.

3315. Streich, Hildemarie. "Musikalische und psychologische Ent-sprechungen in der _Atalanta fugiens_ von Michael Maier." _EJ_, 42 (1973), pp. 361-426.

3316. Teague, Ronald Wallace. _Experimental exploration into C. G. Jung's concept of synchronicity: the role of meaningfullness in clairvoyance._ (Doctoral dissertation). Calif. School of Professional Psychology, 1973.

3317. Tuttle, Mary Caroline. _An exploration of C. G. Jung's psychological types as predictors of creativity and self-actualization._ (Doctoral dissertation). University of Calif., Berkely, 1973.

3318. Ulanov, Ann Belford. "Birth and rebirth." _JAP_, 18:2 (1973), pp. 146-64.

3319. _____. "The self as other." _J of Religion and Health_, 12:2 (1973), pp. 140-68.

3320. Van Loo, Elizabeth. _Jung and Dewey on the nature of artistic experience._ (Doctoral dissertation). Tulane University, 1973.

3321. Vitale, Agosto. "Saturn: the transformation of the father." In _Fathers_ (see *3335 below).

3322. Walcott, William. "Confessions of a male chauvinist animal." _PP_, 4:2 (1973), pp. 122-34.

3323. Wallace, Edith. "Conventional boundaries or protective terme-nos." _Art Psychotherapy_, 1:2 (1973), pp. 91-99.

*3324. Weaver, Rix. _The old wise woman: a study of active imagina-tion._ New York: G. P. Putnam's Sons for the C. G. Jung Foun-dation, 1973.
Rev. Amy I. Allenby. _JAP_, 20:1 (1975), p. 82.

*3325. Wethered, Audrey G. _Drama and movement in therapy_. London:
MacDonald and Evans, 1973.
Rev. A. G. Mountford. _Harv_, 19 (1973), pp. 76-77.

3326. Whitbeck, Caroline. "Theories of sex difference." _Philosophi-
cal Forum_, 5 (1973), pp. 54-80.

3327. Whitmont, Edward C. "Prefatory note to Jung's 'Reply to Buber'."
Spring 1973, pp. 188-95.

3328. Williams, Mary. "Comment on P. King's paper." _JAP_, 18:1 (1973),
pp. 9-10.

3329. _____. "The indivisibility of the personal and collective
unconscious." _Science_ (see *3223 above), pp. 76-82. (see 2105
above)

3330. Wolff, Philipp. "Thoreau goes West: footnote to a footnote."
Spring 1973, pp. 283-88.

3331. Woolger, Roger. "Against imagination: the _Via Negativa_ of Simone Weil." _Ibid_., pp. 256-72.

3332. Zahan, Dominique. "L'univers cosmo-biologique de l'Africain."
_EJ_, 42 (1973), pp. 205-36.

3333. Zaja, Luigi. "Observations in transit between Zurich and Milan." _Spring_ 1973, pp. 274-81.

3334. Zeller, Max. "Femininity discovered: dreams of two women." _PP_.
4:2 (1973), pp. 182-94.

3335. Varia. _Fathers and mothers: five papers on the archetypal
background of family psychology_. New York: Spring Pubs.,
1973.

1974

*3636. Adler, Gerhard, ed. _Success and failure in analysis_. New York:
G. P. Putnam's Sons for the C. G. Jung Foundation, 1974.
Rev. A. S. Thomson. _JAP_, 20:2 (1975), p. 230.

3337. Allenby, Amy I. "Encounter with archetypes." _Harv_, 20 (1974),
pp. 47-59.

3338. Arnold-Carey, L. "Zum Problem des Bewältigung von Realschuld."
_AP_, 5:2 (1974), pp. 113-21.

3339. Arthus, André. "Images de naissance--documents oniriques." _CPJ_, 2 (Sum. 1974), pp. 13-23.

3340. Asher, Charles. _Dream responses to the Jungian training process_. (Diploma thesis). CGJI, New York, 1974.

3341. Assagioli, Roberto. "Jung and psychosynthesis." _J of Humanistic Psychology_, 14:1 (1974), pp. 35-55. (see 2420 above)

3342. Begg, Ean. "Gnosis and the single vision." _Harv_, 20 (1974), pp. 88-102.

3343. Berry, Patricia. "An approach to the dream." _Spring_ 1974, pp. 58-79.

3344. Bess, Bruce Hovis. _A Jungian model of psychosocial development_. (Doctoral dissertation). Calif. School of Professional Psychology, 1974.

3345. Bickman, Martin Elliott. _Voyages of the mind's return: a Jungian study of Poe, Emerson, Whitman, and Dickinson_. (Doctoral dissertation). University of Pennsylvania, 1974.

3346. Birkhäuser, Peter. "Analytische Psychologie und die Problem der Kunst." _AP_, 5:3 (1974), pp. 194-203.

3347. Blöcker, Günther. "Schule der Weisheit, C. G. Jung in seinen Briefen." _Merkur_, 28:1 (1974), pp. 85-122.

3348. Blomeyer, Rudolf. "Aspekte der Persona." _AP_, 5:1 (1974), pp. 17-29.

3349. _____. "Die Konstellierung der Gegenübertragung beim Auftaschen archetypischer Träume: (b) Kasuistik." "The constellation of the countertransference in relation to the presentation of archetypal dreams: (b) Clinical aspects." _Success_ (see *3336 above), pp. 85-108. (see 2911 above for German edition)

3350. Booth, Gotthard. "Jung's and Rorschach's contributions toward a psychological typology." In _Toward a discovery of the person_. Robert W. Davis, ed. Burbank, Calif.: The Society for Personality Assessment, 1974.

*3351. Bradway, Katherine, et al. _Male and female, feminine and masculine_. San Francisco: CGJISF, 1974.

3352. Brooks, C. E. "The group as corrective for failure in analysis." _Success_ (see *3336 above), pp. 144-52.

*3353. Campbell, Joseph. _The mythic image_. Princeton, New Jersey: Princeton University Press (Bollingen Series C), 1974.
    Rev. Joseph L. Henderson. _Quad_, 8:1 (1975), pp. 69-70.

3354. Casey, Edward S. "Toward an archetypal imagination." _Spring_

1974, pp. 1-32.

3355. Clausse, Simone, et al. "Le sentiment." CPJ, (Spring 1974), pp. 51-58.

3356. Coukoulis, Peter P. A comparative investigation of the guru-disciple relationship and the Jungian analyst-analysant relationship. (Doctoral dissertation). Calif. Institute of Asian Studies, 1974.

3357. Debrunner, Hugo. "Changes in the hand lines of C. G. Jung." M. Gubitz, trans. Spring 1974, pp. 193-99. (see 624 above for German edition)

3358. Diekmann, Hans. "Archetypische Gesichtspunkte in der modernen Kunst." AP, 5:3 (1974), pp. 183-93.

*3359. _____. Individuation in Märchen aus 1001 Nacht. Stuttgart and Öffingen: Adolf Bonz, 1974.
   Rev. H. J. Wilke. AP, 6:1 (1975), pp. 87-88.

3360. _____. "Die Konstellierung des Gegenübertragung beim Auf-taschen archetypischer Träume: (a) Untersuchungsmethoden und Ergebnisse." "The constellation of the countertransference in relation to the presentation of archetypal dreams: (a) Research methods and results." Success (see *3336 above), pp. 52-84.

3361. _____. "Der Traum und das Selbst des Menschen." AP, 5:1 (1974), pp. 1-16.

3362. _____. "Zur Erich Neumanns Arbeit über 'Das Gericht' von Franz Kafka." Ibid., 5:4 (1974), pp. 249-51.

3363. Diekmann, Ute. "Ein archetypischer Aspekt in der auslösenden Situationen von Depressiven." Ibid., 5:2 (1974), pp. 97-112.

3364. Dourley, J. P. "Carl Jung and contemporary theology." Ecumenist, 12 (Sept.-Oct. 1974), pp. 90-95.

3365. _____. "Trinitarian models and human integration: Jung and Tillich compared." JAP, 19:2 (1974), pp. 131-51.

3366. Dreifuss, Gustav. "Can we evaluate analysis in terms of success and failure?" Success (see *3336 above), pp. 3-11. (see 3211 above)

3367. Duddington, Alexander. "Humour: the non-material alexipharmic." Harv, 20 (1974), pp. 23-36.

3368. Edinger, Edward F. "American Nekyia." Quad, 17 (1974), pp. 7-33.

3369. Foote, Edward. "Who was Mary Foote?" A. K. Donoghue, trans.

Spring 1974, pp. 256-68.

3370. Fordham, Michael. "Defences of the self." JAP, 19:2 (1974), pp. 192-99.

3371. _____. "Ending phase as an indicator of the success or failure of psychotherapy." Success (see *3336 above), pp. 45-51.

3372. _____. "Jung's conception of transference." JAP, 19:1 (1974), pp. 1-21.

3373. _____. "Jungian views of the body-mind relationship." Spring 1974, pp. 166-78.

3374. _____. "Simbolismo nella prima e secunda infanzia." Riv di Psicologia Analitica, 5:2 (1974), np.

3375. Frank, Margit van Leight. The principle of individuation in Kierkegaard's philosophy. (M. A. dissertation). McGill University, 1974.

*3376. Franz, Marie Louise von. Number and time: reflections leading toward a unification of depth psychology and physics. Evanston, Ill.: Northwestern University Press, 1974. (see *2794 above for German edition)
Rev. Edward H. Russell. Quad, 8:1 (1975), pp. 60-65.
Nathan Schwartz. Quad, 8:1 (1975), pp. 61-69.

*3377. _____. Shadow and evil in fairy tales. New York: Spring Pubs., 1974.

*3378. Frey-Rohn, Liliane. From Freud to Jung. New York: G. P. Putnam's Sons for the C. G. Jung Foundation, 1974. (see *2694 above for German edition)
Rev. James A. Hall. Quad, 17 (1974), pp. 53-54.
Anneliese Schwarzer. Library J, 100 (15 April 1975), p. 769.
Unsigned. Choice, 12 (April 1975), p. 292.

3379. Friedricksmeyer, E. "Bertram's episode in Hesse's Glass bead game." German Rev, 49 (Nov. 1974), pp. 284-97.

3380. Gaillard, Christian. "Du côté de la main gauche." CPJ, 3 (Fall 1974), pp. 34-41.

3381. Gelb, L. N. "Man and the land: the psychological theory of C. G. Jung." Zygon, 9 (Dec. 1974), pp. 288-99.

3382. Gillet, Geneviève Guy. "Le corps." CPJ, 1 (Spring 1974), pp. 40-50.

3383. _____. "Documents cliniques: l'ombre chez les enfants." Ibid., 3 (1974), pp. 42-50.

3384. Gordon, Rosemary. "A last word: comments on the Rorschach, synchronicity and relativity." In Person (see 3350 above), pp. 79-83.

3385. Grinnell, Robert. "In praise of the 'Instinct for unholiness': intimations of a moral archetypal." Spring 1974, pp. 168-85.

3386. Guggenbühl-Craig, Adolf. "Hat Analyse als therapeutisches Instrument versagt?" "Has analysis failed as a therapeutic instrument?" Success (see *3336 above), pp. 12-29.

3387. Hänisch, I. von. "Tiefenspychologische Aspekte der Tarzanfigur." AP, 5:2 (1974), pp. 122-34.

3388. Haft-Pomrock, Yael. "Psyche and soma in chirology: personality changes in analysis as reflected in the hand." Spring 1974, pp. 179-92.

3389. Hall, Marlene Laverne. Consciousness and the unconscious: Henry James and Jungian psychology. (Doctoral dissertation). University of Notre Dame, 1974.

3390. Hannah, Barbara. "Some glimpses of the individuation process in Jung himself." Quad, 16 (1974), pp. 26-35.

3391. Hannum, Hunter G. "Archetypal echoes in Mann's Death in Venince." PP, 5:1 (1974), pp. 48-59.

3392. Hart, David L. "The time of transformation." Ibid., pp. 21-33.

3393. Henderson, Joseph L., and Wheelwright, Joseph B. "Analytical psychology." Chapt. 38, B. In American handbook of psychiatry. 2nd ed. New York: Basic Books, 1974.

3394. Heydt, Vera von der. "Religious aspects of Jung's work." Harv, 20 (1974), pp. 60-70.

3395. Hillman, James. "Anima II." Spring 1974, pp. 113-46.

3396. _____. "Archetypal theory: C. G. Jung." In Operational theories of personality. A. Burton, ed. New York: Brunner/Mazel, 1974. (see 3542 below)

3397. _____. "On the necessity of abnormal psychology." EJ, 43 (1974), pp.

3398. _____. "Three ways of failure and analysis." Success (see *3336 below), pp. 30-36. (see 3112 above and 3554 below)

3399. Hobson, Robert F. "Loneliness." JAP, 19:1 (1974), pp. 71-91.

3400. _____. "The therapeutic community disease." Success (see *3336 above), pp. 153-66.

3401. Hogle, George H. "Family therapy: when analysis fails." _Ibid._,
       pp. 167-77.

3402. Holt, David. "Jung in Britain." _Harv_, 20 (1974), pp. 12-22.

3403. _____. "The timing of analysis." _Success_ (see *3336 above),
       pp. 37-44.

3404. Ho Lung, Richard R. _'Life's Womb'_: _a Jungian archetypal study
       of five novels by Joseph Conrad_. (Doctoral dissertation).
       Syracuse University, 1974.

3405. Hood, John M. "Modern mythology: _2001 AD, A Space Odyssey_."
       _PP_, 5:2 (1974), pp. 146-57.

3406. Hubback, Judith. "Notes on manipulation, activity and handling."
       JAP, 19:2 (1974), pp. 182-91.

3407. Humbert, Elie G. "Le concept d'ombre." _CPJ_, 3 (1974), pp. 16-
       29.

3408. _____. "Image et réalité de soi d'après C. G. Jung." _CPJ_, 1
       (1974), pp. 25-38.

3409. _____. "Images et réalité..." (continued) _CPJ_, 2 (1974),
       pp. 56-62.

3410. Jacobi, Jolande. "Freud et Jung." _Bull de Psychologie_, 27:1-4
       (1973-74), pp. 26-31. (see 1247 above for English and list of
       other editions)

3411. Jarrett, James L. "Dialectic as 'Tao' in Plato and Jung." _Dio-
       tima_, 2 (1974), pp. 73-92.

*3412. Johnson, Robert A. _He! A contribution to understanding mascu-
       line psychology_. King of Prussia, Pa.: Religious Publishing
       Co., 1974.

3413. Johnson, Toby. "The cage of years." _PP_, 5:2 (1974), pp. 164-71.

3414. Jung, Eberhard. "Zur gleichgeschlechtlichen Übertragungs- Ge-
       genübertragungskonstellation unter Berücksichtigung der Aris-
       leus-Vision." _AP_, 5:3 (1974), pp. 204-24.

3415. Kettner, Melvin G. "Ugly duckling complex: a symposium." _PP_,
       5:2 (1974), pp. 117-32.

3416. Kilmann, R. H., and Taylor, V. " Contingency approach to labo-
       ratory learning: psychological types vs. experiential norms."
       Human Relations, 27:9 (1974), pp. 891-909.

3417. King, P. "Notes on the psychoanalysis of older patients." _JAP_,
       19:1 (1974), pp. 22-37.

3418. Kirsch, James. "Imagination and reality." PP, 5:1 (1974), pp. 34-47.

3419. Köberle, Adolf. "Ursache und Heilung ekklesiogener Neurosen." AP, 5:1 (1974), pp. 55-61.

3420. Kraemer, William P. The enemy within-without. Psychotherapy and morals. London: GofPP Lecture # 175, July 1974.

3421. Kreinheder, Albert. "Contemporary psychology as seen by a Jungian analyst." PP, 5:1 (1974), pp. 9-20.

3422. Langegger, F. "Vivaldis 'La Notte', moderne Schlafforschung und Nachtmeerfahrt." AP, 5:3 (1974), pp. 161-82.

3423. Le Bars, Alain. "De la formation des analystes--réflexion." CPJ, 2 (1974), pp. 5-12.

3424. _____. "Le voyageur et son ombre." Ibid., 3 (1974), pp. 30-33.

3425. McCully, Robert S. "The Rorschach, synchronicity, and relativity." In Person (see 3350 above), pp. 33-45.

3426. _____. "Tantric imagery and Rorschach perception." Rorschachiana Japonica (Tokyo), 16 (1974), pp. 123-34.

3427. Maduro, Ronaldo, J., and Martinez, Carlos F. "Latino dream analysis: opportunity for confrontation." Social Casework, 55:8 (1974), pp. 461-69.

3428. Mann, Ulrich. "Adolf Köberle, der akademische Lehrer." AP, 5:1 (1974), pp. 45-47.

3429. Micklem, Niel. "Authority and illness." Harv, 20 (1974), pp. 3-11.

3430. _____. "On hysteria: the mythical syndrome." Spring 1974, pp. 147-65.

3431. Mitroff, Ian I. "Science's apollonic moon: a study in the psychodynamics of modern science." Ibid., pp. 102-12.

3432. Mollinger, Robert N. "Hero as poetic image." PP, 5:1 (1974), pp. 60-67.

3433. Moreno, Mario. "The archetypal foundation of youth protest as a cultural and individual phenomenon." Success (see *3336 above), pp. 185-97.

3434. Morgan, E. R. "Dynamic order." Thought, 77 (July 1974), pp. 359-64.

3435. Nagel, Hildegard. "Faces of time." Spring 1974, pp. 47-59.

3436. Nell, Renée. "The reflections of the liberation movement in the unconscious." Inter Mental Health Research Newsletter, 16:1 (1974), pp. 2-5.

3437. Neumann, Erich. "Franz Kafka: Das Gericht. Eine tiefenpsychologische Deutung." AP, 5:4 (1974), pp. 252-306.

3438. Nicholas, John. "The temenos: a personal reflection." Harv, 20 (1974), pp. 37-46.

3439. Nichols, Sallie. "The wisdom of the fool." PP, 5:2 (1974), pp. 97-116.

3440. Noel, Daniel C. "Veiled Kabir: C. G. Jung's phallic self-image." Spring 1974, pp. 224-42.

3441. Perry, John Weir. "What we may expect of acute schizophrenia." Success (see *3336 above), pp. 129-35.

3442. Plaut, Albert B. J. "Part-object relations and Jung's luminosities." JAP, 19:1 (1974), pp. 165-81.

3443. Pontius, Anneliesa A. "Threats to assassinate the king-president while propitiating mother." Ibid., pp. 38-53.

3444. Pye, Faye. "Images of success in the analysis of young women patients." Success (see *3336 above), pp. 198-205.

3445. Redfearn, J. W. T. "Mandala symbols and the individuation process." Ibid., pp. 120-28.

3446. Rhi, Bou-Yong. "Analysis in Korea, with special reference to the question of success and failure in analysis." Ibid., pp. 136-43.

3447. Rodriguez, Noelie Maria. The archetypal vision: a Marxist and Jungian study of mural art. (Doctoral dissertation). University of Calif., Los Angeles, 1974.

3448. Rudolph, A. "Jung and Zarathustra; an analytic interpretation." Philosophy Today, 18 (Win. 1974), pp. 312-18.

3449. Rupprecht, Carol Schreier. "The martial maid and the challenge of androgyny." Spring 1974, pp. 269-93.

3450. Sanford, John A. The man who wresteled with God; a study of individuation based on four Bible stories. King of Prussia, Pa.: Religious Publishing Co., 1974.

*3451. Schärf-Kluger, Rivkah. Psyche and Bible: three Old Testament themes. New York: Spring Pubs., 1974.

3452. Seifert, Theodor. "Die Gruppentherapie im Rahmen der Analytischen Psychologie." AP, 5:1 (1974), pp. 30-44.

3453. _____. "Zur Methodologie und Begriffsbildung in der Analytischen Psychologie C. G. Jungs." _AP_, 5:3 (1974), pp. 225-33.

3454. Singer, June K. "Creativity in Blake and Jung." _Harv_, 20 (1974), pp. 71-87.

3455. Snider, Clifton Mark. _The struggle for the self: a Jungian interpretation of Swinburne's 'Tristram of Lyonesse'_. (Doctoral dissertation). University of New Mexico, 1974.

3456. Solié, Pierre. "Mai 68..." _CPJ_, 2 (1974), pp. 24-32.

3457. Spier, M. "La trinité; essai sur Jung." _Studies in Religion/ Sciences Religieuses_, 3:4 (1974), pp. 173-74.

3458. Stettner, J. W. "What to do with visions." _J of Religion and Health_, 13:4 (1974), pp. 229-38.

3459. Teboul-Wiart, Hélène. "Relation." _CPJ_, 1 (1974), pp. 17-24.

3460. Toudic, Yves. "Désir et politique." _CPJ_, 2 (1974), pp. 42-56.

3461. Tuby, Molly. "Work." _Harv_, 20 (1974), pp. 103-21.

3462. Verne, Georges. "La relativisation du moi comme critère de succès de l'analyse jungienne." "The relativization of the ego as a criterion for success in Jungian analysis." _Success_ (see *3336 above), pp. 206-29.

3463. Vivas, E. "On aesthetics and Jung." _Modern Age_, 18 (Sum. 1974), pp. 246-56.

3464. Walcott, William. "Psychotherapeutic success with 'Hippies'." _Success_ (see *3336 above), pp. 178-84.

3465. Walser, Hans H. "An early psychoanalytic tragedy--J. J. Honegger and the beginnings of training analysis." _Spring_ 1974, pp. 243-55.

3466. Watkins, Mary. "The waking dream in European psychotherapy." _Ibid._, pp. 33-57.

3467. Wehr, G. "Tiefenpsychologische Bibelinterpretation als Aufgabe." _AP_, 5:1 (1974), pp. 48-54.

3468. Whitmont, Edward C. "Analysis in a group setting." _Quad_, 16 (1974), pp. 5-25.

3469. Wilhelm, Helmut. "Wanderings of the spirit and Hexagram 56 in the _I Ching_." _Spring_ 1974, pp. 80-101.

3470. Wilke, H. J. "Neurosentheoretische Überlegungen zur Struktur und Dynamik depressiver Erkrankungen." _AP_, 5:2 (1974), pp. 81-96.

3471. Williams, Mary. "Before and after the flood." JAP, 19:1 (1974), pp. 54-70.

3472. _____. "Success and failure in analysis: primary envy and the fate of the good." Success (see *3336 above), pp. 109-19.

3473. _____. "Transcience and eternity." PP, 5:2 (1974), pp. 158-63.

3474. Zabriskie, Philip T. "Goddesses in our midst." Quad, 17 (1974), pp. 34-45.

3475. Zeller, Max. "Dismemberment, death and individuation." PP, 5:2 (1974), pp. 132-45.

3476. "Inexorability of eros." TLS, 3766 (10 May 1974), pp. 489-92.

3477. "Rencontre de l'ombre: témoignage d'un analysant." CPJ, 3 (1974), pp. 51-61.

1975

3478. Adler, Gerhard. "Aspekte von Jungs Persönlichkeit und Werk." AP, 6:3 (1975), pp. 205-17.

3479. _____. "Aspects of Jung's personality and work." Harv, 21 (1975), pp. 1-11.

3480. _____. "Aspects of Jung's personality and work." PP, 6:1 (1975), pp. 11-21.

3481. _____. "C. G. Jung in a changing civilization." JAP, 20:2 (1975), pp. 97-101.

3482. Allan, J., and Macdonald, R. "The use of fantasy enactment in the treatment of an emerging autistic child." Ibid., 20:1 (1975), pp. 57-68.

3483. Allenby, Amy I. "Begegnung mit Archetypen." AP, 6:4 (1975), pp. 541-55.

3484. Allwohn, Adolf. "Das Ethos der Schattenannahme." AP, 6:1 (1975), pp. 57-63.

3485. Arthus, André. "Documents Oniriques." CPJ, 4 (1975), pp. 47-52.

3486. Bancroft, Mary. "Jung and his circle." PP, 6:2 (1975), pp. 114-

27.

3487. Baumann-Jung, Gret. "Some reflections on the horoscope of C. G. Jung." F. J. Hopmann, trans. _Spring_ 1975, pp. 35-55

3488. Benert, Annette Larson. _Passion and perception: a Jungian reading of Henry James._ (Doctoral dissertation). Lehigh University, 1975.

3489. Bennet, Edward Armstrong. "The quality of leadership." _Quest,_ (1975), pp. 16-22.

3490. Berner, R. L. "Etienne Leroux: a Jungian introduction." _Books Abroad,_ 49 (Spring 1975), pp. 255-62.

3491. Berry, Patricia. "The rape of Demeter/Persephone and neurosis." _Spring_ 1975, pp. 186-98.

3492. Blomeyer, Rudolf. "Identität, Identifizierung, Individuation." _AP,_ 6:3 (1975), pp. 260-76.

2493. Boe, John. "To kill Mercutio." _Quad,_ 8:2 (1975), pp. 97-106.

3494. Borelli, J. "Dreams, myths, and religious symbolism." _Thought,_ 50 (March 1975), pp. 56-66.

3495. Branson, David Howard. _Individuation: transcendence of Jungian types, life change and illness._ (Doctoral dissertation). University of Washington, 1975.

3496. Broadribb, Donald. "Aboriginal shamanism." _Quest,_ (1975), pp. 110-31.

3497. Brome, Vincent. "H. G. Wells and C. G. Jung." _Spring_ 1975, pp. 60-62.

3498. Brooks, Vernon E. "What does analytical psychology offer those with no access to analysis?" _Quad,_ 8:2 (1975), pp. 117-29.

3499. Burney, Cecil Edward. _A study of Jungian psychological type, body characteristics, value preference and behavioral preference._ (Doctoral dissertation). U. S. International University, 1975.

3500. Cahen, Roland. "Rencontre de Carl Gustav Jung: l'homme et l'oeuvre." _AP,_ 6:3 (1975), pp. 240-59.

*3501. Cohen, Edmund D. _C. G. Jung and the scientific attitude._ New York: Philosophical Library, 1975.

3502. Corbin, Henry. "The imago templi and secular norms." R. Horine, trans. _Spring_ 1975, pp. 163-85.

3503. D'Aquili, Eugene. "The influence of Jung on the works of Claude

Lévi-Strauss." J of the History of the Behavioral Sciences, 11:1 (1975), pp. 41-48.

3504. Daw-Koh, Janice. "Images of the self." Quest, (1975), pp. 97-107.

3505. Diekmann, Hans. "Typologische Aspekte im Lieblingsmärchen." AP, 6:3 (1975), pp. 318-35.

3506. Dreifuss, Gustav. "The binding of Isaac--the Akedah (Genesis 22)." JAP, 20:1 (1975), pp. 50-56.

3507. _____. "Zeitgenößische jüdische Geschichte und ihr archety-pischer Hintergrund." AP, 6:3 (1975), pp. 428-36.

3508. Edinger, Edward F. "American nekyia II." Quad, 8:1 (1975), pp. 5-32.

3509. _____. "The meaning of consciousness." Ibid., 8:2 (1975), pp. 33-48.

3510. Eschenbach, U. "Symbolik und Dynamik des Unbewußten im kindli-schen Spiel." AP, 6:2 (1975), pp. 89-120.

3511. Fierz, Heinrich Karl. "Methodik, Theorie und Ethik in der ana-lytischen Psychotherapie." Ibid., 6:1 (1975), pp. 64-76. (see 3087 above)

3512. Fordham, Michael. "Memories and thoughts about C. G. Jung." JAP, 20:2 (1975), pp. 102-13.

3513. _____. "On interpretation." AP, 6:3 (1975),pp. 277-93.

3514. Franz, Marie Louise von. "C. G. Jung and the problems of our time." Quest, (1975), pp. 4-15. (see 2691 above)

*3515. _____. C. G. Jung: his myth in our time. W. H. Kennedy, trans. New York: G. P. Putnam's Sons for the C. G. Jung Foun-dation, 1975. (see *3095 above for German edition)
     Rev. J. S. Gordon. NY Times Book Rev, (27 June 1975), p. 7.
     D. L. Hart. Library J, 100 (Aug. 1975), p. 1427.
     Unsigned. Choice, 12 (Jan. 1976), p. 1502.
     Unsigned. Economist, 259 (3 April 1976), p. 133.

3516. _____. "Le cri de Merlin: Jung's myth." PP, 6:1 (1975), pp. 22-36.

3517. _____. "Individuation and social contact in Jungian psycho-logy." Harv, 21 (1975), pp. 12-27.

3518. _____. "Psyche and matter in alchemy and modern science." Quad, 8:1 (1975), pp. 33-49.

3519. _____. "Der unbekannte Besucher in Märchen und Träumen." AP, 6:3 (1975), pp. 437-49.

3520. Geigerich, Wolfgang. "Ontogeny = phylogeny? A fundamental critique of Erich Neumann's analytical psychology." Spring 1975, pp. 110-29.

3521. Gillet, Geneviève Guy. "L'inceste à travers 'Les metamorphoses de l'ame et ses symboles'." CPJ, 4 (1975), pp. 5-16.

3522. Göllner, R. "Empirische Überprüfung einiger Aussagen über Einstellungs- und Funktionstypen von C. G. Jung." AP, 6:2 (1975), pp. 149-65.

3523. Goldenberg, Naomi R. "Archetypal theory after Jung." Spring 1975, pp. 199-220.

3524. Greene, Thayer. "Confessions of an extrovert." Quad, 8:2 (1975), pp. 21-32.

3525. Groesbeck, C. J. "The archetypal image of the wounded healer." JAP, 20:2 (1975), pp. 122-45.

3526. Groff, William Stanley. The effectiveness of systematic desensitization in the reduction of test anxiety in Jungian thinking versus feeling personality types. (Ed. D. dissertation). Auburn University, 1975.

3527. Hai, Dorothy Marcia. Some Jungian typological concepts: an audio visual approach for communicating type recognition skills. (Ed. D. dissertation). University of Massachusetts, 1975.

3528. Hannum, Hunter G. "Mann's Joseph novels: a journey toward individuation." PP, 6:2 (1975), pp. 163-75.

3529. Harding, M. Esther. "Conversations with Jung 1922-1960." Quad, 8:2 (1975), pp. 7-20.

3530. Harris, Dorothy. "A layman's approach to Jung's psychology." Aquagencies (Cape Town), 1975.

3531. Harris, Jay E., and Pontius, Anneliese A. "Dismemberment murder: in search of the object." J of Psychiatry and Law, 3:1 (1975), pp. 7-23.

3532. Hart, David. "Bewitchment: the story of Tamlane." Harv, 21 (1975), pp. 84-93.

*3533. Henderson, James L. A bridge across time. London: Turnstone, 1975.

3534. Henderson, Joseph L. "C. G. Jung: a reminiscent picture of his method." JAP, 20:2 (1975), pp. 114-21.

3535. Hensen, George. "Jung and modern psychology." The Questioner, 3 (June 1975), pp. 14-15.

3536. Herman, Lisa. "One transactional analyst's understanding of Carl Jung." Transactional Analysis J, 5:2 (1975), pp. 123-26.

3537. Hess, Gertrude. "König Hirsch, das Erosproblem in einer modernen Dichtung." AP, 6:3 (1975), pp. 472-81.

3538. d'Heurle, A., and Feimer, J. "A new image of the psyche: the archetypal psychology of James Hillman." Cross Currents, 25 (Fall 1975), pp. 289-98.

3539. Heydt, Vera von der. "A session with Jung." Harv, 21 (1975), pp. 108-10.

3540. Hill, John. "Individuation and the association experiment." Spring 1975, pp. 145-51.

3541. Hillman, James. "Abandoning the child." LE (see *3544 below), pp. 5-48. (see 2961 above)

3542. _____. "Archetypal theory: C. G. Jung." Ibid., pp. 170-95. (see 3396 above)

3543. _____. "Betrayal." Ibid., pp. 63-81. (see 2173 and 2279 above)

*3544. _____. Loose Ends: primary papers in archetypal psychology. New York: Spring Pubs., 1975.

3545. _____. "Methodological problems in dream research." LE (see *3544 above), pp. 196-209. (see 2028 above)

3546. _____. "Negative senex and a Renaissance solution." (see 3553 below)

3547. _____. "A note on story." Ibid., pp. 1-4.

3548. _____. "On the psychology of parapsychology." Ibid., pp. 126-37.

3549. _____. "Pathos: the nostalgia of the puer eternus." Ibid., pp. 49-62.

3550. _____. "Plotine, Ficino, and Vico as precursors of archetypal psychology." Ibid., pp. 146-69.

*3551. _____. Re-visioning psychology. New York: Harper and Row, 1975.

3552. _____. "Schism as differing visions." LE (see *3544 above), pp. 82-97. (see 3110 above)

3553. _____. "Senex destruction and a Renaissance solution." Spring 1975, pp. 77-109.

3554. _____. "Three ways of failure and analysis." LE (see *3544 above), pp. 98-104. (see 3112 and 3398 above)

3555. _____. "Toward the archetypal model of the masturbation inhibition." Ibid., pp. 105-25. (see 2370 and 2585 above)

3556. _____. "Why 'Archetypal' psychology?" Ibid., pp. 138-45. (see 2817 above)

3557. Hitchcock, John. A comparison of 'complementarity' in quantum physics with analogous structures in Kierkegaard's philosophical writings, from a Jungian point of view. (Doctoral dissertation). Graduate Theological Union, 1975.

3558. Holt, David. "Jung and Marx: alchemy, Christianity, and the work against nature." Harv,21 (1975), pp. 46-62.

3559. _____. "Projection, presence, profession." Spring 1975, pp. 130-44.

3560. Hurwitz, Siegmund. "Ahasver, der Ewige Wanderer. Historische und psychologische Aspekte." AP, 6:3 (1975), pp. 450-71.

3561. Immoos, Thomas. "'Die Sonne leuchtet um Mitternacht.' Ein literarischer und religionsgeschichtlicher Topos in Ose und West." AP, 6:3 (1975), pp. 482-500.

3562. Jacobi, Jolande. "Der Baum als Symbol." Ibid., pp. 336-67.

3563. Jacobs, Edward C. "A note on Thoreau and Jungian psychology." Spring 1975, pp. 63-66.

3564. Jacoby, Mario. "Autorität und Revolte--der Mythus vom Vatermord." AP, 6:4 (1975), pp. 524-40. (see 3253 above)

3565. Jones, Joyce Marie. Jungian concepts in the poetry of T. S. Eliot. (Ed. D. dissertation). East Texas State University, 1975.

3566. Jung, Eberhard. "Kann die Analytische Psychologie einen Beitrag zum Verständnis der Rauschmittelproblematik leisten?" AP, 6:1 (1975), pp. 12-25.

3567. Kadinsky, David. "Der Symbolbegriff bei C. G. Jung." Ibid., pp. 1-11.

3568. Kapacinskas, Thomas J. "The Exorcist and the spiritual problem of modern woman." PP, 6:2 (1975), pp. 176-83.

*3569. Kerényi, Carl. Zeus and Hera; archetypal image of father, husband and wife. C. Holme, trans. Princeton, New Jersey:

Princeton University Press (Bollingen Series LXV), 1975. (see
*3127 above for German edition)

3570. Kilmann, R. H., and Thomas, K. W. "Interpersonal conflict-hand-
ling behavior as reflections of Jungian personality dimensions."
Bibl Psychol Report, 37 (Dec. 1975), pp. 971-80.

3571. Kirsch, Hildegard. "Crossing the ocean: memories of C. G.
Jung." PP, 6:2 (1975), pp. 128-34.

3572. Kirsch, James. "Remembering C. G. Jung." Ibid., 6:1 (1975),
pp. 54-63.

3573. _____. "Woman and her changing image of self." Quest,
(1975), pp. 23-43.

3574. Kirsch, Thomas B. "A clinical example of puer aeternus identification." JAP, 19:2 (1975), pp. 151-65.

3575. Kreinheder, Albert. "Alchemy and the subtle body." PP, 6:2
(1975), pp. 135-43.

3576. Läppel, J., and Press, G. "Krankendemonstration in der Ausbild-
ung analytischer Psychotherapeuten." AP, 6:2 (1975), pp. 121-
35.

*3577. Layard, John. A Celtic quest--sexuality and soul in individua-
tion. Zurich: Spring Pubs., 1975.

3578. Lewy, E. "Lesefrüchte. Über C. G. Jung." Lexis, 3 (1975) p.
75.

3579. Lockhart, Russell A. "'Mary's dog is an ear mother': listening
to the voices of psychosis." PP, 6:2 (1975), pp. 144-62.

3580. McCully, Robert S. "Contributions of Jungian psychotherapy toward understanding the creative process." Geigy Pharmaceuti-
cals, 1975.

3581. McGlashan, Alan. "Chaos and rhythm." Harv, 21 (1975), pp. 63-
73.

3582. Marc, Olivier. "L'espace-mère et ses representations." CPJ, 4
(1975), pp. 43-46.

3583. Marc, Varenka. "Le Jeu de Sable." Ibid., pp. 53-56.

3584. Marcoen, A. "Enkele Elementen van het Wetenschappelijke Zelfver-
staan van C. G. Jung." Tijdschrift Filosofie, 37 (Sum. 1975),
pp. 420-44.

*3585. Meier, Carl Alfred. Bewußt sein. Olten and Freiburg: Walter,
1975.

*3586.   _____. Experiment und Symbol; Arbeiten zur komplexen Psychologie C. G. Jungs. Elisabeth Rüf, ed. Olten and Freiburg: Walter, 1975.

3587.   Mendelsohn, J. "Psychotherapie eines Kinderheims des Ichud-Hakibbuzim." AP, 6:3 (1975), pp. 368-85.

3588.   Meschkowski, Herbert. "Mathematik und Realität bei Georg Cantor." Dialectica, 29 (1975), pp. 55-70.

3589.   Micklem, Niel. "Medicine and melancholy." Harv, 21 (1975), pp. 74-83.

3590.   Miller, David L. "Ad maiorem gloriam Castaliae. Hermann Hesse and the Greek gods and goddesses." Spring 1975, pp. 152-62.

3591.   Mindell, Arnold. "The Golem." Quad, 8:2 (1975), pp. 107-15.

3592.   Moore, N. "The transcendent function and the forming ego." JAP, 20:2 (1975), pp. 164-82.

3593.   Moskos, George Michael. The individual and individuation in Flaubert's fiction: a Jungian analysis. (Doctoral dissertation). University of Wisconsin, Madison, 1975.

3594.   Mountford, Gwen. "Three touchstones." Harv, 21 (1975), pp. 28-44.

3595.   Naftulin, Donald H., et al. "Four therapeutic approaches to the same patient: a study of the Traux variables." Amer J of Psychotherapy, 29:1 (1975), pp. 66-71.

3596.   Newton, Kathleen. "Separation and pre-Oedipal guilt." JAP, 20:2 (1975), pp. 183-93.

3597.   O'Brien, Sally. "Berlioz and the anima archetype." Quest, (1975), pp. 77-96.

*3598.   Odajnyk, Walter. Jung on politics. New York: Harper and Row, 1975.

3599.   Perry, John Weir. "Jung and the new approach to psychosis." PP, 6:1 (1975), pp. 37-53.

3600.   Plaut, Albert B. J. "Object constancy or constant object?" JAP, 20:2 (1975), pp. 207-15.

3601.   _____. "Where have all the rituals gone?" Ibid., 20:1 (1975), pp. 3-18.

3602.   Pontius, Anneliese A. "Zerstückelungsmord als unbewußtes Ritual." AP, 6:2 (1975), pp. 136-48.

*3603.   Post, Laurens van der. Jung and the story of our time. New

York: Pantheon, 1975.
>Rev. L. Lebowitz. Nation, 221 (15 Nov. 1975), pp. 504-05.
>J. Olney. New Republic, 173 (6 Dec. 1975), pp. 25-26.
>R. Z. Sheppard. Time, 106 (1 Dec. 1975), p. 83.

3604. _____. "The myth of the journey." Quest, (1975), pp. 132-38.

3605. Pye, Faye. "A brief study of an Hasidic fairy tale." Harv, 21 (1975), pp. 94-104.

3606. Rogé, Emile. "Tantra--Oedipe et Inceste." CPJ, 4 (1975), pp. 37-42.

3607. Russell, Edward H. "Parapsychic luminosities." Quad, 8:2 (1975), pp. 49-72.

3608. Schärf-Kluger, Rivkah. "Einige psychologische Aspekte des Gilgamesch-Epos." AP, 6:3 (1975), pp. 386-427.

3609. Scholl, John Newman. Task performance of small groups compared on the basis of Jung's psychological types. (Ed. D. dissertation). Temple University, 1975.

3610. Seidman, P. "Die herakleische Versuchung der Psychotherapie." AP, 6:4 (1975), pp. 556-68.

3611. Seifert, Theodor. "Archetypus und inneres Modell der Welt. Ein Beitrag zur Integration von Analytischer Psychologie und empirische Verhaltenswissenschaften." Ibid., 6:3 (1975), pp. 294-317.

3612. _____. "Die Analytische Psychologie im Rahmen der empirisch-psychologischen Forschung." Ibid., 6:4 (1975), pp. 507-23.

3613. _____. "Notwendigkeit und Reichweit erfahrungswissenschaftlicher Verfahren in der Analytischen Psychologie." Ibid., 6:1 (1975), pp. 26-44.

3614. Seligman, E. "The case for a versitile approach to analytical practice." JAP, 20:2 (1975), pp. 194-206.

*3615. Shapiro, Kenneth J., and Alexander, Irving E. The experience of introversion: an integration of phenomenological, empirical, and Jungian approaches. Durham, N.C.: Duke University Press, 1975.

3616. Sharp, Daryl. "Index for The feminine in fairytales." Zurich: Spring Pubs., 1975.

3617. _____. "Index for The interpretation of fairytales." Zurich: Spring Pubs., 1975.

3618. Singer, June K. "The age of androgyny." Quad, 8:2 (1975), pp. 79-96.

3619. Sloan, William. "Jung and Rhine: a letter by William Sloan." Ibid., pp. 73-78.

3620. Sobosan, Jeffrey G. "Kierkegaard and Jung on the self." J of Psychology and Theology, 3:1 (1975), pp. 31-35.

3621. Solié, Pierre. "Oedipe et transgression." CPJ, 4 (1975), pp. 28-36.

3622. Spencer, M. J. "The instinct for the mysteries." JAP, 20:2 (1975), pp. 146-63.

3623. Sperber, M. "The daimonic: Freudian, Jungian and existential perspectives." Ibid., 20:1 (1975), pp. 41-49.

*3624. Staude, John Raphael. Psyche and society: Freud, Jung and Lévi-Strauss; from depth psychology to depth sociology. London: 1975.

3625. Steffney, John. "Symbolism and death in Jung and Zen Buddhism." Philosophy East and West, 25 (Spring 1975), pp. 175-85.

3626. Storr, Anthony. "The significance of Jung." TLS, 3828 (25 July 1975), p. 830.

3627. Teboul-Wiart, Hélène. "Le complexe mère." CPJ, 4 (1975), pp. 17-27.

*3628. Ulanov, Ann Belford, and Barry. Religion and the unconscious. Philadelphia: Westminster Press, 1975.

3629. Vandermeersch, P. "The archetypes: a new way to holiness; the work of C. G. Jung." Cistercian Studies, 10:1 (1975), pp. 3-21.

3630. Veith, Ilza. "Freud, Jung, and Paracelsus: historical reflections." Perspectives in Biology and Medicine, 18:4 (1975), pp. 513-21.

3631. Wallach, Judith. The quest for selfhood in Saul Bellow's novels: a Jungian interpretation. (Doctoral dissertation). University of Victoria (Canada), 1975.

3632. Weaver, Rix. "The feminine principle." Quest, (1975), pp. 44-76.

3633. Weir, Dennis Michael. The relationship of four Jungian personality types to a stated preference for a high unconditional positive regard as a counseling approach. (Doctoral dissertation). Southern Illinois University, 1975.

3634. Wells, H. G. "C. G. Jung." Spring 1976, pp. 56-60.

3635. Welsh, George S. "Adjective check list descriptions of Freud and Jung." J of Personality Assessment, 39:2 (1975), pp. 160-68.

3636. Wheelwright, Joseph B. "A personal experience of Jung." PP, 6:1 (1975), pp. 64-73.

3637. Willeford, William. "Jung's polaristic thought in its historical setting." AP, 6:3 (1975), pp. 218-39.

3638. _____. "Toward a dynamic concept of feeling." JAP, 20:1 (1975), pp. 18-40.

*3639. Zeller, Max. The dream: the vision of the night. Janet Dallett, ed. Los Angeles: APCLA, 1975.

3640. _____. "The task of the analyst." PP, 6:1 (1975), pp. 74-78.

3641. Zielen, V. "Das Suchtproblem unter anthropologischen Aspekten." AP, 6:1 (1975), pp. 45-56.

3642. Zimmer, Heinrich. "The Chakras of Kundalini Yoga." Spring 1975, pp. 33-34.

*3643. Zumstein-Preiswerk, Stefanie. C. G. Jungs Medium. Die Geschichte der Helly Preiswerk. Munich: Kindler, 1975.

1976

3644. Bär, E. "Archetypes and ideas. Jung and Kant." Philosophy Today, 20 (Sum. 1976), pp. 114-23.

3645. Canale, J Andrew. The effect of situationally controlled suggestibility on Jungian personality types. (Ed. D. dissertation). Boston University School of Education, 1976.

3646. Durand, Gilbert. "The image of man in Western occult tradition." J. A. Pratt, trans. Spring 1976, pp. 81-103.

*3647. Franz, Marie Louise von. Individuation in fairytales. Zurich: Spring Pubs., 1976.

3648. Graves, Barbara Lynne. Understanding rebirth and the symbols which express it: a study of Carl Jung and Paul Tillich. (D. Min. dissertation). School of Theology at Claremont, 1976.

3649. Grinnell, Robert. "Jung at Yale." Spring 1976, pp. 155-56.

*3650. Hannah, Barbara. C. G. Jung: a biographical memoir. New York: G. P. Putnam's Sons, 1976.

3651. Harrison, Noble Wayne. Validation of Jung's typological framework. (Doctoral dissertation). University of Mississippi, 1976.

3652. Heisig, James W. "Depth-psychology and the homo religiosus." Irish Theological Q, (1976 ?).

3653. Hillman, James. "Some early background to Jung's ideas: notes on C. G. Jung's medium by Stefanie Zumstein-Preiswerk." Spring 1976, pp. 123-36.

*3654. _____. Suicide and the soul. Zurich: Spring Pubs., 1976. (see above, *2174 for English and *2369 for German editions)

*3655. Johnson, Robert A. She! a contribution to understanding feminine psychology. King of Prussia, Pa.: Religious Publishing Co., 1976.

3656. Kelly D. "Jung and the medicine wheel." Philosophy Today, 20 (Sum. 1976), pp. 107-13.

*3657. Kerényi, Carl. Hermes--guide of souls. Zurich: Spring Pubs., 1976.

3658. Lathrop, Donald D. "Jung and Perls: analytical psychology and gestalt." In The growing edge of gestalt therapy. E. W. L. Smith, ed. New York: Brunner/Mazel, 1976.

3659. Lewis, Dennis Charles. Jungian theory and marital attraction. (Doctoral dissertation). University of Notre Dame, 1976.

3660. Lopez-Pedrazo, Rachel. "The tale of Dryops and the birth of Pan: a psychotherapeutic approach to eros between men." Spring 1976, pp. 176-90.

3661. McCully, Robert S. "A Jungian commentary on Epstein's case (wet shoe fetish)." Archives of Sexual Behavior, 2 (1976), pp. 185-88.

3662. McGuire, William. "Footnotes on Jung and transcendentalism." Spring 1976, pp. 136-40.

3663. Miller, David L. "Fairy tale or myth." Ibid., pp. 157-64.

3664. Plover, Gustav. "Psychotherapie." Kultur, 13:9 (1976), pp. 514-18.

3665. Portmann, Adolf. "Recollections of Jung's biology professor." J. M. Stoner, trans. Spring 1976, pp. 137-47.

3666. Ritsema, Rud. "The Quake and the Bound: a study of the 51st and 52nd hexagrams in the I Ching." Ibid., pp. 191-212.

3667. Singer, June K. Androgyny: toward a new theory of sexuality. Garden City, New York: Doubleday, 1976.

3668. Spiegelman, J Marvin. "Psychology and the occult." Spring 1976, pp. 104-22.

3669. Stein, Murray. "Narcissus." Ibid., pp. 32-53.

3670. Stein, Robert M. "Body and psyche: an archetypal view of psychosomatic phenomena." Ibid., pp. 66-80.

3671. Walker, Mitchell. "The double, an archetypal configuration." Ibid., pp. 165-75.

3672. Wolff-Windegg, Philipp. "C. G. Jung, Bachofen, Burckhardt, and Basel." Ibid., pp. 148-54.

3673. Ziegler, Alfred J. "Rousseauian optimism, natural distress and dream research." Ibid., pp. 54-65.

Undated

3674. Baudouin, Charles. "Quelques aspects nouveaux du problème de la personne." Rev Philosophique de France et Etranger, pp. 307-21.

3675. Daking, D. C. Jungian psychology and modern spiritual thought. London: Anglo-Eastern Publishing Co.

3676. Gruessen, J. J. The philosophic implications of C. G. Jung's individuation process. Washington: Privately printed.

3677. Hang, Thadeé. La struttura dell'anima nella psicologia de C. G. Jung. (Doctoral dissertation). Università Cattolica del Sacro Cuore, Milan.

3678. Hanhart, E. "Konstitution und Psychotherapie." Psychiatr Neuro Suisse, 134:1 (?), pp. 1-19.

3679. Hart, David L. The challenge of the anima illustrated in certain fairy tales. (Diploma thesis). CGJI, Zurich.

3680. Hess, Gertrude. Das Problem der Einstellungstypen in der Wissenschaft vom angeborenen Verhalten. (Diploma thesis). CGJI, Zurich.

3681. Hillman, James. Emotion and representations: the contribution of analytical psychology to the theory of emotion. (Diploma thesis). CGJI, Zurich.

3682. Howes, Elizabeth Boyden. The contribution of Dr. C. G. Jung to our religious situation and the contemporary scene. Guild for Psychological Studies, # 1.

3683. Marjasch, Sonja. 'The garden of Cyrus' von Sir Thomas Browne. (Diploma thesis). CGJI, Zurich.

3684. Penna, José O. de Meira. "Psicologia e urbanismo." Humboldt, 2:4, pp. 68-74.

3685. Sas, Stefan. Die Figur des Hinkenden in der Mythologie. (Diploma thesis). CGJI, Zurich.

3686. Smart, Frances E. The child archetype. (Diploma thesis). CGJI, Zurich.

*3687. Wickes, Frances G. De innerlijke Wereld van het Kind. E. Camerling, trans. Amsterdam: L. J. Veen. (see *48 above for English and list of other editions)

BOOK REVIEWS
OF WORKS BY JUNG

RJ1. Helbig, __. "PuPP" Reichsmedizinalanzeiger, (1902), p. 513.

RJ2. W. "PuPP" Wiener Medizinische Blätter, (1902), p. 745.

RJ3. Unsigned. "PuPP" Medizinische Rundschau, (1902), p. 1230.

RJ4. Unsigned. "PuPP" Neue Medizinische Presse, 3 (1902), p. 270.

1903

RJ5. Henneberg, __. "PuPP" Centralblatt für Nervenheilkunde und Psychiatrie, (1903), pp. 73-74.

RJ6. Infeld, __. "PuPP" Wiener Medizinische Presse, (1903), p. 1151.

RJ7. Kron, __. "PuPP" Deutsche Medizinalzeitung, (1903), p. 772.

RJ8. Pilcz, __. "PuPP" Wiener Klinische Rundschau, (1903), p. 473.

RJ9. Strasky, __. "PuPP" Centralblatt für die Grenzgebiete der Medizin und Chirurgie, 6 (1903), p. 47.

RJ10. Voss, __. "PuPP" St Petersburg Medizinische Wochenschrift, (1903), p. 3.

RJ11. Unsigned. "PuPP" Wiener Klinische Wochenschrift, 16 (1903), p. 353.

RJ12. Unsigned. "PuPP" Korrespondenzblatt, (1903), p. 83.

1904-1909

RJ13. Gross, Hans. "Assoz" Suddeutsche Allgemeine Zeitung, (28 March 1906), np.

RJ14. Pfister, __. "PuPP" Deutsche Arzte-Zeitung, (1905), p. 204.

RJ15.   Raecke, __. "PuPP" J für Psychologie und Neurologie, 3 (1904), pp. 95-96.

RJ16.   Sommer. "PuPP" Z für Psychologie und Physiologie der Sinnesorgane, 36 (1904), p. 234.

RJ17.   Weygandt, __. "PuPP" Psychiatrisch-neurologiesch Wochenschrift, 7 (1905), p. 124.

RJ18.   Ziehen, __ "PuPP" Deutsche Medizinsche Wochenschrift, 30 (1904), p. 516.

RJ19.   Unsigned. "Praecox" Dominion Medical Monthly, (1909), np.

RJ20.   Unsigned. "PuPP" Medical Weekly, (1908), pp. 15-17.

1911-1912

RJ21.   Adler, Alfred. "Kind" Zentralblatt, 1 (1911), pp. 122-23.

RJ22.   Jones, Ernest. "Die Assoziationsmethode" Ibid., 2 (1911), p. 48.

RJ23.   Unsigned. "Neue Bahnen der Psychologie" NZZ, (13 Jan. 1912), np.

1913

RJ24.   Ferenczi, Sandor. "Wandlung" Inter Z für Ärztliche Psychoanalyse, 1 (1913), pp. 391-403.

RJ25.   Furtmüller, C. "Darstellung" Zentralblatt, 4 (1913), pp. 86-90.

RJ26.   Sichler, A. "Darstellung" Archiv für Systematische Philosophie, 20:1 (1913), pp. 112-18.

RJ27. Abraham, Karl. "Darstellung" Berlin: Psychoanalytische Ver-
       lag, 1914.

RJ28. _____. "Darstellung" In Clinical papers and essays on psy-
       choanalysis. H. C. Abraham, ed. London: Hogarth; New York:
       Basic Books, 1955, pp. 101-05. (Trans of RJ27)

RJ29. Ferenczi, Sandor. "Typen" Inter Z für Ärztliche Psychoanalyse,
       2 (1914), pp. 86-87.

RJ30. Jones, Ernest. "Psychoanalysis" Ibid., pp. 83-86.

1915-1916

RJ31. Ferenczi, Sandor. "Psychologische Abhandlungen." Ibid., 3
       (1915), pp. 162-66.

RJ32. Sichler, A. "On the importance of the unconscious in psychopa-
       thology." "On psychological understanding." Zentralblatt, 6
       (1915), np.

RJ33. Unsigned. "Unc" New Republic, 7 (6 May 1916), pp. 21-22.

RJ34. Unsigned. "Unc" NY Times, (21 May 1916), np.

RJ35. Unsigned. "Paps" Edinburgh Medical J, (July 1916), np.
                          J of Education, (July 1916), np.
                          Outlook, (13 May 1916), np.

1917-1918

RJ36. Mitchell, T. W. "Paps" Proc Soc for Psychical Research, 30:75
       (1918), pp. 169-73.

RJ37. _____. "Unc" Ibid., pp. 134-69.

RJ38. Unsigned. "Unbew" NZZ, (20 Oct. 1917), np.

Berner Bund, (16 Oct. 1917), np.

1919

RJ39. Hug-Hellmuth, Hermine von. "Über Psychoanalyse beim Kinde."
Kinderpsychologie und Pädagogik, BFPA, (1914-19), np.

RJ40. Meyer, Adolf F. "Unbew" Nederlandsch Tijdschrift voor Genees-
kunde, 1 (1919) pp. 10 ff.

RJ41. Ophuijsen, J. W. H van. Discussion of RJ40. Ibid., pp. 818-20.

RJ42. Reik, Theodor. "Unbew" Das Unbewußte,BFPA, (1914-19), np.

1923

RJ43. Hermann, Imre. "Typen" Inter Z für Ärztliche Psychoanalyse,
9 (1923), pp. 529-31.

RJ44. Isham, Mary Keyt. "Types" NY Times Book Rev, (10 June 1923),
np.

RJ45. Murry, J Middleton. "Types" The Nation and the Athenaeum, (17
March 1923), np.

RJ46. Reich, Wilhelm. "Typen" Inter Z für Ärztliche Psychoanalyse,
9 (1923), pp. 532-34.

RJ47. Sapir, Edward. "Types" The Freeman, (7 Nov. 1923), np.

RJ48. Sinclair, M. "Types" English Rev, 36 (May 1923), pp. 436-39.

RJ49. Watson, John B. "Types" New Republic, (7 Nov. 1923), np.

RJ50. Bernfeld, Siegfried, "Analytische Psychologie und Erziehung." Zeit für Psychoanalytische Pädagogik, 1 (1927), pp. 280-83.

RJ51. Thorburn, J. M. "Types" Monist, 34 (Jan. 1924), pp. 96-111.

1928

RJ52. Fenichel, Otto. "Die Bedeutung des Vaters für das Schiksal des Einzelnen." Inter Z für Ärztliche Psychoanalyse, 14 (1928), p. 278.

RJ53. Graber, Gustav Hans. "Unbew" Ibid., p. 131.

RJ54. Harding, M. Esther. "Essays" The Dial, (1928), np.

RJ55. _____. "Essays" The Nation, 127:3310 (12 Dec. 1928), pp. 664 ff.

1929

RJ56. Bertine, Eleanor. "Essays" "Contribs" New Republic, (6 Jan. 1929), np.

RJ57. Eder, David M. "Essays" Inter J of Psycho-Analysis, 10 (1929), pp. 468-70.

RJ58. Harding, M. Esther. "Contribs" NY Times Book Rev, (12 May 1929), np.

RJ59. _____. "Essays" NY Times, (June 1929), np.

RJ60. Unsigned. "Contribs" Commonweal, (6 Feb. 1929), np.

RJ61. Unsigned. "Contribs" NY Times Book Rev, (12 May 1929), np.

RJ62. Unsigned. "Contribs" The Observer, (14 April 1929), np.

RJ63. Unsigned. "Essays" "Contribs" <u>TLS</u>, (31 Jan. 1929), np.

1930-1931

RJ64. Horton, L. H. "Contribs" <u>J of Abnormal and Social Psychology</u>, 24 (1930), pp. 441-59.

RJ65. Schmitz, Oscar A. H. "Welt" <u>Stuttgarter Neues Tagblatt</u>, (25 Aug. 1931), np.

RJ66. Unsigned. "Welt" <u>NZZ</u>, (10 May 1031), np.

1932

RJ67. Barth, Hans. "Die Beziehungen der Psychotherapie zur Seelsorge." <u>NZZ</u>, (3 Aug. 1932), np.

RJ68. Bonifas, H. "Symboles" <u>Rev Fr Psychoanalytique</u>, 5 (1932), pp. 459-61.

RJ69. Paneth, Ludwig. "Gegen" <u>Nervenarzt</u>, 5 (1932), pp. 249-52.

RJ70. Unsigned. "Die Beziehungen der Psychotherapie zur Seelsorge." <u>Basler Nachrichten</u>, (17 Sept. 1932), np.

1933

RJ71. Adams, Grace. "Mod" <u>New Republic</u>, (12 June 1933), np.

RJ72, E. S. W. "Mod" <u>Methodist Times</u>, (16 Nov. 1933), np.

RJ73. Erwin, Edmon. "Mod" <u>NY Rev of Literature</u>, (16 Sept. 1933), np.

RJ74. Forman, Henry James. "Mod" <u>NY Times</u>, (26 Nov. 1933), np.

RJ75. H. I'A. F. "Mod" <u>Manchester Guardian</u>, (19 Sept. 1933), np.

RJ76. Joad, C. E. M. "Mod" The Spectator, (20 Oct. 1933), np.

RJ77. Mairet, Philip.   "Mod" New English Weekly, (2 Nov. 1933), np.

RJ78. Penrose, L. S. "Mod" New Statesman, (30 Sept. 1933), np.

RJ79. Stone, M. Eleanor. "Mod" No place or pages (Sept. 1933).

RJ80. Strickland, Francis L. "Mod" The Christian Century, (1 Nov. 1933), np.

RJ81. Wood, H. G. "Mod" British Weekly, (21 Sept. 1933), np.

RJ82. Unsigned. "Mod" The Listener, (26 Oct. 1933), np.

RJ83. Unsigned. "Mod" NY Times, (24 Aug. 1933), np.

RJ84. Unsigned. "Mod" The Republican, (Jan 1933), np.

1934

RJ85. Campbell, Joseph. "Myth" Rev of Religion, 16 (1934), pp. 169-73.

RJ86. Hedley, S. Dimock. "Mod" J of Religion, (July 1934), np.

RJ87. Hesse, Hermann. "Wirklichkeit der Seele." Neue Rundschau, 45: 2 (1934), pp. 325-28.

RJ88. Unsigned. "Mod" Pax, 23 (Feb. 1934), p. 270.

1935-1936

RJ89. Christoffel, H. "Allg" Schweiz Medizinische Wochenschrift, (1935), np.

RJ90. Muret, Maurice. "Wotan" J de Débats, (14 May 1935), np.

RJ91. Unsigned. "Wotan" Argauer Tagblatt, (14 March 1936), np.

RJ92. Unsigned. "Wotan" Bund Abend Blatt, (17 March 1936), np.

RJ93. Unsigned. "Wotan" _Gazette de Lausanne_, (25 March 1936), np.

1937-1938

RJ94. Barrett, Clifford. "Rel" _NY Times Book Rev_, (20 March 1938), np.

RJ95. Grensted, L. W. "Rel" _The Church Q Rev_, 252 (July-Sept 1938), np.

RJ96. Preutte, Lorine. "Rel" _NY Herald Tribune_, (9 Oct. 1938), np.

RJ97. Savarin, P. "Analytische Psychologie und Erziehung." _Imago_, 23 (1937), pp. 241-42.

RJ98. Unsigned. "Rel" _Tablet_, 171:403 (26 March 1938), np.

RJ99. Unsigned. "Rel" _Time_, (7 March 1938), np.

1939

RJ100. Boisen, A. T. "Rel" _Amer J of Sociology_,44 (1939), pp. 612-13.

RJ101. Ellard, A. G. "Rel" _Thought_, 14 (1939), pp. 335-36.

RJ102. Lasswell, H. D. "Rel" _Psychoanalytic Q_, 8 (1939), pp. 392-93.

RJ103. Unsigned. "Rel" _Religious Rev_, 3 (June 1939), pp. 22-24.

1940

RJ104. Forman, Henry James. "Integration of the Personality." _NY Times Book Rev_, (21 Jan. 1940), np.

RJ105. Spender, Stephen. "Integ" _New Statesman and Nation_, (27 Aug.

1940), np.

1941

RJ106. Belton, Leslie. "Integ" The Aryan Path, (Feb. 1941), np.

RJ107. Kaufman, M. R. "Integ" Psychoanalytic Q, 10 (1941), pp. 652-56.

RJ108. Märker, Friedrich. "Gött" Die Literatur, (April 1941), np.

RJ109. Unsigned. "Gött" Die Weltwoche, (19 Sept. 1941), np.

1942-1947

RJ110. Heym, Gerard. "Paracelsica" Ambix, 2:3-4 (1946), pp. 196-98.

RJ111. Mulde, N. "Freud" Stimmen der Zeit, 189 (June 1942), p. 428.

RJ112. Pfeiffer, Johannes. "Rel" Die Sammlung, 1:5 (Feb. 1946), pp. 317-20.

RJ113. White, Victor. "Über" "Aufs" Blackfriars, 28 (1947), pp. 138-40.

RJ114. Unsigned. "Aufs" Kultur, 15:6 (1947), pp. 113-17.

RJ115. Unsigned. "Über" Ibid., 15:7 (1947), pp. 89-93.

1948

RJ116. Heym, Gerard. "Alch" Ambix, 3:1-2 (1948), pp. 64-67.

RJ117. Hough, Graham. "Contem" New Statesman and Nation, 35 (29 May 1948), p. 439.

RJ118. Rigassi, Georges. "Aspects du drame" <u>Gazette de Lausanne</u>, (18 Dec. 1948), np.

RJ119. Unsigned. "Contem" <u>Sower</u>, 167 (April 1948), pp. 40-42.

1949

RJ120. Boutonier, J. "Aspects du drame" <u>Psyche</u> 4 (1949), pp. 780-82.

RJ121. Fechter, Paul. "Geistes" <u>Die Neue Zeitung</u>, (4 June 1949), np.

RJ122. Gray, R. D. "Alch" <u>The Listener</u>, (15 Dec. 1949), np.

RJ123. Kudszus, Hans. "Geistes" <u>Der Tagesspiegel</u>, (27 Nov. 1949), np.

RJ124. Unsigned. "Ener" <u>Neues Winterthurer Tagblatt</u>, (17 March 1949), np.

RJ125. Unsigned. "Über" <u>Schweiz Monatshefte</u>, (Jan.-July 1949), np.

1950

RJ126. Adler, Gerhard. "Ener" <u>Brit J Mych</u>, (June 1950), np.

RJ127. Unsigned. "Gest" <u>Neues Winterthurer Tagblatt</u>, (25 Oct. 1950), np.

RJ128. Unsigned. "Erz" <u>Schweiz Lehrerzeitung</u>, (21 April 1950), np.

RJ129. Unsigned. "Gest" <u>Thurgauer Zeitung</u>, (7 Oct. 1950), np.

1951

RJ130. Fessler, L. "Seele" <u>Psychoanalytic Q</u>, 20 (1951), pp. 463-64.

RJ131. Jaffé, Aniela. "Aion" (7 Dec. 1951), np.

RJ132. Unsigned. "Aion" Das Bücherblatt, (21 Sept. 1951)

RJ133. Unsigned. "Aion" Der Landbote, (3 Nov. 1951), np.

RJ134. Unsigned. "Aion" Luzerner Neuste Nachrichten, (22 Sept. 1951), np.

RJ135. Unsigned. "Gest" TLS, (8 June 1951), np.

RJ136. Unsigned. "Aion" Der Wendepunkt, (Oct. 1051), np.

1952

RJ137. Buri, Fritz. "Hiob" National-Zeitung, (27 April 1952), np.

RJ138. Hoch, Dorothee. "Hiob" Kirchenblatt für die Reformierte Schweiz, 108 (1952), pp. 165-68.

RJ139. Jaffé, Aniela. "Aion" Bull APCNY, 14:6 (1952), np.

RJ140. Kehoe, Richard. "Job" Dominican Studies, 5 (1952), pp. 228-31.

RJ141. Marti, Kurt. "Hiob" Kirchenblatt für die Reformierte Schweiz, 108 (1952), pp. 168-69.

RJ142. Weizäcker, Viktor von. "Hiob" Psyche, 2 (1952), p. 30.

RJ143. White Victor. "Aion" Dominican Studies, 5 (1952), pp. 240-43.

1953

RJ144. Haberlandt, H. "Hiob" Wissenschaft und Weltbild, 6 (1953), pp. 52-58.

RJ145. Heym, G. "CW12" Tablet, 202 (5 Sept. 1953), p. 230.

RJ146. Ludlow, R. "CW7" Catholic Worker, 20 (Oct. 1953), p. 5.

RJ147. Michaelis, Edgar. "Job" Rev de Théologie et de Philosophie,

3 (1953), pp. 183-95.

RJ148. Raine, Kathleen. "CW12" Decision, 128 (8 June 1953), pp. 2 ff.
        New Republic, 128 (18 May 1953), pp. 17-18.

RJ149. Ramnoux, C. "Myth" Rev Philosophique, 143 (1953), pp. 440-42.

RJ150. Rudin, Josef. "Hiob" Orientierung, 17 (1953), pp. 41-44.

RJ151. Semmelroth, Otto. "Hiob" Scholastik, 28 (1953), p. 139.

RJ152. Werner, M. "Hiob" SZP, 12:1 (1953), pp. 74-76.

1954

RJ153. Evans, Erastus. "Job" London: GofPP Lecture # 78, 1954.

RJ154. Gernet, L. "Myth" Annee Sociologique, 3rd series (1953-54),
        pp. 314-20.

RJ155. Jaeger, Martha. "CW7" J of Religious Thought, 11:2 (1954), p.
        175.

RJ156. Kroner, F. "Natur" Dialectica, 8:30 (1954), pp. 173-79.

RJ157. Nagel, Hildegard. "Job" Spring 1954, pp. 1-12.

RJ158. Southard, S. "CW16" Rev and Expositor, 51 (1954), pp. 559-60.

RJ159. Stocker, A. "Symboles" Pensée Catholique, 34 (Dec. 1954), pp.
        57-69.

RJ160. Waller, H. "Nature" Psychoanalytic Rev, 41 (1954), pp. 389-
        90.

RJ161. White, Victor. "Reflec" Blackfriars, 35 (Jan. 1954), p. 32.

RJ162. _____. "CW12" Ibid., 35 (Mar. 1954), p. 125.

RJ163. _____. "CW7" Loc. cit.

RJ164. _____. "Winz" Loc. cit.

RJ165. Widmann, G. "Gegen" Philos Lit Anzeig, 7:4 (1954), pp. 180-
        88.

RJ166. Willson, D. "CW12" J of Religious Thought, 11:1 (1953-54),
        pp. 82-83.

RJ167. Wise, C. A. "Reflec" Ibid., 11:2 (1954), pp. 178-79.

1955

RJ168. Bernhardt, W. H. "Job" Ibid., 12 (1955), pp. 127-28.

RJ169. Block, M., and Laszlo, Violet de. "The Collected Works of C.
G. Jung: a review article." Rev of Religion, 19 (Mar. 1955),
pp. 150-59.

RJ170. Crehan, J. "Job" Theological Studies, 16 (Sum. 1955), pp.
414-23.

RJ171. Elkisch, F. "Job" Tablet, 205 (5 Feb. 1955), p. 135.

RJ172. Rairbairn, W. R. D. "Reflec" Inter J of Psycho-Analysis,
36 (1955), p. 362.

RJ173. Fordham, Michael. "Job" BJMP, 28 (1955), pp. 271-73.

RJ174. Hartwig, Theodor. "Hiob" Befreiung, 3 (1955), pp. 103-11.

RJ175. Lambert, Kenneth. "Job" JAP, 1:1 (1955), pp. 100-08.

RJ176. Piper, O. A. "CW7" Princeton Seminary Bull, 48 (Jan. 1955),
pp. 38-39.

RJ177. Prince, G. Stewart. "Collected Works" JAP, 1:1 (1955), pp.
97-99.

RJ178. Slochower, Harry. "Job" The guide to psychiatric and psychological literature, 2:1 (1955), np.

RJ179. Vincent, A. "Myth" Rev Scientifique de la Religion, 29:2
(1955), pp. 146-63.

RJ180. Watkin, E. "Job" Dublin Rev, 229 (Aut. 1955), p. 337.

RJ181. White Victor. "CW17" Blackfriars, 36 (Feb. 1955), p. 31.

RJ182. _____. "CW16" Ibid., (Jan. 1955), p. 591.

RJ183. Allwohn, Adolf. "Typen" Zeit für Religions- und Geistesge-schichte, 8 (1956), pp. 361-64.

RJ184. Haynes, R. "Nature" Tablet, 207 (11 Feb. 1956), p. 134.

RJ185. Hiltner, Seward. "Job" Pastoral Psychology, 6 (1956), pp. 82-83.

RJ186. Moloney, R. "Nature" Month, 15 (June 1956), p. 360.

RJ187. Piotrowski, Z. A. "CW17" Psychoanalytic Rev, 43 (1956), pp. 252-53.

RJ188. Plaut, Albert B. J. "Nature" JAP, 1:2 (1956), p. 209.

RJ189. White, Victor. "Nature" Blackfriars, 37 (Feb. 1956), p. 83.

RJ190. _____. "Job" Suppl de la Vie Spirituelle, (1956), pp. 199-209.

1957

RJ191. Blanton, S. "CW5" J of Religious Thought, 14 (Spring-Sum. 1957), pp. 179-80.

RJ192. Booth, Gotthard. "CW11" Pastoral Psychology, 8 (Jan. 1957), pp. 63-64.

RJ193. Evans, Erastus. "Geistes" Ibid., (Feb. 1957), pp. 33-46.

RJ194. Fairchild, R. W. "Reflec" J of Pastoral Care, 11 (Fall 1957), pp. 174-75.

RJ195. Johnson, Paul E. "CW1" Pastoral Psychology, 8 (May 1957), pp. 60-61.

RJ196. _____. "CW7" Ibid., (Oct. 1957), pp. 57-58.

RJ197. Scott, R. D. "CW5" JAP, 2:2 (1957), pp. 201-06.

RJ198. White, Victor. "CW1 and 5" Blackfriars, 38 (Oct. 1957), p. 442.

RJ199. Unsigned. "Ener" Etudes, 294 (Aug. 1957), p. 129.

1958

RJ200. Allers, Rudolf. "Self" Critic, 16 (July 1958), p. 43.

RJ201. Clark, W. H. "Self" Pastoral Psychology, 9 (June 1958), pp.
        61-62.

RJ202. Fordham, Michael. "The transcendent function." JAP, 3:1
        (1958), p. 81.

RJ203. Greer, I. M. "CW5" J of Pastoral Care, 12 (Fall 1958), p.
        197.

RJ204. Hofmann, Hans. "CW5" Harvard Divinity Bull, 23 (1957-58),
        pp. 180-82.

RJ205. Klink, T. W. "CW1" J of Pastoral Care, 12 (Fall 1958), pp.
        196-97.

RJ206. LeBlanc, A. "Self" Catholic World, 187 (Sept. 1958), p. 468.

RJ207. Moloney, R. "Self" Month, 20 (Oct. 1958), pp. 219-24.

RJ208. _____. "CW11" Loc. cit.

RJ209. Salzman, L. "Nature" J of Pastoral Care, 12 (Spring 1958),
        pp. 56-58.

RJ210. Stafford-Clark, D. "CW1" JAP, 3:1 (1958), pp. 71-73.

RJ211. Unsigned. "CW11" Catholic Educational Rev, 56 (Oct, 1958), p.
        449.
        Dominicana, 43 (Win. 1958), p. 333.

1959

RJ212. Fordham, Michael. "Self" JAP, 4:1 (1959), pp. 65-67.

RJ213. Laing, R. D. "Self" Ibid., pp. 64-65.

253

RJ214. Plaut, Albert B. J. "CW11" Ibid., pp. 68-73.

RJ215. Spiegelberg, F. "CW11" Ibid., pp. 78-83.

RJ216. Toynbee, Arnold. "Self" Ibid., pp. 63-64.

RJ217. Wessel, H. "Mod Myth" Deutsche Zeit für Philosophie, 7:2 (1959), pp. 350-52.

RJ218. White, Victor. "CW11" JAP, 4:1 (1959), pp. 73-78.

1960

RJ219. Benner, Edward A. "CW9-II" JAP, 5:2 (1960), pp. 159-65.

RJ220. Home, H. J. "Sauc" Inter J of Psycho-Analysis, 41 (1960), pp. 83-84.

RJ221. Johnson, Paul E. "CW5" Pastoral Psychology, (May 1960), pp. 63-64.

RJ222. Vann, G. "CW9" Catholic Educational Rev, 58 (Sept. 1960), p. 421.

1961

RJ223. Bevand, Richard. "Typen" Action et Pensée, 37:3 (1961), pp. 65-96.

RJ224. Edwards, A. "CW3" JAP, 6:2 (1961), p. 168.

RJ225. Hobson, Robert F. "CW9-I" Ibid., p. 161.

RJ226. Hoffmann, Hans. "CW4" Harvard Divinity Bull, 25 (April-July 1961), pp. 22-23.

RJ227. Stokvis, B. "Psychotherapie für den praktischen Arzt." Rev Méd Psychosom, 3:2 (1961), pp. 102-03.

RJ228. Unsigned. "CW3" Blackfriars, 42 (June 1961), p. 279.

RJ229. Unsigned. "CW8" Ibid., (May 1961), p. 230.

RJ230. Gordon, Rosemary, "CW8" JAP, 7:2 (1962), pp. 157-61.

RJ231. Schrag, C. O. "CW8" J of Religious Thought, 18:2 (1961-62), pp. 186-88.

RJ232. Unsigned. "CW4" Blackfriars, 43 (April 1962), p. 193.

RJ233. Unsigned. "CW4" Catholic Educational Rev, 60 (Jan. 1962), p. 63.

RJ234. Unsigned. "CW3" Loc. cit.

1963

RJ235. Adler, Gerhard. "MDR" JAP, 8:2 (1963), pp. 173-74.

RJ236. _____. "MDR" The Listener, (18 July 1963), p. 2506.

RJ237. Barrett, Mayr L. "MDR" Library J, 88 (15 June 1963), p. 2506.

RJ238. Barrett, William. "MDR" Atlantic, 211 (June 1963), p. 13.

RJ239. _____. "MDR" Christian Century, 80 (8 May 1963), p. 619.

RJ240. _____. "MDR" Economist, 208 (20 July 1963), p. 268.

RJ241. Brown, J. A. C. "MDR" New Statesman, 66 (12 July 1963), p. 48.

RJ242. Edinger, Edward F. "MDR" Sat Rev Lit, 46 (1 July 1963), p. 23.

RJ243. Eysenck, H. J. "MDR" Spectator, (19 July 1963), p. 86.

RJ244. Fromm, Erich. "MDR" Scientific American, 209 (Sept. 1963), p. 283.

RJ245. Glover, Edward. "MDR" NY Times Book Rev, (19 May 1963), p. 3.

RJ246. Kent, Edward A. "MDR" Book-of-the-Month-Club News, (May 1963), p. 16.

RJ247. Kibel, Alvin C. "MDR" Midstream, (Dec. 1963), p. 99.

RJ248. _____. "MDR" Partisan Rev, (Fall 1963), p. 453.

RJ249. König, Karl. "ETG" Die Drei, 33 (1963), pp. 37-44.

RJ250. Layard, Doris. "MDR" Blackfriars, 44 (Dec. 1963), p. 531.

RJ251. Osborne, Charles. "MDR" London Magazine, (Sept. 1963), p. 87.

RJ252. Paulding, Gouverneur. "MDR" NY Herald Tribune Books, (12 May 1963), p. 1.

RJ253. Raine, Kathleen. "MDR" The Listener, (22 Aug. 1963), p. 284.

RJ254. Rey, J. H. "CW4" JAP, 8:2 (1963), pp. 175-80.

RJ255. Thurneysen, E. "ETG" Kirche in der Zeit, 18:10 (1963), pp. 422-27.

RJ256. _____. "ETG" Kirchenblatt für die Reformierte Schweiz, 119 (1963), pp. 162-65, 178-81.

RJ257. Unsigned. "MDR" Tablet, 217 (3 Aug. 1963), p. 841.

RJ258. Unsigned. "MDR" Time, 81 (10 May 1963), p. 100.

RJ259. Unsigned. "MDR" TLS, (2 Aug. 1963), p. 592.

RJ260. Unsigned. "MDR" Virginia Q Rev, 39 (Aut. 1963), p. 139.

RJ261. Unsigned. "ETG" Der Wedepunkt im Leben und Leiden, 40 (1963), pp. 131-35.

1964

RJ262. Adler, Gerhard. "MDR" Spring 1964, pp. 139-46.

RJ263. Edelheit, Henry. "MDR" Psychoanalytic Q, 33 (1964), pp. 561-66.

RJ264. Girard, L. E. "Man" Main Currents in Modern Thought, 21:2 (1964), pp. 44-45.

RJ265. Havens, J. "MDR" Pastoral Psychology, 14 (Jan. 1964), pp. 61-62.

RJ266. Leavy, Stanley A. "MDR" Psychoanalytic Q, 33 (1964), pp. 567-74.

RJ267. Mumford, Lewis. "MDR" New Yorker, (23 May 1964), p. 155.

RJ268. Norbury, F. B. "MDR" J of Religion and Health, 3 (April 1964), pp. 289-90.

RJ269. Unsigned. "Relig" Lumen, 19 (June 1964), p. 336.

1965

RJ270. Allwohn, Adolf. "Relig" Zeit für Religions- und Geistesge-
schichte, 17:3 (1965), pp. 284-85.

RJ271. Edinger, Edward F. "CW14" JAP, 10:2 (1965), pp. 192-93.

RJ272. Haynes, R. "Man" Tablet, 219 (9 Jan. 1965), p. 40.

RJ273. Heymann, Karl. "ETG" Abhandlungen zur Philosophie und Psychologie, 8 (1965), pp. 14-20.

RJ274. Hobson, Robert F. "CW14" JAP, 10:2 (1965), pp. 189-92.

RJ275. MacIntyre, A. "Man" NY Rev of Books, 4 (25 Feb. 1965), p. 5.

RJ276. Philipson, M. "Man" New Republic, 152 (16 Jan. 1965), p. 22.

RJ277. Schlette, H. R. "Relig" Zeit für Missionswissenschaft und
Religionswissenschaft, 49:3 (1965), pp. 242-43.

RJ278. Tuinstra, C. L. "Relig" Nederlandsch Theologisch Tijdschrift,
20 (Oct. 1965), pp. 67-68.

RJ279. Unsigned. "Man" Booklist, 61 (15 Jan. 1965), p. 446.

RJ280. Unsigned. "CW10" TLS, (7 Jan. 1965), p. 11.

RJ281. Unsigned. "Man" Loc. cit.

RJ282. Unsigned. "CW10" Virginia Q Rev, 41 (Win. 1965), p. xxiv.

1966

RJ283. Johnson, Paul E. "Man" Pastoral Psychology, 17 (May 1966),
pp. 59-61.

RJ284. Layard, John. "CW10" JAP, 11:1 (1966), pp. 69-72.

RJ285. Pascal, E. "Job" (in Italian) Protestantesimo, 47:3 (1966),

pp. 215-22.

RJ286. Rieff, Philip. "CW5, 10, 11 and 16" An Amer Academy Science, 366 (July 1966), p. 199.

RJ287. Whitney, James G. "CW10" JAP, 11:1 (1966), pp. 72-73.

1967

RJ288. Edinger, Edward F. "CW15" Library J, 92 (1 March 1967), p. 1020.

RJ289. Haendler, Otto. "C. G. Jungs 'Gesammelten Werken'." Wege zum Menschen, 19:10 (1967), pp. 383-86.

RJ290. Heavenor, E. S. P. "Job" Scottish J of Theology, 20 (1967), pp. 120-21.

RJ291. Heldinger, Ulrich. "Hiob" Theologische Zeit, 23 (1967), pp. 340-52.

RJ292. Unsigned. "CW15" Virginia Q Rev, 43 (Spring 1967), p. 112.

1968

RJ293. Gough, C. L. "MDR" Modern Churchman, ns 11 (July 1968), pp. 264-65.

RJ294. Richardson, M. "Proc" New Statesman, 76 (25 Oct. 1965), p. 550.

RJ295. Wolff, Otto. "Hiob" Dialog Über den Menschen. Stuttgart: 1968, pp. 153-68.

RJ296. Unsigned. "Proc" TLS, (10 Oct. 1968), p. 1151.

RJ297. Unsigned. "CW15" Ibid., (4 Jan. 1968), p. 17.

RJ298. Unsigned. "CW15" Ibid., p. 10.

1969

RJ299. Haynes, R. "Prac" <u>Tablet</u>, 223 (18 Jan. 1969), p. 59.

RJ300. Henderson, Joseph L. "CW13" <u>JAP</u>, 14:2 (1969), pp. 189-92.

RJ301. _____. "Prac" <u>Quad</u>, 3 (1969), pp. 7-8.

RJ302. Partos, L. "Dyn" <u>Lumen</u>, 24 (March 1969), p. 171.

RJ303. Starobinski, __. "Schelm" <u>Critique</u>, (Dec. 1969), p. 1033.

RJ304. Unsigned. "Prac" <u>Kenyon Rev</u>, 31 (Spring 1969), p. 285.

RJ305. Unsigned. "Prac" <u>NY Rev of Books</u>, 12 (16 Jan. 1969), p. 4.

RJ306. Unsigned. "CW12" <u>TLS</u>, (6 March 1969), p. 251.

1970-1971

RJ307. Storr, Anthony. "Port" <u>Book World</u>, (21 Nov. 1971), p. 8.

RJ308. Strauss, Ruth. "Prac" <u>JAP</u>, 15:2 (1970), pp. 186-89.

RJ309. Welch, M. "Reflec" <u>Ibid.</u>, 16:2 (1971), p. 213.

RJ310. Unsigned. "Types" <u>TLS</u>, (26 Nov. 1971), p. 1489.

RJ311. Unsigned. "Reflec" <u>Virginia Q Rev</u>, (Aut. 1971), p. 187.

1972

RJ312. Newson, J. "Reflec" <u>Teilhard Rev</u>, 7 (Feb. 1972), p. 28.

RJ313. Partos, L. "Gegen" <u>Lumen</u>, 27 (March 1972), p. 167.

RJ314. Welch, M. "CW15" <u>JAP</u>, 17:1 (1972), pp. 93-94.

RJ315. Wheelwright, Joseph B. "CW6" <u>Ibid.</u>, 17:2 (1973), pp. 212-13.

RJ316. Davies, R. "Let-I" NY Times, (25 Feb. 1973), p. 31.

RJ317. Edinger, Edward F. "F-J Let" Library J, 98 (15 Dec. 1973), p. 3628.

RJ318. Heydt, Vera von der. "Br-I" Erasmus, 25:19-20 (1973), p. 674.

RJ319. Roazen, Paul. "Let-I" Nation, 216 (25 June 1973), pp. 822-23.

RJ320. Stewart, R. S. "Let-I" Sat Rev Sci, 1 (May 1973), pp. 62-63.

RJ321. Unsigned. "CW2" TLS, (21 Sept. 1973), p. 1080.

RJ322. Unsigned. "Let-I" Ibid., (19 Oct. 1973), p. 1271.

RJ323. Unsigned. "Let-I" Virginia Q Rev 49 (Aut. 1973), p. 164.

1974

RJ324. Brown, C. A. "Let-I" J of Religion, 54 (Jan. 1974), pp. 95-96.

RJ325. Brown, Frederick. "F-J Let" Harper's, 249 (Aug. 1974), p. 88.

RJ326. Dicks-Mireaux, M. J. "CW2" JAP, 19:2 (1974), p. 207.

RJ327. Heydt, Vera von der. "Let-I" Ibid., 19:1 (1974), pp. 110-13.

RJ328. Lebowitz, Martin. "F-J Let" Nation, 219 (6 July 1974), p. 24.

RJ329. Meyers, Jeffrey. "F-J Let" Commonweal, 101 (11 Oct. 1974), p. 41.

RJ330. _____. "F-J Let" Economist, 251 (29 April 1974), p. 125.

RJ331. _____. "F-J Let" Encounter, 42 (June 1974), p. 39.

RJ332. Nye, Robert. "F-J Let" Christian Science Monitor, (5 May 1974), p. 5.

RJ333. Prescott, P. "F-J Let" Newsweek, 83 (29 April 1974), pp. 95-96.

RJ334. Pye, Faye. "Let-I" Harv, 20 (1974), pp. 124-25.

RJ335. Roazen, Paul. "F-J Let" New Statesman, 87 (12 April 1974), p. 516.

RJ336. Rycroft, Charles. "F-J Let" NY Rev of Books, 21 (18 April 1974), p. 6.

RJ337. Trilling, Lionel. "F-J Let" NY Times Book Rev, (21 April 1974), p. 1.

RJ338. Wheelwright, Joseph B. "F-J Let" PP, 5:2 (1974), pp. 171-76.

RJ339. Wilke, H. J. "Br-I-III" AP, 5:2 (1974), pp. 146-47.

RJ340. Unsigned. "F-J Let" Choice, 11 (Oct. 1974), p. 1218.

RJ341. Unsigned. "F-J Let" New Yorker, 50 (15 April 1974), p. 151.

RJ342. Unsigned. "F-J Let" TLS, (10 May 1974), p. 489.

1975

RJ343. Fordham, Michael. "F-J Let" JAP, 20:1 (1975), pp. 79-80.

RJ344. Jung, Eberhard. "Über" AP, 6:2 (1975), p. 185.

INDICES

266

Cabbala, 575, 800, 920, 1296,
   1408, 1518, 1727-28, 1855,
   2214, 2319, 2877
Camus, A., 2661
Cancer, 2341, 2428
Cantor, G., 3588
Caritas, 752
Carus, C. G., 2813
Caruso, I. A. 3007
Case histories, 3576
Cassirer, E., 2800
Cat, 1990-91
Catharsis, 1012
Catholic analyst, 2126
Catholicism, 841, 1820, 1913,
   2809, 2869
Cattell, R. B., 2490, 2727
Causality, 3256; see also Syn-
   chronicity
Cave, 813
Cayce, E., 619
Celtic myth, 205, 319, 3577
Center symbolism, 625
Chagal, M., 1134
Chakra symbolism, 2197
Character, 31, 1876, 2819
Chaucer, 3068
Child, 2662
   analysis, 226, 1332, 2262
   art, 2375
   birth, 992, 1093
   Gifted, 1902
   psychology, 48, 76, 203, 325,
      403, 410, 449, 633, 706, 712,
      778, 838, 1037-38, 1199,
      1335, 1337, 1341, 1637, 1669,
      1724, 1783, 1874, 1987, 2006,
      2059, 2148, 2151-52, 2169,
      2186, 2327, 2413, 2554, 2611,
      2689, 2722-23, 2740, 2786,
      2804, 2884, 2938, 2980, 2982,
      3021, 3067, 3140, 3220-21,
      3284, 3383, 3482, 3510, 3587
   childhood memory, 2298
China, 163, 237
Chinese literature, 1528
   philosophy, 3271
Chirology, 83, 624, 3357, 3388
Christ, 279, 2353-54, 2760, 3118,
   3304-05
   and the Self, 1686, 1832, 2122,
   2270, 3093
Christianity, 223, 429, 866,
   1028, 1215, 2344, 2436

Early, 139, 266
   Sacramentalism in, 527
   Symbolism in, 379, 3064
   see also particular figures or
   topics; New Testament; Psychol-
   ogy and religion; Religion;
   Theology
Christmas, 2801
   tree, 1346
Church, 1552, 1752, 2423, 2738
Cinema, 640, 2807, 2903, 3405,
   3568
   Evil in the, 1853, 2511
Circumcision, 1797, 2255, 2321
Cloud symbols, 2987, 3129
Coincidence, 826, 3131; see also
   Synchronicity
Collective consciousness, 2495-96
Collective unconscious, 54, 67,
   116, 140, 233, 261, 353, 490,
   549, 644, 679, 742, 865, 881,
   1031, 1816, 2105, 2493, 2495-96,
   2524, 2747, 2750, 2781, 2876,
   3237, 3245, 3329
Collectivity, 78, 93
Collins, C., 2962
Color, 3116-17, 3167
   in biology, 3156
   in Christianity, 3064
   symbolism, 3075, 3082, 3164,
   3169, 3187
   in the unconscious, 2033, 2407
Communication, 1948, 2346, 2860
Community, 1550
   psychology, 2548
Compassion, 1118, 1421
Complementarity, 2589, 2763, 2897,
   3150, 3557
Complex, 170, 366, 1366, 1584,
   1926, 1968, 1970, 2153, 2424
Compulsion, 1720
Concepts in science, 2870
Confession, 1202
Conflict situations, 684
Conjunctio, 1535, 1749; see also
   Wholeness
Conrad, J., 1235, 3404
Conscience, 1441-42, 1446, 1513,
   1515, 1526, 1530, 2768-69, 2772,
   2815, 2869, 2871, 2887, 2893,
   3229
Consciousness, 396, 523, 573, 943,
   2042, 2239, 2441, 2798, 3509,
   3585

integration (cont.), 2253
psychology, 1098
Egypt, 297, 309, 336, 781, 1080-81,
1133, 2304, 2597-98, 2711, 2824
Einstein, A., 3022
Elections, 1684
Eleusis, 212, 236, 1140, 1912,
2285, 2478
Eliade, M., 2864
Eliot, T. S., 358, 1117, 1238,
1355, 2446, 2916, 3565
Emerson, R. W., 2257, 2260,3345
Emotion, 1683, 2581, 2801, 2855,
3009, 3059
Empedocles, 1290
Enantiodromia, 2647; see also
Opposites
Encounters, 615
Entelechy, 3033
Entropy, 2746, 2873; see also
Psychic energy
Envy, 2075, 3114, 3185
Ephesis, 212
Epistemology, 1759, 3023
Eranos, 235, 1020, 1023, 1075,
1095, 1146, 1450
Eros, 3099, 3230, 3476
Eternal youth, 2906; see also
Puer
Eternity, 703, 1328, 2644, 3195
3473
Ethics, 3, 388-89, 503, 940, 1314,
1656, 2477, 2726, 2948, 3017,
3087, 3100, 3511; see also
Values; Evil; Good/Evil
Eucharist, Symbol of the, 322,
991
Euripides, 1405
Evil, 319, 1607, 1672, 1765, 1785-
86, 1806, 1819, 1845, 1852-53,
1871, 2155, 2264, 2271, 2287,
2433, 2449-50, 2460, 2479, 2485,
2511-12, 2522, 3377; see also
Good/Evil
Evolution, 2204, 2677, 3144
Eye, 1710, 1813
Exorcism, 2017, 2571
Extraversion, 2490; see also In-
troversion/Extraversion
Ezekiel, 671
Failure in analysis, see Success
in analysis
Fairy tales, 707, 846, 994, 1122,
1225, 1344, 1471, 1672, 1785,

1826, 1975, 2155, 2351, 2449,
2458, 2532, 2683, 2790, 2797,
2921-22, 3097, 3235, 3377, 3505,
3519, 3605, 3616-17, 3647, 3663
Faith, 595, 1046, 1556, 2211, 2892
Falling, Dreams of, 3008
Family, 296, 3225, 3335
Fantasy, 2804, 2814, 3149, 3482
Fatima, 210, 1118
Fate, 408, 904, 2273, 2757, 3043
Father, Archetype of, 981, 2390,
2979, 3239, 3310, 3321, 3335,
3569
Jealous, 2992
Murder of the, 3564
Problems of the, 1035
Faust, 79, 2394
Feeling, 2810, 2963, 3142, 3355,
3526, 3638
Fellini, F., 2903
Feminine, 2925, 3016, 3035, 3097,
3632
Fear of the, 1598
inferiority, 2702, 2811
psychology, 90, 144, 147-48, 207,
407, 448, 547, 554, 655, 747,
790, 833, 851, 853, 904, 942,
981, 1058, 1259, 1261, 1263,
1300, 1302, 1375, 1471, 1603,
1630, 1633, 1839, 1984, 2246,
2303, 2517, 1594, 2702, 2802,
2811, 3084, 3203, 3234, 3265,
3274, 3298, 3334, 3616, 3655
Fetishism, 1414
Fichte, J. G., 427
Ficino, 3550
Filicide, 3069
Fire symbolism, 635
First principles, 2406
Flaubert, G., 3593
Flood symbolism, 324, 1148, 2640,
3471
Folklore, 2683
Fool, The, 2759, 2791, 3439
Foote, Mary, 3369
Forgetting, 2619
Four elements, 2004
Francis de Sales, St., 2664
Free will, 1931, 2741
Freud, S., 4, 16, 22, 31, 36, 38,
42, 66, 96, 100, 104, 115, 121,
129, 351, 400, 409, 444, 461, 479,
486, 533, 540, 544, 584, 602, 617,
628, 679, 689-90, 695, 709, 753,

Hermaphrodite, Archetype of, 858;
  see also Androgyny
Hermeneutics, 1323, 2134, 2549,
  2705, 3299
Hermes, 293, 3657
Hero, Archetype of, 269, 271, 530,
  1701, 2132, 3151, 3242, 3432
Hesse, H., 2055, 2216, 2404, 2476,
  3379, 3590
Hillman, J., 3538
Hindu, 286, 301-02; see also
  India
  history, 2237
  symbolism, 127
History, 23, 734, 788, 798, 1291,
  1726, 1770, 3507
Hitler, A., 230; see also National
  Socialism
Hoffman, E. T. A., 636
Holiness, 3629
Holy Spirit, 752, 1211
Homo-eroticism, 1590, 1817
Homosexuality, 1612, 1838, 2708,
  3099, 3660
Honegger, J. J., 3465
Hope, 2069, 2917
Hugh of St. Victor, 912
Humanism, 443, 1404
Humor, 2846, 3205, 3277, 3367
Hunger, 1609, 1835
Hypokrites, 2587, 2909-10
Hysteria, 1300, 3430
I-Ching, 746, 1299, 1422, 1424,
  1738, 1870, 2520, 2866, 2889,
  3020, 3159, 3184, 3302, 3469,
  3666
Ideals, 1443, 1646
Ideas, 386, 967, 2233, 3644
Identity, 2250, 2654, 3492
Ideology, 1443, 1646
Idolatry, 2818
Ignatius, St., 139
Image, 1339-40
  and energy, 794
Imagination, 108, 2777, 2930,
  2966, 3074, 3293, 3331, 3354,
  3664
Immortality, 223, 646, 2193
Impotence, 2121
Incarnation, 281
Incest, 371, 2325, 3312-13, 3521,
  3606
Incubation, 1124, 2491
India, 172, 180, 184, 219, 244,

India (cont.), 329, 931, 975,
  1119, 1328, 1742-43, 2236, 2652-
  53, 2659; see also Hindu
  Indian myth, 128, 2502
  Indian psychology, 1801
  Indian religion, 97, 869
Individual, 1777, 2442, 3270,
  3275, 3593
  and the group, 202, 316-17, 1467,
  1868, 2714, 2926
Individuality, 78, 93
Individual Psychology, 55; see also
  Adler
Individuation, 52, 168, 285, 289,
  296, 431, 436, 474, 542, 614,
  1048, 1050-51, 1064, 1107, 1292,
  1394, 1413, 1462-63, 1486, 1556,
  1593, 1630, 1641, 1731, 1741,
  1750, 1787, 1809, 1896, 2064-47,
  2157, 2165, 2283, 2353-54, 2363,
  2389, 2409, 2466, 2476, 2487,
  2554, 2558, 2626, 2634, 2641,
  2687, 2692, 2695, 2701, 2722-23,
  2755, 2764, 2791, 2805, 2844,
  2909-10, 2932, 2944, 3005, 3024,
  3028, 3157, 3175, 3218, 3359,
  3375, 3390, 3445, 3450, 3462,
  3475, 3492, 3495, 3517, 3528,
  3540, 3577, 3593, 3647; see also
  Wholeness
Inferior function, 60, 1062, 1983,
  2942; see also Functions
Initiation, 157, 228, 240, 694,
  704, 1009, 1562, 2456
Instinct, 225, 564, 597; see also
  Drives
Institutions, 150
Intentionality, 2734
Introspection, 469, 583
Introversion, 2727, 3173, 3311,
  3615
  Introversion/Extraversion, 659,
  769, 848, 1480, 1564, 1780,
  2124, 2137, 2647, 3132, 3149;
  see also Extraversion
Intuition, 1009, 2062
Iran, see Persia
Irrationalism, 2850
Issac, 1453, 2928, 3506
Isis, 215
Islam, 193, 210, 232, 308, 334,
  372-73, 418, 420, 455, 621, 724,
  935-36, 1022, 1118, 1125, 1217,
  1323, 1386, 1451, 1881, 2195,

Islam (cont.), 2616
Jahweh, 238
James, H., 3389, 3488
Japanese myth, 2188
Jerusalem, 672
Jews, see Judaism
Joachim von Fiore, 1211
Joan of Arc, 2737
Job, 784, 807, 900, 957, 968,
    1190, 1360, 1473, 3047
John Climachus, St., 668
John of the Cross, St., 514
Jones, E., 3198
Journey myth, 3604
Joyce, J., 1986, 2332, 2661, 2886,
    3076
Judaism, 62, 124, 409, 1364, 1615,
    1720, 1937, 2255, 2402, 2642,
    2744, 2822, 2887, 2919, 2971,
    3018, 3169, 3229, 3263, 3507,
    3591; see also Cabbala; Hasidism;
    Messianism
  Jewish psychology, 565, 1877
  Symbols in, 710, 1648
  Women in, 3145
Judgment, 168
Jung, C. G.
  in Britain, 3402
  and contemporary thought, 348
  Contribution and influence of,
      433, 998, 1224, 1576, 1884,
      1900, 1946-7, 2001, 2007, 2092,
      2100, 2482, 2499, 2534, 2751
  and the East, 1120, 3191
  Empiricism of, 1007, 1295, 1872,
      2008, 3219, 3501
  in France, 103
  Handwriting of, 145
  Institute, 685, 1650
  Library of, 2010, 2219, 2789
  and National Socialism, 354, 457,
      505, 526, 560, 570, 575, 587-
      89
  and psychoanalysis, 1
  and religion, 1160, 1162, 1209,
      1218, 1279, 1289, 1361-62,
      1415, 1638, 1830, 2209, 2315,
      2372, 2454, 2494, 2749, 2771,
      3394
Kabeiroi, 328, 1092
Kafka, F., 1502, 3362, 3437
Kant, I., 149, 1818, 2484, 3013,
    3644
Keller, G., 2368

Keppler, J., 793, 1142, 3022
Kibbutz, 3587
Kierkegaard, S., 3375, 3557, 3620
King Lear, 1810
Kinship, 322, 606, 1497, 2391
Klee, P., 2492
Knox, J., 2917
Köberle, A., 3428
Kokoschka, O., 3259
Kretschmer, E., 848, 2831
Krishnamurti, J., 648, 744
Kubbla Kahn, 1679
Kundalini Yoga, 77, 2462, 2660,
    3642
Labyrinth, 639
Language, 2086, 2582, 2780, 2860
Lao-Tse, 164
Latin American dreams, 3427
    literature, 3193
Law, 3291
Leadership, 3489
Leibniz, G. W. 1818, 2484
Leonardo, 1602
Leroux, E., 3490
Lévi-Strauss, C., 2678, 3503, 3624
Liberation movements, 3436
Libido, 17, 35, 66, 2473, 2490
Life, 1711, 2833, 3015
    and death, 2206
Light, 310, 1327, 1713, 1917, 3167
Literary criticism, 2712, 2775,
    3119
Literature, 629, 952, 1942, 2361,
    2524, 2656, 2773, 2987, 3129
Little Prince, 1041
Liturgy, 612, 971, 2878; see also
    Mass
Logic, 234
Logos, 978, 2862, 3230
London, J., 1097, 2838
Loneliness, 916, 3399
Lorenz, K., 731
Lourdes, 1436
Love, 27, 327, 515, 1214, 2201,
    2882
LSD, 2766
Luther, M., 2044
Macbeth, 2191, 2287
Machine, 2718, 2845
Macrocosm/Microcosm idea, 1671,
    2263
Madagascar, 1219
Magic, 538, 1298, 1421, 1546, 1869,
    2232, 2680; see also Bewitchment

Mother archetype, 1602, 2145, 2478, 3335; see also Great Mother
Mother/child relationship, 1824, 2306, 3286
complex, 3624
imago, 1874, 2250, 3208, 3582
Mother-in-law, 1586
Motivation, 1356
Mozart, W. A., 854
Murder, 3531
Music, 644, 682, 854, 897, 1734, 1744, 1859, 1994, 3315; see also particular musicians
Musical man, 1873
Mysteries, 342, 452, 899,1109, 1153, 1170, 1912, 2610, 3622; see also Eleusis; Ephesis; Isis
Christian, 339
Origin of, 329
Mystery, 2141
Mysticism, 113, 130, 188, 355, 502, 514, 612, 1407, 1427, 1460, 1551, 1562, 1670, 1829, 2278, 2348, 2515, 2624, 2906, 3205
Byzantine, 892, 2136
Christian, 92, 375, 1678, 1879, 1950, 2472, 2620
Hasidic, 780
Islamic, 334, 936, 1125, 1217, 2195
Jewish, 1171, 1517, 1727, 3169
Orphic, 176
Orthodox, 2025
Myth, 276, 337, 529, 558-59, 572, 611, 656, 925, 1069, 1114, 1207, 1221, 1237, 1664, 1680, 1770, 1799, 1806, 1994, 2006, 2170, 2202, 2345, 2367, 2390, 2431, 2458, 2479, 2539, 2577, 2597, 2667, 2676, 2678, 2743, 2773, 2862, 3050, 3069, 3096, 3215, 3283, 3352, 3494, 3663
in China, 123, 2635
in Japan, 2188
Narcissism, 347, 1139, 2388, 2935, 3092, 3669
National Socialism, 247, 263, 268, 354, 409, 457, 505, 526, 570, 575, 587, 2684, 2927; see also German problem; Jung and National Socialism
Natural Law, 2128
Nature, 413, 867, 2509, 2568

in Islam, 418, 420, 935, 2616
and spirit, 424-25, 3249
Navaho myth, 1112, 1237, 3168
Negativism, 2
Neo-platonism, 349, 2568
Nerval, G. de, 736
Neumann, E., 1313, 1379, 3362, 3520
Neurosis, 4, 18, 43, 432, 434, 1128, 1894, 2184, 1210, 1405, 3045, 3419, 3491
Neutrality, 260
New being, 964
New Testament, 467, 1882, 2301
Newton, I., 401
Nicholas Cusanus, 673
Nietzsche, F., 287, 474, 1543, 1848, 2241, 1340, 2661, 2850, 1947, 3061, 3106, 3448
Nightmare, 3081, 3107, 3109
Night sea journey, 25, 3422
Nihilism, 1613
Niklaus von Flüe, 404, 1342, 1570
Niobe, 562
Nirvana, 162
Nordic art, 524
Nothing, 1294
Novalis, 2875
Number, 107, 999, 2794, 3376
Object relations, 2855, 3009
Objective psyche, 152, 705, 1173, 1459, 1465, 1498, 3014
world, 3303
Occultism, 1266, 3089, 3646, 3668
Oedipus, 325, 2993, 3606, 3621
Old Testament, 243, 466-67, 511, 671, 1375, 1790, 2461, 2510, 2994, 3080
1001 nights, 3359
Oneness, 2334
O'Neill, E., 2378
Opposites, 166, 242, 645, 1081, 1191, 1758, 3155, 3637; see also Enantiodromia
Oracle, 1078
Order, 150, 2625
Organic life, 1272, 3015
Organism, 1147
Origen, 464, 1822
Original self, 1782
Orphism, 176, 346, 563, 1193, 3158
Ortega y Gasset, J., 2207
Orthodoxy, Eastern, 813
Osiris, 336, 1133

Oswald, L. H., 2504
Ovid, 2920
Pan, 3107, 3109
Panic, 3081
Pannwitz, L., 1519
Paracelsus, 3630
Paradise, 2000
Parapsychology, 264, 603, 1691, 1856, 1910, 2079, 2314, 2468, 2715, 3256, 3548, 3607, 3643
Parent/child relation, 608
Parental imago, 410, 2275
Pascal, B., 1641
Pastoral care, 74, 380, 423, 670, 681, 767, 802, 835, 911, 917, 1850, 1860, 2163, 2201, 2290, 2364, 2401, 2408, 2720, 2952
Patient, 2194, 2396, 2690, 3090, 3262, 3356
Patristics, 378, 734, 796, 823, 954, 1402
Paul, St., 154, 267, 279, 424, 1556-57, 2537, 3304-05
Peace, 1437, 1504, 1506, 1510, 1516
Perception, 3152
Perls, F. J., 3658
Persecution, 1887
Persephone, 1621, 3491
Perseus, 1094
Persian religion, 335, 374, 531, 620, 821, 1020, 1126, 1553, 1655, 1705, 1769, 2918
Person, 1723
Persona, 2243, 2280, 2312, 3348
Personal unconscious, 679, 2105, 3329
Personality, 140, 158, 264, 303, 314, 605, 683, 729, 857, 982, 1359, 1525, 2038, 2675, 3160, 3162-63, 3176
Peter Pan, 2697
Peyote, 3136
Phenomenology, 1187
Philo, 377, 953
Philology, 840
Philosophy, 17, 166, 673, 696, 1110, 1818, 1858, 2045, 2214, 2218, 2229, 2330, 2651, 2863, 3014, 3146, 3373; see also particular philosophers; topics in philosophy
Eastern, 2981
of religion, 2295

of science, 1907, 3300
Physics, 159, 783, 793, 1966, 2003, 2176, 2281, 2399, 2741, 2794, 3167, 3266, 3376, 3557; see also Science; Synchronicity; Time
Piaget, J., 2403
Pictures, 2198
Plato, 386, 427, 2779, 3411
Platonism, 280
Play, 3155, 3510
Plotino, 3550
Plotinus, 196, 2214
Pneuma, 377, 381, 953
Poe, E. A., 3345
Poetry, 131, 696, 1238, 1276, 1355, 1413, 1927, 1932, 2282, 2631, 3188, 3250, 3432; see also particular poets
and religion, 1357
Poliphilo, 439, 626
Politics, 1538, 1616, 3289, 3460, 3598
Pollock, J., 3186
Poltergeist, 2005, 2105, 2336
Pompeii, 1330, 1456
Possession, 2571
Power, 2201, 2588, 2950-51
Prayer, 1359
Preaching, 270
Precognition, 1489, 2036
Preiswerk, H., 3643
Priesthood, 2832, 3126
Primitive society, 1590, 1817
Primordial man, 452
Prisons, 2322-23
Projection, 911, 934, 1192, 1267, 1288, 1596, 2268, 2555, 3248, 3559
Projective techniques, 1099; see also Rorschach
Prometheus, 414, 658, 1277, 1589, 2039
Prophecy, 1881, 2265, 3264
Protestantism, 1493, 1913, 2044, 2871
Psychology
Abnormal, 3397
Behavioral, 3272
and Catholicism, 318, 618
Clinical, 2002
Community, 2548
Existential, 765, 815, 2131, 3623
Gestalt, 398, 523, 3658
Individual and collective, 483

Psychology (cont.)
  and religion, 249-50, 288, 312,
    491, 543, 722, 738, 809, 845,
    872, 893, 901, 918, 945, 1045,
    1163, 1168, 1176, 1228, 1458,
    1485, 1559, 1587, 1642, 1651,
    1660, 1698, 1703, 1709, 1712,
    1723, 1725, 1736, 1843, 1846,
    1866, 1892, 2070, 2085, 2088,
    2090, 2208, 2242, 2267, 2300,
    2338, 2342, 2379, 2423, 2459,
    2472, 2480, 2489, 2518, 2556,
    2637, 2750, 2762, 2795, 2917,
    2949, 2954, 2989

  Psychological development, 604
  see also Child psychology; Fe-
    minine psychology; Greek psy-
    chology; Group psychology; Mas-
    culine psychology
Psyche, 307, 791, 910, 966, 1057,
  1222, 1233, 1264, 1403, 1707,
  1736, 2457, 2571, 2573, 2655,
  2795, 3115, 3451, 3518, 3670
Psychic energy, 290, 488-89, 725,
  777, 805, 1005, 1632, 2022, 2580
Psychosis, 763, 902, 1031, 1179,
  2551, 2722, 3579, 3599
Psychosomatic medicine, 564, 1087,
  1169, 1925, 2051, 2414, 2523,
  3670
Psychosynthesis, 56, 2420, 3341
Psychotherapy, Goals in, 55, 59,
  787, 844
Puer aeternus, Archetype of, 1569,
  2159, 2357, 2463, 2792, 3111,
  3242, 3549, 3574; see also Eternal youth
Puppets, 712
Puzzle-tree, 2299
Pyramids, 133
Quaternity, 939, 2139-40, 2333,
  2484
Rank, O., 1082, 1597
Reality, 3418
Rebirth, 221, 240-41, 244, 643,
  2227, 2617, 3648
Redemption, 186, 196, 669, 891,
  1225, 1810, 2658, 3051
  in Buddhism, 195
  in Gnosticism, 187
  in India, 180, 184, 1119
  in Manicheism, 183, 2628
  in Orphism, 176
Regression, 2148

Relationship, 566, 592, 877, 1312,
  1439
Relativity, 3384, 3425-26
Religion, 34, 153, 174, 200, 229,
  360, 423, 440, 459, 461, 513,
  532, 592, 611, 670, 696, 714,
  803-04, 850, 880, 885, 899, 906,
  983, 997, 1049, 1069, 1160, 1165,
  1188, 1209, 1250, 1279, 1289,
  1310, 1321, 1345, 1361-62, 1381,
  1415, 1438, 1440, 1527, 1542,
  1544-45, 1625, 1664, 1735, 1799,
  2141, 2164, 2181, 2210, 2304,
  2401, 2410, 2574, 2605-06, 2882,
  2905, 3023, 3050, 3098, 3120,
  3217, 3260, 3628; see also particular religious figures; religious figures
  Ancient, 562, 1250, 1371, 2366
  east and west, 94, 1871, 2522
  Greek, 638, 1250
  History of, 625, 770, 1006, 2072
  Origin of, 758, 785
  and the unconscious, 392, 627,
    1390, 2158, 2452
  Religious experience, 1180, 2851,
    2937
    instinct, 1303
    knowledge, 256
    man, 97, 2415
Rembrandt, 2972
R. E. M. states, 2608
Renaissance, 412, 439, 923, 3553
Renewal, 1548, 1553, 1561, 1601,
  1613, 1954, 3010
Repression, 1001
  and Christianity, 484, 1468
Responsibility, 1448, 2231
Resurrection, 223, 232
Revolt, 3253, 3564
Reynard the Fox, 1370
Rhine, J. B., 3619
Rhythm, 3581
Rilke, R. M. 2527
Ring, The, 1994
Ritual, 110, 558, 649, 1408, 2874,
  3101, 3601
  American Indian, 666
  Animal, 664
  Islamic, 621
Rogers, C., 2530, 2879
Romanticism, 613
Rorschach, H., 216, 848, 884, 988,
  1098-99, 1129, 1373, 2124, 2839,

276

Rorschach (cont.), 2995-97, 3209, 3273, 3350, 3384, 3425; see also Projective techniques
Rousseau, J. J., 3673
Russia, 1995
Sabbatai Zwi, 1070
Sacrament, 611
  Sacramentalism, 527, 1648
Sacrifice, 929, 1104-05, 1423
Salvation, 677, 931
Sandspiel, 2475, 2829, 2982; see also Methods of therapy
Sartre, J. P., 762, 2677, 2850
Satan, 939, 1429, 2461, 2510, 3080
  as archetype, 1166
Saturn, 3321
Saul, King, 466, 511, 1167
Schelling, F. W. J., 882, 2120
Schism, 3110, 3552
Schizophrenia, 6, 676, 727, 773, 856, 1030, 1268, 1313, 1387-89, 1395, 1500, 1867, 1944, 2093, 2152, 2418, 1752, 3031, 3441
Schopenhauer, A., 2244, 2850
Schleiermacher, F., 2906
Science, 426, 459, 482, 517, 719, 795, 805, 1142, 1376, 1537, 1764, 2154, 2406, 2228, 2560, 2870, 3022-23, 3142, 3217, 3223, 3300, 3431, 3501, 3518, 3624; see also Biology; Physics
  Myth in, 577
  Symbolism in, 2003, 2281
Second half of life, 616, 623, 1766, 1774, 2168, 2515, 3040, 3417; see also Aging; Mid-life crisis
Self, 113, 149, 470, 520, 590, 687-88, 706, 729, 838, 856, 905, 956, 973, 977, 1018, 1194, 1206, 1232, 1341, 1433, 1563, 1590, 1593, 1657, 1663, 1668, 1686, 1771, 1789, 1802, 1817, 1832, 1891, 1929, 2008, 2122, 2151, 2270, 2505, 2530, 2535, 2707, 2735, 2808, 2837, 3092-93, 3152, 3214, 3219, 3221, 3265, 3319, 3361, 3370, 3408, 3504, 3620
  Not-self, 2514
  realization, 1449, 1753, 1805, 2477, 2530, 3146, 3317
  representation, 3085
Secondary sources, Problems with, 1883

Senex, Archetype of, 2463, 2816, 3111, 3553
Sensation function, 2890
Separation, symbolism of, 1704, 1863, 2221, 3001, 3207, 3596
Serpent, 231, 1109, 2593
Seven Sermons, 2147, 2373, 3104
Sexuality, 888, 2883, 3226, 3577, 3667; see also Male/Female
Shadow, Archetype of, 269, 362, 654, 789, 1001, 1055, 1344, 1605, 1714, 1776, 2061, 2146, 2262, 2301, 2748, 2837, 2947, 3114, 3220, 3305, 3377, 3383, 3407, 3424, 3477, 3484
  Therapist's, 2567
Shakespeare, W., 347, 395, 1054, 1132, 1231, 1915, 1920, 2376, 2634, 2960, 3054, 3249, 3493
Shamanism, 2142, 2832, 3496
Shamash, 316
Sickness, 1593, 3051, 3429, 3641
Sin, 677, 2301
Skin, 3138
Slave, Archetype of, 2931
Sleep, 3003, 3422
Smoking, 3566
Social psychology, 1036, 1464, 2548
Society, 3275
Sociology, 795, 1003, 3624
Socrates, 907, 3086
Son, His father's, Archetypal situation of, 3055-56, 3194
Sophia, 820
Soul, 64, 70, 184, 246, 383, 391, 554, 748, 764, 771, 824, 855, 946, 993, 1046, 1074, 1090, 1172, 1321, 1429, 1700, 1723, 1736, 1985, 2027, 2070, 2174, 2317, 2538, 2582, 2663, 2670, 2710, 2974, 3174, 3577
  Energy of the, 65
South Africa, 1401, 1839
Space/Time, 2281; see also Physics; Time
Spiral, Symbolism of, 384
Spirit, 29, 149, 372, 374-75, 378, 383, 390, 412, 456, 597, 923, 954, 969, 1205, 1643, 1791, 2419, 2616, 3568
  in Biology, 422, 949
Spittler, C., 1927
Steiner, R., 716, 3180-81
Stranger, 1259, 3002

Transcendence (cont.), 3592
Transference, 444, 453, 755, 934,
976, 979, 1009, 1037, 1050-51,
1061, 1063, 1144, 1184, 1267,
1270, 1286-87, 1326, 1335-36,
1596, 1612, 1838, 1869, 2020,
2031, 2178, 2324, 2350, 2541,
2564, 2713, 2975, 3028, 3067,
3135, 3210, 3227, 3255, 3279,
3372, 3414; see also Counter-
transference
Trickster, Archetype of, 1275,
1498, 1500, 1608
Trinity, 280, 721, 1213, 2139,
2140, 2337, 2657, 3365, 3457
Truth, 2110, 3303
Twins, 1536
Types, Psychological, 26, 30, 32,
41, 53, 89, 120, 125, 239, 273,
303, 323, 361, 405-06, 445-46,
487, 507, 544-46, 551, 696, 715,
769, 884, 890, 894, 988, 1475,
1847, 1980, 2062, 2123-24, 2137,
2222-24, 2240, 2248, 2365, 2398,
2405, 2407, 2421, 2633, 2776,
2844, 2879, 2946, 3005, 3077,
3091, 3132, 3139, 3148, 3153,
3173, 3202, 3288, 3317, 3350,
3416, 3495, 3499, 3522, 3524,
3526-27, 3570, 3609, 3633, 3645,
3651
in marriage, 326
U. F. O., 1474, 1488, 1499, 1531,
1540
Unconscious, 3, 31, 51, 58, 82,
229, 248, 392, 485, 523, 609,
627, 662, 674, 684, 702, 799,
871, 873, 941, 947, 959, 978,
1076, 1174, 1298, 1390, 1419,
1538, 1600, 1620, 1696, 1723,
2033, 2154, 2158, 2232, 2560,
2618, 2686, 2734, 2782, 2796,
2819, 2830, 2894, 2900, 2959,
2973, 3126, 3138, 3189, 3207,
3278, 3329, 3436, 3510, 3628;
see also Collective unconscious;
consciousness
Unity of the psyche, 3329
Unus Mundus, 2559
Upanishads, 195
Urban, W., 2800
Utopia, 1520, 2000, 2040, 2067,
2108
Valéry, P.,2116

Values, 253, 653, 917, 3499; see
also Ethics; Morality
Van Gogh, V., 980, 1000
Vedanta, 2328
Vermeer, J., 2972
Vico, G., 3550
Vietnam, 3019
Violence, 397, 399, 2434, 2486,
2820, 3261, 3443; see also Aggres-
sion;
Virgin, Archetype of, 371, 3137;
see also Mary
Visions, 3458
Vivaldi, A., 3422
Wagner, R., 1994
Wandering Jew (Ahasver), 3560
War, 399; see also World War II
Weil, S., 3331
Wells, H. G., 3497
Welty, E., 1692
Wheel symbolism, 122; see also Man-
dala Symbolism
White child, Symbol of, 2621
Whitman, W., 2665, 3345
Wholeness, 1399, 1454, 2953, 3103,
3329; see also Conjunctio; One-
ness
Williams, T., 2880
Wingenfeld, B., 1226
Wisdom, 1840
Wise old woman, Archetype of, 3324
Witch, 449
Women, 90, 147-48, 207, 254, 726,
960, 1040, 1058, 1177, 1550, 1766,
1791, 2246, 2303, 2802, 2998,
3002, 3232, 3265, 3274, 3444,
3474, 3568, 3573; see also Femi-
nine psychology
Individuation in, 285
Word, The, 2767, 2778
Word-association test, 5-6, 211,
216, 759, 1155-56, 1505, 1968,
3052, 3138, 3540
Work, 3461
World War II, 252, 257-60, 265, 277,
289; see also War
Writer's block, 2179
Yantra, 989
Yeats, W. B., 2096, 2661, 2967,
3190, 3246, 3290
Zarathustra, 3448
Zen, 867, 963, 1695, 2225, 2472,
2707, 3026, 3252, 3625
Zeus, 3127, 3569

Abegg, E. 321, 975
Abel, A. 686
Abenheimer, K. M. 347, 395, 474, 750, 1205, 2525, 2895
Abood, E. 2895
Abraham, K. RJ27, RJ28
Adams, G. RJ71
Adelman, G. R2427
Adler, A. RJ21
Adler, G. 104-05, 199, 261, 348, 396-97, 475, 521-22, 590, 687-88, 751, 976-79, 1206, 1306-07, 1535, 1748-50, 1959-61, 2114, 2337-38, 2416, 2526, 2763-64, 2897-99, 3336, 3478-81, R2285, R2319, R2390, R2670, R3131, RJ126, RJ235-36, RJ262
Adolf, H. 2527
Aeppli, E. 591
Affeman, R. 1308
Agoston, T. 1751
Aigrisse, G. 980, 1876, 2115-16, 2417, 3188
Aldridge, M. 1536
Alex, W. 1962, 2418, 1900-01, 3189
Allberry, C. R. C. 221
Allchin, W. H. 2902
Allee, A. S. R2576
Allen, C. 1207, 1435
Allen, J. L. 3190, 3482
Allenby, A. I. 592, 877, 981-82, 1208-09, 1752, 1963-64, 2117, 2339, 2419, 3053, 3337, 3483, R2315, R2274, R2409, R2434, R2802, R3324
Allers, R. 810, RJ200
Allwohn, A. 878, 3484, RJ183, RJ270
Alm, I. 130, 174, 1965
Altizer, T. J. J. 983, 1537, 2765
Alveredes, F. 222
Amann, A. 2528
Amman, P. 2903
Angers, W. P. 1638
Anghinetti, P. W. 2661
Anrich, E. 1966
Aramus, R. 593.
d'Arcy, M. 752
Arens, R. 3191

Arluck, E. W. 1639
Arnold-Carey, L. 3338
Aronson, A. 3054
Arthus, A 3339, 3485
Asher, C. 3340
Assagioli, R. 1753, 2420, 3341
Assatiani, M. M. 1
Aumüller, A. 594, 1967
Aurigemma, L. 2905, 3192
Avendano, F. 3193
Axele, __. 753
Aylward, J. C. 984-85, 1436, 2118, 2239, R2726, R2877
Bach, H. I. 689-90, 754, 811-12, 3055-58, 3194
Bachant, J. L. 3059
Backhaus, W. 1538
Bacon, L. 131, R292
Baeck, L. 430
Bänziger, H. 431, 595, 691
Bär, E. 3644
Baird, 1640
Baker, I. F. 2766
Baker, L. E. 262
Baldus, D. R2974
Ball, E. D. 2421
Bally, G. 106
Balmer, H. H. 3060
Bamberger, J. E. 2529
Bambrough, R. 3195
Bancroft, R. 3061
Bannerju, S. 1210
Barberousse, E. H. 2240
Barefield, R. S. 2530
Barker, C. 432, 1309, 1754, 2262, 3062
Barnes, H. E. 23, 349
Baroni, C. 2241, 2340
Barrett, C. 200, RJ94
Barrett, M. L. RJ237
Barrett, W. RJ238-40
Barron, L. R1017
Bartmeier, L. H. RJ67
Barth, T. 986
Bartning, G. 1187
Barz, H. 2422-23, 3063
Bash, K. W. 523, 596, 755-56, 879, 987-89, 1539, 1755
Battegay, R. 398, R1366
Baudouin, C. 85-7, 132, 201, 350, 597-98, 692, 990, 1310, 1641,

1756-58, 1968-70, 2424, 3674
Baum, J. 322, 524, 991
Baumann, C. 525, 992, 2119
Baumann, H. H. 133, 175
Baumann-Jung, G. 3487
Baynes, C. A. 187, 693
Baynes, C. F. 526
Baynes, H. G. 36, 134-35, 246,
 263-64, 351, 476, 599-610, 993,
 2663
Beach, B. Y. 2425, 2531, R3296,
 R3312
Beck, I. 2664
Becka, R. 1759
Begg, E. C. M. 3342, R3083,
 3108
Beirnaert, L. 527, 611-12, 880,
 1642
Beit, H. von. 994, 2532
Belton, L. RJ106
Bender, H. 1540
Benedetti, G. 1541
Benert, A. L. 3488
Benko, S. 2905
Bennet, E. A. 881, 995, 1761,
 1878, 1971, 2426-27, 2533,
 3489, RJ219
Bennett, A. A. G. 1760
Bennette, G. 2341, 2428
Benoit, R. 2665
Benz, 813, 882, 996, 1211, 1437-
 38, 1542-43, 1879, 2120, 2342,
 2666, 2767, 2906, 3064, 3196
Berlucchi, C. 323
Berner, R. L. 3490
Bernet, W. 997, 2343, 2429
Bernfeld, S. RJ50
Bernhard, D. 2907-08
Bernhard, E. 1972, 2667
Bernhardt, W. H. RJ168
Bernoulli, R. 107, 136, 1643
Berry, P. 3197, 3343, 3491
Bertine, E. 15, 202, 247, 265,
 324, 399, 433, 477-78, 528,
 694, 757, 998, 1311-12, 1439-
 40, 1544-45, 1644, 2534, RJ56
Bertram, G. 2909-10
Bertrand, R. 999
Bess, B. H. 3344
Bévand, R. RJ223
Beveridge, W. E. 758
Beyme, F. 1313, 1973, 2430
Bianchi, I. 137
Bickman, M. E. 3345

Bier, W. C. R1362
Billinsky, J. M. 2668
Binder, H. 434
Binswanger, H. 1974, 2243
Binswanger, K. 1000, 1212, 2121
Birkhäuser, P. 3346
Birkhäuser, S. 1975
Bishop, J. G. 2344
Bitter, W. 479, 695, 883, 1001,
 1546, 2669-70, 3065
Bixler, R. H. 759
Black, R. A. 3066
Blake-Palmer, G. 1880
Blanton, S. RJ191
Bleuel, J. 1213,
Bleuler, E. 2
Block, M. RJ169
Blöcker, G. 3347
Blomeyer, R. 2911-12, 3067, 3198,
 3348-49, 3492, R2546, R2694,
 R3060
Blum, E. 1441, 2768
Bockus, F. M. 2122, 2535
Bodamer, J. 1002
Bodkin, M. 108, 696
Boe, J. 3492
Böhler, E. 1003, 1314-17, 1442-
 44, 1645-46, 2345, 2769
Böhme, W. 2913
Bohm, E. 1004
Boisen, A. T. RJ100
Bomar, P. H. 3199
Bonaventura, E. 352
Bonifas, H. RJ68
Bonime, W. 1005
Booth, G. 3350, RJ192
Borelli, J. 3494
Bosanquet, C. 2770
Boss, M. 760, 814, 1647
Boutonier, J. RJ120
Bradshaw, C. 3351
Bradway, K. 2123
Bram, J. R861
Brand, R. 1762, 1976
Brann, H. W. 2244
Branson, D. H. 3495
Brantmay, 1445
Brawer, F. B. 2124
Braybrook, N. 2536, 2671-72
Breuss, E. 138
Brierly, M. R292
Briner, M. 287
Brinkmann, D. 613
Broadribb, D. 2431, 2673, 3496

281

Brock, P. van den. 884
Brome, V. 2432, 3497
Brooks, H. C. 2125, 2245, 2771, 3352
Brooks, V. E. 3498
Brower, B. 1763
Brown, C. A. 3068, RJ324
Brown, F. RJ325
Brown, J. A. C. RJ241
Brunner, A. 815, 1006
Brunner, C. 614, 1977
Buber, M. 109, 761-62, 816-17, 1648
Buder, H. 1978
Bügler, K. 763, 1979
Bumke, O. 203
Buonaiutti, E. 88, 110, 139, 176, 188, 204, 223, 266-67, 885, 2537
Burchard, E. M. L. 1764
Burger, N. K. R1556
Buri, F. RJ137
Burkhardt, H. 1980
Burney, C. E. 3499
Burns, C. 2126
Burrow, T. 16
Burt, C. 2127
Butler, B. R2877
Buytendijk, F. J. J. 615
Bychowski, G. 2128
Byles, M. B. 1649
CGJIZ. 764, 1446, 1547, 1650, 1765, 2129, 2433, 2538, 2772
Cairnes, H. 2674
Cahen-Salabelle, R. 616, 1007-09, 1318, 1651, 1981, 2914, 3201, 3500
Calluf, E. 2675
Cambon, G. G. 529
Camerling, E. 1010
Cammerloher, M. C. 111, 1652
Campbell, J. 530, 886, 1011, 1319-20, 1548, 1653, 2130, 2539-40, 2676, 2773, 3353, RJ85
Campbell, P. 1447
Campbell, Rob. 697
Campbell, Ruth. 2434
Canale, J. A. 3645
Cannon, A. 2541
Carloni, G. 3069
Carlson, R. 3202
Carlsson, A. 2774
Carol, H. 1982

Carp, E. A. D. E. 400, 480, 1012, 2677
Carpintero, F. J. 3070-71
Carson, J. R3296
Caruso, I. 765, 1321, 2131
Casey, E. S. 3354
Castillejo, I. C. de. 1013, 1214, 1448, 1549, 1654, 1766, 1983-84, 2132, 2246, 2346, 3072, 3203
Cazeneuve, J. 1014-15
Chamberlin, J. M. 1215
Champernowne, H. I. 1550, 2347, 2915
Chang, C-Y. 1016, 1216, 1449
Chein, I. 303
Childs, G. H. 435
Choisy, M. 617-18, 698
Chouinard, T. 2775, 2916
Chrichton-Miller, H. 24
Christoffel, H. 436, RJ89
Christou, E. 887, 1985
Cirlot, J. E. 818, 3073
Citroen, P. 2542
Clark, G. 3204
Clark, J. M. 1551
Clark, R. A. 819, 1017-19, 1767-68
Clark, T. C. 619
Clark, W. H. RJ201
Clausse, S. 3355
Clift, W. B. 2917
Cline, R. A. 2247
Cogni, G. 888
Cohen, E. D. 3501
Coleman, E. 1986
Collins, M. 1987
Collum, V. C. C. 205
Conray, F. M. 2248
Cook, D. A. 2776
Cooley, R. 2678
Cope, G. F. 1552
Corbin, H. 531, 620-21, 699, 820-21, 889, 1020-22, 1217, 1322-23, 1450-51, 1552, 1655, 1769, 1881, 1988, 2133-34, 2249, 2348, 2435, 2679, 2777-78, 2918, 3074-75, 3205-06, 3502
Corman, 890
Corrie, J. 25, 37
Corti, W. R. 1023, 1324, 1452, 1554
Cossa, P. 1555
Coukoulis, P. P. 3356
Covitz, J. 2919
Cowan, T. 3076

282

283

Gaffney, J. 2015
Gaillard, C. 3380
Galdston, I. 1473, 1674
Gammon, M. 3228
Gantner, J. 2362
Garthe, O. W. 50
Gebhard, D. R2065
Gebsattel, V. E. von. 443, 829, 2162
Gelb, L. N. 3381
Gemelli, A. 1044-45, 1229
Gernat, A. 38
Gernet, L. R1069, RJ154
Gerster, G. 1046, 1346, 1474, 1675
Giegerich, W. 3520
Giehrl, H. E. 2797
Giese, F. 39
Gilen, L. 2452
Gillet, G. G. 3382-83, 3521
Gilli, G. 145
Gillibert, J. 2695
Giorgini, C. 2696
Girard, L. E. RJ264
Glover, E. 486, 540, 709, 909, RJ245
Göllner, R. 3522
Goetz, B. 1895
Götz-Heinrich, H. 51
Goldberg, J. 3099
Goldbrunner, J. 250, 541-42, 1047-49, 1787-88, 1896, 2163-65, 2267, 2363-64, 2562
Goldenberg, N. R. 3523
Goldstein, D. 3229
Gomes, F. S. 3230
Goodenough, E. R. 710
Goodheart, S. P. 4
Gordon, J. S. R3515
Gordon, R. 1789, 1897, 2016, 2268, 2453, 2563-64, 3100, 3231, 3384, R2007, R2174, R2510, R2997, R3054, R3178, R3314, RJ230
Gorlow, L. 2365
Gottschalk, H. 1676
Gough, C. L. RJ293
Graber, G. H. 52, 448, 1050-51, RJ53
Granjel, L. S. 543
Grapp, F. 1475
Graves, B. L. 3648
Gray, H. 326, 361, 404-06, 445-46, 487, 544-45

Gray, R. D. RJ122
Gravenitz, J. von. 2565
Greene, T. A. 3524, R3035, R3174
Greer, I. M. RJ203
Gregori, E. 2269
Grensted, L. W. RJ95
Griffin, G. M. 2270
Grill, 1052
Grinnell, R. 2798, 3232, 3385, 3649
Grønbeek, W. 2949
Groesbeck, C. J. 3525
Groff, 3526
Gross, D. H. 2017
Gross, H. RJ13
Gruessen, J. J. 3676
Grütter, E. 1572
Guggenbühl-Craig, A. 2166, 2271, 2566-67, 2799, 2950-51, 3101-02, 3386
Gun, G. S. R1556
Gut, G. 2272
Gutscher, K. 775
Haberlandt, H. 910, RJ144
Hadot, P. 2568
Haendler, O. 270, 830, 911, 1230, 1573-74, 1898-99, 2952, RJ289
Hänisch, I. von. 3387
Hafner, T. 546
Haft-Pomroch, Y. 3388
Hai, D. M. 3527
Hainline, R. R2434, R2703, F 2977
Hall, C. S. 2569, 3233
Hall, J. A. R3314, R3378
Hall, M. L. 3389
Hall, R. C. 2800
Hallman, R. J. 2697
Hammerschlag, H. E. 1053
Hammersley, J. R292
Handel, S. R3083
Hang, T. 3677
Hanhart, E. 3678
Hanna, C. B. 2454
Hannah, B. 630, 711, 831-33, 912-13, 1054-55, 1231, 1790, 2018-19, 2167-68, 2455, 2571, 2698-99, 2953, 3390, 3650
Harding, M. E. 27, 90, 146-48, 207, 227, 251, 271, 289-90, 362, 407-08, 447-48, 488-89, 547-48, 776-77, 1056-58, 1232-34, 1347-53, 1476-77, 1575-77, 1791-92, 1900, 2020-22, 2274-75, 2572-73, 2801-02, 2955-56, 3234, 3529,

Holton, G. 1907, 2176, 2281, 2589
HoLung, R. R. 3404
Homans, P. 2705
Home, H. J. RJ220
Hondius, J. M. 491-92
Hood, J. M. 3405
Hoop, J. H. van der. 31, 95, 152, 715, 2819
Hoppin, H. (C). 274, 450, 493, 632
Horia, V. 3113
Horton, L. H. RJ64
Hostie, R. 918-19, 1069, 1360-62, 1685, 1798-99, 2590
Hough, G. 2967, 3249-50, RJ117
Howes, E. B. 1244, 1686, 2372, 2591, 3682
Hubback, J. 2373, 2706, 2820, 3114, 3251, 3406, R3039, R3188
Hübscher, A. 552, 837
Hug-Hellmuth, H von. RJ39
Hull, R. F. C. 2821, 2968
Humbert, E. G. 2969-70, 3407-09
Hummel, G. 3115, R2408
Hupfer, J. 716
Hurwitz, S. 780, 920, 1070, 1482, 2592, 2822, 2971, 3560
Hutin, S. 921, 1245
Huyghe, R. 2972, 3116
Iandelli, C. L. 2593
Ikin, A. G. 177
Illing, H. A. 1071, 1246, 1363-65, 1483
Immoos, T. 3561
Infeld, __. RJ6
Isham, M. K. RJ44
Izutsu, T. 2465, 2707, 2823, 3117, 3252
Jaccard, P. 1072
Jackobsohn, H. 781
Jackson, M. 1687-88, 1800, 1908, 2031-32. 2177-78, R1391, R1417
Jacobi, J. 255, 292, 304-5, 366-67, 451, 494, 553-57, 633-35, 717, 838, 1073-79, 1247-49, 1366, 1484-87, 1584-85, 1689-90, 2033-34, 2179-83, 2374, 2466, 2594-96, 2708-10, 2973-74, 3118, 3410, 3562
Jacobs, E. C. 3563
Jacobs, H. 1801
Jacobsohn, 1080-81, 2597-98, 2711, 2824

Jacobson, R. 1586
Jacoby, Marianne. 922, 1802, 3119, R2371, R2383, R2470, R2475, R2694, R2710, R3223
Jacoby, Mario. 2467, 2712-14, 2975, 3120, 3253-55, 3564
Jaeger, Martha, 1082, RJ155
Jaeger, Marc A. 2035
Jäger, O. 1803
Jaffé, A. 636, 1083-85, 1488-90, 1691, 1909-10, 2036-37, 2183, 2468-70, 2599, 2600, 2715, 2825, 2976-78, 3121-22, 3256, RJ131, RJ139
Jahoda, G. 2471
James, E. O. 558
Jarrett, J. L. 3411
Jenkins, 2826
Jensen, A. E. 559
Joad, __. RJ76
Johnson, H. K. 839
Johnson, P. E. 1587, RJ195-96, RJ221, RJ283
Johnson, R. A. 3412, 3655
Johnson, S. R2454
Johnson, T. 3413
Johnston, W. 2472
Joly, 840
Jones, C. 560
Jones, E. RJ22, RJ30
Jones, J. M. 3565
Jones, W. M. 1692
Jordan, D. C. 2284
Jordens, J. 2473
Jorés, A. 1804
Journet, C. 1086
Jung, A. 1087, 1805, 2184, 2601, R1361
Jung, C. G. 2185, 2602
Jung, Eber. 2979, 3257-58, 3414, R479, R2618, R2796, R3078, R3095, RJ345
Jung, Emma. 119, 275, 1088, 1367-69, 1693, 2474, 2716-17, 2827
Kadinsky, D. 2038, 2186, 2718, 2828, 2980, 3567
Kaegi, W. 412, 923
Kalff, D. M. 1370, 2187, 2475, 2829, 2981-82, R2786
Kalsched, D. E. 2476
Kantor, 32
Kapacinskas, T. J. 3568
Karpf, F. B. 190
Katz, W 2983

287

288

Lander, K. F.   307, 330
Landers, J. J.   928
Laney, J. H.   3136
Lang, J. B.   6, 154, 294
Lang, R.   785
Langegger, F.   3422
Lantero, E. H.   498
Laroque, P.   720
Larson, C. A.   1699
Lasswell, H. D.   RJ102
Laszlo, V. de.   155, 277, 787,
   844, R246, R292
Lathrop, D. D.   3658
Lauer, H. E.   1700
Lauffenburger, __.   644
Lauterborn, E.   2837
Lawrence, J.   R2827
Laws, F.   209
Layard, D.   R1736, RJ250
Layard, J.   192, 331-32, 371, 499,
   645, 929, 1104-05, 1497-98,
   1590-91, 1701-02, 1817, 3137,
   3577, R1275, R1556, RJ284
Leavy, S. A.   R873, RJ266
LeBars, A.   3423-24
LeBlanc, A.   RJ206
Lebois, A.   1106
Lebovici, S.   2380
Lebowitz, L.   R3603
Lebowitz, M.   RJ328
LeComte, M.   1107
Lecourt, J.   2483
Lee, C.   3271
Leeuw, G. van der.   500, 567, 646,
   1380, 2193
Lehman, M.   2293
Leibbrand, W.   721, 1108
Leisgang, H.   231, 647, 1109
Le Lay, Y156, 1110
Lemke, G.   1111
Léonard, A.   722, 845, 1381
Leslie, R. C.   R1232
Lévy-Bruhl, L.   157
Lewis, A.   1382
Lewis, D. C.   3659
Lewis, E.   2611, R3223
Lewy, E.   3578
Linera, A. A. de.   415-16, 454
Link, M. S.   1112
Linssen, R.   648
Liran, B.   1703
Little, D.   278
Lockhart, R. A.   3272, 3579
Lockwood, M.   333

Löwenich, W. von.   2044
Löwith, K.   788, 1818, 2484
Londero, C.   1592
Long, C. E.   R30
Looser, G.   2381
Lopez-Pedraza, R.   3660
Lorenzo, __.   2721
Lossen, H.   1255
Loy, R.   7
Lubbeke, H.   64
Ludlow, R.   RJ146
Lüthi, K.   R2840
Lyddiatt, E. M.   1113
Lynch, T. A.   2994
Lynn, P. C.   R3174
Maag, V.   1819, 2485
Macavoy, J.   1383
McClintock, J. I.   2838
McCully, R. S.   1920, 2839, 2995-
   97, 3273, 3425-26, 3580, 3661
Mace, C. A.   1256
McGlashan, A.   1122, 1921, 2294,
   2382, 2486, 3581
McGuire, W.   3662
Macintosh, D. C.   256
MacIntyre, A.   R1556, RJ275
Mackworth, J.   1593
McLeish, J.   1820
MacMonnies-Hagard, B.   295
McPherson, T.   2295
MacQuarrie, J.   2045
Maduro, R. J.   3427
Maeder, A.   8-10, 19, 501, 1384
Märker, F.   RJ108
Maguire, A.   3138
Mahla-Helwig, R.   1114
Mahler, M. S.   2046-47, 2487, 2722-
   23
Mahoney, M. F.   2383
Mahr, W.   723
Mailhiot, B.   1115
Mairet, P.   930, 1257, RJ77
Malamud, R.   2998
Malinine, 1258
Mallet, C.-H.   846
Mance, J.   2999
Mandler, G.   2296
Mann, H.   2612, 3139
Mann, K.   257-58, 296, 417, 1922,
   2488-89
Mann, U.   2297, 2840, 3000, 3428
Manuel, A.   1821
Marc, O.   3582
Marc, V.   3583

2869, RJ150
Rudolf, A. 1848, 3448
Rüf, E. R2579
Rüsch, F. 2212
Rütting, H. 3166
Rumpf, L. 1933
Rupprecht, C. S. 3449
Russell, E. H. 3607, R3376
Rychner, M. 1406
Rycroft, C. RJ336
Saburovitsh, A. 1279
Sänger, A. 2740, 3021
Sager, N. 2508
Salfield, D. J. 1280, 1724
Salzman, L. RJ209
Sambursky, S. 2399, 2509, 2741,
   2870, 3022, 3167, 3303
Sandner, D. F. 3168
Sands, F. 1157, 1849
Sanford, J. A. 668, 2400, 2639,
   3023, 3304-05, 3450
Santis, M. I. de. 2742
Sapir, E. RJ47
Sargent, J. O. 1281
Sas, S. 2213, 3685
Saurat, D. 1158
Savage, D. S. 956
Savarin, P. RJ97
Sborowitz, A. 510, 737-38, 1159,
   1282, 2316
Schär, H. 312, 380, 423, 669-70,
   798, 1160-65, 1283, 1515, 1850-
   51, 2077, 2317, 2401, 2871
Schärf-Kluger, R. 466, 511, 671,
   1166-67, 1725, 2078, 2510,
   2640, 3451, 3608
Scharf, C. 81
Scharfenberg, J. 1934-35
Scharpff, W. 1168
Schatten, E. 124
Schechter, D. E. 2641
Schirren, J. 739
Schlappen, M. 1852, 2511
Schlette, H. R. RJ277
Schmaltz, G. 1169
Schmid, G. 82
Schmid, K. 1614, 1853, 2318,
   2512
Schmidbauer, W. 2743
Schmidt, E. W. 957
Schmidt, K. L. 381, 424, 467,
   672
Schmitt, P. 313, 342, 382-83,
   425, 673, 1170

Schmitt, W. 1854
Schmitz, O. A. H. 44, 57-58, RJ65
Schnackenberg, __. 83
Schneider, E. 799
Schneider, H. W. 1516, 1726
Schoch-Bodmer, H. 384
Schoedel, W. R. 1936
Schöler, J. P. 2079
Schöneck, G. F. 512
Scholem, G. G. 579, 800, 863,
   1171, 1284, 1407-07, 1517-18,
   1615, 1727-28, 1855, 1937, 2214,
   2319, 2402, 2642, 2744, 2872,
   3169
Schrag, C. O. RJ231
Schrödinger, E. 426, 958
Schulz, G. 1519
Schulze, W. A. 2745
Schwander, O. 1856
Schwartz, C. 864
Schwartz, N. J. 2746, 3170-71,
   R3376
Schwartzbaugh, R. 2747, 2873
Schwarz, U. 1616
Schwarzer, A. 3378
Schweizer, E. 2080, 3024
Schweizer, L. 1172
Schwermer, J. 1617
Scott, R. D. 1285, RJ197
Scott, T. A. 2403
Scott, W. C. M. 580
Scott-Maxwell, F. 1409, 2643,
   3306
Scrutton, M. R1017
Seidemann, P. 1618, 3610
Seifert, F. 165-67, 674, 959,
   1173-74, 1619, 2215, 2320
Seifert, T. 3172, 3307, 3452-53,
   3611-13
Seillière, E. 45
Seitz, F. 1857
Selesnick, S. T. 2081
Seligman, E. 3614, R2546
Seligman, P. 2321, 2644, R2356,
   R2734
Sellery, J. 2874, R3035
Sellner, T. F. 2875
Semmelroth, O. RJ151
Sen, I. 314
Serrano, M. 2216, 2404
Sergeant, E. S. 73, 343
Servadio, E. 1410
Servier, J. 3025
Sestier, J. 2082

Sykes, G. 1523
Syřištová, E. 1944
Tate, D. 1524, 1863
Tatlow, A. 1525
Teague, R. W. 3316
Téboul-Wiart, H. 3459, 3627
Tedeschi, G. 679, 2752, 3031
Teillard, A. 344, 515-16, 1182
Teirich, H. R. 680, 1183-84
Tenny, R. 3032, R2275, R2376,
   R2383, R2726, R2953, R3203,
   R3264
Tenny, E. V. 2091
Tenzler, J. 2515, 2649
Thayer, E. 282
Thiry, A. 1415
Thompson, C. 2092
Thomson, A. S. R3336
Thorburn, J. M. 1662, 2226, RJ51
Thorton, E. 2328, 2516, 3033
Thum, B. 741
Thurneysen, E. 681, RJ255-56
Thurnwald, R. 240
Tillich, P. 964, 1732, 2227
Torrie, A. 2093, R1362
Toudic, Y. 3460
Tourney, G. 1290
Towers, B. 2753
Toynbee, A. 965, 1291, RJ216
Tramontin, J. A. 742
Traux, L. 3034
Trevi, __. 2329
Trilling, L. RJ337
Trüb, H. 118, 470, 1864
Tuby, M. 3461
Tucci, G. 868
Tuinstra, C. L. 99, RJ278
Tuttle, M. C. 3317
Uchizono, R. S. 2228
Ueberwasser, W. 1623
Uexküll, T. von. 2885
Ushadel, W. 802, 1865, 2408
Ulanov, A. B. 2517, 2650, 3035,
   3318-19, 3628
Underwood, R. A. 1945
Urban, P. 2651
Uslar, D. von. 1733
Valett, R. E. 1946-47
Valengin, A. 315, 682
Van den Berge von Eysinga, G. A.
   869
Vandermeersch, P. 3629
Van der Veldt, J. R1044
Van Loo, E. D. D. 3320

Vann, G. RJ222
Vasavada, A. U. 1292, 2094, 2229-
   31, 2652-53
Vaszquez, F. 2754
Végh, S. 1734
Veith, I. 3630
Velazquez, J. M. 1866
Vergote, A. 2518
Verne, G. 2095, 2755, 3462
Vestdijk, S. 1185
Vetter, A. 84, 185
Victoria, M. 1186, 1293
Vidal, G. 2409
Vincent, A. RJ179
Vinchon, J. 966
Virolleaud, C. 215, 241, 316
Vitale, A. 3321
Vivas, E. 3463
Vlaikovič, S. 3036
Vogel, G. 1416
Voss, RJ10
Walls, H. G. van der. 216
Waelhens, A. de. 1187
Walcott, W. O. 2332, 2886, 3037,
   3322, 3464, R3264
Walder, P. 743, 870
Waldighofer, J. 585
Walker, D. A. R1556
Walker, M. 3671
Walker, N. 1417
Wall, R. J. 2096
Wallace, A. F. C. 2410
Wallace, E. 3323
Wallach, J. D. L. 3631
Waller, H. RJ160
Walser, H. H. 3465
Walter, E. J. 2333
Wandler, J. 100
Wap Van Pesch, __. 744
Washburn, D. E. 1948
Watkin, E. 1188, RJ180
Watkins, M. 3466
Watson, J. B. RJ49
Watts, A. W. 242
Weaver, R. 3324, 3632
Weeks, D. R2065
Wehr, G. 2756, 3038, 3180-81,
   3467, R2717
Weizäcker, V. 1294, RJ142
Weidlé, W. 1949
Weir, D. M. 3633
Weiss, J. G. 2097
Welch, M. 2654, R2454, RJ309,
   RJ314

2110, 2238
Züblin, W. 1199, 1874
Zulliger, H. 1637
Zumstein-Preiswerk, S. 3643
Zunini, G. 2415, 2762